A Precarious Happiness

A Precarious Happiness

Adorno and the Sources of Normativity

PETER E. GORDON

The University of Chicago Press
Chicago and London

The University of Chicago Press, Chicago 60637
The University of Chicago Press, Ltd., London
© Suhrkamp Verlag AG 2023
All rights reserved by and controlled through Suhrkamp Verlag Berlin. No part of
this book may be used or reproduced in any manner whatsoever without written
permission, except in the case of brief quotations in critical articles and reviews.
For more information, contact the University of Chicago Press, 1427 E. 60th St.,
Chicago, IL 60637.
Published 2023
Printed in the United States of America

32 31 30 29 28 27 26 25 24 23   1 2 3 4 5

ISBN-13: 978-0-226-82857-2 (cloth)
ISBN-13: 978-0-226-82919-7 (e-book)
DOI: https://doi.org/10.7208/chicago/9780226829197.001.0001

Library of Congress Cataloging-in-Publication Data

Names: Gordon, Peter Eli, author.
Title: A precarious happiness : Adorno and the sources of normativity /
    Peter E. Gordon.
Description: Chicago : The University of Chicago Press, 2023. |
    Includes bibliographical references and index.
Identifiers: LCCN 2023006680 | ISBN 9780226828572 (cloth) |
    ISBN 9780226829197 (ebook)
Subjects: LCSH: Adorno, Theodor W., 1903–1969. | Critical theory. |
    Normativity (Ethics)—Philosophy.
Classification: LCC B3199.A34 G675 2023 | DDC 193—dc23/eng/20230421
LC record available at https://lccn.loc.gov/2023006680

♾ This paper meets the requirements of ANSI/NISO Z39.48-1992 (Permanence of Paper).

For Lucy

Was wäre Glück, das sich nicht mäße an der unmeßbaren Trauer dessen was ist?

[What would any happiness be, which did not measure itself according to the immeasurable sorrow of what is?]

—THEODOR W. ADORNO, *Minima Moralia*,
Aphorism §128, "Regressionen"

Contents

Preface to the English Edition: Adorno's Legacy

The philosopher and social theorist Theodor Wiesengrund Adorno died more than a half century ago, in the late summer of 1969. By contemporary standards his life was not long: he did not survive to see his sixty-sixth birthday. But during the time that was given to him his achievements were astonishing. He not only enriched and transformed the canon of modern European philosophy; he also contributed to debates in empirical sociology, literary and cultural criticism, and musicology, and he left behind not less than three collected volumes of musical compositions, including pieces for string quartet, orchestra, and even sketches for an opera. It should hardly surprise us that Jürgen Habermas, who had been his close student and assistant at the Institute for Social Research, was not embarrassed to call Adorno "the only genius I have ever met." The young "Teddie" (as he was known among family and friends) was delicate in physique and often the object of ridicule at school. But he could rely on the loving attention of his parents, who nourished his gifts and sought to assure that the prodigy would emerge from the chrysalis. His father, Oscar Wiesengrund, an assimilated German Jew, worked as a wine exporter; and as a boy Teddie would play with friends among the bottles stored in the cellar. Much later, the image of a *Flaschenpost*, or message in a bottle, would reappear as a preferred metaphor for critical theory—a hopeful if desperate image of lessons cast into the future.

Early in his life the rebellious son of the Frankfurt bourgeoisie attached himself with fierce conviction to the new trends in aesthetic and philosophical modernism. Adorno found his initial inspiration in Nietzsche, Kafka, and Kraus, writers whose gifts for aphorism and paradox would serve as models for his own dialectical criticism. In his early years at the University of Frankfurt he developed a style of philosophical reflection that drew not only from the rich sources of German Idealism, from Kant to Hegel, but also from thinkers such as Kierkegaard, Feuerbach, and Marx, who turned against the idealist confidence in reason and plunged philosophy into the turmoil of this-worldly existence. Though his enduring debt to the great systems of classical idealism is self-evident, so too is the spirit of irony that he brought to his readings of the philosophical canon. Long before him, the poet Heinrich Heine had captured this very same spirit in an amusing rhyme: "Zu fragmentarisch ist Welt und Leben! Ich will mich zum deutschen Professor begeben!"[1] Like Heine, Adorno no longer believed in the world's coherence. Its fissures and its fragmentation were not flaws for which purely academic philosophy could provide a remedy; they became the very signature of the modern age.

It is one of the defining paradoxes of Adorno's thought that he was a radical steeped in tradition. In the twilight years of traditional humanism, Adorno seemed to welcome its demise even while he became the very embodiment of European erudition. Most of all, Adorno was the child of his mother, Maria Calvelli-Adorno, a talented opera singer who was determined to see that her son receive a musical education. In the 1920s the young man's aesthetic passions took him to Vienna, where he studied composition with Alban Berg and strengthened his bond with the musical modernism of Arnold Schoenberg and the Second Viennese School. His commitment to the tradition of European art music is an essential and defining feature of his work, and it is not something that can be set aside as a merely personal idiosyncrasy. Indeed, music is a virtual paradigm for his dialectical understanding of human experience.

It is somewhat ironic that so many of his books, despite their stylistic difficulty and their willful resistance to facile categorization, now enjoy the ambivalent prestige of classics. But this should hardly surprise us when we recall that Adorno himself appropriated the archive of bourgeois experience in a dialectical fashion. The theorist of negativity and rupture also cherished the high-bourgeois Proust for the intimacy and sensuality of his literary works. The partisan of musical atonality also professed an undying love for Beethoven, and he spent much of his later years collecting the notes for a never-published study that was to demonstrate the sovereign place of the Bonn composer in the musical canon. In all of these respects we can say that Adorno's relationship to the inheritances of European culture was not that of mere opposition; it exemplified a stance of determinate negation insofar as it aimed to realize the broken promises of modernity.

In his philosophical work and as a public intellectual, Adorno never fully abandoned his conviction that modernity, despite its manifold failures, also contains the resources that are necessary if its promises are to be fulfilled. In the early months of 1969, he was engaged in a contest of political will with student activists on the German Left who looked upon the aging representative of the Frankfurt School with growing suspicion. They recognized of course that they owed him a great debt. In the postwar decades of conservatism and political conformity, Adorno, together with his colleague Max Horkheimer, had helped awaken the spirit of resistance that had swept through the German universities in the later 1960s and had given birth to the "extra-parliamentary opposition." But in the eyes of their students, the high theorists of resistance had failed the crucial test: when faced with radical demonstrators and with an occupation of the Institute's building, Adorno had called on the police to have the protesters expelled. A small but militant faction within the student movement was incensed at this betrayal, and they denounced Adorno for aligning himself with the establishment. The Frankfurt School, it was said, had adopted a posture of political radicalism but refused to draw the political consequences; it did not cross the bridge from theory to practice but resigned itself to the quietism of mere theory alone.[2]

In a February 1969 address on Berlin radio, Adorno sought to defend himself against this charge. It was wrong, he said, to evaluate all ideas only in a practical light and for their worldly consequences. Such an attitude could only strengthen the authority of instrumental reason and the spirit of utility that has come to dominate late-modern capitalist society. When untethered from theory practice becomes pseudopractice; it degenerates into mere actionism and betrays the ideals it meant to realize. Against the imperatives of premature action, Adorno defended what he called "the emphatic concept of thinking [*emphatischer Begriff von Denken*]."[3] When understood in this *emphatic* sense, thinking itself became for Adorno a site of critical leverage against the overwhelming facts of social conformity. "Thinking," he said, "is actually the force of resistance [*die Kraft zum Widerstand*]." Thinking promises this resistance even though, in Adorno's words, it is "not secured, not by the existing conditions, nor by ends yet to be achieved" [*nicht gedeckt, weder von bestehenden Verhältnissen, noch von zu erreichenden Zwecken*].[4]

> Thinking is not the intellectual reproduction of what already exists anyway. As long as it doesn't break off, thinking has a secure hold on *possibility*. Its insatiable aspect, its aversion to being quickly and easily satisfied, refuses the foolish wisdom of resignation. The utopian moment in thinking is stronger the less it—this too a form of relapse—objectifies itself into a utopia and hence sabotages its realization. Open thinking points beyond itself.[5]

For those who have learned from Adorno and continue to draw instruction from his work today, this late defense of "emphatic thinking" as a mode of resistance must appear in an ambivalent light. On the one hand, it speaks to the genuinely utopian impulse that animated Adorno's philosophy and moved him to hold fast to the ideal of a possible world beyond the hopelessness and suffering of the actual one. On the other hand, it seems to defer all action and even denies itself the satisfaction of any determinate utopian ideals, in the fear that such ideals will betray themselves and solidify into an affirmative ideology. More troubling still, this denial of utopia extends so far that it refuses to countenance the prospect that critical thinking can be secured by anything, either in current society or in future ends. It should hardly surprise us that Adorno's defense of critical theory has left many of his readers dissatisfied. Shortly after Adorno's death, Jürgen Habermas published a tribute to his teacher in which he asked "how critical theory can be justified."[6]

In the more than fifty years since his death, this question retains its urgency. In all of his work, Adorno adopts a critical posture: we should not accept present conditions as authoritative merely because things happen to be the way they are. Against Hegel, Adorno refuses to award the actual the prestige of the rational. The enormity of social suffering already invalidates any such identity. Under the name of a "negative dialectics," he resolutely denies the authority of the given: he seeks to expose the untruth in what presents itself as truth, the negativity in what claims to be seamless identity. What makes this posture so difficult, however, is his apparent refusal to appeal to any independent and fully *intact* norms that could serve as sources of critical leverage against untruth. He is especially resistant to the demand that he furnish a rational *justification* for his critical posture, because he believes that reason itself has been compromised by the one-sided and coercive process of social rationalization. Deontological ethics would require an appeal to discursive concepts. Moral philosophy as Kant understood it can be possible only if one remains committed to the concept of a universal law. Adorno, however, will not tolerate such requirements. The formalist approach already reflects the subject's domination over the object. Whatever normative standards we may have, Adorno seems to believe that they could not be made available to us in merely conceptual form.[7] He concludes that critical thinking is "not secured [*nicht gedeckt*]" at all. The power of what exists is so pervasive that it blocks any appeals to normativity in both the present and the future. This may seem to leave Adorno's readers without *any* normative orientation whatsoever. But we cannot rest content with this skepticism. If Adorno is willing to forgo any and all normative standards, then those who do not accept his criticism can simply dismiss his claims as arbitrary and without consequence. The question concerning the sources of normativity in Adorno's thought is not one we can easily escape.

In the present book, I explore one possible response to this problem. Briefly, I argue that Adorno's work is animated by a normative commitment to happi-

ness or human flourishing. No doubt this claim places me at odds with some
of the philosopher's most discerning readers, who have faulted his work for
its alleged deficit of normative standards. My chief argument here is that
Adorno is not a mere "negativist." He does not believe that the world is so
deeply immersed in the false that he is unable to give a philosophical account
of the normative commitments that underwrite his own critical efforts. On the
contrary, I hope to show that a distinctive and comprehensive vision of human flourishing animates his critical practice. This understanding of human
flourishing is broadly materialist, in the sense that it involves what he calls an
"emphatic" concept of the human being as a sensual and embodied creature
who holds fast to the possibility of our species-wide happiness.

Adorno's commitment to this idea redeems him from the charge of thoroughgoing negativism and from the related concern that he failed to offer
any normative resources for critical theory. Admittedly, Adorno believed that
such foundations could not be fully secured. The very longing for philosophical "security" was yet another symptom of the modern will to dominate nature.
We must therefore distinguish between *sources* and *justifications*. Although
Adorno is constantly alert to sources of normativity in worldly experience, he is
skeptical as to whether these experiential sources admit of rational validation.
This means that his philosophical efforts are unlikely to satisfy readers who
feel that critical theory must find its justification in some kind of rationalist
foundationalism or, at the very least, a theory of post-foundationalist rational
communication. Adorno remained mistrustful of all such ambitions chiefly
because he believed that the damaged condition of modern society must also
compromise our claims to incorrigible normative insight. Here we discover
the moment of self-reflexivity in his philosophical criticism: if Adorno ab-
jured the task of laying out a comprehensive and systematic defense of his
normative commitments, this is because he refused to exempt himself from
the society he described. In a world that is so disfigured by human suffering
our experience of happiness must also remain precarious and incomplete.
Philosophy too cannot remain immune from such difficulties. If it is not to
lose hope in the possibility of social transformation, it must discover within
our experience itself the normative resources it needs to gain critical leverage
against it.

In modern society, however, these resources are growing ever more scarce
and uncertain. Social theorists may therefore feel tempted to dismiss the
question of normative justification altogether and devote themselves instead
to the purely negative task of documenting how our norms have failed. This,
I believe, may explain why the practice of historical genealogy has enjoyed
widespread acclaim especially in recent years: it offers the superficial allure

of emancipatory criticism even while it recuses itself from the burdens of normative justification. Untroubled by paradox, it knows what it is against even if it does not know what it is for. And if it is pressed to provide some explanation as to why it finds a given condition intolerable, it dismisses the request with a wave of the hand. The mere feeling that something is wrong is supposed to suffice.

In this book I hope to redeem Adorno from the misleading impression that his philosophy offers only a negative account as to how society has failed. Unlike other critics of modernity, Adorno condemns the social world for its failure only because he measures that failure against a maximalist demand for happiness or human flourishing. He admits that this demand has not been met, but he cleaves to the ideal even when confronted with the likelihood of catastrophic failure. No doubt my argument as I have summarized it here may draw down upon my head the accusation that I wish to turn Adorno into a utopian. To this accusation I can only say that a thinker is utopian only if he deludes himself into believing that utopia beckons to us in undamaged perfection from just over the horizon. Clearly Adorno believed no such thing, and when commenting on false utopianism in philosophy he could be just as lacerating as Marx himself.[8] But I will insist nevertheless that his unrelenting criticism was only possible because he appealed, however obliquely, to an ideal of human flourishing that remained precarious and largely unrealized.

I would be the first to admit that happiness is only one term among many for the ideal of human flourishing that underwrites his efforts. In his various writings on philosophy, sociology, and aesthetics, Adorno refers to this ideal by different names that cover a remarkably broad semantic range. With little regard for their distinctive implications, he writes of "happiness," "the true society," "the right life," "the reconciled condition," or even "peace." He also invokes an ideal of "*a genuinely emancipated humanity [der real befreiten Menschheit].*"[9] These various phrases are no doubt vague and overlapping in their significance, and Adorno can rarely be troubled to sort out their various meanings. In a discussion with Ernst Bloch concerning the significance of utopia, he even denies that such clarification is possible: "I would say that what is essential about the concept of utopia is that it does not consist in a certain, single selected category that changes itself and from which everything constitutes itself, for example, in that one assumes that the category of happiness is the key to utopia." Adorno feels no greater confidence in freedom as the organizing term: "Not *even* the category of freedom can be isolated. If it all depended on viewing the category of freedom *alone* as the key to utopia, then the content of idealism would really mean the same as utopia, for idealism seeks nothing else but the realization of freedom without actually including the realization of happiness in the process. It is thus within a context that *all these categories* appear and are connected."[10]

Anyone who wishes to discover the pulsing heart of normativity that animates Adorno's social criticism will be tempted to conclude from his own confessions that he offers no single concept and no clear guidance as to how the various concepts might cohere. He seems content to appeal indiscriminately, and often rather obliquely, to an unrealized condition of human flourishing in which all facets of our being would find their "boundless fulfillment [*die schrankenlose Erfüllung*]."[11] While recognizing Adorno's own reluctance to fasten upon a single term, I will refer to this normative ideal as *happiness*, on the proviso that it is meant in a truly comprehensive sense, not unlike the Greek idea of εὐδαιμονία, or *eudaemonia*.[12] This condition is capacious and multidimensional in the sense that it implies the satisfaction of both our material needs and our social ideals, and it spans the full range of human experience from the simplest somatic pleasure to the most sophisticated encounter with works of art. This ideal is unabashedly normative in the sense that it serves as a critical standard that finds the given order deficient and expresses what Adorno calls the "source of energy [*Kraftquelle*]" or demand, the imperative that "there should be happiness [*es soll Glück sein*]."[13] To be sure, Adorno would have been the first to say that confining such a broad ideal within a single concept is bound to fail. Indeed, in his conversation with Ernst Bloch (quoted above), he explicitly warns against assigning the category of happiness a singular importance in our reflections concerning utopia.[14] But if we wish to make sense of the normative ideal that underwrites his philosophy, we should not abandon the effort to gain at least some sense of what this ideal implies.

A truly capacious conception of human happiness must include all facets of human experience, including the experience of art. This brings me to a topic that has aroused much controversy, not only among scholars of Adorno's philosophy, but also in the broader circuits of intellectual life where certain misunderstandings or caricatures of Adorno continue to hold sway. Especially in North America, it is a commonplace opinion that the aesthetic sphere can enjoy no exemption from the ideals of personal liberty and free expression that emerged in historical tandem with the principles of laissez-faire capitalism. Given the authority of this opinion, culture in the United States is understood chiefly as "popular culture," while any attempt to introduce standards of aesthetic judgment into the cultural realm is seen as an intolerable violation of democratic principle. Needless to say, this demotic conception of culture holds sway with unusual force when the discussion turns to those forms of commodified music that, since the mid-twentieth century, assumed a primary role in the fashioning of a distinctively American cultural identity. From big-band jazz to rock and roll, American music remains one of the most successful exports of American capitalism across the globe. Ironically, it represents one of the more striking instances of cultural commodification and standardization even while it appears to its consumers as if it were the vehicle of unfettered personal expression. We should therefore not find it surprising that some readers, especially though not exclusively in the United States, may feel moved to dismiss Adorno as an incorrigible snob. His exacting cultural standards are seen as elitist, while his passion for European art music is seen as a mark of social privilege. It is not unusual to come across the verdict that Adorno's idea of autonomous art is little more than a last redoubt of bourgeois aestheticism that indulges in the myth of apolitical transcendence.

Among my tasks in this book is to offer a corrective to this misunderstanding. Despite what is often said about Adorno, it was his view that aesthetic experience can achieve only a *relative* autonomy in relation to social reality: it must draw back from the world precisely so that it can serve as a seismograph of human suffering. If art were to lose this responsiveness to its surroundings it would no longer be art at all. For Adorno, then, art has an intrinsically normative status: it holds out to us both a promise of happiness and a critical standard by which we can take the measure of worldly catastrophe. His aesthetic theory does not signal a retreat from social criticism but a broadening of its reach. But this means that art cannot be exempted from our vision of human flourishing. It was Adorno's view that artworks are not merely commodities that reflect the current tastes of a consumer consciousness that has been disfigured by the market; they are also vessels of unrealized possibility. If we wish to imagine how our shared condition as human beings might be healed of its manifold injustices and distortions, there is little reason to assume that artistic expression would remain as it is. The critical standards that we bring to bear on social reality must extend into the aesthetic sphere as well.

I conclude these prefatory remarks by offering a brief and somewhat more personal explanation as to why I regard this project as philosophically significant. In recent years it is my impression that in academic circles a certain spirit of cynicism has grown ever more pronounced, especially when the conversation turns to the question of normative commitment. Because it is easy enough to document the many ways in which our society has betrayed its own ideals, it should hardly surprise us if many social theorists believe that the purely negative exercise of revealing the complicity between normativity and power already qualifies as a sufficient mode of social critique. But this belief is controversial at best. After all, social criticism is a worthwhile pursuit only if we feel that the social world should be otherwise than it is. To claim that certain conditions (or institutions or practices) are wrong we must be able to say *why* they are wrong and what norms of the right do not obtain, whether these norms are construed as fairness, or the good, or human flourishing. In social criticism it should therefore at least be possible to give an account of our underlying commitments. This is a question we must be willing to explore if we are not contented with the world as it is and we do not permit ourselves to succumb to disabling melancholy. Adorno understood this. On the opening page of *Minima Moralia* in the dedication to his friend Max Horkheimer Adorno writes that we must have the courage to enter a field of inquiry that "from time immemorial was regarded as the true field of philosophy, but which, since the latter's conversion into method, has lapsed into intellectual neglect, sententious whimsy and finally oblivion: *the teaching of the right life* [*die Lehre vom richtigen Leben*]."[15] In this book I wish to take this claim seriously as an interpretive guide into Adorno's philosophy.

Against Gnosticism

On May 12, 1959, in the opening lecture of his summer semester lecture series on Kant's *Critique of Pure Reason*, Adorno begins with a series of rather enigmatic remarks. He informs his students that it is a "fiction" that they do not already possess knowledge of the topic. A magnum opus such as Kant's first *Critique* radiates a tremendous authority such that all students already know at least something of its canonical meaning. But Adorno then reverses the claim and warns his students against any presumption of knowledge, for "whenever one aspect of a philosophy becomes public knowledge it tends generally to obscure its true meaning rather than to elucidate it." Conventional interpretation and received wisdom do not always assist us in revealing the inner truth of a philosophy, since the facile slogans by which a given work gains its reputation are tokens of mere exchange rather than understanding. Ideas too have an exchange value that substitutes for and may even obscure their use value. "The formulae to which philosophies are commonly reduced tend to reify the actual writings, to sum them up in a rigid fashion and thus to make genuine interaction with them all the harder."[1] Here we are confronted already with a curious instance of Adorno's habit of reading philosophy in its social matrix: he begins his lectures on the first *Critique* by admonishing his students that if they wish to appreciate the truth of Kant's masterpiece they must break through the hardened crust of popular wisdom that has gradually transformed it into a commodity.

A similar warning may be relevant when we seek to understand Adorno's own philosophical legacy. Today it is a commonplace view that Adorno was a totalizing skeptic about moral knowledge and moral conduct. Adorno, it is said, was a philosopher of thoroughgoing negativity who looked upon the modern world as a *Verblendungszusammenhang*, a dark and seamless context of deception that permits no glimpse of possible alternatives. This "negativist" interpretation holds great appeal not least because certain well-known passages in Adorno's writing, especially in the aphorisms in *Minima Moralia*, seem to offer unmistakable confirmation of its truth. Consider, for instance, what is surely the boldest and most notorious dictum "There is no right living in the false [*Es gibt kein richtiges Leben im falschen*]."[2] This single phrase, appealing in its compression and Nietzschean power, has become such a commonplace reference in the literature on Adorno that it has hardened into something of a cliché, and it should come as no surprise that it was even eternalized on the bas-relief plaque on the apartment building in Frankfurt's Westend where Adorno spent the final years of his life. There is perhaps no better metaphor for the ossification of his thought. Meanwhile, a popular variation on the negativist theme is also evident in the commodification of Adorno-as-persona. The philosopher's face has been reproduced on fetishized tchotchkes, on coffee cups and T-shirts, where he appears as a scowling contrarian who gives the entire world his "thumbs down." This is a rather ironic twist of fate: the culture industry has taken its last revenge against the theorist who first sought to diagnose its ills.

It is the chief assignment of this book to explain why this widespread understanding of Adorno is mistaken and to offer a corrective. It is true, of course, that Adorno was a critic of social reification in all spheres of human experience—in our public conduct, in our moral thinking, in our aesthetic experience, and even in the smallest moments of everyday life. But it is crucial to note that Adorno did not see the totality of our social world as plunged into absolute darkness. Notwithstanding his reputation for pessimism, he did not believe that humanity lacks any and all normative sources that might offer a glimpse of a better world. Admittedly, Adorno rarely permits himself to indulge in fantasies of utopia. Like Marx, his allusions to hope are tempered by grim realism and an acknowledgment that the modern experience of happiness all too frequently serves as a social apologia. But his restraint in speaking about the right life should not be mistaken for thoroughgoing skepticism. Even in *Minima Moralia*, the book that is infamous for its obiter dicta that would seem to affirm only the ubiquity of the false, Adorno is not embarrassed to begin the dedication to his friend Max Horkheimer with the rather striking claim that even at a moment of historical catastrophe his melancholy science retains its connection to the now-endangered philosophical practice that he calls "the teaching of the right life [*die Lehre vom richtigen Leben*]."[3]

Such perplexing statements, I shall argue, are only intelligible if we abandon the conventional view of Adorno as a philosopher of thoroughgoing negativity. Just as Adorno counseled his students to avoid any reification of Kant's philosophy, so too as readers of Adorno's work our interpretive practice must remain alive to its contradictions. We must avoid the reification that sets in when we content ourselves with the formula that he is a diagnostician of absolute reification. His own written corpus is analogous to the social world it describes: it is not a seamless portrait of a seamless world. Rather, it is a dialectical philosophy that is shot through with fragments of normativity that point beyond the landscape of our current suffering. If his writing gives us only a partial and precarious glimpse of the happiness we seek, this is because in the society that surrounds us the promise of happiness is likewise precarious. In an unhappy world, all happiness is interlaced with despair.[4]

In this introductory chapter I have three distinct aims. First, I wish to explore some of the major features of the negativist interpretation, specifying what I believe to be a charitable reconstruction of its merits. Second, I explain why, despite these merits, the negativist interpretation must be set aside as inaccurate. Third and finally, I present an overview of an alternative interpretation that I consider both more accurate as a portrait of Adorno's thinking and more defensible as a model for social criticism.

The Negativist Interpretation

In the first part of Goethe's *Faust* (1790) we are introduced to the enigmatic character of Mephistopheles, who describes himself as follows:

> Ich bin der Geist der stets verneint,
> Und das mit Recht, denn alles was entsteht,
> ist Werth, daß es zu Grunde geht.[5]

> [I am the Spirit that ever negates,
> And rightly so, for *all that comes to be,*
> *deserves to go under.*]

The lines are well known and scarcely demand exposition. What might intrigue us about this passage is that, in words that anticipate Hegel's *Phenomenology of Spirit* only seventeen years later, Mephistopheles introduces himself as a spirit of unrelenting negation, then provides the further claim that his negative action is justified because in the entirety of the temporal world there is *nothing* that does not merit destruction. This implies a thoroughly negative verdict on all that exists: all becoming is mere transience (*Vergänglichkeit*), and all that is must pass away. But destruction is also creation. Although he is a spirit of negation, Mephistopheles nonetheless recognizes that he serves a productive role in the unfolding of divine purposes: he declares himself "a part of that power, that always wants evil but always creates the good [*ein Teil von jener Kraft, die stets das Böse will und stets das Gute schafft*]." Here we are confronted with a primitive statement of dialectical logic, where negation (in Hegelian terminology) is *determinate* and not merely *abstract*: the transience that is destroyed is also sublated (*aufgehoben*) and survives on a higher plateau of world reason. The key to determinate negation is that it makes use of the negative in an *anticipatory* way: it looks upon the apparent negativity of current conditions and finds *within those very conditions* a genetic clue and a point of departure for what has *not yet* become actual.⁶

I return to the distinction between abstract and determinate negation later in this chapter. But let me pause for a moment to entertain the comparison between Mephistopheles and Adorno. Although the suggestion may seem surprising, we should recall that in the 1947 novel *Doktor Faustus*, Thomas Mann's modern revision of the Faustian drama, the devil appears in many guises, and at one point he transforms himself into an apparition that bears some resemblance to Adorno himself. Mephistopheles has "horn-rimmed spectacles" on his "hooked nose," and his brow is "pale and vaulted"; he is a "member of the intelligentsia," a "writer on art," and "a theoretician and critic who composes, as far as thinking allows him." It was the literary critic Hans Mayer who first suspected an allusion to Adorno, prompting the philosopher to ask Mann if the resemblance were intentional. Mann insisted, however, that the true model for this apparition was not Adorno but Gustav Mahler.⁷ We can infer that the description was most likely a composite that unites the philosopher and the composer into a single demonic figure. Even if the description does not perfectly suit Adorno, Mann's denial did not inhibit Adorno from delighting in the apparent homage: following the discovery, he once signed a letter "the devil."⁸

But the comparison is of more than biographical interest. From a philosophical perspective, the comparison is revealing insofar as it captures the way in which Adorno's work has often been understood. Many readers have found it tempting to think of Adorno as Mephistopheles incarnate. On this interpretation, Adorno looks upon the entirety of the social landscape with the stern eyes of a judge who recognizes that none of it can hold any value, and that "*all* that comes to be" deserves only annihilation. Now if this interpretation is valid, then we must naturally ignore the further claim by Mephistopheles that he belongs to a power "that forever wills the bad and creates the good." Instead we must find in Adorno a spirit of merely *abstract* negation, a critic who sees only darkness in the world and does not allow for the possibility that what is apparently negative may be turned toward the good. This image of Adorno corresponds to what I will call the *negativist interpretation*:

it suggests that for Adorno the social world is wholly false and that we find in it nothing that could possibly serve as an anticipatory clue to the "right life." The negativist interpretation presents us with two interlocking philosophical difficulties, epistemic and practical. First, if the world is wholly false, then it is not clear how we possess any contrasting normative standards by which we can even identify it as false. Second, if it is wholly false, then it may seem that we find ourselves trapped in a social world that lacks any and all resources for its overcoming. The very practice of social critique begins to look as if it were simply impossible.

Notwithstanding these philosophical difficulties, the negativist interpretation has enjoyed much authority in the literature on Adorno, for the obvious reason that appreciable evidence in his work would appear to support its claims.[9] Consider, for instance, the extraordinary statement from the 1963 lectures on moral philosophy, in which Adorno denies that we possess incorrigible knowledge of what he calls "absolute good."

> We may not know what absolute good is or the absolute norm, we may not even know what man is or the human or humanity—but what the inhuman is we know very well indeed. I would say that the place of moral philosophy today lies more in the concrete denunciation of the inhuman than in vague and abstract attempts to situate man in his existence.[10]

> [Wir mögen nicht wissen, was das absolute Gute, als die absolute Norm, ja auch nur, was der Mensch oder das Menschliche und die Humanität sei, aber was das Unmenschliche ist, das wissen wir sehr genau. Und ich würde sagen, daß der Ort der Moralphilosophie heute mehr in der konkreten Denunziation des Unmenschlichen als in der unverbindlichen und abstrakten Situierung etwa des Seins des Menschen zu suchen ist.][11]

The meaning of this passage may appear incontrovertible. Adorno rejects any attempts to ground moral philosophy in concepts of the "absolute good" or the "absolute norm," because all such concepts presuppose some secure ideal of human flourishing. Our difficulty today, however, is that we have little evidence of human flourishing, and we may therefore lack confidence in the availability of humane norms that conventional moral reflection would seem to require.

Elsewhere Adorno expressed this agnostic view in even stronger terms: "Every image of humanity, other than the negative one, is ideology."[12] It would seem to follow that a critique of our bad reality cannot begin with an appeal to positive norms of humanity, since no such norms can be found in social reality as it currently exists. Rather than seek to secure our moral claims in such normative evidence, we should instead take as our starting point the widely available evidence of inhumanity. Moral philosophy would do best to pursue a *via negativa*. If we cannot ground our moral criticism in an *absolute* ideal of the human, we should instead confine ourselves to the purely negative practice that Adorno calls a "concrete denunciation of the inhuman."[13]

I shall return to this passage later in the book, and I will argue that upon closer examination it does not entail the posture of thoroughgoing normative skepticism that some readers have supposed. For the time being, however, it may suffice to note that Adorno rejects only the appeal to the "absolute" good or the "absolute" norm—and this is a crucial specification insofar as it leaves open the possibility that we might appeal to damaged or imperfect instances of normativity. All the same, this passage is hardly unique, and there is a great deal of further evidence from Adorno's work that might be adduced in support of the negativist interpretation; indeed, if there were no such corroboration it seems unlikely that it could ever have gained the authority it now enjoys. The image of Adorno as a skeptic about normativity is not implausible, and it has hardened into conventional wisdom for a variety of reasons. The negativist interpretation does not always speak to the specific problem of constructing a moral philosophy without reference to some positive ideals of human flourishing. Seen in a broader perspective, it also speaks to our more general impression that Adorno was a thoroughly antiutopian thinker who did not believe that anything about our present social order could warrant our hope for its overcoming. Some scholars have thus concluded that Adorno painted himself into a corner of self-defeating skepticism since he had lost all confidence in the very practice of rational criticism itself. This impression too finds some textual support in those more hyperbolic passages in his work where he seems to suggest that the social world has simply closed down all possibilities of critical insight, even of the purely negative kind. In *Minima Moralia*, for instance, Adorno declares, "There is not a crevice in the cliff of the established order into which the ironist might hook a fingernail."[14] Here we could infer that Adorno not only offers a thoroughgoing *condemnation* of modern society; he portrays it as a closed and self-affirmative system that affords no conceptual space whatsoever for our own critical efforts. The epistemic and practical problems mentioned above thereby join together.

How Adorno could possibly sustain such an awkward philosophical posture is a question I will address momentarily. Be that as it may, the general impression that underwrites the negativist interpretation is that Adorno saw the modern world as normatively indifferent, that is, as lacking any internal sources of normativity that could furnish us with the critical energies we would require if we wished to identify its errors or take some practical action

to remedy them. It is this general impression that is also responsible for the
view of Adorno as a late-modern gnostic who looked upon all of contemporary society as fallen and beyond all possible redemption.[15] The gnostic
image of modernity as fallen or morally vacuous also appears in the famous
caricature of Adorno by Lukács, who described the philosophers as men
of great wealth and cultural privilege who could dream of no better life for
themselves than taking up a permanent residence in the "Grand Hotel Abyss,"
from which they could gaze upon the abyss of mere nothingness or senseless-
ness while treating themselves to the finest meals and entertainment.[16] To
be sure, not all versions of the negativist interpretation indulge in cultural
caricatures or accusations of mystical dualism. Common to all such views,
however, is the basic understanding of Adorno as a thinker who cannot locate in modern society any immanent sources of normativity that could be
mobilized for its favorable transformation. Three distinctive versions of this
negativist interpretation stand out for their philosophical acumen, and they
merit closer examination here.

Performative Contradiction

In his 1985 book, *The Philosophical Discourse of Modernity*, Jürgen Habermas
presents us with a series of chapters that explore various stages in the unfolding history of modern European philosophy. The analysis begins with Hegel
not because he is necessarily the first philosopher of the modern age (and
surely he is not) but rather because it would be plausible to say that he was the
first philosopher "for whom modernity became a problem."[17] Hegel understood as perhaps no philosopher before him that modernity is special insofar
as it untethers itself from the unexamined sources of traditional or inherited
normativity, and it assigns itself a distinctive requirement; namely, "*it has to
create its normativity out of itself.*"[18]

   This criterion serves as the operative standard by which Habermas judges
the achievements of each contributor to post-Hegelian philosophy. Habermas grants that the young Hegel still held open the possibility of conceiving
of the ethical totality as an intersubjectively established context of communication. But he faults the mature Hegel for an inflationary model of reason that is conceived as an all-knowing subjectivity. This inflationary model
eventually informs Hegel's understanding of politics: the state appears as a
"higher-level subjectivity" insofar as it stands above and beyond its individual
constituents.[19] The upshot of Habermas's analysis is that Hegel answered the
challenge of modernity's need for normative self-grounding only by inflating spirit into the arrogant and overwhelming force of "absolute knowing."

This inflationary model of an all-encompassing metasubject ultimately viti-
ates the ongoing practice of modern criticism since the essential truths of the
age have been decided in advance. "Hegel's philosophy satisfies the need of
modernity for self-grounding only at the cost of devaluing present-day reality and blunting critique."[20] Habermas argues that this anticritical or finalistic
image of modernity is due to the fact that Hegel remained trapped in the
philosophy of the subject.

Although it is hardly necessary here to reconstruct each of the succeed-
ing steps in Habermas's discussion, the general lesson of the book is that the
philosophical discourse of modernity as it developed after Hegel tended to
recapitulate the error of its founder insofar as it placed unwarranted emphasis
on the isolated subject. This error is especially noticeable in Nietzsche's attempt to install the will to power as a quasi-metaphysical principle for all of
reality. This inflationary understanding of power remains committed to critique, but it is a genealogical exercise that appears only as a theatrical gesture
of unmasking; it loses its genuinely critical purpose because it dissolves truth
into a purely aesthetic criterion. Criticism for the sake of reason becomes
little more than criticism for the sake of an unfettered will that celebrates its
ecstatic freedom like a modern-day Dionysus. Like Hegel, Nietzsche operates
with an inflationary philosophy of the subject that isolates it from the intersubjective practice of rational criticism. For Habermas, Nietzsche therefore
marks the "entry into post-modernity" insofar as his thought lays bare fatal
problems that will recur in later chapters in the history of philosophy, most
notably in Heidegger, Bataille, Derrida, and Foucault.[21]

In his genealogical critique of subject-centered philosophy, Habermas follows the analysis of Nietzsche with a chapter that is devoted to Adorno and
Horkheimer, especially to their coauthored *Dialectic of Enlightenment*, a text
that was completed in 1944 and then published officially in 1947, when the trau-
matic experiences of the war weighed heavily on their thoughts. Not without
justification Habermas calls it "their blackest book."[22] No doubt still in a state
of astonishment at the revelation of the crimes at Auschwitz, its authors try
to grapple with the painful question as to how rational modernity could have
resulted in such barbarism or how enlightenment could revert to myth. For
Habermas their conclusion is paradoxical. Even while they still wish to exercise a species of critique their genealogical strategy borrows from Nietzsche
the confusing equation between reason and power. Their skepticism places in
doubt the very possibility of rationality itself and therefore risks a thoroughgoing condemnation of modernity as such. They simply ignore the enduring force of rational criticism, and they underestimate those still-untapped
sources of normativity in modern society that hold out the possibility for an

emancipatory transformation *from within*. Adorno and Horkheimer see in reason little more than an instrument for self-preservation. By unmasking reason as nothing but power, the "suspicion of ideology becomes *total*, but without any change of direction. It is turned not only against the irrational function of bourgeois ideals, but against the rational potential of bourgeois culture itself."[23]

One might speculate that Habermas reaches this conclusion in part because he reads *Dialectic of Enlightenment* as if it were composed as a comprehensive argument and not as a series of "philosophical fragments" (as its subtitle would suggest). This encourages him to draw lessons from the book that are perhaps more definitive than the authors may have intended. On the presupposition that the book makes the pretense of total synopsis (after the model of Hegel's absolute knowing) one may therefore feel tempted to agree with Habermas that its negative verdict on modernity is no less totalizing and finalistic than the affirmative philosophy of spirit that serves as its implicit target. Nor can we dismiss the question of whether Adorno and Horkheimer intended these fragments as a *summa* that contains a freestanding philosophical doctrine. It could be that by treating the book in isolation from the broader history of twentieth-century critical theory certain distorting effects are introduced into our interpretation of its claims. We should recall, for example, the joint discussion over the book in 1946, when Horkheimer alluded to their plans for a *second* volume and described their shared task not as a wholesale condemnation of the enlightenment but as its "rescue [*Rettung*]."[24] A further question, however, is whether we are justified in seeing the book as a unified statement given the fact of its joint authorship. Evidence assembled by Rolf Tiedemann and remarks by Gunzelin Schmid Noerr would suggest that the fragments emerged from a conversation that did not wholly succeed in effacing differences between the two participants.[25] Given these many concerns it is also fair to ask whether we can read the book as an accurate expression of Adorno's distinctive philosophical commitments.

Notwithstanding these various questions, however, we cannot deny that *Dialectic of Enlightenment* has cast a long and singular shadow over the history of critical theory, and Habermas is quite right to assign it a prominent place in the philosophical discourse of modernity. For Habermas the book offers further evidence as to how the philosophy of the subject continues to hold sway in the broader philosophical tradition. Adorno and Horkheimer redescribe the history of reason as the history of instrumental reason; reason sheds its capacity for critical self-reflexivity and becomes an instrument that serves only the subject's own strategic purposes. Reason assists humanity in its effort to gain mastery over nature but simultaneously represses the nature that also belongs to the human being. Mastery over nature accordingly means self-mastery, setting the stage for all of the repressive pathologies that will characterize bourgeois modernity. In homage to Kant, the authors describe reason's betrayal of its own self-posited ends as a dialectic: the drive for total freedom culminates in a condition of total unfreedom; reason oversteps itself and falls into error.

For Habermas this argument raises a specter of unworkable paradox. If reason is unmasked as *nothing more than* instrumental reason, then the authors can no longer offer a justification for the rational status of their own critique: "ideology critique does not have anything in reserve to which it might appeal."[26] Nietzsche could at least declare himself emancipated from the fetters of reason altogether and claim that his efforts were justified only from the aesthetic point of view. Adorno and Horkheimer, however, are unwilling to take this final step into mere aestheticism. Although they allow for no moment in the history of enlightenment that is not already complicit with power, they still want to hold fast to the original gesture of the enlightenment as a practice of critical unmasking. But this gesture loses its substantive meaning as a revelation of truth. Here the enlightenment turns against itself and calls into question the validity of its own foundation: "critique becomes total."[27] It is here that Habermas identifies the problem of performative contradiction: "To be sure, this description of the self-destruction of the critical capacity is paradoxical, because in the moment of description it still has to make use of the critique that has been declared dead. It denounces the enlightenment's becoming totalitarian with its own tools."[28]

Habermas is charitable enough to grant that Adorno at least recognized this paradox even if he did not attempt to resolve it. But for Habermas the mere acceptance of paradox can hardly suffice to redeem Adorno from the charge of performative contradiction. Instead of seeking a way beyond this impasse Adorno merely dwells with "the embarrassment of a critique that attacks the presuppositions of its own validity."[29] For Adorno (and Horkheimer), all that remains is the vision of a rationalized modernity in total eclipse. Because all available norms of rational validity have been exposed for their complicity with power the authors of the "philosophical fragments" leave us with the impression of totalitarian immanence that lacks all normative resources, excepting perhaps those that survive as the memory of an embattled theology or the mimetic preserves of modernist art. Notwithstanding these nonrational traces of hope, the administered society assumes the general appearance of a *huis clos* from which there is little prospect for criticism let alone escape.[30] Habermas believes that this grim verdict on modernity is both exaggerated and premature, since it paints a one-sided picture of modernity that refuses to acknowledge the emancipatory potentials of critical reason that still inhere *within* modernity itself. Adorno and Horkheimer would only have the right to their fatalistic conclusion if they had shown that "there is no way out."[31]

Whether this is an accurate interpretation of their book is a question I address later on. For the time being I only want to recall the basic motive that drives Habermas in his critique.[32] Following both Kant and Hegel, he is committed to the basic criterion that modernity can only claim its distinctive validity if it subscribes to norms that it has created *for itself and out of itself*. This historicized criterion of self-authorization rules out any criteria that are not immanent to modern society in all of its manifold complexity, and it sets up the expectation that the fate of our society rests entirely in our own hands.[33] Implicit in this criterion, then, is a premise of self-actualizing spirit whose rational capacities are parceled out equally to all participants of a modern democracy. But this premise will hold valid for all of us only insofar as we sustain our belief in *immanent normativity*, namely, the belief that modern society still bears within itself at least some normative content that we can mobilize for the purposes of its transformation. What Habermas finds most disquieting in *Dialectic of Enlightenment* is that its authors seem ready to declare that within the bounds of our now-inescapable modernity all such content has been evacuated. Inspired in part by Weber's analysis of disenchantment and one-sided rationalization, Adorno and Horkheimer conclude that rationalized modernity suffers from a profound and perhaps even fatal normative deficit that modernity cannot be expected to remedy on its own.[34]

Honneth and Recognition

The philosopher Axel Honneth, the most prominent figure in the "third generation" of critical theory, shares with Habermas the general opinion that however much we may continue to prize the philosophical legacy of Adorno and Horkheimer, we must nonetheless conclude that they failed to provide their critical theory with a convincing justification for its normative commitments. Honneth's argument merits closer examination.[35]

According to Honneth, "Adorno had founded the point of departure for his critique of society so decisively on Marx's critique of fetishism that *he could no longer find any trace of an intramundane transcendence in the social culture of everyday life*."[36] This was a common failing among those who belonged to the circle of first-generation critical theory. As a consequence, Adorno and his colleagues lapsed into a disabling skepticism regarding the normative foundations for their own critical practice. They remained caught in a "Marxist functionalism" that "misled them into accepting such a *closed* theoretical sphere of capitalist domination and cultural manipulation that there could be no room for a domain of practical-moral critique." The result was a normative aporia in critical theory. "These approaches were theoretically dependent upon a pre-theoretical resource for emancipation whose very existence could no longer be proved empirically." According to Honneth, this problem of a normative deficit in critical theory reached its unworkable conclusion in Adorno's philosophy: "Critical Theory's turn to Adorno's historico-philosophical negativism marked the historical point at which the endeavor to link critique back to social history failed completely. In the reflections contained in *Dialectic of Enlightenment*, the only remaining place for something like intramundane transcendence was in the experience of modern art."[37] This philosophical aporia in Adorno's argument has left critical theory with its greatest unresolved challenge. The "fundamentally negativist orientation" that is held in common by both Adorno and Horkheimer "gave rise to a problem that ever since has stood at the head of every renewed attempt to link up with Critical Theory." This is a problem we must still confront today. "If the Left Hegelian model of critique is to be retained at all, we must first re-establish theoretical access to the social sphere in which an interest in emancipation can be anchored pre-theoretically."[38] Critique can proceed only if it can find an *immanent* point of departure for this emancipatory interest. "Without some force of proof that its critical perspective is reinforced by a need or a movement within social reality, Critical Theory cannot be further pursued in any way today, for it would no longer be capable of distinguishing itself from other models of social critique in its claim to a superior sociological explanatory substance or in its philosophical procedures of justification." Its claim to superiority over rival critical projects is possible only if it can furnish its "standards of critique" with an "objective foothold in pre-theoretical praxis."[39]

Like Habermas, Honneth believes that Adorno saw social reality as a closed and self-identical system. But the thesis of total falsehood left Adorno without any strong resources for explaining what positive norms this system has violated. For if social reality is a realm of seamless falsehood, then it follows that "there could be no room for a domain of practical-moral critique."[40] Honneth's basic view is that Adorno sees all subjects of our current order as caught up in the "context of delusion" and "permeated by instrumental attitudes" to such a degree that he remains doubtful as to whether "collective knowledge of capitalist reality" is truly possible.[41]

In his interpretation of Adorno, however, Honneth differs from Habermas in at least one important respect; namely, Honneth ascribes to Adorno a minimal and negativist standard for social criticism in the form of *suffering*. Adorno never attempts a full-scale philosophical explanation as to why suffering can serve as a critical standard, and he seems skeptical as to whether any such explanation could be rationally compelling. But it is Honneth's opinion that in many places in his work Adorno unmistakably appeals to suffering as a kind of presupposition for critical practice: "The concept of 'suffering' that Adorno employed is not meant in the sense of noting an explicit, linguistically articulated experience; rather, it is 'transcendentally' presupposed everywhere there is the justified suspicion that human beings experience a loss of their self-realization and happiness through the restriction of their rational capacities."[42]

Adorno's chief philosophical difficulty, according to Honneth, is that Adorno never bothers to explain *why* suffering can serve as a critical norm. "There are references to the unavoidability of somatic impulses of suffering in numerous places, but a justification of their normative or social-critical revaluation is always left out."[43] Any charitable reconstruction of Adorno's philosophy would therefore need to supplement its argumentation to furnish our intuitive objections to suffering with the normative and conceptual justification they demand. In an important paper from 2006 Honneth seeks to do just this. He argues (convincingly) that Adorno can appeal to suffering as a kind of negative norm for social criticism only because he borrows from Freud a rudimentary and largely implicit anthropology, according to which the human being is understood as having basic desires and impulses toward somatic satisfaction that our current social relations have blocked. "Adorno manages to enrich his concept of suffering by imperceptibly equipping it with components of Freud's psychoanalysis. Through this categorial supercharging, suffering as an impulse with which subjects react to capitalist living conditions becomes the prereflective desire to be freed from conditions that fetter our potential for imitative reason."[44]

It is here, Honneth claims, that Adorno lands himself in a philosophical aporia. If he wishes to construe suffering as a negative *norm*, Adorno needs to see the "impulsive reaction" of suffering as having a "cognitive content," at least in the sense that the reaction already expresses "the perception of a restriction of reason."[45] But according to Honneth, Adorno fails to provide this cognitive content. The best Adorno can do is allude to suffering as if it served as a self-certifying standard. In *Negative Dialectics* he writes that "the bodily moment registers the knowledge, that suffering should not be, that things should be different."[46] Honneth comments, "This sentence already anticipates the second step Adorno must have taken in order to be able to construct an immanent connection between 'suffering impulses' and subjective resistance: the feeling of pain must rudimentarily include not only the knowledge that one's own potential for reason can only be realized in a restricted way, but at

the same time the wish to be freed from this felt deformation."⁴⁷ From Freud
Adorno borrows the idea that neurotic suffering itself already expresses a
demand for recovery. Honneth concludes that in Adorno's philosophy the
deformation of suffering humanity already implies a protest against the conditions that caused it. "Transferred to the critique of capitalism within which
Adorno speaks of the 'suffering' of subjects, the result of this line of thinking is that the negative feelings of a deformation of reason always bring with
them a wish to be freed from social pathologies. To this extent, to put it more
strongly, suffering impulses guarantee the subjects' ability to resist the instrumental demands of the capitalist form of life."⁴⁸ Moreover, Adorno appeals to
memories of love and mimetic attachment in childhood in order to furnish
the image of an undistorted humanity against which he can measure the extent of present distortion: "Even the adult who acts in total conformity with
the instrumental pressures of the capitalist form of life retains a weak memory of the origins of his thinking in early moments of empathy and care. It
is a residuum of experience of this kind on which Adorno in different places
bases his confidence that, despite their delusions, subjects still possess an interest in the liberation of their reason."⁴⁹

My own interpretation in this book shares much in common with Honneth, but I do not feel he goes far enough in acknowledging the concept of
undistorted humanity that pervades Adorno's criticism.⁵⁰ Honneth interprets
Adorno primarily as a theorist of *negative normativity*, in the sense that human *suffering* together with the corelated phenomena of "social pathologies"
are supposed to serve as the negative standards against which we can develop
our implicit image of undistorted humanity. As I explain further on, this
negativist interpretation may not fully capture the complexity of Adorno's
work.⁵¹ To be sure, Honneth has noted that Adorno also appeals to scenes
from childhood as images of undistorted humanity. But these fleeting memories of *temps perdu* are hardly unique, nor would it have been plausible if
Adorno had placed such an extraordinary emphasis on only one type of experience. Throughout his philosophy we find intimations as to what undistorted experience would be, and it is in fact crucial to his argument that such
experiences are not found in only one specific and narrowly circumscribed
domain of experience but are distributed across the entire landscape of everyday life, both individual and collective. Despite this point of disagreement,
however, I share with Honneth a key insight, namely, that Adorno places
great importance on the survival of an undistorted and intersubjective bond.
In his own philosophy Honneth understands this bond in terms of *recognition*, a phenomenon that he has explored tirelessly and in great detail so as
to provide critical theory with the robust normative justification it requires.

My argument in this book might be construed as an elaboration of Honneth's insight. While recognition serves an indispensable role in social theory it is best understood as the formalized and conceptually elaborated description of a prior affective bond. Specifically, I argue that Adorno's philosophy already provides us with an account of our basic *responsiveness* to others and to the surrounding world. This mimetic capacity for responding to what is around us can be interpreted as the affective *precondition* for recognition: any ethical relation between subjects must presuppose that the subject retains the capacity to hold itself open in a state of vulnerability to the experience of others as subjects. I refer to this as Adorno's *ethics of vulnerability*.[52]

I am not the only one to pursue this line of argument. The perspective developed here also owes a significant debt to J. M. Bernstein's excellent 2001 study in which the case is made for Adorno as an exemplar of "ethical modernism." Bernstein offers an especially powerful interpretation of what he calls "fugitive ethical experience," and he explores the normative status of such experiences insofar as they possess what he calls a "promissory character." The argument developed here differs from Bernstein in several respects, notably in the attempt to integrate aesthetic theory and aesthetic experience into the broader framework of Adorno's ethics of vulnerability.[53] Before I turn to my own interpretation, however, it is worthwhile to consider a third interpretation that pursues the negative interpretation to the fullest extent possible.

Living Less Wrongly

Alongside Habermas and Honneth, we owe to Fabian Freyenhagen an immeasurable debt for his 2013 book, *Adorno's Practical Philosophy: Living Less Wrongly*, a lucid and thoughtful study that I would rank among the most consistently argued attempts to reckon with the problem of normativity in Adorno's thought.[54] At first glance the interpretations by Habermas and Freyenhagen would appear to have little in common. Habermas faults Adorno and Horkheimer for yielding to a species of totalizing skepticism insofar as they no longer place any trust in the emancipatory promise of enlightenment. They hold on to the unmasking gesture of ideology critique but fail to retain any rational standards of justification for this critical practice and thereby lapse into performative contradiction. The resulting portrait of rationalized modernity lacks any immanent sources of normativity: the Enlightenment is thus redescribed as *totalitarian*.

Freyenhagen confronts head-on the problem of normativity in Adorno's work, but he does not accept Habermas's verdict.[55] He offers a charitable reconstruction of Adorno that seeks to redeem his work from the charge of performative contradiction even while he takes seriously the image of Adorno as a totalizing skeptic about positive norms.[56] He claims that Adorno is a "thorough negativist," in at least two distinct but interlocking senses.[57] Adorno is a negativist in the *substantive* sense insofar as he sees our current society as fundamentally bad or wrong; but he is also a negativist in the *epistemic* sense, insofar as he denies that as members of a bad society we can have any knowledge of the good. These two senses are united in a doctrine that Freyenhagen calls "meta-ethical negativism." Namely, Adorno believes that he can account for normativity "even in the absence of knowing the good, the right, or any positive value."[58] Not only does Adorno deny our knowledge of the good, but he even denies our capacity to articulate or imagine any counterfactual vision of human flourishing. Freyenhagen states this point in the strongest possible terms. The current social world is *"so deeply delusional that we cannot even conceptualize or imagine* what realized humanity would consist in."[59]

This negativist interpretation of Adorno's work presents us with an obvious puzzle, because in the absence of at least *some* critical standard it is difficult to see how Adorno could ever say that any given arrangement of society is objectionable or wrong. The very condemnation of our social conditions as false would seem to presuppose some knowledge, however rudimentary or partial, as to what it would be like for those conditions to be true. Freyenhagen seeks to rescue Adorno from this difficulty by appealing to a "potential" of basic human functioning that remains unrealized in our false society but nonetheless permits us to identify what is false. Adorno might accordingly be understood as advocating a kind of "negative Aristotelianism." In other words, Adorno believes that there is an unfulfilled but damaged potential in the human being that serves as a practical postulate. We know that humanity presently lives in a destitute condition: we exhibit what Freyenhagen calls a "widespread shortfall" from our "basic functioning." But this sense of shortfall nonetheless implies an *unrealized potential*. This potential has the status of an Aristotelian *ergon*, except for the important qualification that it is not yet available to us as a robust concept. "We cannot currently know *anything positive*" about this potential, Freyenhagen says, though he also admits that without it *"we cannot make sense of the world."*[60] Freyenhagen concludes that our normative orientation can only be negative: it is directed *against the bad rather than toward the good*. The best Adorno can counsel is therefore a minimalist ethics of "living less wrongly."

The starting point for such a minimalist ethics assumes the form of what Adorno calls "a new categorical imperative," namely, that all citizens in the state of their unfreedom should arrange their "thoughts and actions" such that Auschwitz or similar events could never again occur.[61] It is crucial to note that Adorno deploys the term "Auschwitz" in this statement not as an exclusionary gesture that inflates one catastrophe into an incomparable standard of evil. Adorno's formula insists on the possibility of comparison because he recognizes that the singularity of individual suffering does not rule out a more comprehensive perspective on the suffering of all humanity. Freyenhagen offers a painstaking analysis of this formula, and he takes special care to explain how Adorno's "new" categorical imperative differs from Kant's "old" categorical imperative in crucial respects. Most importantly, Adorno rejects the demand that the new categorical imperative admits of discursive *grounding*, and he goes so far as to say that the call for such grounding would be "outrageous."[62]

Freyenhagen offers a powerful and on many counts persuasive case for the negativist interpretation of Adorno's ethics. He takes to heart the famous claim that "there can be no right living in the false," and he reads it in the most expansive sense, as an argument against any and all attempts to locate any robust acquaintance with the good in the midst of a bad world. Freyenhagen admits that this negative ethics is therefore a "minimalist ethics," but he insists that within a pervasively wrong society we should not expect anything like "moral certainty" or a "full set of practical guidance."[63] He nonetheless insists that even without the moral certainty that would come from knowledge of the good, we can locate within our bad conditions a species of normativity that is sufficiently strong as to justify our rejection of those conditions. "The bad has its own negative normativity insofar as it demands to be mitigated or overcome and it demands this irrespective of the content of the good."[64] Freyenhagen's neo-Aristotelian idea of an unrealized potential equips us with all the normativity we require insofar as we can reject current conditions as bad "in virtue of the kind of beings we are and could become."[65] This idea of an unrealized potential furnishes Adorno with what Freyenhagen sees as a "negativist philosophical anthropology." We only possess knowledge of our present *inhumanity*; but regarding the question as to what our realized humanity might actually consist in we are condemned to ignorance.[66]

At first glance it may seem as if Habermas and Freyenhagen share few points in common. Habermas reads Adorno as a thoroughgoing skeptic: because he permits his unmasking efforts to invalidate even the norms it was meant to serve, Adorno leaves himself with no normative grounds whatsoever for objecting to current conditions. His broader philosophical project is therefore incoherent and founders on the shoals of paradox. Although Freyenhagen shares with Habermas the basic view that Adorno was a skeptic about positive normative standards, he seeks to defend Adorno's philosophy against Habermas's dismissive verdict. Despite his skepticism Adorno can still appeal to a quasi-Aristotelian principle of unrealized human potential, and because he is equipped with this purely negative normativity he can object to current conditions as wrong since they inhibit us from becoming what we should be. Notwithstanding the many points of disagreement between them, however, we should not neglect the basic fact that Freyenhagen and Habermas have in common a crucial view. They both read Adorno's normative skepticism as *totalizing*. For Habermas this means that Adorno refuses all appeals to a better alternative and sees us as captives in a *huis clos* from which there can be no hope for escape. For Freyenhagen this means Adorno sees current society as "so deeply delusional that we cannot even conceptualize or imagine what realised humanity would consist in."[67] Both Habermas and Freyenhagen start from the premise that Adorno cannot locate any reliable sources of positive normativity within our current world.

Social Uniformity

In the previous section I offered a brief (and, I trust, charitable) summary of the "negativist" interpretation as it is represented by Habermas and Freyenhagen. Despite their many differences, both authors interpret Adorno as a philosopher who sees us as living in a social order that is thoroughly false. Habermas concludes that we should reject Adorno's social theory as incoherent, while Freyenhagen seeks to defend Adorno by means of a *negative* normativity that is directed against the bad rather than toward the good. Both authors portray Adorno as a thinker who sees social reality as bad without qualification or remainder. In other words, they interpret Adorno's skepticism about positive sources of normativity as *totalizing*. In what follows I wish to explain why I think the totalizing interpretation is inaccurate.

The totalizing interpretation suffers from three disadvantages. First, and most generally, it ascribes to Adorno a certain understanding of the *uniformity* of our social world. On this view Adorno apparently saw modern society as a seamless whole without breaks or contradictions. But we know that Adorno was a relentless critic of all claims to social uniformity, and throughout his writing he tends to dismiss the image of social uniformity as ideological or false. Already in his 1931 lecture, "The Actuality of Philosophy," Adorno declares that philosophy is confronted with the task of interpreting a world that is "incomplete, contradictory, and fragmentary [*unvollständig, widerspruchsvoll und brüchig*]."[68] Throughout his career he sustains this basic attitude of skepticism regarding any and all images of the social world as an unbroken whole. In his 1968 introductory lectures to sociology, Adorno faults

Talcott Parsons for endorsing a "harmonistic tendency" that obscures our insight into social contradiction. We should reject Parsons and his harmonistic vision because "within the seamlessness of exposition [*Bruchlosigkeit der Darstellungsform*] and the systematization of social phenomena" there lurks a tendency to explain away "the constitutive contradictions on which our society rests [*die konstitutiven tragenden Widersprüche der Gesellschaft*]," or, in other words, an ideological attempt "to conjure them out of existence."[69] This argument against social uniformity is not confined to Adorno's sociological work. It is essential to his understanding of dialectical criticism itself. In his 1958 course of lectures, "An Introduction to Dialectics," he encourages his students to recognize that a properly philosophical understanding of reality must begin by rejecting the premise that it is "seamless [*bruchlos*]"; they should instead construe society "in virtue of fractures that inhere in reality itself [*vermöge der Brüche, die ihr selber innewohnen*]."[70] As he famously announces at the conclusion to *Minima Moralia*, the critic's task is not to affirm the unity of the world but to reveal all of its "Risse und Schründe," its rifts and crevices.[71]

We must therefore conclude that Adorno rejects all images of social uniformity, whether such images present the world as uniformly true or as uniformly false. The first of these two alternatives is clearly intolerable for Adorno, since any attempt to portray the world as uniformly true must cover up instances of social irrationality and obstruct our awareness of human suffering. In his 1964 lectures, "Philosophical Elements of a Theory of Society," Adorno rejects the appearance of social uniformity as ideological or deceptive because it presents us with a pacifying image of generalized happiness. Huxley's *Brave New World*, for instance, presents us with the illusion of uniform satisfaction as if "everyone is happy nowadays." Adorno describes this attitude as "affirmative" insofar as it asserts a "false identity" between objective conditions and subjective consciousness. The assertion of such an identity is the chief task of ideology, or what Adorno elsewhere calls "the affirmative lie of culture."[72] In *Dialectic of Enlightenment*, we are presented with a modernized variation on the classical theory of ideology in the guise of the culture industry. Much like the Marxist understanding of ideology, the culture industry seeks to justify current forms of domination while obscuring any awareness of suffering. Entertainment, Adorno explains, is "society's apologia."[73] The culture industry works by affirmation: it smooths over all instances of social irrationality and serves up palliatives for all members of society so that they come to identify completely with their own social order. "To be entertained means to be in agreement."[74] But this appearance of affirmation and social uniformity is clearly an illusion. The moment one looks beneath "the surface of this happy agreement" one finds that the "false identity" is in fact "broken" in "countless places."[75]

The theory of the culture industry provides us with a powerful illustration as to why Adorno rejects any image of society as uniformly true. But we must also understand why Adorno cannot accept the image of society as uniformly negative or *false*. His attitude toward this uniformly negative understanding of the social order may strike us as rather more surprising, especially if we have been convinced by the widely shared view of Adorno as a totalizing negativist. One instance where Adorno addresses some difficulties with the false uniformity thesis appears in his discussion of the Italian sociologist Vilfredo Pareto, who Adorno criticizes for his theory concerning "*the totally ideological character of all society-related consciousness.*"[76] Adorno believes that this theory is clearly mistaken for the simple reason that Pareto's image of a uniformly false society is no less "harmonistic" than is Parsons's image of a uniformly true one. Here we are confronted with a striking irony. Although at first glance the two sociologists may seem to be sharply opposed, it turns out they have committed the very same error by smoothing over moments of dissonance in social reality. In this sense the totalizing theory of false consciousness is no more accurate than the totalizing theory of true consciousness. As Adorno explains, the idea of pervasive social falsehood encourages us to imagine social reality as an unbroken surface without immanent contradictions. But he rejects this image of total falsehood not least because such an image "*makes it impossible to distinguish between true and false.*" The true and the false, however, are terms of mutual entailment: "one cannot talk of false consciousness unless the possibility of a right consciousness also exists."[77] A totalizing theory of *false* consciousness is therefore no more coherent than the ideological portrait of a society as seamlessly true.

The Challenge of Self-Reflexivity

I have argued so far that it would have been implausible for Adorno to subscribe to any image of society as wholly uniform, whether this social uniformity was characterized as wholly true *or* wholly false. My arguments are meant to motivate the larger claim that Adorno could not have been a thoroughgoing skeptic about all available sources of normativity. But the specific puzzle of social uniformity also alerts us to a further and related problem: namely, the theory of total normative skepticism cannot easily respond to the challenge of self-reflexivity.

The challenge of self-reflexivity is of relevance to any social theory. By "self-reflexivity," I mean the principle that any general theory of society must be able to explain the possibility of its own appearance.[78] A theory of society can be defined as comprehensive when it claims to offer a general portrait of society as a whole and refuses to break social reality into pieces that can be understood entirely on their own. A comprehensive theory could not content itself, for example, with an explanation of the economy that sees the economic sphere as a discrete portion of the human world that obeys its own separable and independent laws. Such a separation of social reality into discrete domains is one way of understanding the Marxian problem of "fetishism," and, moreover, it is one instance of the broader epistemic and metaphysical error that occurs whenever we assign subject and object to mutually isolated spheres and believe that we can describe some particular portion of the social world without also describing ourselves. By contrast, if a social theory is genuinely comprehensive, it must be inclusive *without reservation*; and this means that it cannot exempt itself from the reality it wants to know. Here we confront the criterion of self-reflexivity. To satisfy this criterion, a social theory must provide a portrait of the social world in which it would at least be possible to imagine the emergence of that social theory itself.

This requirement would seem to rule out as illegitimate any social theory that purports to describe the whole of social reality as a seamless and unified domain that is plagued by false consciousness. Such a totalizing account of false consciousness would suggest that no member of a given society has a clear view of what her own society is actually like. But any such account would thereby fall into a trap of self-refuting relativism: it would mean that the social theorist could not exempt herself as a member of society from the charge of false consciousness and her theory would be robbed of its claims to truth. Marx himself was well aware of this problem, which is why he tried to develop his critique of society as an *immanent* critique that sought to identify only internal features of the social world that pointed beyond itself to its future transformation. This readiness to see internal contradictions satisfied the requirement of self-reflexivity: without internal contradictions the Marxist model of social reality would have been flattened out into a seamless whole, and it could not have explained how any members of a given society could gain an epistemic grasp of its contradictions. In *The Communist Manifesto*, Marx and Engels express the self-reflexivity principle in socio-historical form, charting the appearance of what they call "bourgeois ideologists" who have broken away from their own class and have "raised themselves to the level of comprehending theoretically the historical movement of [the social] whole."[79] Marxism, at least in some of its more philosophically subtle forms, has been notably alive to the problem of self-reflexivity, and it has responded to this problem with a dialectical model of social theory that refuses to isolate the theorizing subject from the object of its analysis.

For Adorno, Horkheimer, and the other affiliates of the Institute for Social Research, the problem of self-reflexivity was a central concern. In his 1937 essay, "Traditional and Critical Theory," Horkheimer brought all of his philosophical energy to bear on this problem, and he insisted that no theory of society could claim to be genuinely "critical" if it did not understand itself as emerging from, and dialectically entangled in, its own social surroundings.[80] No social theory can absent itself from its own description of the world, since social description too is *a socially embedded practice*. Without self-reflexivity, a social theory splits off the social observer from the social object as if the object were brute nature; the observer assumes the illusory transcendence of a quasi-Cartesian mind, and the exercise of social theory tends to betray all of the embarrassments associated with positivism.

In sum, the challenge of self-reflexivity reminds us that no critique of society can be valid if it does not offer a portrait of the social world in which that very critique would be possible. My question here is whether Adorno's theory can succeed in responding to this challenge. Naturally, our answer very much depends on how we construe his theory. One familiar interpretation suggests that Adorno rejected the classical model of false consciousness because he felt that modern society no longer has any need for illusion; instead it simply affirms society in its present form: "There are no more ideologies in the authentic sense of false consciousness, only advertisements for the world through its duplication [*Verdoppelung*]."[81] The classical theory of ideology presupposed a difference between ideology and reality, but this gap has now closed.[82] According to this new theory, ideology has given way to candid affirmation, and no experiences testify to the possibility of alternatives. "All phenomena rigidify, become insignias of the absolute rule of that which is."[83] Although this is a striking proposal, it still does not explain why this "duplication" itself is one that we should criticize and from what vantage any such criticism could arise. The normative question of whether our world merits our rejection or our assent remains unanswered. Another interpretation would be that Adorno sees the entirety of our social world as one of thoroughgoing falseness or delusion. But it would seem that such a description immediately presents us with a familiar puzzle of self-reference. If Adorno saw his social surroundings as a context of thoroughgoing delusion, then ipso facto his own theoretical ambition to offer a descriptively accurate portrait of this reality would fail. The theory of total negativity refutes itself the instant it stakes a claim to truth. This is what Habermas had in mind when he charged Adorno and Horkheimer with performative contradiction. Unlike

Habermas, Freyenhagen thinks he can succeed in eluding the trap of self-refutation by saying that Adorno does not need to stake any claims to truth at all; he only needs to claim knowledge of the false. In Freyenhagen's terms, Adorno must therefore be an "epistemic negativist."

But there are good reasons to doubt whether this response actually succeeds in rescuing Adorno from the charge of self-refutation. Freyenhagen's solution raises at least two further puzzles that merit our attention. First, it is readily apparent that Adorno believes his own social theory is *true* in the robust sense, since it presumably gives us an accurate portrait of what our social world is actually like. But in a totally false world why would we expect that true descriptions would persist? And how would the very norm of truth survive given the context of thoroughgoing delusion? Freyenhagen's answer (based on his negative Aristotelian understanding of our frustrated human nature) would seem to be that despite his epistemic negativism Adorno still enjoys some knowledge about the human *potential* that our society has damaged. The best we can say about this answer is that it conflicts with the thesis of epistemic negativism. For if Adorno can claim to know *anything* about this potential, then he already knows more about the human condition than the context of total delusion would allow. The second puzzle about this response is that it looks as if even Adorno's *knowledge* of the false already equips him with rare and privileged insight into the nature of our social world that is not generally available.[84] But the best we can say about this second answer is that it fails the challenge of self-reflexivity. It exempts Adorno from the context of allegedly total social delusion from which his own theory was born.[85] For both reasons, then, it seems that if the negativist reading were true, Adorno's critical efforts could not meet the requirements of self-reflexivity.

Presuppositions of Public Criticism

Before concluding this topic, it is important to mention yet another reason we should reject the interpretation of Adorno as a totalizing negativist about social norms. Although I do not wish to dwell in this book on facts of biography, we should recall that in the postwar era Adorno contributed a great deal to public conversations regarding the political culture of the Federal Republic. In public speeches both in person and on the radio, Adorno took upon himself the task of addressing problems of general concern to his fellow citizens in Germany and to the wider community of students and scholars abroad. Consider, for instance, the conversation with Hellmut Becker on the topic "Education for Maturity" (*Erziehung zur Mündigkeit*) that was broadcast on August 13, 1969, only a few days after the philosopher's death.[86] Adorno begins the conversation with reference to Kant's well-known essay, "What Is Enlightenment?" and he does not hesitate to say that maturity is vital to democracy, since democracy presupposes "the capacity and courage of each individual to make full use of his reasoning power."[87] This was only one of many radio conversations to which Adorno contributed at a rate of approximately one a year under the general rubric "Educational Questions for Today." Such conversations presuppose a certain idea of democratic pedagogy. It may strike some readers as odd to describe Adorno as a "public intellectual," and it is a term that we should use with caution since he expressed strong reservations concerning the fetish of intellectual *engagement*.[88] But Adorno nonetheless had to believe that it was at least possible to intervene in public consciousness for the purposes of its beneficial transformation. This is surely the case in his remarks on maturity as a prerequisite for democracy and is no less the case when we recall his various public lectures on topics such as "Education after Auschwitz" and "The Meaning of Working through the Past."[89]

It is not at all clear if the negativist interpretation allows conceptual space for Adorno's commitment to the practice of democratic pedagogy.[90] As Volker Heins has argued, this practical pedagogy is "predicated on the Enlightenment-era faith in the educability of the public."[91] We must therefore ask whether such a presupposition can be harmonized with Adorno's philosophical claims or whether we must instead accept the suggestion (as expressed by Habermas) that there were "two Adornos," the sociological pessimist and the democratic activist.[92] This distinction would presumably correspond to the difference between the formal philosopher and the public intellectual. My own view is that this suggestion is untenable, since there is no bright line that would permit us to distinguish between the two modes of argumentation: Adorno's written texts bear traces of informal and semipublic commentary, while the lectures often serve as dress rehearsals for more "formal" publications. Rather than resort to any such dualism, I consider it far more plausible to follow the suggestion by Heins that "the differences between the two bodies of work are differences in context and style, not in kind."[93]

The practice of democratic pedagogy therefore illustrates what I would call the informal logic of public action. When one intervenes discursively in the nexus of public affairs one implicitly commits oneself to an understanding of public consciousness as variable rather than fixed. Otherwise one's own interventions can have little purpose beyond the narcissistic satisfactions of theatrical self-expression. Now if one were to condemn *all* of public consciousness as total falsehood one would violate this informal logic. In Adorno's case it strains credulity to claim that he imagined himself exempt from the world he described.[94] As a dialectician he knows that even before he has begun to speak the theorizing subject is already implicated in the social world he means to understand and is already entangled in innumerable social meditations. Against Karl Mannheim's celebration of *freischwebende Intelligenz*, Adorno wrote that "the very intelligentsia that pretends to float freely is fundamentally rooted in the very being that must be changed."[95] Philosophers of a different kind may arrogate to themselves the right to withdraw from the world and condemn it to its *Seinsverlassenheit*. But for the social theorist this option is not available. "Theory" is not the piety of thinking at a mountainside retreat; it is a mode of socially embedded praxis.

The Possibility of Immanent Critique

The preceding considerations should lead us to conclude that something must be wrong in the standard understanding of Adorno as an epistemic negativist or a totalizing skeptic regarding the sources of normativity. Although the negativist interpretation has generated an exceptionally compelling body of scholarship, I fear that it has also burdened the community of interpretation with various philosophical puzzles that are based on a false premise. The image of Adorno as a totalizing skeptic is an intriguing philosophical construct, but as a portrait of Adorno's own philosophical commitments it is inaccurate.

If we now ask ourselves what essential features of Adorno's own philosophy are missing from the negativist interpretation, the remarks offered above should have prepared us for the answer. The negativist interpretation misses the crucial fact that Adorno does not see the social world as a seamless whole. Rather, Adorno sees society as a broken or fragmented landscape that contains contradictions. But to say that society contains contradictions is just to say that some of its norms stand in conflict with others. Although the far greater share of these norms simply confirm society as it is, others challenge their authority. These immanent contradictions have a normative and anticipatory status insofar as they point beyond the present order to a better one. Adorno's chief work as a critical philosopher is largely negative but not in the merely descriptive sense as if he meant only to portray the world in all its negativity. Rather his task is negative in a distinctively dialectical sense, insofar as he means to expose moments of contradiction in order to break up the illusion of a normatively uniform whole. The strategy he adopts for this practice is that of *immanent critique*. He believes that this critical approach will free us up to experience not just our pervasive suffering but also instances of promise or possibility that point the way beyond our present condition to a future of human flourishing.[96]

The suggestion that Adorno should be seen as practicing a species of immanent critique has other proponents in the secondary literature, including scholars such as Rahel Jaeggi and Brian O'Connor.[97] To his credit, Freyenhagen is willing to acknowledge that this alternative has considerable merit even while he lays out a vigorous case against it.[98] My own view is that the understanding of Adorno as a theorist of immanent critique is not only a more faithful description of his stated philosophical aims. But also, quite apart from what Adorno himself may have intended, it is more defensible as an account of critical practice. After all, it is one thing to provide a summary of what we believe Adorno wished to do, but it is quite another thing to claim that what he was doing was viable.

This distinction helps us appreciate a major point of disagreement among his interpreters. The case of Seyla Benhabib is instructive. Although she is in certain respects unsympathetic to Adorno's overall philosophical project, she nonetheless offers an excellent summary of its aims. "The task of the critic," she writes, "is to illuminate those cracks in the totality, those fissures in the social net, those moments of disharmony and discrepancy, through which the untruth of the whole is revealed and *glimmers of another life become visible.*"[99] Those who understand Adorno as a theorist of immanent critique can agree with Benhabib's description even if they disagree with her conclusion that Adorno's project cannot succeed because (as both Habermas and Benhabib have argued) it falls into performative contradiction. My own defense of Adorno positions me in an unusual place among his many readers. I agree with Habermas that if Adorno's philosophy can be defended, it must appeal to some sources of normativity; but I disagree with him that Adorno fails to identify such sources. Meanwhile, I agree with Freyenhagen that Adorno's project is philosophically defensible; but I disagree with him that this defense can only go through if we abandon the premise that Adorno is somehow restricted to knowledge of the false. Freyenhagen's argument runs into a further difficulty because if he is right, then Adorno should not be permitted to appeal to any positive norm of human flourishing. But the neo-Aristotelian idea of a "potential" is just such a norm. After all, actualizing such a potential is something we believe that human beings *should do.* This philosophical difficulty just underscores a more general point, that what may strike us as purely negative language in social theory is seldom consistently negative at all, and it often bears within itself an implicit commitment to the better and the true.[100] In some well-known cases this commitment remains largely hidden—hence the charge of "crypto-normativity."[101] But in the case of Adorno's philosophy, I believe this accusation is wide of the mark.

The Question of Exaggeration

In the preceding discussion I have confined myself to rather general remarks as to why we should prefer the immanent-critical interpretation of Adorno's philosophy over the negativist interpretation. But it must be admitted that Adorno's writing is sufficiently multivalent as to provide us with considerable warrant for both lines of interpretation. At times he claims that our critique of the wrong or the false is possible only if we presuppose a standard of the right or the true, while on other occasions he argues with nearly equal vigor that it is philosophically misguided or politically repressive to demand that critique be tethered to a better alternative. His inconsistency on this question is so pronounced that occasionally he seems willing to endorse both views even within the very same sentence. In the radio address, "Critique," from late May 1969 (one of his very last statements in public), he observes, "It is *by no means always* possible to add to critique the immediate practical recommendation of something better, *although in many cases critique can proceed by way of confronting realities with the norms to which those realities appeal.*"[102] In this address Adorno seems adamant that "progressive thought" is mistaken to place undue confidence in the immanent movements of reality, since the "higher form" of society can "*no longer be read out of reality as a concrete tendency.*"[103] Yet he concludes the very same address (with a reference to Spinoza) with the bold confirmation that "the false, once determinately known and precisely expressed, is *already an index of what is right and better* [*das Falsche, einmal bestimmt erkannt und präzisiert, bereits Index des Richtigen, Besseren ist*]."[104]

The resolution to this interpretive puzzle is by no means obvious. On the one hand, we are told that (a) it is entirely possible for critique to be immanent since we can find current reality deficient when it is measured against available norms. On the other hand, we are told that (b) critique cannot possibly be immanent because our current order contains no internal normative tendencies that point toward a preferred alternative. Because these two interpretations would appear to be mutually exclusive, we are faced with a stark choice: (a) and (b) cannot both be true. When confronted with such a basic conflict in textual evidence, we may feel tempted to conclude that Adorno's larger philosophical project is caught in an unworkable antinomy, or, more simply, that its claims are as changeable as the wind.

But there is another and more charitable option. To appreciate what is at stake in this debate we must look more closely at how Adorno employs the rhetorical device of exaggeration. Favorable remarks on exaggeration can be found throughout his writing, most famously in *Minima Moralia* where he declares that "nothing is true in psychoanalysis except the exaggerations."[105] In a no less famous commentary on the "dark writers of the bourgeoisie" from *Dialectic of Enlightenment* we are told that "only exaggeration is true."[106] This passage is especially instructive insofar as it is suggested there that critics such as Nietzsche and de Sade should be understood not as ruthless antagonists of the Enlightenment but as its advocates. Unlike the positivist philosophers who openly profess their fidelity to enlightenment even while they hasten its descent into unreflective instrumentalism, the "dark writers" at least have the courage to reckon honestly with reason's contradictory effects. We must therefore read their criticism in a dialectical manner: Their "secret purpose" was not merely negative; they meant "to lay bare the utopia which is contained in every great philosophy, as it is in Kant's concept of reason: the utopia of a humanity which, itself no longer distorted, no longer needs distortion."[107]

The various motives and meanings that inform Adorno's "art of exaggeration" has inspired much discussion.[108] I am broadly in agreement with critics such as Bert van den Brink that exaggeration in Adorno's work is a rhetorical device with an emancipatory intent insofar as it is meant to assist us in our effort to "escape the attenuating coercion of the given." But this suggests that when is it directed toward the ends of human freedom, exaggeration sustains its alliance with enlightenment. The purpose of exaggeration is not to describe what is the case but rather to motivate our *criticism* of what is the case. In his 1961 essay, "Open Delusion Society," Adorno states this point succinctly: "All thinking is exaggeration, in so far as every thought that is one at all goes beyond its confirmation by the given facts."[109] Although many other instances from Adorno's work could be cited to support the claim that exaggeration has a critical function, one further example may suffice. In the 1959 essay, "The Meaning of Working through the Past," Adorno notes that many citizens would prefer to surrender the challenge of autonomy and simply submit to the mindlessness of the collective. But he offers this remark not as a mere description but with a monitory intent; it is meant chiefly as a warning about the world that is still coming into being. Adorno explains that he has "exaggerated the somber side, following the maxim that only exaggeration per se today can be the medium of truth."[110]

The first thing to notice about this "maxim" is that it too is clearly an exaggeration. Elsewhere in his work Adorno lays aside his well-honed rhetorical skill in the art of exaggeration and adopts the sober-minded tones of a social philosopher who wishes to convey with precision the full complexity of the surrounding world. Since it is readily apparent that Adorno does not always exaggerate, we must conclude that he is exaggerating when he says that exaggeration is the unique medium of truth. But the maxim should also arouse our suspicions for a rather different and more straightforward reason. The very idea of an exaggeration already involves a distinction between a statement and the conditions to which it refers. After all, an exaggeration is an exaggeration *of* something. To say that one has exaggerated is just to say that one has strayed from a faithful description of actual conditions by enhancing certain features and dimming down others. Adorno admits that he has done precisely this: he explains in a quasi-confessional mode that he has placed special stress on the "somber [*das Düstere*]" aspect. I therefore propose that we think of exaggeration as a technique of anticipatory critique. Adorno means to direct our attention toward the emerging features of social reality that may soon metastasize into the universal if they are permitted to continue. His exaggerations serve a critical purpose insofar as they serve as monitory statements about the world that is now coming into being. In this respect his exercises in exaggeration share much in common with the genre of dystopian fiction (such as Aldous Huxley's *Brave New World*, a novel that Adorno found intriguing) in which incipient problems of society today are projected into a possible future.[111]

We can resolve the apparent antinomy in Adorno's writing between total negativism and dialectical immanence if we understand his statements of total negativism as exaggerations in the sense I have sketched above. They are not intended as faithful descriptions of the world as it is; rather, they are meant to alert us to emergent possibilities in our present society that are growing ever more pronounced and may eventually terminate in total eclipse. In the discussion that followed his lecture "The Meaning of Working through the Past," Adorno was pressed to explain what he meant in suggesting that exaggeration could serve as a means for teaching and education. In response he says that he wishes "to forestall a misunderstanding" and that he would not wish "to accept the responsibility for recommending exaggeration in education." He admits that he "perhaps exaggerated" but then explains:

> Exaggeration seems to me to be a necessary medium for social-theoretical and philosophical presentation, because the moderate, normal surface existence in general conceals such potentials and because in the face of neutral average everydayness to indicate *the threat laying below it at first blush always has the character of exaggeration*. I would urgently warn *against exaggeration* in pedagogical work, for instance. On the contrary, I would say the less the idea of propaganda here even arises, the more stringently one holds to the facts—which God knows speak for themselves, or against themselves—the better.[112]

In this response Adorno draws a clear distinction between *threats,* on the one hand, and current *facts,* on the other. This suggests that exaggerations have an anticipatory status that is comparable to the immanent possibilities that play such a prominent role in the Marxian theory of history, except that Adorno's exaggerations are anticipations of social catastrophe rather than social fulfillment. We should note that when Adorno is being careful and avoids the temptation of aphorism, he does not endorse the famous thesis that there is "no right living." In *Problems of Moral Philosophy* he speaks of an emerging tendency rather than a final condition: he alerts us to "the thematic that should form the basis of every deeper reflection on moral or ethical questions, namely the question whether culture, or whatever culture has become, permits something like the good life [*so etwas wie richtiges Leben*], *or whether it is a network of institutions that actually tends more and more to thwart the emergence of such right living.*"[113] The unmistakably temporal and anticipatory status of exaggeration in Adorno's writing must be kept in mind, or we would be forced to conclude that he has violated the requirement of self-reflexivity by describing a world in which his own critical insights would be impossible. Exaggeration can serve the interests of critique only so long as there remains a gap between exaggeration and description. Unfortunately, Adorno does not always write in a fashion that acknowledges this gap; he thereby redescribes the world as a uniform whole when the stated purpose of his social criticism is to expose this uniformity as deceptive.[114] We must conclude that his very skill in the rhetorical art of exaggeration often does his philosophical claims a disservice, insofar as readers can easily miss the moment of critical anticipation in his exaggerations and misconstrue them as merely descriptive reports about the present world.

Marx's Critical Method

At this point it is relevant to mention a further consideration that argues in favor of the immanent-critical interpretation. This concerns affinities between Adorno and the broader traditions of historical materialism and neo-Marxism. Such affinities, to be sure, should not be inflated beyond measure. Adorno was far too idiosyncratic and heterodox a thinker to permit us to categorize his work as part of the official canon of Marxist doctrine, and even the more capacious term "Western Marxism" may obscure what is most instructive in his philosophy.[115] But I would nonetheless insist on one salient point of connection. Historical materialism is distinctive perhaps most of all for its singular principle of dialectical immanence, namely, the principle that historical change emerges from the immanent contradictions of history itself.[116] This principle is an obvious homage to the Hegelian thesis that spirit does not shy away from the negative. Rather, it is a power that "looks the negative in the face [and] tarries with it." This tarrying is "the magical power that converts the negative into Being."[117] Marx inherited this principle: he believed that it is possible to identify moments of tension or contradiction within current social reality that are signs of a future that will eventually win its self-realization. It is true, of course, that Marx bitterly resisted the contamination of his socialist theory by what he called "utopian" themes, since he denied that, within our own historical moment, it is possible for us to claim full and incorrigible knowledge of the values and arrangements that we need only apply to the as-yet unrealized future.[118] His colleague Engels was arguably even more explicit in rejection of utopian tendencies in nineteenth-century socialist thought; he believed that utopianism violated the principle of historical immanence by inflating socialism into "an absolute truth that is independent of time, space, and of the historical development of man."[119]

Notwithstanding such criticism, however, both Marx and Engels adhered to the principle that the present contains contradictory tendencies that have the status of promissory notes on the future. Only this principle of dialectical immanence can support the well-known Marxist view that proletarian political consciousness first develops *within bourgeois society itself.* In his inaugural address to the International Workingmen's Association in 1864, for example, Marx offered full-throated praise for the Ten Hours' Bill as "the victory of a *principle,*" because "it was the first time that in broad daylight the political economy of the middle class succumbed to the political economy of the working class."[120] Such praise for an internal principle suggests that, despite his antiutopianism, Marx adhered to a theory of immanent contradiction that permitted him to gain at least partial epistemic familiarity with future-directed norms or themes that already lie at hand within the historically dynamic present. Marx never denied such familiarity. In fact, he believed that the present must first generate all of its internal contradictions to the fullest possible extent before the sum of such contradictions brings the present to an end. In the *Critique of Political Economy* (1859) he wrote, "No social order ever perishes before all of the productive forces for which there is room in it have developed, and new, higher relations of production never appear before the material conditions of their existence have matured in the womb of the old society itself."[121] In his 1871 essay on the Paris Commune, Marx further explains that the working class "[has] no ready-made utopias to introduce," and it has "no ideals to realize." But he affirms that it is still the task of the working class "to set free the elements of the new society with which the old collapsing society is pregnant."[122]

The well-known obstetrical metaphor—of the present that is pregnant with the future—confirms Marx's understanding of history as a process that does not proceed by mere negation but rather gestates the immanent forces that will eventually produce a new reality. Now it would be exceptionally strange if Marx had denied that inhabitants of a given epoch could enjoy *any* epistemic familiarity with such productive forces prior to the event of revolution. Fortunately, Marx never expressed such an extravagant skepticism about the immanent norms that pointed toward an epoch's self-overcoming.[123] Much like Hegel, Marx wished to identify the "ought" that already inheres within the "is," the rational that lies coiled and still unrealized as a latent moment in the actual. Marx endorsed this dialectical principle of immanent normativity as early as 1843 in his well-known letter to Arnold Ruge: "The critic can start from any form of theoretical or practical consciousness, and develop out of the actual forms of existing reality the true reality as what it ought to be, that which is its aim."[124] No matter how vigorously he rejected utopianism, Marx strongly believed in the possibility of mobilizing the normative commitments of present-day consciousness as a resource for the realization of the future. By locating the "ought" within what "is," he could affirm a dialectical continuity between present and future.[125] As he explained to Ruge, "We develop new principles to the world *out of its own principles.*"[126]

The Idea of Normative Surplus

The idea of dialectical immanence alerts us to the phenomenon that Axel Honneth calls a "normative surplus." The idea of a normative surplus conveys a certain irony in the historical dynamics of social norms. Any society can be understood as a normative order in the sense that it subscribes to certain basic standards or moral goods. Those who are most successful or the primary beneficiaries of this normative order will insist that the standards in question have been realized to the fullest possible extent: they will say that even if the realization of those standards may have involved a long and arduous trial of historical attempts, their society has now arrived at the intended match between the standards and actual conditions such that no further modifications are necessary. However, an irony occurs where it becomes evident that the standards can be interpreted as implying a further transformation beyond what the current beneficiaries may have intended. This happens when those who are not the current beneficiaries recognize that the standards have implications that hitherto have gone largely unnoticed or have been dismissed as illegitimate, utopian, et cetera. These implications exemplify a normative surplus in the current normative order. Subordinated groups can then invoke this surplus when they wish to explain the legitimacy of their demand for further social transformation.

A classical illustration of this phenomenon can be found in Marx's remarks on the difference between political and human emancipation. In his essay on the "Jewish question," Marx expresses unambiguous support for the emancipatory ideals of civic inclusion and equality as codified in the eighteenth-century revolutions of Europe and North America.[127] Only on very rare occasions does Marx subscribe to the skeptical view that such ideals are nothing but ideology.[128] Rather, he tends to endorse these ideals insofar as they formalize the then-dominant conception of freedom for all citizens within the framework of an emergent capitalist order. Admittedly, Marx sees this bourgeois model of freedom as merely formal and thus incomplete. He insists that the bourgeois (political-legal) model must be both annulled and dialectically fulfilled in a higher species of genuinely comprehensive or "human" freedom. But this is not to say that Marx ever *denies* the legitimacy of bourgeois freedom. On the contrary; he embraces it, and he goes so far as to claim that any state that does not honor it is not yet *fully* bourgeois. In *The Holy Family* he writes that "states which cannot yet *politically* emancipate the Jews must be rated by comparison with accomplished states and must be considered as underdeveloped."[129] Implicit in this claim is a normative model of history that assigns to the bourgeoisie a necessary role in volatilizing all elements of society to the point where freedom signifies nothing more than freedom for egoistic self-assertion and private property.

At this point the idea of a normative surplus comes clearly into view. Marx recognizes that the standard of freedom that is seen as the organizing norm of bourgeois society has further implications that cannot be fully realized within the individualistic framework of bourgeois society. These implications, however, are constitutive of the idea of freedom itself. Freedom means not only the formal (political and legal) freedom of the propertied citizen; it also means the substantive freedom of the fully realized human being. What the bourgeoisie identifies as freedom is therefore one-sided and self-contradictory even while it contains a "surplus" or unfulfilled promise. To this idea of a normative surplus, however, Marx adds the further claim that the bourgeois ideal of freedom simultaneously functions as ideology. Political freedom is not only indifferent toward human freedom, but actually helps solidify inequalities in socioeconomic status. Marx is therefore able to say that (a) political emancipation is a precondition for human emancipation, even while he is also able to say that (b) political emancipation serves apologetic and ideological purposes because it obstructs our understanding of the need for any further change. In sum, Marx recognizes that the ideal of freedom in bourgeois society is intrinsically dialectical: it is *at once ideology and more than ideology*. Following Honneth, we can say that the bourgeois idea of freedom carries a normative surplus that points beyond the constraints of bourgeois society. And, following Marx, we should add that the normative surplus of current standards is often obscured to such a degree that we are discouraged from imagining that any further transformation in society would be necessary or desirable. The final irony is that *this very surplus* can become ideological: the promise of a "way out" of the current order can serve an apologetic function insofar as any deeper insight into our own unfreedom is transformed into a fantasy that permits that unfreedom to persist unchallenged.

Adorno's version of critical theory subscribes to all three of these claims. Bourgeois society is understood as (1) a self-affirmative order in which dominant norms serve a largely apologetic or ideological function. But it is also understood as (2) a self-contradictory order that contains a normative surplus that expresses a genuine ideal of human flourishing even while that ideal remains unrealized. Like Marx, however, Adorno adds the further irony that (3) even the normative surplus in bourgeois society can serve the purposes of ideology, insofar as it offers us the illusion of an escape that may help obscure the problems of our current condition. For Adorno it is the culture industry that serves this ideological function. All the same, Adorno never goes so far as to deny the normative surplus altogether, nor does he believe that this surplus itself is necessarily and nothing but an ideological fantasy. On the contrary, it is crucial to Adorno's argument that this surplus has a dialectical character: it points beyond the present even while it *also* obstructs our deeper awareness of what is presently wrong: "All happiness to this day promises what never yet was, and the belief in its immediacy gets in the way of its coming to be."[130] It would therefore be a mistake to interpret Adorno as a modern gnostic, since he never permits himself to lapse into a one-sided or totalizing critique of happiness as *mere* ideology. On the contrary; he sustains the difficult posture of a dialectician who recognizes the normative surplus that is contained *within* ideological representations or practices. What is not yet fully realized nonetheless serves as a sign for its future realization.

In sum, it seems to me relatively uncontroversial to say that Adorno subscribes to a principle of dialectical immanence. He does not roundly condemn the entirety of our present life as false, nor does he claim that we are condemned to total ignorance as to what a true life would be like. Rather, he is willing to acknowledge that within our present order, and even within the bounds of individual experience, we can identify moments that are "non-identical" or disharmonious with the overall structure of things. Like Marx, he regards these moments of contradiction as immanent signs of future possibility. For Adorno even the smallest and seemingly insignificant elements of our current experience therefore become what he calls "rehearsals of the right life [*Uebungen zum richtigen Leben*]."[131] If we confine our discussion at least momentarily to this single theme we can justifiably conclude that Adorno deserves a seat among other social theorists in the neo-Marxist tradition.

Aesthetics and Dialectical Immanence

Acknowledging these broad similarities hardly implies that Adorno should be characterized as a Marxist in the doctrinal or political sense, but it does suggest that we should be alert to further points that Adorno may have shared in common with Marx and other theorists in the tradition of historical materialism. In this regard we must acknowledge the enormous importance Adorno assigns to the problem of aesthetics. In the official edition of his collected writings a full half of the published volumes are devoted to questions of music, and several other volumes address problems of literature. Adorno delivered several lecture courses on aesthetics, and at the time of his death he was working on the major treatise, *Aesthetic Theory*, published posthumously in 1970. Since that time it has been a temptation among critics to echo the hostile verdict of Hans-Jürgen Krahl, who disparaged his teacher's flight into "aesthetic abstractions."[132] But the great emphasis Adorno placed on aesthetic experience cannot be dismissed as a bourgeois indulgence or a withdrawal into Parnassus. On the contrary, in his treatment of music and literature Adorno consistently upheld the interpretive principle of dialectical immanence: no different from other spheres of human life, all aesthetic creation is "ideology and simultaneously more than mere ideology."[133] An artwork is no doubt a product of its own epoch, but it also contains within itself a normative surplus that bursts free of its surroundings. Only this normative surplus can explain why Adorno (following Stendhal) found in art "une promesse du bonheur," or a promise of happiness.[134]

This very same idea was not unknown to Marx himself. In the *Grundrisse* Marx commented on the twofold quality of artworks, for instance, those from ancient Greece, namely, that they are "bound up with certain forms of social development," yet "they still afford us artistic pleasure" and therefore "*they count as a norm and an unattainable model [als Norm und unerreichbare Muster gelten]*."[135] With his dialectical understanding of the relation between aesthetics and historical conditions, Marx readily admitted that "a man cannot become a child again, or he becomes childish." The art of the past at least in this sense belongs to the past. But Marx did not permit this historicist conceit to obstruct or altogether vitiate our appreciation of past artworks. Rather, he recognized that art is the carrier of normative lessons that exceed the moment of their genesis and anticipate a better if still unrealized world. "But does [a man] not find joy in the child's naiveté, and must he himself not strive to reproduce its truth at a higher stage?"[136] Marx posed this question chiefly to make explicit his hostility to any historicism that would lock the artwork away in a hermetically sealed past. He insisted instead on the historical dialectic that permits an artwork's *truth* to exceed the moment of its origin. Adorno will later build on this thematic of normative recuperation not only in relation to the truth-value of aesthetic experience; it will also reappear in his analysis of childhood experience. This dialectical understanding of the relationship between past normativity and the surplus of meaning that remains available to future generations is a major theme that connects Adorno to the Marxist tradition, and if we fail to recognize its importance a considerable share of Adorno's philosophy will remain unintelligible.

The Stakes of Social Criticism

Ultimately what is at stake is a question of far greater importance than the interpretive matter as to whether we have succeeded in getting Adorno right. The more urgent question is whether the philosophical vision we ascribe to Adorno corresponds to our own possible understanding of what our current social world is like. It is precisely on this point that the immanent-critical interpretation enjoys a crucial advantage since it alerts us to the available moral and political resources that we desperately need if we wish to raise any objections to the way our world is now arranged. Such considerations confront us with an urgent question. Do we believe that such resources are available, or shall we surrender to thoroughgoing skepticism as to the prospects for transformation? No doubt the current state of the world leaves us with a great many reasons to believe that skepticism is warranted. War and suffering, domination and discrimination, cruelty and hatred—these are all such pervasive features of our local and global situation that we may often feel inclined to say with Dante that we have entered the inferno and that all hope must be abandoned. As a description of our world such a verdict is no doubt tempting; it is only natural if the record of human conduct in the modern era often leaves us with the hopeless impression that we are poised on the edge of an abyss. Precarity has become an everyday experience. But it is nonetheless of greatest importance that we distinguish between the condition of precarity and a condition of thoroughgoing Gnosticism. We should not and cannot permit ourselves to accept a description of the social world that rules out the possibility of its criticism.

For those who continue to believe that social theory has some role to play in the improvement of society the stakes could not be higher. Immanent critique proceeds on the assumption that the current world offers at least *some* internal resources for its radical transformation. Without such resources we would have little warrant for our assumption that things can ever be different than they are. But without such an assumption it is difficult to understand why we would claim that anything about the current world is objectionable at all. A social order that is simply given to us in the way that it is and does not allow for even the slightest sense of an alternative hardens into brute facticity, and it takes on the illusory character of "second nature." The central task of critical theory is to break up the reified appearance of second nature and restore to us our understanding of society as a world that human beings have made. But we must assume that anything that we have made remains susceptible to its remaking. Only if we see society as a human creation can we sustain our awareness that it might be arranged altogether differently from the way it happens to be arranged now. But it is just this sense of a difference—between what the world is and what it ought to be—that permits us to stand back from our surroundings in a posture of critical evaluation. Criticism presupposes this posture of "oughtness" or normativity without which we could do little more than affirm the world as it is given. The world is not everything that is the case.

Temporality and Normativity

Adorno was a thinker of the normative precisely because, as Iain Macdonald has so scrupulously explained, he adhered to the category of *possibility*.[137] If he was skeptical about the likelihood of realizing an alternative future, he did not permit his doubts to sabotage his commitment to the demand that things ought to be different than they currently are. One could argue that this demand has an intrinsically temporal logic: to look at the world in a normative posture is to presuppose that its status can be modified and is susceptible to change. Such considerations may help us explain why Adorno could never completely disavow the concept of progress even if he admitted its "antinomian" character. In his 1964–65 lectures on the theory of history and freedom, he warns that if we embrace the concept of progress without qualification and insist that it is immanent to the historical continuum, we convert history into an object of idolatry. Yet he also warns that if we insist that progress is transcendental to history and deny its temporal character, it thereby "evaporates into ahistorical theology." Adorno resists both of these alternatives, but he nevertheless holds fast to a qualified concept of progress as a hope for this-worldly improvement:

> The temporal nature of progress, its simple concept—for progressing is simply inconceivable outside time—binds it to the empirical world. *Without such a temporal dimension, in other words, without the hope that things might improve with time, the heinous aspects of the world and its ways really would become immortalized in thought and creation itself would be turned into the work of a gnostic demon.*[138]

If Adorno resists this gnostic temptation, it is because he holds fast to the logic of the normative, with its implicitly temporal hope for a future that would be different from how the world is presently constituted. Such considerations moved him to offer a striking affirmation of our need for progress, not as an determinate concept or empirical truth, but simply as a normative standard that belongs to the very logic of social action: "Too little that is good has power in the world for the world to be said to have achieved progress, but *there can be no good, not even a trace of it, without progress.*"[139]

Incidentally, it is worth recalling that the topic of Gnosticism was of great interest to Adorno, and he was especially fascinated by the concept of the evil demiurge who appears in gnostic teaching as the creator of the fallen world. In a 1959 letter to Hans Jonas (the scholar perhaps best known for his study of Gnosticism) Adorno writes that "Valentinus' gnosticism is just as important to me as Marcion's, in which only a very specific motif interests me specially: the denunciation of the demiurge."[140] According to Adorno, the gnostic idea of the created world as a realm of radical evil has a literary analogue in the works of Samuel Beckett, in whose imagination the entirety of human life appears as little more than a "death sentence."[141] Beckett's universe is bereft of all hope except perhaps for the singular hope "that there would be nothing." But Beckett rejects this nihilistic hope as well. Out of this "fissure of inconsistency" Beckett turns the "image-world of nothingness [*Bilderwelt des Nichts*]" into a "something that secures his poetry." The poetic result is indistinguishable from the gnostic image of creation: "Gnostically [Beckett's work] regards the world as it has been created as radically evil and its repudiation the possibility of a different, not yet existent one. So long as the world is as it is, then all images of reconciliation, peace and quiet resemble those of death. The smallest difference between nothingness and that which has come to rest, would be the refuge of hope."[142]

It is well known that Adorno held Beckett in high esteem and ranked his works among the greatest artifacts of literary and theatrical modernism. But this fact only compounds the difficulty of recognizing the real differences between them. After all, the possibilities that may be available in aesthetic representation are in crucial respects distinct from those that may be available for a social theory that must meet certain standards of argumentative consistency. Although the comparison to Gnosticism may shed a helpful light on Beckett's literary achievement, when we consider the social world as it is portrayed in Adorno's own philosophy the comparison introduces more confusion than light. Despite its evocative power, Gnosticism does not offer an accurate description of what Adorno believes the world is like; rather, it is the name for a theoretical *temptation* that he must overcome if he wishes to understand the world in all its irreducible complexity.[143] To be sure, he does not always succeed in resisting this temptation. This may explain why he occasionally portrays his world as a place of thoroughgoing falsehood that lacks any internal resources for its transformation. It remains an open question as to whether we should accept Adorno's startling claim that Beckett portrays the whole of social reality as a "concentration camp."[144] But even if we were to consider this a plausible characterization of Beckett's work, we might nonetheless insist that it does not correspond to Adorno's own vision of social reality. Adorno does not see the social world as a fallen realm that appears as if it had been created by an evil demiurge. On the contrary, he sees it as shot through with contradiction and promise.[145] The difference is crucial, since if Adorno believed that the world were *thoroughly* false he would have to look beyond its walls to discover the resources for its transformation. But then he would have to abandon the practice of immanent criticism altogether.[146]

Concluding Remarks

Since its founding nearly a century ago, critical theory has defined itself as an intrinsically normative practice in two interlocking ways. First, it refuses to accept the false affirmation of society; and second, its critical stand against the false is animated by an enduring if implicit appeal to the true. That is, it is animated by the idea of a society that would be worthy of humankind.[147] The resources that are still available to us for such a normative practice have indeed grown scarce. Our moral language itself has grown impoverished and is too often put toward purely strategic ends. Those who contribute to social theory today often seem all too ready to announce the wholesale corruption of our normative ideals, as if the mere documentation of corruption could serve as an *Ersatz* for critique. But genealogical efforts have no purpose if they are not guided by at least some normative standards, even if these standards are partial or compromised. To demonstrate through historical reconstruction how even our most humane ideals have been turned toward inhumane ends has little meaning if we cannot explain what ideals in this history have thereby been violated. A genealogy without normativity consumes its own critical intent: it yields only cynicism and an attitude of condescension toward those who still believe that things could be better than they are. If we do not wish to abandon ourselves to disabling cynicism, we must hold fast to our ideals even as we acknowledge how thoroughly they have been compromised.

In this introductory chapter I have said a great deal about why I believe other interpretations of Adorno are mistaken. In the chapters that follow, I propose an alternative reading of Adorno that I believe better accords with the philosopher's own intentions. The key to my interpretation is the view that Adorno sees the world not as a seamless whole but as a landscape that is shot through with contradictions. Through the practice of immanent critique Adorno seizes upon these contradictions to expose moments that point beyond our current despair to a world in which happiness or human flourishing would at last be realized. My interpretation depends on the strong premise that even in our present situation we can identify moments of happiness that embody this possibility even if under current conditions such happiness remains precarious. Adorno, I will argue, was not a totalizing skeptic about human flourishing. Indeed, his criticism of present society would not have been possible if it did not appeal even in an oblique way to a normative concept of flourishing, or what he called the human being "in the emphatic sense."[148] This concept equipped him with the contrasting standard he needed to gain some critical distance from his social surroundings and judge them deficient. This standard was hardly minimal; it suggests a *maximalist* demand that the world finally become what it should be. Just as Marx believed that the present contains anticipations of the future, so too Adorno believed that even in the midst of the false it is nonetheless possible to gain some knowledge of what a fulfilled humanity would consist in. Moments of contradiction are more than contradictory; they have an anticipatory status insofar as they point the way toward a generalized condition of happiness that humanity in general is denied: they are rehearsals for the right life.

Immanent Critique

In the introduction I suggested that Adorno succeeds in meeting the challenge of self-reflexivity in social theory. He can meet this challenge by appealing to sources of normativity that are features of his own social world. I further argued that self-reflexivity is a criterion that any social theory must address if it does not wish to fall into one of two possible errors, namely, (a) arrogating to itself a privileged access to moral and political insights that are generally occluded from its other inhabitants; or (b) falling into a self-sabotaging trap where the world is criticized in toto such that one can no longer explain how this very criticism is possible. Adorno was highly sensitive to these charges and explicitly addressed the seeming paradox, that "even the implacable rigor with which criticism speaks the truth of an untrue consciousness remains imprisoned within the orbit of that against which it struggles."[1] To avoid the errors of both elitism and performative contradiction, we need to be able to explain how Adorno's own critical practice is possible within the social conditions he describes. My argument in this book is that Adorno's social theory succeeds in meeting this challenge insofar as it exemplifies the practice of immanent critique. In this chapter, I wish to explore the precise meaning of immanent critique, its logic and its broader implications for Adorno's understanding of the sources of normativity.

Beethoven's *Fidelio*

To explain the idea of immanent critique in greater detail, I would like to begin this chapter by examining an essay that Adorno wrote in 1955 titled "Bourgeois Opera."[2] The essay is of interest not only as an inquiry into musical aesthetics but also as a contribution to the general question as to how Adorno thought about the immanent sources of normativity. The most relevant portion of the essay is one that concerns *Fidelio*, Beethoven's only successful venture into the operatic form.

Composed in 1805, *Fidelio* is a document of hopeful classicism that tells the story of Leonore, a devoted and heroic wife who rescues her husband, Florestan, from a Spanish prison. In act 2, we encounter Florestan in his cell when he sings a lament: "Gott! Welch Dunkel hier [God, how dark it is]"; but he consoles himself with the image of his wife, Leonore, about whom he sings: "Ein Engel, Leonoren, der Gattin, so gleich, Der führt mich zur Freiheit ins himmlische Reich. [An angel Leonore! so like my wife, who'll lead me to freedom in the heavenly kingdom]." As musicologists have observed, the theme of redemption that animates the opera may express the composer's own longing both for personal love and for release from the isolation of his deafness, causes of sadness that brought him to the edge of suicide just a few years before, as we know from his 1802 "Heiligenstadt Testament." In Beethoven's libretto, however, the longing for redemption transcends the sphere of individual psychology and assumes a broader political significance. Act 1 concludes with the well-known scene in which prisoners are permitted a momentary respite in the sunlight, where they sing, "O welche Lust [O what a joy]"; they are then conducted back into the darkness and must bid the sunshine farewell: "Leb wohl, du warmes Sonnenlicht."

Such details serve as a helpful overture to my discussion of immanent critique. It is well known that Beethoven's musical legacy remained a constant preoccupation for Adorno throughout his life, not least because Adorno believed that he could hear in the very form of Beethoven's music a formal analogue to his own dialectical thinking. "One can no longer compose like Beethoven," Adorno wrote, "but one must *think* as he composed."[3] From early in his career until the very last years of his life, Adorno compulsively resumed only to repeatedly abandon the drafts and notes for a never-finished study of Beethoven that he hoped would rank among his greatest achievements. An analysis of Beethoven's compositions would confirm the power of immanent critique by revealing the unresolved dialectic on the level of musical structure itself.

But Adorno was also drawn to the more programmatic aspect of Beethoven's musical works. In "Bourgeois Opera," Adorno offers some comments on the libretto to *Fidelio* as a specimen of the Enlightenment and its emancipatory ideals. In the late-modern era, Adorno explains, when the Enlightenment may seem to have betrayed its true promise and the disenchanted world seems to have confined us to an iron cage, we may feel tempted to think of freedom as a world-transcendent or metaphysical ideal that stands absolutely opposed to present darkness. On this interpretation, our world appears as if it were a closed prison, and the idea of freedom appears as its total negation. We should not find this metaphysical distinction at all surprising, since freedom has grown so improbable that we are tempted to imagine it as an otherworldly norm that has the status of an unrealized and perhaps unrealizable utopia: an *ought* (*Sollen*) that starkly contradicts the *is* (*Sein*). But Adorno warns us against this interpretation. The dream of our liberation becomes little more than a powerless consolation when it is conceived as an abstract principle that stands "opposed to history."[4] For this reason we should not be appeased by the opera's finale, when trumpets announce the arrival of the minister Don Fernando. This denouement offers little more than an authoritarian solution; it does not actually realize our hope for freedom, it violates it. If the idea of freedom still holds any validity, then this idea cannot be understood as transcending social reality. Rather, some intimation of this idea, however partial or incomplete, must be discovered *within* that very reality.

Adorno is keenly aware of the fact that the opera does not succeed in re-solving a problem that is so fundamental to philosophy; but he clearly believes that it points toward the proper solution. The fanfare of *Fidelio* "consummates almost ritualistically the moment of protest that breaks open the eternal hell of the prison cell and puts an end to the rule of force." As an actual solution to the problem of unfreedom, however, this ritual proves unsatisfactory, since it appeals to Don Fernando as a system-transcendent authority (despite the intriguing detail that he entrusts the keys to Leonore so that she can fulfill the merely ceremonial role of liberating her husband). *Fidelio* thereby illus-trates what Adorno calls the "interlocking of myth and Enlightenment" that characterizes not only bourgeois opera but all of bourgeois ideology as such. But this bad dialectic should not inhibit us from recognizing the unrealized promise that still inheres in the Enlightenment. Although it is doubtless the case that we are locked away, like Florestan, in a social order of near-total domination, nevertheless our "imprisonment in a blind and unself-conscious system" cannot be dissociated from "*the idea of freedom [that] arises in its midst*."[5] Adorno's conclusion is striking:

> Metaphysics is not an unchanging realm to be grasped by looking out through the barred windows of the historical; it is the glimmer—albeit a powerless glimmer—of *light which falls into the prison itself.*[6]

If we wish to understand why Adorno aligns himself with the practice of im-manent critique, these lines merit careful scrutiny. He speaks here directly to the question as to whether his critical work can appeal to any *internal* sources of normativity or whether he has denied himself any knowledge of the good in the midst of the bad. In the passage above, his answer is unambiguous. Notwithstanding his grim assessment of social possibility, he does not abstain from the suggestion that we have at least some grasp of the good, or what he calls "metaphysics." To be sure, he does not mean to affirm metaphysics in the traditional sense, since in the modern era metaphysics has lost the prestige of invariance or timeless perfection. Metaphysics now appears in a chastened form of a once-Platonic Idea that has surrendered the Platonic illusion of world-transcendence. He conveys this conclusion via the conventional metaphor of light. Metaphysics in the distinctively modern sense retains its meaning as an ideal of freedom, but it is now compromised by the social conditions in which it appears. Freedom no longer appears as a light that would beckon to us as if from beyond those conditions. Rather, it is a light we glimpse *within those very conditions.*

Nothing in this argument suggests that Adorno has permitted himself a lapse into utopian idealism. He admits that the light that we once ascribed to the idea of freedom has now grown dim or even "powerless." He also seems ready to acknowledge the dialectical compromise that results once the metaphysical idea and history become mutually intertwined. Values that are immanent to history are no doubt vulnerable to historical distortion, and even our noblest ideals can be enlisted for ends that contradict their stated aims. But even while he recognizes this risk he nonetheless reserves his greatest criticism for the ideological function of norms that appear to *transcend* history. Such norms on his view have lost all credibility and efficacy. The only ideals that can retain their power (or even grow *more* powerful) are those that have become fully embedded in the historical continuum: "The more powerful it becomes, the deeper its ideas embed themselves in history; the more ideological it becomes, the more abstractly it stands opposed to history."[7] The general thrust of this argument is dialectical: normative ideals that once claimed a metaphysical status have now lost their world-transcendent authority and survive chiefly as supports for ideology. Normative ideals can enjoy a critical power if and only if they are discovered in the immanent space of history itself.

It should be readily apparent that Adorno's reflections on bourgeois opera are not only about opera, nor are they relevant only to aesthetic experience. They also provide us with an entry point into his general reflections on the possibility of immanent critique, and they announce what we might call the desideratum for his own critical practice. Critique as Adorno understands it must look for the sources of its own possibility not outside the social field but *within* it, in the "powerless glimmer of a light that shines in the prison itself [*ohnmächtige Schein des Lichts, der ins Gefängnis selber fällt*]." The imagery from Beethoven's opera is especially apt insofar as it accords with Adorno's general impression that the modern world is gradually transforming into what he elsewhere calls an "open-air prison."[8] A crucial difference, however, is that, unlike the closed prison as it is described in *Fidelio*, an open-air prison can dispense with the bars of a traditional cell, such that it becomes increasingly difficult to distinguish between what is found inside the prison and what lies beyond it. This difference only heightens the conceptual challenge of immanent critique, since modern conditions are said to be slowly effacing the boundary between transcendence and immanence. But Adorno nonetheless holds fast to the possibility that he can identify small spaces of illumination in the growing darkness, and he situates his own critical practice precisely in those narrow crevices.

The Micrological Glance

Adorno characterizes this critical practice as a certain way of looking upon the social world: a "micrological glance." The aim of such a practice is to dispel the illusion of unity that governs our modern experience and discourages us from thinking that conditions could be otherwise than they are. The illusion works chiefly by effacing the intrinsic difference among particulars and reducing them to mere instances of an all-powerful social logic. Adorno's critical practice seeks to challenge this logic by fastening our attention on precisely those small differences since they bear within themselves the promise of an alternative. The best characterization of this practice appears in the famous concluding passage of *Negative Dialectics*, where Adorno writes, "The micrological glance demolishes the shells of that which is helplessly compartmentalized according to the measure of its subsuming master concept and explodes its identity, the deception, that it would be merely an exemplar."[9] Against the illusion of seamless perfection, Adorno wishes to uphold the mere fragment or remnant, not as a mere part of the established whole, but rather as a sign of unrealized possibility. Only this can explain his conviction that "the smallest innerworldly markings would be relevant to the absolute."[10] Features of immanent social reality assume a quasi-transcendent or even metaphysical meaning insofar as they point toward a social world radically different from our own.[11] Although Adorno disavows any fidelity to traditional metaphysics, he adheres to a secularized metaphysics that turns toward the world rather than away from it into a beyond. At the conclusion of this chapter, I explain how this conception of secularized metaphysics assumes the form of an "immanent transcendence." The practice of immanent critique thereby acquires a redemptive meaning: it is a mode of thinking that demonstrates its "solidarity" with "metaphysics at the moment of its fall."[12]

The practice of micrological criticism can succeed only if Adorno assumes a certain relationship between the fragment and the unrealized future,
or what he calls "the absolute." He characterizes this relationship as "metaphysical" only in the sense that it connects a present condition of immanence
to that which transcends or points beyond that immanence. In other words,
by fastening his attention on our current social reality, Adorno believes that
he can locate *within* the historical present small elements that have an *anticipatory character*. In his lectures on history and freedom he offers a succinct
summary of this idea. By fixing one's micrological gaze upon the fragment, the
historian can help dispel the illusion of social necessity: the historian "detects
in these fragments the trace of possible developments, of something hopeful
that stands in precise opposition to what the totality appears to show."[13] Adorno's practice of immanent critique would seem to require that he connect
the present to the future, by locating in the fragment an anticipatory trace of
what still remains unrealized. This anticipatory structure assures us that the
practice of criticism of the present does not devolve into pure negativity or
pessimism. Our micrological efforts must be turned toward identifying particular fragments of hope in the midst of generalized hopelessness.

The Non-Identical

Earlier I suggested that Adorno's practice of immanent critique commits him
to the idea that our social world is not a seamless unity; rather, it is shot
through with elements that are disharmonious with the social whole. His
nonaffirmative stance toward current society is premised on the notion that
it is not the reconciled whole that it pretends to be. We must remain steadfast
in our resistance to its apologetic claims, and we must recognize that it is not
actually harmonious at all; rather, it is characterized by the persistence of unreconciled negativity. It is at precisely this point that Adorno's disagreement
with the traditional dialectic comes into view. Hegel understands the dialectic as a logic of reconciliation that culminates in an "identity of identity and
non-identity."[14] The history of spirit passes through negativity and sublates all
negative moments into the mediated whole of "absolute knowing." Adorno
refuses to accompany Hegel all the way to dialectical *Vollendung*, or completion, and he turns against the triumphalist reading of history as a narrative
that concludes with the self-satisfaction of spirit.[15]

This refusal is overdetermined. No doubt it reflects Adorno's reckoning
with actual historical events: after the manifold horrors of the mid-twentieth
century Adorno can no longer accept Hegel's attempt to retain the basic
logic of historical theodicy. He summarizes this refusal in the well-known

phrases from the final chapter of *Negative Dialectics*, where we read that "after Auschwitz" any attempt to construct history as a meaningful narrative has been reduced to "sanctimonious prattle."[16] If Hegel still believed that it was possible to find "meaning" in immanence, this was only because he affirmed this immanence as the worldly manifestation of transcendent spirit. But such a construction becomes an apologia for absolute negativity, and it even serves as an ideological justification for ongoing atrocity. Adorno condemns this historical logic as "injustice to the victims."[17] But his refusal should also be understood in philosophical terms as a critique of historical closure itself. Adorno can no longer accept any idea of history that would ascribe to it a coherent and unified meaning. Hegel may have believed that history could only gain intelligibility once it was seen from the vantage of a purely retrospective reason, but Adorno believes that such a vision already presupposes the achievement of a comedic denouement. What Hegel reads as comedy would in fact be despair, because it imagines history as a space of pure immanence without alternatives. In *Negative Dialectics*, Adorno thus rejects the Hegelian idea of historical closure: "Not absolutely closed is the course of the world; nor is absolute despair [*Nicht absolut geschlossen ist der Weltlauf, auch nicht die absolute Verzweiflung*]."[18] This critique goes to the very heart of Hegel's philosophy: it rejects any and all attempts to portray the present world as hospitable to spirit. Adorno believes that this portrait is inverted: what Hegel calls intelligibility is actually opaque; what Hegel calls fulfillment is actually a nightmare of thoroughgoing closure. But the critique is not directed only against Hegel; it takes aim at *any* philosophical interpretation that would assign to our present experience the unity of a single meaning, whether positive *or* negative. It contests *both* Hegelian theodicy *and* its Gnostic reflection.

The critique of pure closure has origins that lie deep in Adorno's early thinking. Already in his 1924 thesis, "The Transcendence of the Thing and the Noematic in Husserl's Phenomenology," the twenty-one-year-old student of Hans Cornelius focuses on the division in Husserl's work between "Being as consciousness" and "Being as Reality."[19] Still committed to the neo-Kantian perspectives of his teacher, Adorno sees in Husserlian phenomenology an idealistic ambition to identify reality with the contents of consciousness even while these contents nonetheless refer to the "absolute transcendence" of the "thing-world."[20] In this interpretation, transcendent reality appears as a Kantian *Ding-an-sich*: a glimpse of materialism first arises on the distant horizon within the landscape of Kantian idealism. This critique of idealism and the turn toward a material residuum that exceeds the mind's ambitions to absolute knowledge was to become an enduring theme in all of Adorno's work. In his 1931 inaugural lecture at the University of Frankfurt, Adorno announces that he wishes to dispel the illusion that "the power of thought is sufficient to grasp the totality of the real."[21] He opposes the illusion of a "rounded and closed reality [*einer runden und geschlossenen Wirklichkeit*]."[22] Against the pretensions of idealism, he recommends a new style of philosophy that will forgo the law-giving claims of autonomous reason. Rather, it will fasten our attention on those places where "irreducible reality breaks in upon it."[23] This idea of a breakthrough of what is "irreducible" is repeated everywhere in Adorno's mature philosophy. In his 1958 lectures on dialectics, he announces his strong opposition to the "closed dialectic [*geschlossenene Dialektik*]" of the German idealist tradition, and he proposes in its stead an "open dialectic [*offene Dialektik*]."[24] The arrogant claims of absolute spirit are now dismissed as attempts to dominate the plenitude of nonconceptual reality. The older model had the ambition of embracing all negativity within a coherent and stabilized system that unites being and thought. The open dialectic breaks the spell of systematicity; it acknowledges the insufficiency of the concept when confronted with the persistence of what Adorno calls the "non-identical."

The concept of the non-identical may be described as the concept of that which escapes the net of conceptuality. No doubt this may strike some readers as paradoxical.[25] But the idea of something that lies beyond the limits of full intelligibility already enjoys a central role in philosophy well before Adorno, and it is especially prominent in the doctrine of transcendental idealism. One might even surmise that Adorno developed this idea thanks to his intimate understanding of Kant's *Critique of Pure Reason* (which he had first studied under Siegfried Kracauer's tutelage even before he had left gymnasium). According to Kant, the mind can claim knowledge of appearances only insofar as these are conditioned by the pure forms of intuition (space and time) together with the forms of understanding (the categories). Beyond the realm of appearances there lies the unknown and unknowable realm of the thing-in-itself (*Ding-an-sich*). The two domains are *not* metaphysically distinct. Kant takes care to explain that they are merely two aspects of the same object: the object *as it appears* must be distinguished from *that very same object* as it may be quite apart from the conditions of its appearing.[26] Kant insists on this point precisely because he has to defend himself against the accusation that his philosophy has dissolved the entire world into mere appearance: the thing-in-itself may lie outside the realm of appearance, but as a conceptual posit its persistence saves transcendental idealism from lapsing into absolute idealism. The world for Kant is nevertheless more than its appearance. The significance of this idea can hardly be exaggerated as it marks the crucial difference between Kant and his German idealist successors. Most significant of all, the distinction between appearance and the thing-in-itself imposes a sharp limit on our claims to knowledge. We can *think* of the things that are unconditioned by our own cognitive faculties, though we can never claim to know them. Human reason suffers a "peculiar fate" insofar as it is burdened with questions that due to the very limits of human reason it is unable to answer. Notwithstanding Kant's reputation as an arch-rationalist, what emerges from this doctrine is a disposition that Rae Langton has called *Kantian humility*. The mind knows that it does not know all.[27]

The above considerations are of great relevance for our interpretation of Adorno's philosophy. Specifically, Adorno finds in the Kantian idea of the thing-in-itself the impetus for his own turn toward the non-identical. The affinity is especially noticeable when we examine his 1959 lectures on Kant's *Critique of Pure Reason*, where Adorno expresses qualified praise for Kant as a philosopher who does not seek to transgress the "threshold [*Schwelle*]" between mind and world. Our thought does not penetrate all the way to the core of what there is; rather, "it remains attached to something to which it refers."[28] The doctrine of the Kantian "block [*Block*]" prevents transcendental idealism from inflating into the later version of idealism that acknowledges no such limit or constraint. Adorno's praise is evident: with the distinction between the realm of appearance and the realm of the intelligible, Kant hints toward what Adorno calls a "*materialist motif.*"[29] Adorno understands, of course, that Kant hardly meant to bring transcendental idealism to the dialectical point of reversal where it would negate itself and terminate in materialism. Adorno's claim is simply that Kant was forced by the logic of his own argumentation to introduce the theme of "something that cannot be further reduced."[30] Although it does not openly surrender to materialism, *Critique of Pure Reason* becomes "the first great attempt in modern times—or perhaps we should say the first and also the last great attempt, and one doomed to failure—*to master through mere concepts all that cannot be mastered by concepts.*"[31] The paradoxical result is a doctrine that simultaneously extols the power of the concept to establish identity but is nonetheless "compelled to acknowledge the fact of *non-identity* [*Nichtidentität*]."[32]

To be sure, any attempt to assign a determinate meaning to the concept of the non-identical will confront a serious difficulty. Definition presupposes the possibility of subsuming the particular under a universal. But the non-identical is the concept of that which refuses to be subsumed under a universal. In this sense it may indeed appear as though the non-identical presents us with the paradox: it is the concept of that which escapes conceptual determination. Adorno does not ignore this potential difficulty, though he hardly considers it fatal to his argument, chiefly because he can draw upon the analogy to the Kantian thing-in-itself. Just as the concept of the thing-in-itself is the concept of an *indeterminate* object beyond the realm of appearance, so too the concept of the non-identical is the concept of that which does not accommodate itself to the realm of identity. But this means that the non-identical is a purely *negative* category. The non-identical is that which resists conceptual determination; its definition inheres in nothing but this very resistance. Here the analogy to the Kantian doctrine of the thing-in-itself is of great relevance. Just as Kant upholds the thing-in-itself to defend himself against the charge of idealism, Adorno assigns the concept of the non-identical a crucial role in his philosophy because it marks the precise point of resistance against the power of identity. Both concepts serve as tokens of epistemic humility; they are signs that the mind is not closed in upon itself but is both dependent on and open to the nonconceptual world.[33] But we can press this analogy a step further. Just as Kant requires the thing-in-itself as an assurance against idealistic solipsism, Adorno needs the non-identical as an assurance that things can be different from how they are. For Kant, the threat of solipsism is largely epistemological: if we were to cast away the concept of the thing-in-itself, we would find ourselves adrift in a sea of self-created appearance. For Adorno, however, the threat is also social: if we were to surrender the concept of the non-identical, we would be lost in the realm of ideological appearance and would have no leverage for negating the illusions of a self-affirmative society.

Non-Identity and Critique

In Adorno's thought the non-identical becomes the *point d'appui* for the practice of immanent critique. But without further specification it is not entirely clear how this practice is supposed to proceed. After all, it seems obvious that Adorno cannot simply hold up the concept of the non-identical as if this could suffice to impugn his social surroundings. We can easily see why such a strategy would be insufficient: the task of criticism must be to direct our attention to distinct *instances* where society has failed. As Adorno explains at the conclusion to *Negative Dialectics*, the micrological glance cannot rest content with such instances of non-identity as if they were mere *exemplars* of a universal concept. The concept of the non-identical thus presents Adorno with a philosophical dilemma since it seems to be little more than an empty placeholder for something more determinate. It is merely "the opposition between whatever is held down and the universal domination that is condemned to identity."[34] The dilemma is apparent: how can the non-identical remain a merely generic category if it is defined precisely by its opposition to generic categories? Adorno can finesse this dilemma only because he is not actually concerned with the non-identical in its generic form at all. The idea of the non-identical does not refer to one determinate thing; rather, it serves as a mere token for nonconceptual particulars that manifest themselves in infinite variety and differentiation across the wide landscape of human experience.

Here I believe we confront one of the more intriguing facets of Adorno's philosophy. Because Adorno's critical practice depends on the appeal to non-identity, he needs to offer some specification as to how non-identity actually makes itself available to us in our experience. At this point the analogy between the non-identical and things-in-themselves breaks down: Kant was free to define the thing-in-itself as that which remains untainted by the conditions of possible experience; but Adorno cannot protect the non-identical from the all-embracing conditions of the social whole. This leaves him in a difficult position. If the non-identical enters into the space of social appearances, then it is surely marked by the conditions of its appearance and it ceases to be the purely or absolutely non-identical. Now, if the non-identical were somehow to remain a pristine fragment that was unaffected by its social surroundings, then Adorno would be guilty of rendering the non-identical as an image of utopia, an island of truth in the midst of the false. But everything we know about Adorno warns us against that possibility. His unreserved antipathy to the cult of authenticity (*Eigentlichkeit*) reflects his strong conviction that falsehood permeates our lived experience and disallows the fantasy of an undamaged communion with Being.[35] If he was sincere when he declared that "there is no right living in the false," then we cannot ascribe to him the fantasy of pure and uncontaminated non-identity.

The answer to this problem is clear. Adorno never seeks to isolate the non-identical from the conditions of its appearance, and he resists the utopian trap of imagining the non-identical as an island of perfection. Rather, he embraces the thought that the non-identical itself cannot help but manifest the damage of its surroundings. In an imperfect world the non-identical too must bear the marks of worldly imperfection.[36] He explains this thought in an important passage from his lectures on history and freedom:

> All the non-identical phenomena that are expelled as a result of the domination of the identity principle are nevertheless mediated by the power of that principle. What persists are the stale remnants left over once the process of identification has taken its share. *And even these stale remnants are left mutilated, scarred by the power of the principle of identity.* The spell cast by the identity principle, by the world spirit, to formulate it even more emphatically, perverts whatever is different—and even the smallest quantity would be incompatible with the spell if it were still pure.[37]

This passage should suffice to put to rest any concern that Adorno adhered to the consoling idea of the non-identical as an island of perfection untouched by the power of the social whole. On the contrary, Adorno insists that what appears as "other" to the whole not only suffers from the fact of its exclusion, but it also assumes some of the characteristics of what it wished to escape: "this other then becomes something evil and pernicious."[38] Incidentally, this argument bears a noteworthy resemblance to a claim that is found in *Dialectic of Enlightenment*, where we are reminded that nature itself cannot survive in a pristine state when it is subjected to rational domination. The romantic dream of a return to uncontaminated nature ignores the bitter truth that this nature too has succumbed to the spell of reason. All that remains to us are "scraps of a subjugated nature that have been spewed out by the process of domination," but these are "just as deformed as those that are ground down by the machinery."[39]

At this point it is important to note that Adorno believes his reasoning aligns at least to a certain extent with that of Hegel. The passage quoted above, concerning the "spell" that is cast by the identity principle, appears in the midst of a longer discussion where Adorno adopts a charitable stance toward his predecessor. Hegel, he explains, was not only an advocate of the social totality, but "he [also] wished to remind us of *what is left out of the totality*."[40] Hegel rightly understood that any moment of exclusion impugns the totality itself as abstract, as incomplete and therefore false. But he also understood that this very exclusion sets the stage for the realization of the totality in its completion and truth. On the one hand, "the non-identical itself is taken possession of by the spell while, on the other hand, it becomes the factor that enables the abstract spell to be attenuated."[41] Adorno assigns great importance to this idea, since it suggests that the dialectician can find in even the most distorted fragment of non-identity the anticipation of a better world. "Thus reflection on difference would *help towards reconciliation*."[42] But the argument is admittedly puzzling. Hegel was able to see the negative as an *animus* in the dialectic only because he believed that reason has an intrinsic drive toward self-realization. Thanks to this premise, Hegel can argue that negativity already implies its sublation (*Aufhebung*) and reconciliation (*Versöhnung*). Reason's encounter with difference becomes not simply an obstruction it happens to confront, but a problem it needs to resolve. This raises an important question. Can Adorno too embrace such a premise?

The conventional response to this question is a resounding *no*. Adorno vehemently rejects the Hegelian premise that the non-identical somehow anticipates reconciliation, because he believes that a false totality wholly obstructs our awareness of what genuine reconciliation could be. I want to argue that this conventional response is mistaken, or, the very least, it is a drastic overstatement. I have already addressed the problem of exaggeration in the introduction. Here, however, I should like to examine a slightly different problem. The difficulty with this conventional response is that the term "false" is unavoidably contrastive.[43] More precisely, it already implicates us in a space of normativity where the characterization of our current world as false presupposes some notion of what it would be like for it to be true. Adorno makes precisely this point in the essay, "Critique," where he writes (in conscious allusion to Spinoza) that "the false, once determinately known and precisely expressed, is already an index of what is right and better."[44] True and false are not merely contrastive; they are mutually implicative.[45]

Adorno pursues this argument even into the very heart of his analysis of concepts. Consider, for instance, the following passage from *Negative Dialectics*, where Adorno comments on a conventional problem of epistemology, namely, the problem of how we should construe the relationship between our concepts and the worldly objects to which they refer. On the one hand, he criticizes the concept's ambition to dominate the object; on the other, he sees this very ambition as a distorted demand for genuine reconciliation.

> It is hubris, that identity would be, that the object in itself [*Sache an sich*] would correspond to its concept. But its ideal is not to be simply thrown away: in the reproach that the thing would not be identical with the concept lives, too, the longing that it would like to be so. In this form the consciousness of non-identity contains identity. Indeed the supposition of this, all the way down to formal logic, is the ideological moment in pure thinking. In it however the moment of truth of ideology is also hidden, *the injunction that no contradiction, no antagonism ought to be* [*In ihm jedoch steckt auch das Wahrheitsmoment von Ideologie, die Anweisung, daß kein Widerspruch, kein Antagonismus sein solle*].[46]

Adorno's point in this passage is that even the false or ideological claim to an identity between concept and object bespeaks the utopian promise of a relation that would be more than mere domination. Adorno clearly believes that this promise has a normative character: it is a "longing [*Sehnsucht*]" or even an "injunction [*Answeisung*]" that there *ought to be* no antagonism. The passage, I would suggest, provides us with an instructive specimen of immanent critique: by revealing the negative, it impugns the claim to identity as false; but, just as importantly, this very accusation also presupposes the idea of an identity that would be true. This is what Adorno calls the "truth moment" in all ideology. When we criticize an ideology as false, we already commit ourselves to the normative ideal of truth. Ideology and normativity are intertwined.

Notwithstanding these considerations, little in the argument above actually serves as a *guarantee* that our ideal could be realized. The logical presupposition of the true does not save us from the skeptical challenge that our hopes might turn out to be mere delusion. But if Adorno cannot furnish even the slightest assurance that reconciliation is possible, we are left once again with the grim thought that the ideal might never come into being. After all, what could immanent critique hope to gain by fastening our attention only on what is "evil" or "pernicious"? If Adorno believes that the non-identical is no less damaged than the social whole from which it has been expelled, it seems implausible to insist that the non-identical could ever serve as a harbinger of better things. The best we could hope for would be a candid recognition of the false, not an anticipation of the true. This skeptical challenge would seem to suggest that we should content ourselves with a purely minimalist interpretation of Adorno's moral teaching, and we might very well conclude that he never meant to equip us with anything more than the dispiriting counsel that we "live less wrongly."[47] But it is the burden of my argument to show that this minimalist interpretation is misleading, as I explain below.

Rehearsals of the Right Life

I argued above that Adorno does not limit himself to a purely negative interpretation of the non-identical. In other words, he does not believe that the task of immanent critique is limited to documenting only what is false or bad about our present society. I further argued that he understands the very concept of the false as implicating us in a space of normativity where the false also involves a contrasting (if mostly implicit) appeal to the true. This is why he believes that criticism of the false has an anticipatory character: to condemn our current conditions as bad is to allude however obliquely to conditions that would be good. Nevertheless, it would of course be mistaken to understand this argument merely as a matter of logical implication. For our criticism to have any traction within our social world, concepts alone will not suffice. As I will explain at greater length in the following chapter, Adorno is sufficiently materialist in his philosophical commitments to believe that any criticism of the present order must secure its warrant by pointing to evidence that is available for us not just in conceptual form, but in the texture of our lived experience.

Fortunately, Adorno has a rich understanding of the kind of evidence that might satisfy this requirement. An instructive example can be found in the enchanting entry, "Kaufmannsladen," from *Minima Moralia*, where Adorno muses on the significance of children's games.[48] The topic may strike the reader as marginal to the task of social criticism. But of course Adorno recognizes this. In fact, it is precisely the apparent triviality of the subject matter that makes it such an advantageous point of departure if we wish to understand how immanent criticism should proceed. The commentary begins on a sober note by acknowledging the overwhelming power of the market. "Acquisition," he writes, "commandeers" virtually all of our daily activities and transforms them into mere means so that their particularity is effaced and they are reduced to "interchangeable, abstract labour-time."[49] The logic of exchange is so powerful that the "equivalence form" begins to disfigure not only our conduct but also our individual perception. Adorno does not portray capitalism only as an economic system; he sees it as a disenchanted world that has drained our experience of nearly all color and light:

> What is no longer irradiated by the light of its own self-determination as "joy in doing," pales to the eye. Our organs grasp nothing sensuous in isolation, but notice whether a color, a sound, a movement is there for its own sake or for something else; wearied by a false variety, they steep all in grey, disappointed by the deceptive claim of qualities still to be there at all, while they conform to the purposes of appropriation, indeed largely owe their existence to it alone. Disenchantment with the contemplated world [*Die Entzauberung der Anschauungswelt*] is the sensorium's reaction to its objective role as a "commodity world."[50]

This may be about as close as Adorno ever comes to endorsing the Weberian portrait of capitalism as a "stahlhartes Gehäuse," or steel-hard casing. In the disenchanted world objects must obey the logic of exchange: their use value dissolves, and their intrinsic character must then submit to the law of *Zweckrationalität*, or instrumental reason.

It is therefore all the more striking to follow Adorno as he muses on the significance of children's games as activities that apparently serve no purpose at all. "In his purposeless activity the child, by a subterfuge, sides with use-value against exchange value. Just because he deprives the things with which he plays of their mediated usefulness, he seeks to rescue in them what is benign towards people and not what subserves the exchange relation that equally deforms humanity and things."[51] With his micrological glance Adorno is not embarrassed to fasten our attention on even the smallest and least significant objects such as children's toys. His analysis, poignant in its specificity, is meant to disclose the most innocent particulars as allegories for a universal redemption: "The little trucks travel nowhere and the tiny barrels on them are empty; yet they remain true to their destiny by not performing, not participating in the process of abstraction that levels down that destiny,

but instead abide as allegories of what they are specifically for."[52] The significance of such childish objects is that they seem to have escaped, or at least
have momentarily evaded, the instrumentalist imperative that governs the
adult's world:

> Scattered, it is true, but not ensnared, they wait to see whether society will
> finally remove the social stigma on them; whether the vital process between
> men and things, praxis, will cease to be practical. The unreality of games gives
> notice that reality is not yet real. They are unconscious rehearsals for the right
> life [*Sie sind bewußtlose Übungen zum richtigen Leben*].[53]

I have drawn attention to Adorno's analysis of children's toys because it is
illustrative of the general practice of immanent critique. Three themes in
this analysis stand out as especially instructive: marginality, negativity, and
anticipation.

1. With regard to *marginality*, Adorno believes that the critic can benefit by
    looking not at the center of society but to its edges and its gaps, where
    certain activities or experiences persist that are disharmonious with the
    organizing logic of the social whole. Adorno recognizes, of course, that
    something as trivial as the games of a child may seem undeserving of criti-
    cal interest. But it would seem that this is precisely his point. In their ludic
    innocence the activities of children are "scattered [*versprengt*]" but not yet
    fully "caught [*verstrickt*]" in the dominant order. From the relative safety
    of its social margins they embody ways of being that the dominant order
    has largely suppressed.

2. The disharmonious character of such activities alerts us to the theme of
    negativity. The games of children are negative in the sense that they resist
    the general logic of exchange. Adorno's specification of this theme allows
    for various interpretations, both passive and active. Children's games ex-
    hibit a kind of *passive* negativity insofar as they are seen as not participat-
    ing in the dominant order: they merely "wait" at the margins for society
    to change so that they can assume a more generalized importance. But
    they also exhibit negativity in a more *active* sense, insofar as they actually
    deprive objects of their overly practical status and thereby assist in the
    "rescue" of a suppressed alternative. We should not miss the crucial point,
    then, that children's games are negative only in the sense that they negate
    the false and thereby stand for an unrealized truth.

3. This alerts us to the most significant theme, *anticipation*. Children's games
    are understood as having an anticipatory status insofar as they can be
    said to signify future conditions within the present. Adorno thinks that
    their negativity already implies this anticipatory status, and this is the
    case whether or not such games exhibit a kind of negativity that is merely

passive (in the sense of mere waiting) or active (in the sense of actually seeking rescue). In either case, children's games are understood as embodiments of an alternative way of being human that has not yet found a fuller and more generalized realization. This is why Adorno calls them "allegories" or "exercises [*Übungen*]" for "the right life."[54]

These three themes—marginality, negativity, and anticipation—all contribute to Adorno's conception of social critique. But he assigns paramount importance to anticipation, a theme that recurs with manifold variations throughout his work. Its significance is due to the fact that it alerts us to the normative demand that animates the overall practice of immanent critique, namely, the demand that our life should finally become one that would be worthy of human beings. It is not incidental that the allusion to the "right life" appears in *Minima Moralia*, a work that is perhaps better known for the dark epigram by Ferdinand Kürnberger that stands on the first page of part 1: "Life does not live [*Das Leben lebt nicht*]."[55] But we should not commit the mistake of thinking that these two portions of the book are mutually contradictory. Adorno endorses the view that life in its present form does not live, but he *also* holds on to the anticipatory theme that *within* our currently nonliving life we can identify marginal and oppositional ways of being that point to an alternative life that could be lived in the true sense. He grants that these ways of being are not wholly satisfactory in their current form because the overall structure of our current life is false. Indeed, this is the actual meaning of the statement, "There is no right living in the false." But this claim should not be misunderstood as an outright ban. The significance of children's games is that they are instances of normative anticipation, and these instances afford us a momentary glimpse of what a right life might be.

Immanent and Transcendent Critique

Before turning to the next chapter, it will be helpful to consider in greater depth what is ultimately at stake in the claim that Adorno's philosophy exemplifies the practice of immanent critique. In the current literature on Adorno's philosophy, opinion on this matter is divided.[56] In a lucid and wide-ranging study, Titus Stahl provides a systematic reconstruction of the tradition of immanent critique, and he suggests that we can identify an important continuity that extends from Hegel to Marx to Frankfurt School critical theory. Meanwhile, James Gordon Finlayson has raised important objections to the continuity thesis: he argues that Adorno cannot endorse the practice of immanent critique chiefly because he is committed to what Finlayson calls "austere negativism." In what follows I wish to take up some of the threads of this controversy so as to motivate my claim that Adorno adheres to the practice of immanent critique.

In the well-known early essay "Cultural Criticism and Society," Adorno offers some intriguing observations on the distinction between immanent and transcendent critique, and he expresses a strong preference for the former. To appreciate why he endorses immanent critique, we must first be clear as to what would qualify a critique as immanent rather than transcendent. According to Adorno, a transcendent critique is one that "assumes an Archimedean position above culture and the blindness of society, from which consciousness can bring the totality, no matter how massive, into flux." Adorno concedes that at first glance "the transcendent method, which aims at totality, may *seem* more radical than the immanent method."[57] If the transcendent critic looks more radical, this is perhaps due to the impression that such a critic appears ready to condemn *everything* without remainder, whereas the immanent critic "presupposes the questionable whole."[58] Given the lamentable condition of the world, we might therefore appreciate why the transcendent critic's posture of totalizing condemnation would appear justified. "The attack on the whole draws strength from the fact that the *semblance* of unity and wholeness [*Schein von Einheit und Ganzheit*] in the world grows with the advance of reification." If the critic does not wish to "succumb in advance to the fetishization of the intellectual sphere," then one could imagine that a "position transcending culture is in a certain sense presupposed."[59]

Despite this acknowledgment of its apparent merits, however, Adorno ultimately rejects the strategy of transcendent critique. His grounds for doing so are fairly straightforward: there just is *no such thing* as an "Archimedean standpoint" beyond the social whole. To assume such a position would be to arrogate to oneself a privileged but wholly imaginary vantage outside one's own social reality. But this sets up a false and undialectical dualism between the critic and the critic's world. As Adorno explains, "The choice of a standpoint outside the sway of existing society is as fictitious as only the construction of abstract utopias can be."[60] Transcendent critique seeks to justify this fictitious standpoint in various ways, by appealing (for instance) to the ostensibly nonsocial standard of a wholly uncontaminated nature:

> The transcendent criticism of culture, much like bourgeois cultural criticism, sees itself obliged to fall back upon the idea of 'naturalness', which itself forms a central element of bourgeois ideology. The transcendent attack on culture regularly speaks the language of *false escape* [*die Sprache des falschen Ausbruchs*], that of the 'nature boy'. It despises the mind and its works, contend-

ing that they are, after all, only man-made and serve only to cover up 'natural' life.[61]

But Adorno dismisses these sorts of transcendent appeals, since the ideal of
an uncorrupted nature that lies beyond social artifice is no less a fiction than
the social ideologies it wishes to escape. Transcendent critique thus fails what
I have called the challenge of self-reflexivity. It imagines critique as emanating from a position that is exotic to the world it describes. But it is a cardinal
principle of Adorno's philosophy that the critic has no other place to stand
than the world itself. It follows that transcendent critique is impossible.

Once he has exposed transcendent critique as illusory, it may seem as
if Adorno has no choice but to endorse the strategy of immanent critique.
He confirms that immanent critique is "more essentially dialectical" than
transcendent critique since it does not posit a dualistic contrast between the
wholly false society and an extra-social or world-transcendent standard of
truth. Rather, immanent critique "takes seriously the principle that it is not
ideology in itself which is untrue but rather its pretension to correspond to
reality."[62] An ideology asserts a perfect correspondence or identity between its
representations and the world it represents. Adorno rejects any such pretension to identity. He insists that where ideology stakes a claim to such identity
we must vigorously resist that claim, and we must instead seek to expose the
fact of non-identity or contradiction. To accomplish this, however, we cannot
follow the strategy of the transcendent critic and seek normative instruction
in a precinct that would lie outside the realm of ideology. For we have no access to such an external perspective. We must therefore proceed by seeking
out moments of contradiction or non-identity *within* our social reality. The
relevant moments of non-identity will often manifest themselves on the level
of cultural form as internal fractures or dissonances that require the painstaking work of interpretation. "Immanent criticism of intellectual phenomena
seeks to grasp, through the analysis of form and meaning, the contradiction
between the objective idea and that pretension."[63] Immanent critique thus
enjoys a decisive advantage over transcendent critique. Because immanent
critique does not succumb to the illusory search for an Archimedean point
that would transcend social reality, it cannot proceed by identifying contradictions between the world and some set of exotic or world-transcendent
normative standards. Rather, it seeks out such contradictions within social
reality itself. We do not find our social reality defective by judging it deficient in accordance with a critical norm that we bring to it from the outside.
We fasten our attention only on what Adorno calls an "inconsistency [*Inkon-
sistenz*]" that inheres in "*the structure of the existent*."[64]

The decisive advantage of immanent critique as discussed above is that it appeals to internal contradiction. But this does not yet fully express what is truly distinctive about immanent critique. For we still need to understand why it would be so important to take note of internal inconsistency. Adorno offers a clue to the answer when he notes that "dialectic is not a third standpoint but rather the attempt, *by means of immanent critique, to develop philosophical standpoints beyond themselves*."[65] This phrase is admittedly puzzling. To suggest that the task of immanent critique is to *develop* a standpoint beyond itself suggests that something about the current standpoint *already* bears within itself a normative surplus or a demand that has not been fulfilled. As noted above, Adorno does not see our current society as self-consistent or uniform; it offers not just one vision but *competing* visions of what our life should be like. The attentive critic must be alert to these dissonances or inconsistencies, because different moments of the same social reality are expressive of competing normative standards. To be sure, the dominant standards will tend to be affirmative: they will simply endorse the normative authority of the world as it is. But we can also identify other standards, albeit less common and even partially obscured, that call into question or challenge the authority of the prevailing standards and point to alternative possibilities. Adorno does not believe that any of these visions need to be fully articulated as explicit ideologies or moral principles; in fact, they do not need to *state* normative commitments at all. Socially relevant norms do not always appear in the form of full-dress moral philosophies; it is sufficient that they simply *embody* normative claims as to how we should live. Normative claims can be embodied even in the simplest and most everyday modes of conduct. Adorno recognizes that these normative claims are now embattled and may soon disappear. *Minima Moralia*, perhaps his most successful inquiry into the lived and embodied experience, is also a melancholy record of that experience at the moment of its decline. He warns that experience will eventually yield to "the law of pure functionality" that will tolerate "no surplus [*Überschuß*] either in freedom of conduct or in autonomy of things."[66] For the time being, however, we can still rely on this surplus as the necessary point of departure for the practice of criticism.

It is here that social interpretation can play an important role. Adorno thinks that the internal inconsistencies in a given society can be made explicit by the social or cultural critic, who can reveal through interpretation the dissonance or misalignment of competing normative claims and can assist us in bringing out the anticipatory promise of normative "rehearsals" that are implicit in our everyday experience. To say that the task of criticism is to *develop* a philosophical standard is to say that interpretation can bring out just that misalignment. More relevant will be to identify misalignment between dominant norms and suppressed alternatives. Although these alternatives are not fully embodied in current social arrangements, they nonetheless contain a normative surplus that can be developed or made explicit by means of interpretation. Most important of all, however, Adorno believes that the task of criticism is not simply to reveal the breach between surplus and actuality; it is also to demand that this breach be healed. But such a fundamental transformation can only be accomplished by addressing the social conditions that are responsible for this breach. This is because the misalignment between actuality and norm is not due to local and incidental features of our social order; rather, it is due to constitutive problems that afflict the social order as a whole.

If the above reconstruction is correct, then it looks as if Adorno has compelling reasons to endorse the practice of immanent critique. Still it is important to entertain possible objections to the account that I have offered here. The first objection is that Adorno may have changed his mind. It is worth noting that Adorno's discussion of the contrast between immanent and transcendent critique that I discussed above derives from an earlier phase in his career. Finlayson has suggested that "from about 1950 onwards, Adorno begins to doubt the viability of immanent criticism" (though he adds that Adorno "does not do this consistently"). After 1950, Adorno no longer feels confident in the merits of immanent criticism chiefly because he comes to see social reality as "pervasively evil." It is "a single integrated system that is completely denuded of worthwhile ends, and fully instrumentalized, such that no part of it is immune from complicity with forms of domination."[67] This vision of an integrated order of total falsehood is what Finlayson (in broad agreement with Freyenhagen) calls "austere negativism." To support this claim, Finlayson refers to well-known apothegms from *Minima Moralia* such as "There is no right living in the false" and "The whole is the untrue," which he interprets as "literally true statements" of Adorno's social vision. This line of reasoning leads Finlayson to conclude that Adorno eventually came to believe that immanent critique was no longer a viable option:

> If society, as Adorno maintains, is a self-maintaining whole, and if it is also pervasively and irredeemably evil; if nothing in it is free from complicity with the atrocities which have taken place in its midst, then the idea that it contains reliable standards of criticism, however conceived, has to be abandoned. To the extent that they are integrated into the context of immanence, standards of criticism, whatever they are, are not transcendent enough. They are not capable of pointing beyond existing relations to a society that, were it to be realized, would be completely different to, and better than, the presently existing one. To the extent that they belong to the object of criticism—society—they

are continuous with it and contaminated by it. In which case they are not the
appropriate standards for a critical theory of society.[68]

For Finlayson such considerations are decisive: "Adorno clearly acknowledges that given austere negativism, a merely immanent criticism of society
will not do: for it will not realize the aim of critical theory."[69] It follows that we
must reject the continuity thesis (as proposed by Stahl and others) that would
assign Adorno's philosophy a place in the line of immanent-critical thinking
that descends from Hegel to Marx.

   This conclusion is warranted, however, only if we accept the claim that
Adorno sees society as "pervasively and irredeemably evil." As I noted in the
introduction, however, this claim requires that we interpret his most hyperbolic apothegms (such as the notorious one about "no right living") as literal
and accurate descriptions of our current world. It is important to see what is
at stake in this debate. If we were to accept such descriptions as literally true
and if Adorno saw society as pervasively and irredeemably *evil*, then he could
not possibly have appealed to *internal* standards for criticism, for the simple
reason that there would be none. But it would follow that he could not have
endorsed the strategy of immanent critique. Fortunately, a great deal of the
textual evidence suggests that such aphoristic statements are not intended as
literal descriptions at all. Rather they are exaggerations that are meant to alert
us to emerging tendencies of the modern world. Despite occasional lapses
into totalizing or "austere" negativism, Adorno is more often than not careful
to say the modern world is "incomplete, contradictory, and fragmentary [*unvollständig, widerspruchsvoll und brüchig*]."[70] He sustains this view not only in
his earlier writings, but throughout his career and well through the late 1960s.
In *Negative Dialectics*, for example, he objects to the social image of "total determinism" as "mythical," and he insists that even if society now appears to be
uniformly gray and presents itself as a "negative whole," we can nonetheless
discern in it the "scattered trace [*versprengte Spur*]" of a better alternative.[71]
To be sure, such statements may seem unimpressive, since they concede only
the most minimal recognition of immanent alternatives and inconsistencies.
But even the smallest concession would already suffice to disprove the thesis
of total negativism. It would therefore seem that we have enough evidence to
set aside the claim that Adorno was a late-modern Gnostic who saw society
as an unredeemable domain of absolute falsehood or evil. But once we reject
the thesis of austere negativism, the way is clear for Adorno to endorse the
strategy of immanent critique.

   It is perhaps relevant to note in passing that in his more recent work Finlayson seems to have modified his own interpretation. He no longer char-

acterizes Adorno as an austere or totalizing negativist; he is now content to characterize Adorno as a *partial* negativist.[72] Finlayson summarizes partial negativism as the view that "human beings can come to know or conceive of the good and the right, albeit through a glass darkly, such that the access that they have is unreliable and diffuse, and the good or right they know partial and fragmented."[73] But if Adorno is only a partial negativist, then he can still intelligibly appeal to fragmentary instances of the good in the midst of the bad. And in fact this is all that immanent critique actually requires. We cannot ignore the great frequency with which Adorno employs metaphors such as the fragment, the trace, or (on at least one occasion) the broken shard of glass.[74] Such metaphorical language is not merely a poetic indulgence; it belongs to the logical infrastructure of Adorno's conception of immanent critique. The task of interpretation is to fasten upon the smallest fragments of current reality as anticipatory signs of an unrealized and better whole.[75] Still it is surely important to note that the shift to "partial negativism" entails a somewhat different and less damning assessment of our current social arrangements. For once we admit that we have *some* access to instances or fragmentary anticipations of the good (however partial or diffuse), we then have to abandon the expectation that Adorno's version of immanent social criticism can equip us for the encounter with social conditions of thoroughgoing catastrophe. After all, immanent criticism remains a possibility only so long as we sustain at least a slender margin of confidence in the availability of alternatives. As Stahl has observed, "The model of immanent critique was never meant to deal with severely distorted practices, but rather to uncover better *potentials* within practices."[76] To this I would only add that immanent critique in Adorno's sense is perfectly capable of dealing with severe distortion. It is only when the distortion becomes so drastic as to efface *all* alternatives that the practice of immanent critique must lose its efficacy.

Immanent Transcendence

At this point in the argument, we must confront a rather formidable objection. Because Adorno is concerned with global problems that afflict all of modern society, it may seem implausible for him to insist that he can nevertheless identify immanent norms that contradict society. As I already explained earlier in this chapter, Adorno has anticipated this objection: he recognizes that the immanent norms that are necessary for criticism are likewise compromised by the social whole in which they appear: "Even the norms which condemn the organisation of the world are themselves the fruit of this wrong organisation [*Selbst die Normen, welche die Einrichtung der Welt verdammen, verdanken sich deren eigenem Unwesen]."*[77] Given that they cannot transcend the damaged world but owe their appearance to this very world, they too will necessarily exhibit damage. It follows that we should not expect any of the available norms to be absolutely perfect or reliable. No doubt this introduces another complication into the practice of immanent critique. Let us call this the problem of the *false exit*. In any given social order, we are presented with certain norms that may *seem* to afford us the promise of an escape from that order but are in fact little more than further instances of the dominant ideology. These false exits afford us the illusion of transcendence but actually serve to confirm immanence. In his critique of religion Marx provides us with a paradigm of this idea: in his introductory remarks in the *Contribution to the Critique of Hegel's "Philosophy of Right,"* Marx says that religion promises little more than the *"fantastic realization* of the human being," that is, an *"illusory* happiness" that serves as a substitute for *"real* happiness." Even if religion expresses a *"protest* against real suffering," this protest does not open our eyes to the real conditions that produced that suffering. On the contrary, religion works as an "opium" that robs the protest of any worldly consequence and lulls us into an affirmative sleep.[78] Religion is therefore the original version of ideology: it is a fantasy that mobilizes our longing for release only to confirm our oppression.

Adorno follows the model of Marx's criticism of religion but considerably widens its scope. He sees the culture industry as a realm of commodities and standardized experiences that offers a dazzling array of false exits in commodified form. At nearly every turn the culture industry awakens fantasies of self-realization or escape that hold out the promise of happiness only to affirm our imprisonment in the administered world. More sobering still, Adorno believes that the Marxist version of ideology has now yielded to a new species of realism: the false exit no longer appears as a fantasy of release; it merely commands our submission to reality and offers "insignias of the absolute rule of that which is."[79]

It may appear as if the problem of the false exit poses a serious challenge to immanent critique, insofar as the critic wants some assurance that the norm that presents itself as an immanent contradiction to the social whole is genuine and not merely a ruse. Adorno seems to have precisely this problem in mind when he offers the otherwise rather perplexing remark that we should repudiate the choice between immanence and transcendence:

> The alternatives—either calling culture as a whole into question from outside under the general notion of ideology, or confronting it with the norms which it itself has crystallized—cannot be accepted by critical theory. To insist on the

choice between immanence and transcendence is to revert to the traditional logic criticized in Hegel's polemic against Kant.[80]

Although he does not make the point as clearly as he should, Adorno means to say that we should resist the bad and undialectical dualism between immanence and transcendence.[81] Rather, we should embrace what Honneth has called an *immanent transcendence*, or, to adopt terminology from Habermas, a "transcendence from within."[82] Such phrases are not as paradoxical as they may seem. They simply express Adorno's distinctive idea of an immanent normativity that *also* points beyond the sphere of mere immanence. As Honneth explains, "The idea that a critical analysis of society needs to be tied to an innerworldly instance of transcendence represents the legacy of Critical Theory's left-Hegelian tradition."[83] Earlier in this chapter I referred to the anticipatory character of immanent normativity, namely, the context-transcending power of norms that are simultaneously situated but also exceed their socio-historical situation.[84] The idea of an "immanent transcendence" captures this anticipatory character of immanent norms. Thanks to their anticipatory character, immanent norms must be understood as dialectical—as immanent *and* transcendent. Although they appear within our social context, they also point toward the overcoming of that context.

This is due to what we might call the constitutive *precarity* of all critical norms. The standards or experiences that may be available to us in our current situation may appear as promising sources of normativity, but such sources are always at risk of transforming from actual anticipations into false exits. This is why Adorno urges us to reject the stark and undialectical choice between immanent and transcendent critique. The genuinely transcendent moment in immanent transcendence can easily fall back into sheer immanence, such that what appeared to be a genuine door can turn out to be a solid wall. This is perhaps the most ingenious trick of ideology, that it awakens our longing for escape from current society only to turn our devotion to given norms into yet another affirmation of society as it is. What may appear to be a "critical standard [*kritische Maßstab*]" then becomes little more than an uncritical fantasy that binds us more decisively to what was already there.[85]

Adorno is constantly alert to the problem of the false exit. Because he recognizes the precarity of all anticipatory norms, he seldom permits himself to endorse those norms without simultaneously calling their validity into question. In this respect his critical practice remains alive to the perennial threat of ideology and the dialectical contradictions that compromise all our normative commitments. "The existing cannot be overstepped except by means of a universal derived from the existing order itself. The universal triumphs over the existing through the latter's own concept, and, therefore, in its triumph the power of mere existence constantly threatens to reassert itself by the same violence that broke it."[86] Note that Adorno takes care to indicate that the power of affirmative existence is a *threat* to our critical norms; he does not say that these norms *necessarily* lose all validity. Notwithstanding the threat of their compromise, Adorno does not and cannot fully surrender his commitment to the possibility of immanent transcendence.[87] For to do so would be to abandon the raison d'être of social criticism itself.

In order to clarify what is ultimately at stake in the problem of the false exit, I wish to draw on some of the illuminating insights that Rahel Jaeggi offers in her 2014 book, *Critique of Forms of Life*. Jaeggi seeks to defend the practice of immanent criticism as the mode that is best suited to critical theory. She draws a helpful distinction between *immanent criticism* and *internal criticism*.[88] Both of these are methods that criticize society based on standards that are already contained in society itself; so at least in this respect they share in common a basic difference from all varieties of transcendent critique.[89] But they are nonetheless distinctive on several counts.[90] Most importantly, *internal criticism* is one that judges certain practices of a given society deficient in terms of a norm that is already given in that society, but it takes that given norm to be wholly authoritative, and it ignores the further question as to whether those norms really deserve the authority our society has conferred on them. For this reason internal criticism often has noticeably conservative effects: although it may find that society has failed to honor its professed standards, it is content to bring existing social practices into alignment with currently authoritative norms. The very practice of internal criticism thereby helps to reaffirm the authority of those very standards.

Immanent criticism, by contrast, does not limit itself to the misalignment between current practices and norms. Rather, the immanent critic believes that we should direct our critical energy toward our current social practices *and* the norms they are said to embody. It sees society not as fixed but as a *dynamic* ensemble of norms and practices, and it recognizes that the standard of criticism itself may change as criticism proceeds. Here, then, is the crucial difference between internal and immanent criticism: whereas internal criticism ultimately affirms the authority of current standards and aims only to achieve better harmony between them, immanent criticism is potentially *transformative*. It does not assume that the norm to be realized is already present in reality as an ideal.[91] Rather, it starts from the inside of social reality but makes context-transcending claims that seek to transform *both* our current practices *and* our currently authoritative standards. Jaeggi acknowledges, however, that even the currently authoritative standards are not wholly false. For to condemn them as such would rob the immanent critic of a necessary presupposition, namely, that society is not fixed but a *dynamic* "ferment" that bears within itself the possibility of change. "The existing order—including its contradictory character—contains the potential that must provide a starting point for criticism, though only as part of a process of transformation." Pace Freyenhagen and other advocates of thoroughgoing negativism, the immanent critic is therefore convinced (in Jaeggi's words) that *"the 'better' is to be sought in the existing order of things where it already exists in incipient form."*[92]

Jaeggi's distinction between internal and immanent criticism sheds a helpful light on what I have called the problem of the false exit. It is often the case that society presents us with normative standards or ideals that seem highly appealing or authoritative, and we may also find that certain practices do not always honor those ideals. We may therefore feel that our criticism should be directed primarily to the reformist task of calling attention to the discrepancy between those ideals and current practices. The difficulty is that occasionally those ideals *also* deserve critical scrutiny, but because we have invoked them in our criticism of current practices we have thereby helped to solidify their authority. Here we can see how what may appear to us as a standard for social transformation may ultimately *obstruct* that transformation. The norms that animate our criticism are therefore not context-transcendent but context-affirmative. What looks like an exit may very well turn out to be a ruse that only binds us to society as it currently is. Reformism, in other words, can sometimes yield real benefits, but it can also have the effect of stabilizing the currently dominant ideology.

I have called attention to the problem of the false exit because it has serious implications for the way in which Adorno goes about the work of immanent critique. In what follows I wish to argue that Adorno believes that he can point to instances, or "fragments," of the good in the midst of the bad. I argue that these instances of the good appear chiefly in an experiential form, as experiences of material happiness that alert us to the possibility of human flourishing that the world generally denies. These instances are supposed to provide Adorno with the normative standard he requires so that he can find current society deficient, that is, as having failed the demand for human flourishing. But the foregoing discussion alerts us to the danger that those very instances of the good may themselves turn out to be deficient or even illusory. When this is the case immanent critique loses its system-transformative power, and it thereby lapses into the system-affirmative mode of merely "internal" criticism. We are therefore confronted with an important challenge: How can we be *certain* that the norms or standards that guide us in our criticism are not simply false exits, but hold out a genuine promise of context-transcendence or transformation?

The answer to this question is quite simply that we can never be *fully* assured that the promises are genuine ones.[93] The expectation that our confidence in these promises must be unshakable is simply unrealistic, and it ignores the dialectical insight that our standards are no less riven with contradiction than is the rest of our social reality. Adorno would never expect that actual promises of change could appear in pristine isolation from the illusions that conspire against this change. Truth and illusion, we might say, are inseparable. What he calls "ambiguity" is therefore a feature that afflicts all sources of normativity in social criticism. But this ambiguity does not deter him from his critical task. Adorno summarizes this commitment in a remarkable passage from *Minima Moralia* with which I will conclude this chapter:

> So, when we are hoping for rescue, a voice tells us that hope is in vain, yet it is powerless hope alone that allows us to draw a single breath. All contemplation can do no more than patiently trace the ambiguity of melancholy in ever new configurations. Truth is inseparable from the illusory belief that from the figures of the unreal one day, in spite of all, real deliverance will come.[94]

> [So sagt uns eine Stimme, wenn wir auf Rettung hoffen, daß Hoffnung vergeblich sei, und doch ist es sie, die ohnmächtige, allein, die überhaupt uns erlaubt, einen Atemzug zu tun. Alle Kontemplation vermag nicht mehr, als die Zweideutigkeit der Wehmut in immer neuen Figuren und Ansätzen geduldig nachzuzeichnen. Die Wahrheit ist nicht zu scheiden von dem Wahn, daß aus den Figuren des Scheins einmal doch, scheinlos, die Rettung hervortrete.][95]

Human Flourishing

In the previous chapter, I argued that Adorno's practice of immanent critique seeks to focus our attention on marginal and negative elements in human experience, not only because such elements demonstrate what is false in our current social arrangements, but also because such elements anticipate how our society could one day be true. I further suggested that this theme of anticipation alerts us to what we might call the *normative demand* that animates Adorno's immanent-critical practice. The demand is normative in the sense that we criticize the world with the expectation that it should live up to its promise. Such a demand, however, is not imposed on the world from the outside. Rather, it is an *immanent* demand in the sense that we can identify internal features, however marginal or insignificant, that are currently available in our worldly experience and that serve as warrants for our hope that life could at last become what it should be.

All of the above considerations suggest that Adorno's practice of immanent critique is ultimately animated by a normative demand for maximal fulfillment or human flourishing.[1] The demand that life should be lived rightly is simply the demand that our social world should be arranged in such a way as to make it feasible for human beings to realize who they are to the fullest possible extent. The idea of human flourishing has its origins in Aristotle and has been defended by a variety of neo-Aristotelian philosophers such as Martha Nussbaum, Rosalind Hursthouse, and Alasdair MacIntyre. It has also been suggested by David Leopold that the idea of human flourishing plays an important role in the early writings of Karl Marx.[2] Fabian Freyenhagen, whose interpretation I discussed in my introduction, ascribes to Adorno a species of "negative Aristotelianism," because he thinks that Adorno cannot justifiably lay claim to a *positive* concept of human flourishing, so he can only appeal to the thought that human beings have an unrealized potential. Although I agree with Freyenhagen that the comparison with Aristotle can assist us in

understanding Adorno's social philosophy, I disagree that Adorno's concept
of human flourishing is merely negative. On the contrary, I believe we should
characterize Adorno as a *maximalist* in his demand for human fulfillment.[3]

No doubt such a concept may strike us as exorbitant, and a skeptic might
very well object that no such criterion could ever be met. That human beings
should flourish by realizing their humanity in all possible ways surely strikes
a utopian chord that many readers would feel reluctant to associate with Adorno's negative-critical *Denkstil*, or manner of thought. Nor can we ignore the
concern that the concept of human flourishing is tainted by its association
with a capitalist imperative that we exploit every human capacity to the fur-
thest degree, as if the human being were simply another natural resource that
must submit to the principle of maximizing utility. These concerns, however,
should not inhibit us from seeing how Adorno appeals to an ideal of what
humanity can and should become. Nevertheless, Adorno is not an idealist. As
I argued above, he needs to point to material evidence within the bounds of
our current life that can offer some anticipatory glimpse of our flourishing.
He describes such approximative evidence in various ways: as a "rehearsal,"
as an "allegory," or as a "promesse du bonheur." His philosophical reflections
on music and aesthetics all bear witness to this very same vision. Elsewhere
he seeks to describe what he calls "metaphysical experience." Whatever the
domain, all such experiences are meant to fulfill our need for a kind of phenomenological warrant that the promise of human flourishing is not a mi-
rage. Such evidence, then, is anticipatory of the future, but it must be available
here and now and in experiential form. What saves Adorno from the charge
of utopianism is the further specification that the present world imposes a
serious constraint on our ability to experience any such evidence with the
fullness and depth that the ideal of human flourishing would seem to require.
Because the present world is disfigured by human suffering, any present experience of human flourishing will necessarily be precarious and incomplete:
"One must make the most of the possibilities that, by the standards of a truly
emancipated humanity, are *visible in our present situation, however faintly and
negatively.*"[4] We must recognize, however, that this maximalist standard of
human flourishing is precisely what impels Adorno to practice a relentless
criticism of our current life. Because nothing fully measures up to this high
standard, we cannot rest content with the minimalist ideal of a life that is "less
wrong." On the contrary, only a maximalist criterion can justify what Marx
called "the ruthless criticism of all that exists."

In this chapter, I offer an interpretation of Adorno's idea of human flourishing, with the specification that this idea must be understood in a materialist

sense; namely, he does not permit himself an appeal to concepts that correspond to no possible experience in the sensible world. Still he believes that our material existence alone is sufficient to afford us the rudimentary evidence we require if we wish to sustain our hope in the promise of human flourishing. This promise is given to us in instances of human happiness, though we should take care to note that by "happiness" Adorno seems to have in mind an exceptionally rich kind of human fulfillment that would require the unfolding of all our manifold capacities, from the sheer fact of bodily pleasure to the most exalted kinds of aesthetic and intellectual experiences.[5] For happiness of this sort to obtain sensual satisfaction is a necessary but not sufficient condition. "All happiness," he suggests, "aims at sensual fulfillment and wins its objectivity in it. If happiness is blocked in any one of its aspects, then it is no happiness at all."[6]

It is worth noting that without such a maximalist concept it would be difficult to make sense of Adorno's arguments concerning aesthetics, since his standards for what counts as excellence in art and music are so exacting. The kind of happiness that Adorno has in mind is perhaps best captured by the Greek ideal of *eudaemonia*, which acknowledges hedonic experience but insists that bodily pleasure be understood as only one element in a more capacious understanding of human excellence. Just as importantly, *eudaemonia* implies the co-determination of individual and social ideals; no individual can experience full happiness and self-realization apart from the full realization of society, and no society can be said to be fully realized if it does not involve the full satisfaction of all its inhabitants. It follows that no single individual can achieve absolute fulfillment if the individual's social surroundings do not make this experience *genuinely universal*. It is in this sense that Adorno warns us against the consoling illusion of an exclusively individual happiness. As he notes above, a happiness that is distorted (*verstellt*) in any fashion is not genuine happiness at all, though it may serve as an anticipation or "trace" of a universal fulfillment that is not yet at hand. Although we may still acknowledge the bare possibility of individual happiness, we must also recognize that in a damaged world any such individual happiness must necessarily remain partial and interlaced with suffering. To introduce this interpretation, I begin by looking more closely at the ideal of human flourishing itself.

The Emphatic Concept of the Human Being

In his summer semester 1958 introductory lectures on dialectics, Adorno devotes a greater share of his time to a discussion of Hegel's philosophy. The discussion is noteworthy chiefly because Adorno does not leap to criticizing

Hegel; instead he adopts a posture of interpretive charity that permits students to understand the basic principles of Hegelian dialectics in a more or less favorable light. Although Adorno does not suppress his occasional disagreements with Hegel, he seeks to bring out those features of the philosopher's work that are most suitable for lectures that promise an "introduction" to dialectics in general. For my own purposes here, it is worth pausing to consider the seventh lecture (June 12, 1958) where Adorno discusses the prominent role that Hegel assigns to the logical figure of contradiction. Hegel is a philosopher who understands that knowledge emerges out of *contradiction* (*Widerspruch*) rather than (in Adorno's words) "blank identity."[7] Knowledge that is genuinely self-conscious must realize that "every particular instance of knowledge becomes knowledge only through and by means of contradiction."[8] For Hegel contradiction is therefore nothing less than the "*organon of truth.*"[9]

To explain why contradiction plays a role of such importance in the dialectical idea of truth, Adorno offers an example or "model," though he also hastens to warn his students that dialectics does not easily accommodate itself to reasoning by means of examples. To the dialectician the concept of an example is controversial because it presupposes that we already have in our possession the higher or universal category under which the exemplary particular is to be subsumed. But this presupposes that the universal is "firm and positively given" as a kind of "reified result." In the Hegelian dialectic, however, a mundane universal is not pregiven at all; rather, it emerges *from* the particular. "The universal field consists precisely in the life of the particular it grasps within it; it fulfills itself through the particular, it does not merely cover or include the particular but arises out of it."[10] Adorno's phrasing here is unusual: we are told that the universal "has its life [*hat sein Leben*] in the particular"; so it follows that we are forbidden from thinking of any particular as "a merely lifeless example."[11] These provisos notwithstanding, Adorno presses on to offer an example as to how dialectics involves contradiction. The example he provides is that of "the concept of the human being in the emphatic sense [*dem Begriff des Menschen im emphatischen Sinn*]."[12] In what follows I reconstruct Adorno's presentation in order to bring out some of its more intriguing philosophical claims.

Consider the proposition, "X is a human being." If we state this proposition in relation to a certain individual ("Mr. X") then it may seem that the proposition is true in a rather straightforward sense. We possess a universal concept of "human being" (B), and the particular individual who stands before us (A) is simply subsumed under that concept. The proposition "A is B" appears to be true. A difficulty arises, however, once we acknowledge that

A is merely a *representative* of B and does not comprise the whole of it. The "emphatic concept" of the human being would include "everything possible" that is implied in that concept, but the individual X who stands before us does not instantiate all of those various implications. The emphatic concept comprises many features that the individual X evidently lacks. Adorno explains as follows:

> [Hegel] would not simply content himself, therefore, with a primitive biological definition of 'human being,' but would say instead, if we are talking about a truly vital comprehension of the human being as such, that we must think in terms of categories such as freedom, individuation, autonomy, the possession of reason, and a host of other things, all of which are already implicitly contained in the concept of human being as the objective character of the latter.[13]

We are therefore confronted with a serious problem. We began with the thought that "X is a human being" was obviously true. The difficulty arises from the fact that, according to Hegel, the "emphatic dimension is always already involved in the concept of the human being [*im Begriff des Menschen immer dieses Emphatische schon mitgesetzt ist*]." But when we consider the specific individual in question, it is immediately apparent to us that he does not fully satisfy that emphatic concept. But this means that our proposition is true but "at the same time untrue."[14]

Adorno does not pursue this analysis in all its exquisite detail without a broader purpose in view. He means to call attention to the crucial fact that the dialectic embraces both the true and the false in their immanent simultaneity. This simultaneity has to do with the antagonism between concept and reality. The emphatic concept of the human being, for example, "is certainly not yet realized here and now in any particular existing being."[15] Indeed one might go so far as to say that "something like a human being does not yet exist at all," at least insofar as "the emphatic concept of the human being objectively and intrinsically implies."[16] This is why Adorno concludes that "the proposition 'X is a human being' is right or correct[,] . . . but it is also false."[17] This discovery regarding the simultaneity of the true and the false is a general principle of dialectical reasoning as such. But it carries special significance when we consider the antagonism between the emphatic concept of the human being and all the particular human beings who inhabit our world. For we can hardly ignore the distressing fact that no human being who actually exists here and now fully lives up to its emphatic concept. Adorno presents this lack of congruence between concept and reality as a species of normative *failure* insofar as the emphatic concept serves as a standard of truth that no individual human being has yet achieved:

I believe that we need only to apply this proposition really seriously to any human being, to indicate that the individual in question is a human being, and
we will realize this difference at once, will realize that the individual does not
yet really do justice to the concept of the human being in the emphatic sense,
the concept of the human being in terms of absolute truth [*daß er eigentlich
dem Begriff des Menschen im emphatischen Sinn, also dem Begriff des Menschen im Sinn der absoluten Wahrheit*].[18]

This normative failure is unsurprising once we recall that Hegel is a philosopher who cannot conceive of the full realization of the individual apart from
concrete institutions and practices of the social world that individual inhabits. As Frederick Neuhouser has observed, Hegel understands true freedom
as *social freedom*.[19] It follows that the emphatic concept of the human being
cannot be intelligible for us if we do not also refer to the full range of institutions in which this human being gains its concreteness and reality. In Hegel's
emphatic concept of the human being this institutional proviso is presupposed. Such a requirement, however, only enhances our awareness of the
yawning gap between concept and reality. Our emphatic concept makes an
exorbitant demand for an organization of things that exceeds by far what is
currently the case, so it can hardly surprise us that our institutional world as it
is currently arranged must fail that demand and even fail it by a wide margin.
But then the question must arise: How are we able to recognize this failure?
Adorno's startling response is that we can only make sense of the normative
failure if we somehow already have the emphatic concept in our possession.
Our awareness of this failure "presupposes that we already have on hand such
an emphatic concept of the human being, ultimately the concept of a right
and genuine human being, ultimately, indeed, the concept of a right and genuine arrangement of the world in general."[20]

    This conclusion follows from the principle of immanent normativity. The
dialectic cannot appeal to an "ought [*Sollen*]" that wholly transcends "what
is [*was ist*]." It must locate the dynamic sources of transformation *within* the
contradictions of society as these obtain here and now. For Hegel this very
same principle must also apply to our *conceptual* resources. If we can identify a contradiction between how we currently are and our concept of how
we should be, then we must locate *that* contradiction too within our present experience. It is a vital feature of the Hegelian dialectic that no concepts
can be exempted from this requirement, and this is so even for that special
class of concepts that Adorno describes as "emphatic" (a term of art I examine further on). It does not matter if these concepts confront us with a
normative demand. We must nonetheless resist the seductive thought that
such norms would have their origin in a realm of pure thought beyond all

possible experience. For no concepts can make a normative demand on us unless they have already gained at least some traction within the world as it is. Our emphatic concepts too must be somehow *already* available to us within the bounds of worldly experience.

Dialectical Contradiction

Little in the foregoing remarks should strike us as controversial. Adorno offers these remarks only to bring out the central role that immanent contradiction plays in dialectics. But it turns out that immanent contradiction itself must be understood in a twofold sense. First, it means that our worldly experience is riven with contradiction; but, second, it means that this very contradiction already bears within itself the resources for its overcoming. Adorno insists on both of these senses. "All dialectical thought," he explains, finds its original inspiration in a basic experience, namely, "our knowledge of the contradictory or antagonistic character of reality itself [*das Wissen vom widerspruchsvollen, vom antagonistischen Charakter der Realität selber*]."[21] Hegel shared with the Romantics this basic experience of contradiction or "diremption [*Zerrissenheit*]."[22] Unlike the Romantics, however, Hegel believed that no genuine reconciliation of the contradictory world could ever be gained if one were merely to withdraw into the isolation of the subject, nor did he consider it plausible that we could seek a resolution by appealing to world-transcendent principles or ideas. Rather, Hegel understood that the resolution would have to be found "in and through this self-contradictory character itself." But if contradiction is immanent to reality, then so too is reconciliation: "And the idea that this development, this driving force, and ultimately also that which strives for reconciliation, is something itself harbored within the diremption, the negative, the suffering of the world, this idea is equally, as an experience of reality, a sustaining idea of the Hegelian dialectic."[23] This twofold understanding of contradiction is an indispensable theme in all dialectical reasoning. It saves contradiction from being nothing more than a static or motionless condition, and it lends it its truly dynamic character. Contradiction itself, we might say, has its own dialectical structure. It does not signify merely opposition; it signifies *both* opposition *and* its resolution.

In a series of lectures that are meant to provide a general introduction to dialectical thinking, Adorno devotes special attention to this idea because he recognizes its vital importance for *any* understanding of the dialectic, including his own. Indeed, he is careful to explain that he is chiefly interested in the general features of the dialectic as such and not the specific features that applied only to the dialectic in its Hegelian form. He states this point to his students with remarkable candor. "I wish to provide you with a concept of dialectic which is also a *rigorous* conception of dialectic," he explains, "albeit one which cannot be fully captured within the context of idealist theses which have become so problematic for us."[24] Although the presuppositions of the idealist tradition are no longer credible, Adorno urges his students to embrace dialectics in its "materialist version."[25] For both versions of the dialectic share in common a twofold perspective on reality that ascribes to it the simultaneity of unity and division.

To be sure, there is an important difference. For the idealist, reality exhibits this simultaneity insofar as it is a rational system that comprises the mediated unity of internally antagonistic moments. For the materialist, reality exhibits a comparable simultaneity, but it is now understood as an irrational system of social exchange whose operation unifies all of society even while it also generates contradiction. This difference should not be overlooked. According to Adorno, the idealist believes that the simultaneity of unity and division has *already* found its resolution in a higher identity, or, at the very least, it is on the cusp of resolution. Mediation, in other words, appears as a more or less achieved fact. For the materialist, however, the simultaneity of unity and division has not found any such resolution. Conditions of social antagonism that emerge from the process of exchange cannot be contained within the current system and are instead harbingers of its undoing. This difference is expressed in Adorno's distinction between two understandings of the dialectic as either "closed [*geschlossen*]" or "open [*offen*]." Where the closed dialectic of the idealist tradition insists on the *identity* of identity and non-identity, Adorno insists that an open dialectic is one that sustains the *non-identity* of identity and non-identity.[26]

Although he does not deny the importance of this difference, Adorno believes that dialectical reasoning in all of its guises remains committed to the very same idea. Namely, it understands contradiction not as a static fact but as a dynamic and *anticipatory* principle that contains within itself the force for its own overcoming. "To think dialectically," he explains, "is not to confront one proposition of whatever kind with some other contrary opinion from outside. Rather, it is to drive through to the point where it comes to recognize its own finitude, its own falsehood, *and is thereby also driven on beyond itself* [*und dadurch über sich hinaustreibt*]."[27] Here Adorno seems to endorse the motif of immanent transcendence, according to which social reality contains moments that anticipate its own sublation. This idea is easily missed if we understand contradiction as something merely static. But Adorno insists that if we wish to take contradiction seriously, we must understand it too in a resolutely dialectical manner that does not permit it to remain at rest in mere opposition. For this would misconstrue non-identity as yet another identity. Rather, we must see the negation of contradiction as a kind of impulse or drive that already inheres in contradiction itself. This would seem to be the meaning behind his rather pathos-laden claim that "the driving force [*das Treibende*]" or "that which strives for reconciliation [*das, was auf Versöhnung abzielt*]" is not something transcendent to the world or something that is "brought in from the outside [*nicht etwa von außen Hinzugefügtes*]."[28] Rather, it is something that is "harbored within the diremption, in the negative, in the suffering of the world itself [*etwas ist, was selbst in der Zerrissenheit, in dem Negativen, in dem Leiden der Welt eigentlich steckt*]."[29]

The upshot of all such considerations is that we must reject what I have called the "gnostic" or negativist interpretation of Adorno's philosophy. If Adorno does not portray the world as a realm of absolute falsehood, this is because his concept of falsehood is already dialectical in the sense that it contains within itself its own negation. Adorno naturally recognizes that argumentation of this kind may seem to strain the bounds of logic. But he does not regard this as a philosophical embarrassment. Rather, he argues that the dialectic should be understood as more than mere logic since it does not permit the categories of the true and the false to remain in stark opposition. The dialectic is, quite simply, a higher manifestation of reason itself, because it represents reason's ability to think in a self-reflexive and critical manner about its own logical instruments. Dialectics therefore involves a "disintegration of traditional logic by logical means. [*Zerfall der traditionellen Logik mit logischen Mitteln*]."[30] But it performs this disintegration not by "external" critique. Rather, it does so "by an immanent demonstration that in each case, *measured by their own standards* [these logical means] are inadequate to the truth [*durch den Nachweis, daß sie immanent, also nach ihrem eigenen Maß jeweils nicht die Wahrheit seien*]."[31] Only such a dialectical approach will permit us to understand the crucial insight that the true and the false are not strictly opposed. This insight, however, is not only valuable in a formal sense as a sign of reason's capacity for self-reflexivity; it also has important implications beyond merely formal considerations when we turn our attention to our actual surroundings. For if the false and the true are not strictly opposed, then we cannot see the world as a domain of absolute falsehood where the true would obtain only as a world-transcendent standard. The true is not expelled from the world as its gnostic other; rather, the true already inheres in the false.

From these considerations we can conclude that Adorno commits himself to what we could call the idea of truth-immanence. But we can still understand this idea in two distinct ways. We can understand it as (1) a question of *conceptual* entailment or as (2) a question as to what we have a right to expect from our *experience*. First, we might think that truth-immanence is something that we have to presuppose merely as a matter of conceptual entailment, in the sense that in criticizing anything as false we already commit ourselves to the *concept* of the true even if no evidence is available to confirm this concept. Adorno apparently feels that the question of merely conceptual entailment is unproblematic. "Dialectical theory," he explains, "holds fast to the idea of truth."

> A dialectic which was incapable of bringing the standard [*Maß*] of truth to bear so rigorously and persistently upon every claim to knowledge that this latter would dissolve in the face of it would already lack the power without which no dialectical process could ever be grasped at all. *And the idea of truth is already involved in the insight into untruth, namely in the critical motif that is the decisive dimension of dialectic, and its necessary condition.*[32]

Adorno is committed to the idea that criticism of social falsehood is only possible if the concept of truth is already presupposed. Truth in this sense resembles a Kantian postulate, insofar as the very exercise of criticism compels us to accept it, though only from the practical point of view. Truth is "ineluctably and unconditionally posited and intended in [the] moment of critique, in the moment of thought which cannot but press onward."[33]

For Adorno, however, presupposition must mean something more than merely conceptual entailment. His materialism also commits him to the second, far stronger claim that we only have the right to a concept if there is in fact some worldly intuition to which it corresponds. "The truth in question cannot itself be fixed and reified as something beyond the phenomena [*Wahrheit nicht vorgestellt wird als ein Verdinglichtes, Festes jenseits der Phänomene selber*]."[34] Adorno can only endorse the idea of truth-immanence if he believes we can expect to find some support for this truth *within our material experience*. He cannot accept the suggestion that truth could remain *merely* a postulate, since this would still leave it vulnerable to the accusation that it is not immanent at all but is instead something that lies "beyond the phenomena." Such an inference, he explains, would be merely a symptom of "the dichotomous consciousness of the present." In rejecting this inference, he commits himself to the stronger claim that truth must be something more than a mere concept that is presupposed in our thoughts. Rather, *it must be something that could actually be given to us in our experience*: "Truth must be sought *within the life of the phenomena themselves* [*daß die Wahrheit gesucht wird in dem Leben der Phänomene selber*]."[35]

Whether Adorno actually means to endorse the stronger claim without reservation remains uncertain. At times he seems to concede that truth-immanence might amount to little more than a "demand [*Forderung*]" placed on thought alone, while the question of its reality or unreality (*Wirklichkeit oder Unwirklichkeit*) remains a matter of near-indifference (*fast gleichgültig*).[36] More often, however, he accepts both meanings, as if he could not imagine how we would ever endorse the mere *concept* of truth without also seeking at least a partial validation for this concept in our experience. In an important passage from *Negative Dialectics* he comes close to conflating these two meanings. "Consciousness," he writes, "could not despair at all over what is grey, if it did not harbor the concept of a different color, whose *scattered trace is not lacking in the negative whole [Bewußtsein könnte gar nicht über das Grau verzweifeln, hegte es nicht den Begriff von einer verschiedenen Farbe, deren versprengte Spur im negativen Ganzen nicht fehlt]*."[37] This extraordinary passage deserves our notice because it states with admirable economy what we might call the animating principle of Adorno's critical practice. Just as it would be impossible to identify a given object as gray without some familiarity with colors that lie elsewhere on the spectrum, so too our knowledge of what is wrong presupposes at least some familiarity with better alternatives. The metaphors of color and light drive home the point that Adorno seeks not only conceptual but also experiential validation for his normative standards. The prospect that the world might be someday redeemed from its darkness is more than an idle wish. The traces of light that we are able to identify in our present society may be qualified and partial, but we do not hope in vain.

The Normative Status of Emphatic Concepts

I argued above that for Adorno the practice of immanent critique does not confine itself to an identification of what is false. Rather, our condemnation of the false already presupposes some concept or "standard [*Maß*]" of truth. Since Adorno is not an idealist, however, he rejects the view that any such concept could enjoy validity if it had a merely conceptual or world-transcendent character. The concept must find at least a partial validation within worldly experience or "in the phenomena themselves." Adorno recognizes, however, that this stricture leaves him in a position of some philosophical uncertainty, since on his view our worldly experience suffers from pervasive damage and is growing only more damaged with the passage of time. What he calls the "withering of experience" presents a serious challenge insofar as no validation in the actual phenomena can suffice to fully satisfy our conceptual standards.

In an imperfect world all available evidence too will be shot through with imperfection. Nevertheless, Adorno does not feel moved to dismiss the standard altogether simply because of its precarious status. On the contrary, he seems to feel that holding on to such a standard is indispensable to the practice of immanent critique even if nothing in our current experience rises to the level of total satisfaction. For without this standard he would not be able to take the measure of the damage in question.[38]

I have more to say later regarding this philosophical difficulty and the skeptical concerns it may raise. For my present purposes, however, I would like to draw attention to a terminological matter that is central to Adorno's argument. I have suggested that Adorno wishes to hold on to a certain kind of conceptual standard even when he finds only partial and uncertain validation for this standard in worldly experience. When he refers to such a standard, the term of art that Adorno considers most suitable is that of an *emphatic concept*. This term appears with great frequency in his work, and it is nearly always used to signify a concept that plays the role of a higher standard or norm against which we can determine whether a given phenomenon fulfills its own concept. This special usage reflects the etymological background of the word. *Emphatic* is derived from the Greek ἐμφατικός, which is in turn based on ἐμφαίνω, which combines ἐμ (in) with φαίνω (I let shine, or I show). Not incidentally, this verb also lies at the root of the term "phenomenon." If one consults the dialogues of Plato, one can appreciate how the root terms associated with emphasis (e.g., ἐμφανῆ or ἐμφαίνεται in the *Timaeus*, 46a2–b2) convey the important theme of coming-into-appearance.[39] The political theorist Jill Frank has suggested that this theme is used by Socrates in the *Republic* in order to question "any hard and fast distinction between what is thought and what is seen." Thus she argues that (in, e.g., *Republic* 508e) even the idea of the good "appears to be *mediated by experience*."[40]

Whether Adorno was aware of this Greek philological background may strike us as doubtful: his knowledge of Greek philosophy was rather limited. But the association of *emphasis* with that which shows itself *in appearance* is nevertheless philosophically instructive: it underscores the basic point that when Adorno appeals to an emphatic concept he always requires that this concept must somehow manifest itself *in our experience*. However, it may be of greater relevance here to recall the meaning of emphasis in rhetoric: from the Greek noun form ἔμφασις there was derived the Latin *emphasis*, a term that acquired the technical meaning of placing unusual stress on a given word in order to indicate that in a specific context it implies something beyond its customary or everyday meaning. When Adorno employs the term "emphatic," we might understand him as following this rhetorical practice.

He refers variously to "the emphatic concept of experience," "the emphatic concept of the human being," "the emphatic concept of art," "the emphatic concept of knowledge," and "the emphatic concept of truth." He even refers to the generic concept of an "emphatic philosophy."[41] In all these cases Adorno implies a distinction between the conventional meaning of the given concept and its emphatic meaning, where the emphatic meaning serves as a higher standard or norm. This norm is *emphatic* insofar as it implies more than the concept in the conventional sense denotes. An emphatic concept is *normative* insofar as it makes a demand on what is given in our experience that it live up to the higher standard.[42]

If we wish to understand the status of the normative in Adorno's philosophy, this appeal to emphatic concepts is of great importance. Most of all, it assists us in drawing a distinction within social reality between (a) the empirical standards that are socially authoritative and (b) the higher idea that can be said to inhere *in those empirical standards* even though its claims remain largely unfulfilled. In *Negative Dialectics*, for example, Adorno applies this principle to the concept of freedom. He urges us to distinguish between (a) the empirical individuals who may seem to embody freedom at least in a certain measure and under present circumstances and (b) the emphatic concept of freedom that implies something *more than* freedom in the empirical sense:

> The judgement that someone is a free man is related, *thought emphatically* [*emphatisch gedacht*] to the concept of freedom. However, this is for its part more than what is predicated of that man, just as that man, through other determinations, is more than the concept of his freedom. Its concept says not only that it could be applied to all other individuals, as freely defined men. It nourishes the idea of a condition in which the individuals would have qualities, which here and now could be ascribed to no one.[43]

The crucial thought here is that although empirical instances of freedom are no doubt inadequate to its emphatic concept, this inadequacy should not serve as an occasion for dismissing the emphatic concept as illegitimate. The emphatic concept still serves as a guiding norm; or, in Adorno's words, it *nourishes the idea of* a condition in which freedom would become a reality. The distinction between empirical and emphatic concepts is vital to Adorno's philosophy since it allows us to imagine the thought of social conditions that would be otherwise than they are. If we do not wish to surrender to the authority of the given, we must hold fast to emphatic concepts as standards for criticism even when little in empirical reality offers evidence for their legitimacy.

Another illustration of this idea can be found in *Aesthetic Theory*, where Adorno often refers to "art in the emphatic sense."[44] By this, he means art that succeeds in satisfying its own concept. Admittedly, the idea of an emphatic concept of art seems to have two, mutually exclusive implications. On the one hand, the concept of art is highly discriminatory in the sense that it does not permit each and every specimen of art to meet the criterion for its success. Implicit in this concept is the possibility that certain instances of what may *seem* to be art in the conventional sense might not actually be works of art at all. Indeed, Adorno tells us that "the concept of an artwork implies that of its success. Failed artworks are not art."[45] Adorno's idea of an emphatic concept thus sets the bar at such a great height that it rules out of consideration a great many items that we might have thought were obvious examples of the concept in question. On the other hand, however, the idea does not seem discriminatory *enough*. After all, there is a sense in which Adorno thinks that we cannot draw a distinct line between the emphatic and the conventional uses of a concept, since the former is nothing but the self-realization of the latter. It turns out that both sides of this puzzle capture something important about the idea of an emphatic concept. An emphatic concept imposes a normative demand that its conventional instance *should* fulfill. But the conventional instance can be expected to meet this demand only because it is already directed *toward* this fulfillment. The relationship between them is therefore *self-regulative*. To be sure, the concept at issue cannot simply be the one that happens to enjoy an authoritative status under current conditions, since such a concept would be affirmative, not regulative: it would merely affirm what already exists anyway. A genuinely emphatic concept would have to reach out beyond conditions as they are given. This is why Adorno believes that he can intelligibly say that something *should live up to its very own concept*.

The self-regulative logic of emphatic concepts does not apply exclusively to art; the very same logic applies in other domains. Adorno also illustrates this self-regulative function with reference to the concept of enlightenment. Against those who have misunderstood him as issuing an exhaustive or totalizing condemnation of the enlightenment, for example, he takes care to explain that the critique of the enlightenment can proceed only if it is committed to the fulfillment of its own concept. He insists that "we must constantly recognize the dialectic of enlightenment," in the sense that we should acknowledge "all the sacrifice and injustice which the enlightenment has brought in its course." But this means that we must acknowledge these liabilities as moments when the Enlightenment has betrayed its very own promise and has revealed "*that it is still partial, thus actually not yet enlightened enough.*"[46] Such a remark may come as a surprise especially to readers who understand

Adorno as a thoroughgoing skeptic about normative concepts such as reason, enlightenment, and progress. The remark thus offers a welcome corrective. Instead of issuing a totalizing and negative verdict on the Enlightenment, Adorno insists that "it is only by pursuing *the enlightenment's own principle* through *to its end* that these wounds may perhaps be healed."[47] The critique of the Enlightenment is therefore self-regulative: it appeals to its own emphatic concept to show what it is that has been failed even while it also remains fully committed to that same concept so as to remedy the failure.[48]

Once we understand the self-regulative status of emphatic concepts in Adorno's philosophy, we can make better sense of his penchant for self-referential claims that might otherwise strike us as paradoxical or hopelessly self-referential. Consider the well-known claim, "Progress occurs where it ends." The philosopher Amy Allen has interpreted this claim in a rather straightforward sense as if Adorno simply meant to say that the concept of progress has ended in total failure and therefore can no longer play any legitimate role in critical theory.[49] But we will adopt such a totalizing verdict only if we ignore what Adorno sees as the concept's intrinsically dialectical character. He does not mean to say that we should dispense with the concept of progress altogether. Rather, he means that progress *in the emphatic sense* can only succeed if we identify cases of apparent progress as partial and disfigured instances of the higher standard. Adorno is not merely indulging in paradox, nor is he endorsing wholesale skepticism. But we will appreciate how he avoids these fallacies only if we recognize the non-identical or mediated status of the concept in question. This is the case not only for the concept of progress; it is no less the case for other normative concepts that play an important role in his philosophy. Another well-known instance is the seemingly paradoxical epigram by Ferdinand Kürnberger that appears on the opening page of the first part of *Minima Moralia*: "Life does not live [*Das Leben lebt nicht*]."[50] The meaning of this epigram becomes intelligible once we prise apart the two senses of "life" that are condensed into a single statement. We can decompose the epigram into a normative judgment of failure: Life as it is now lived has so far *failed its own concept*; or, stated differently, life does not (yet) live in the emphatic sense. When the epigram is broken into its unreconciled moments it admittedly loses much of its rhetorical force, but it gains just as much in dialectical precision, since we can now appreciate its meaning as an immanent critique of what our life has become. When Adorno informs us that something has *failed its own concept* he means to alert us to the intrinsically dialectical relationship that obtains between an emphatic concept and its distorted manifestation. This relationship, in other words, should not be misconstrued as one of sheer identity; rather, it is best understood as one of *difference-within-identity*. An emphatic concept *both is and is not* identical to its worldly manifestation: it signifies not only what the latter has failed to be but also what it *should* be were it to actually succeed in fulfilling its own concept.

This brings us to one of the more controversial questions in the interpretation of Adorno's philosophy. It is a widespread belief that Adorno surrendered any commitment to concepts such as "enlightenment" or "progress" because he had witnessed the catastrophic end to which such concepts must lead, and he therefore felt moved to conclude that these concepts are thoroughly corrupt and mere masks for power. This skeptical verdict left him with no other choice but to embrace the paradox of a critical practice that lacks all normative concepts or foundations. The foregoing discussion of emphatic concepts can assist us in seeing why this interpretation of his philosophy is mistaken. The error is due to the impression that Adorno understood our present world as unbroken and absolutely false. But this was not his view. Our society is not a seamless or self-identical whole; rather, it is characterized by internal difference and contradiction. Now it turns out that the structure of our concepts bears a close resemblance to the structure of our world. Our concepts too are not seamless or self-identical; rather, they exhibit an internal and contradictory character of difference-within-identity. Adorno can avoid the trap of totalizing skepticism about our normative concepts only because he sees them as dialectical; they express *both* an unresolved demand *and* the world's failure to satisfy that demand.

Normativity and Damage

At this point it is important to confront a serious philosophical objection. Let us suppose that we subscribe to the negativism thesis and we grant its basic claim that for Adorno we inhabit an "evil world," that is, a gnostic world in which we are blocked from any and all experiences of the good. Now if we hold that an emphatic concept must correspond to a possible intuition, then it would seem that no emphatic concept could possibly be available for us as a standard by which to judge the world a failure. Of course, it might be argued that a certain puzzle arises in connection with this scenario, since it is not altogether obvious how we could describe the world as "evil" without at least some contrasting intimation of the good. The world would appear to us just as it did to Hegel in his preface to the *Philosophy of Right*, where we are presented with the well-known image of the owl of Minerva. In the twilight of a given age philosophy would abandon the task of criticism and confine itself to mere knowledge of what is at hand; it would have no other task than to paint the world as "grey in grey."[51] Adorno appears to have precisely this passage from Hegel in mind when he writes that criticism (or even mere "despair") requires a richer palette: "Consciousness could not even despair over the grey, if it did not harbor the notion of a different color, whose dispersed traces are not absent from the negative whole [*Bewußtsein könnte gar nicht über das Grau verzweifeln, hegte es nicht den Begriff von einer verschiedenen Farbe, deren versprengte Spur im negativen Ganzen nicht fehlt*]."[52]

Be this as it may, those who interpret Adorno as a thoroughgoing negativist may still want to object that a mere "trace" of a different color is surely not the same as a robust intuition or experience of the good. Timo Jütten, for example, admits that in the passage quoted above Adorno seems to allow for the possibility that we might experience "fleeting moments of happiness and otherness in our radically evil world." But Jütten insists that such moments are far too ephemeral to serve the needs of moral or political criticism, because "their entanglement with radical evil and their fugitive character mean that they cannot be conceptualized, used, and reproduced in the same way as other events. In particular, Adorno does not think that the phenomena he describes are traces of the good in the sense that they could underwrite a normative ethics."[53] At best such experiences can serve only as (in Jütten's words) "*ephemeral reminders* of the possibility of non-instrumental or non-dominating relationships that offer hope, if they are experienced in this way. They remain promissory of future happiness and otherness."[54]

This objection merits closer scrutiny, since it is expresses what I would call the key premise of the negativist thesis. The premise would appear to be that no "fleeting" or imperfect experience of the good can really count as a genuine instance of the good. The assumption, in other words, is that if we can claim a normatively meaningful experience of "the good" this implies that we have some experience of the good in its uncontaminated perfection. And since we cannot experience any such perfection, then what we experience as the mere possibility of the good cannot *actually* be the good at all. We might still assign it some deflationary status as a "reminder" that our world might some day be better than it currently is. But to assign it such a lowly status is altogether different from granting it any dignified role in our moral and political thinking. From the perspective of (in Jütten's words) "normative ethics," all such experiences must be dismissed as without consequence.

The key premise is perplexing on several counts. Formulated in the most general terms, the assumption would seem to be that "no imperfect version of x can count as an x." To grasp what is mistaken about this assumption we need to recall that for Adorno *everything* in our experience is damaged or imperfect. Indeed, it was his view that all experience is marked by an incorrigible

transience: all worldly being is finite, temporal, and shot through with constitutive imperfection. But the mere fact that our experience is fleeting and
imperfect can hardly suffice to rule out the possibility of its conceptualiza-
tion. To be sure, Adorno does not waver from his claim that our sensual and
time-bound reality possesses a kind of richness and depth that will forever
exceed the limits of mere conceptuality. All subjective experience is therefore experience of a world that exhibits objective "primacy [*Vorrang*]." Now
what is true of all worldly experience is ipso facto true of any experiences
that hold out to us a fleeting glimpse of happiness or the good. It follows that
the "fugitive character" of these experiences should not give us any special
reason to dismiss them as lacking in normative significance. The dismissive
verdict is born of the inference that damaged norms cannot and should not
count as norms at all. But little in Adorno's philosophy can warrant such a
rash inference. To be sure, Adorno readily admits that in our imperfect world
the norms that are available to us will inevitably be compromised. "Even the
norms that condemn the order of the world are themselves are due to its
bad existence [*Selbst die Normen, welche die Einrichtung der Welt verdammen,
verdanken sich deren eigenen Unwesen*]."⁵⁵ But he does not permit this general
truth to vitiate their meaning. Jütten wishes to say that due to their "entanglement with radical evil" none of our experiences could possibly play a role in
our ethical thinking. But Adorno does not draw such a conclusion. On the
contrary, he insists that our experiences can still be enlisted for the purposes
of normative criticism. We must continue to pursue the task of criticism under non-ideal conditions, but this is unsurprising because non-ideal conditions are the only conditions we have.

Stepping back from the details of this dispute, it is worth pondering the
broader, methodological question as to why the fleeting character of human
experience would encourage an attitude of thoroughgoing normative skepticism. Adorno addresses precisely this question in the concluding lecture of
his 1960 lecture course on philosophy and sociology. The lecture course is of
great interest not least because Adorno recognizes that his own thinking is
situated at the hazardous boundary between two disciplines whose methodological and metaphysical assumptions would seem to place them forever at
odds: philosophy asserts validity for concepts that sociology wishes to understand in terms of their genesis alone. If validity and genesis seem impossible
to reconcile, this is because of a long-standing prejudice that is at least as
ancient as philosophy itself. Beginning with Plato if not before, it has been
assumed as a guiding metaphysical premise in philosophy that nothing that
has merely come into being over time can possibly stake a claim to validity.
Only that which is enduring possesses absolute truth, whereas anything that

is ephemeral must succumb to relativism. The sociologist, who seeks to identify the social and historical origins of an idea, is therefore locked in a kind of permanent metaphysical opposition with the philosopher, who wishes to isolate the validity of the idea from the vagaries of society and time.

This methodological quarrel between sociology and philosophy also alerts us to a deeper, more metaphysical question as to whether we are justified in seeking to uphold the conventional distinction between genesis and validity. In the final lecture of the 1960 lecture course on philosophy and sociology Adorno argues that this distinction rests on a metaphysical error. His argument (already articulated in his 1956 *Metacritique of Epistemology*) is that genesis and validity are not strictly opposed but mutually implicative. He insists that "genetic moments are already implicit in the question of validity" and also (correlatively) that "it is equally impossible to separate genetic moments from the claim to validity or justification."[56] To be sure, Adorno is fully aware of the fact that even our most cherished normative concepts have their genesis in time, but he is unwilling to draw the skeptical conclusion that all such concepts can therefore enjoy nothing more than a relativistic meaning. This skeptical conclusion, he notes, is one that derives from an ancient metaphysical prejudice that we can already discern in Plato's philosophy, namely, the prejudice that "what has become cannot be true," whereas "only that which directly and immediately 'is' . . . can properly raise the claim to truth."[57]

To illustrate why this prejudice is mistaken, Adorno offers some remarks on the socio-historical genesis of the bourgeois ideal of freedom. He explains that this ideal first emerged in the context of a historically particular struggle of free owners of mobile property against those whose social authority was conditional upon ownership of land. Bourgeois freedom thus expressed a series of normative claims regarding the validity of social power, but it also expressed normative claims whose validity reached beyond their original context of application. Notwithstanding the specificity of its genesis, this validity could also be turned "against those to whom it had once exclusively been reserved."[58] Adorno does not make explicit the Marxian theme in his argument, but the reference to historical materialism is fairly self-evident. "The bourgeois ideal of freedom already understands itself as an essentially *critical* relationship to what preceded it," in the sense that this ideal "appears as the realization of a freedom that had somehow already been envisaged and projected." It follows that the bourgeois claim to power operates simultaneously as ideology *and* as a critique of ideology: "the genesis or process of development that leads from one form of society to the other cannot actually be separated from the issue of validity or justification."[59] The implication is that validity *emerges out of but also exceeds genesis*. A concept that was generated only to justify bourgeois right also prepares the terrain for the dialectical self-overcoming of bourgeois right; ideology and its critique are both contained within a single concept.

Adorno provides a further illustration of this dialectical relationship between genesis and validity from the history of music. Seen from one perspective, it is obvious that everything that we subsume under the concept of musical experience can be explained in the genetic categories of social history. Richard Wagner once expressed this socio-genetic insight in his dismissive remark that when he heard certain compositions by Mozart "he could not help thinking of the clatter of dishes coming in and out at the great banquets of the princes and archbishops."[60] Adorno generalizes this claim into the sociological principle that even the highest forms of autonomous music as exemplified by Beethoven's symphonies and late quartets are traceable to the "lowly and heteronomous" forms of *Tafelmusik* (table music). Yet at the same time these works must also be heard as "the most consummate expression of the ideal of humanity." If one adopts the merely external perspective of socio-genetic determinism this ideal will remain invisible, but from the internal perspective of musical form we can discern the "autonomous logic" that coexists alongside its social heteronomy. It belongs to the very structure of music that "it contains within itself, in the language of its own forms and structures, everything that points beyond [its] origin."[61]

With such illustrations in mind, Adorno wishes to convey the more general lesson that the principles of genesis and validity are not mutually exclusive but mutually constitutive: the "decisive thing is to try and free yourself as resolutely as possible from the idea that truth cannot be something that has become, from the idea that truth stands motionless on one side, while the realm of factical existence, of change, of becoming, stands on the other."[62] Adorno urges us to see that we can pursue the task of social criticism in the proper fashion only if we overcome this (originally Platonist) prejudice according to which validity and genesis are thoroughly incompatible. On his view, to identify the socio-genesis of a concept does not mean that the concept loses all validity; nor can we insist on the pristine validity of a concept by isolating it from its socio-historical origins. The actual relation between genesis and validity is not dualistic but dialectical. And this is also the case for any and all normative concepts that emerge out of an ideological matrix but also serve the purposes of moral and political criticism.

It follows that we should reject the principle that "a socially and historically compromised instance of norm x cannot count as a valid norm x." As Adorno explains in his 1960 lectures on philosophy and sociology, such a conclusion would be a metaphysical error insofar as it seeks to isolate the validity of a given norm from the social and historical conditions out of which that norm has emerged. This error rests on the assumption that our normative ideals must possess eternal validity and must not bear any signs of their genesis: it seeks to rescue being from becoming, or eternity from time. This is an error insofar as Adorno (not unlike Nietzsche and Marx) sees *all* of social reality as plunged into the endless sea of becoming. To insist on the stark separation of being and becoming would rob Adorno of the conceptual resources that are necessary for the practice of social critique. He would find himself in the position of the Hegelian philosopher who must abandon the task of robust criticism and who conceives of philosophy mostly as an affirmative task that must paint the grey of the world in grey.

Nietzsche, Genealogy, Validity

The above considerations are of some interest not least because they can help us to discern some of the deeper affinities between Adorno and Nietzsche. But if we wish to know what these affinities consist in, it is also important to ward off a commonplace misunderstanding as to how Nietzsche's genealogy works and what critical lessons it is supposed to yield. Some readers of Nietzsche, both sympathetic and unsympathetic, see the method of genealogy as a stratagem of merely skeptical dismantling; that is, they understand it as a method that judges a given norm to be invalid once its historical origins in social power have been exposed. In his lectures on philosophy and sociology Adorno argues that this understanding of genealogy is surely mistaken, since it ascribes to Nietzsche the metaphysical view that only eternal concepts would possess normative authority, whereas any concepts that are born from the flux of becoming would have to be dismissed as invalid. But Nietzsche, of course, was hardly a crypto-Platonist; he reserved his greatest hostility for the metaphysical prejudice, first articulated by Plato, that sought to draw a strong line between being and becoming. In the lectures on philosophy and sociology Adorno invokes Nietzsche, who in the *Twilight of the Idols* condemns this metaphysical prejudice as "the longest error."[63] Nietzschean genealogy should not be understood as an exercise in debunking simply because it reveals the temporal character of ostensibly eternal values. On the contrary: Nietzsche knows that values come into being *historically* for the sake of certain social purposes. Recognizing their historical origin would only vitiate their status as values if one subscribed to the crypto-Platonist view that genuine values must be eternal. Because Nietzsche does not subscribe to this premise he is free to understand the method of genealogy as a normative practice that is oriented to the discovery of *truth*.[64]

Similar considerations are of relevance when we examine the status of normative concepts in Adorno's philosophy. Like Nietzsche, Adorno rejects the crypto-Platonist premise that "nothing which has become is really capable of truth." Adorno calls this premise "the very prototype [of] reifying thought," since it conceives of truth as something fixed or eternal that we can value only if we imagine it as lying in a realm beyond transience and death.[65] As a critic of all reification Adorno readily accepts the sociological or genealogical discovery that our normative concepts are imbricated in the vagaries of social power and becoming. But he does not use this discovery as a license for full-blown normative skepticism. He resists, in other words, the unwarranted and skeptical conclusion that because our normative concepts do not exhibit the perfection of extramundane or eternal forms, we must therefore dismiss them as wholly lacking in merit. To see why such a conclusion would be unwarranted we should begin by acknowledging the quasi-axiomatic truth that according to Adorno *nothing* in human experience exhibits such perfection: all of social reality is marked by transience and damage. The complaint that our normative concepts are socially constituted and imperfect is not really a complaint about those concepts in particular; it is merely a complaint about the constitution of the human world in general, so it is hard to see why such a global description would provide us with a specific warrant for singling out only one class of concepts as lacking in credibility. But this is only the most obvious difficulty with reading Adorno as a thoroughgoing negativist. The deeper and more ironic problem (which I have mentioned above) is that the negativist reading depends on a covert idealism. As Adorno notes, its unstated premise is that "no imperfect norm x can count as an x." This silent premise sets the bar at such a great height that everything must fail the test. Adorno avoids this difficulty because (much like Nietzsche) he flatly rejects the unstated premise. Rather than insist on a stark and quasi-metaphysical distinction between being and becoming, he is ready to acknowledge that transience and imperfection are *general features of all socio-historical experience*. Validity is shot through with genesis, and genesis does not vitiate considerations of validity.

In the concluding minutes of his final lecture on philosophy and sociology, Adorno admonishes his auditors to keep in mind a rather simple point, namely, that the solution to the problems of our social world is not to be found in some fictional precinct outside the world. "For if we really want to resolve these problems, we discover that we are thrown back on our own spontaneity and subjectivity. In a sense the problem lies waiting in the matter itself, but it also lies waiting for us, and *without the requisite intellectual activity on our part it cannot be picked up in the first place*."[66] This does not

mean that we must somehow imagine ourselves to be wholly free and unconditioned beings whose concepts would exhibit the very same unconditioned
perfection. "For the human beings who these problems intrinsically require if
they are to be resolved are the same human beings who belong in turn to the
social totality, who are pre-formed through the categories of this social totality that they bring to the problems." Our concepts, in other words, are born
out of the very same world to which they respond. Validity emerges from
genesis. "Thus human beings impress something of the shape of the society
to which they themselves belong upon the problems with which they are involved."[67] Adorno's lesson is that despite the astonishing damage that is evident in both our concepts and our surroundings, we can nevertheless remain
committed to a species of *immanent* normativity, that is, a species of criticism
that emerges from little more than the internal contradictions of our social
life itself. "The unfolding rationality which prevails within the products of the
mind, which distinguishes what is right and what is false, which drives one
intellectual structure, one philosophy, one principle on towards the next, is
itself identical with the unfolding principle of the society which—as a thoroughly interconnected society bound together by the principle of exchange—
obeys this moment of rationality to the point where it might finally drive
beyond the form of exchange society altogether."[68] This species of immanent
normativity is available to us *in our social experience*, even though it naturally
lacks the prestige of absolute validity. Emphatic concepts themselves are no
doubt imperfect, but if we wish to take the measure of our imperfect world.
they are nonetheless indispensable.

To be sure, Adorno is entirely cognizant of the fact that nothing in our
current social experience fully corresponds to the exacting normative demands that are expressed in our emphatic concepts. Our emphatic concepts
are much like Kantian Ideas insofar as they orient us in our thinking even
while nothing that is currently available to us in our empirical experience can
provide us with a corresponding intuition. For example, we must admit that
no single empirical human being X adequately fulfills the emphatic concept
of a human being. So too no empirical experience of happiness fully realizes the emphatic concept of happiness. But such a misalignment between
emphatic concepts and extant conditions is an altogether expected circumstance, since our emphatic concepts are not descriptive concepts that match
up with the world as it is. Rather, they are normative concepts that express
a moral and political demand for the world to become what it should be.
The current world's failure to realize this demand cannot justify our retreat
into thoroughgoing moral and political skepticism. Adorno is clear that the
lessons of genealogy must not be abused. Genealogical work can assist us

in seeing the social imperfection of even our highest ideals, but it cannot be deployed in a skeptical mode to expose all normativity as a metaphysical illusion.

In his 1965 lectures on metaphysics, he rejects this skeptical conclusion in the strongest possible terms. It is a "metaphysical fallacy," he declares,

> to believe that because culture has failed; *because it has not kept its promise*; because it has denied human beings freedom, individuality, true universality; *because it has not fulfilled its own concept*, it should therefore be thrown on the scrap-heap and cheerfully replaced by the cynical establishment of immediate power relationships. One of the most dangerous errors now lurking in the collective unconsciousness—and the word error is far too weak and intellectual for it—is to assume that *because something is not what it promises to be, because it does not yet match its concept* [*weil es nicht das ist, was es verspricht, weil es nicht sein eigener Begriff ist*], it is therefore worse than its opposite, the pure immediacy which destroys it.[69]

Adorno's critique of totalizing skepticism in the passage above is instructive, insofar as it explicitly appeals to the logic of emphatic concepts. When we observe our world with open eyes the first thing we see is the accumulated evidence of catastrophic failure. The norms to which we have committed ourselves have been realized only in a partial and distorted way: they have not enhanced the human condition so much as they have exacerbated our difficulties and our suffering. We might therefore feel licensed to conclude that "culture" itself has failed and that all of its affiliated concepts (such as freedom, individuality, or true universality) can have no merit whatsoever. Adorno rejects this drastic conclusion precisely because he thinks it misses the non-identical status of our normative concepts. Such concepts are not simply identical with some undifferentiated and all-encompassing medium called "power." While it is assuredly true that these concepts are indeed instruments of power, they are also *more than* instruments of power. Due to this internal tension these concepts are ideology and *simultaneously more than ideology*.[70] And this is why we can think of them as *failing their very own promise*. But this should hardly surprise us when we recall that our concepts are part of our own social order. In their non-identity they exhibit the same dialectical character as society itself.

It should be admitted that Adorno's use of emphatic concepts raises a serious concern as to how such concepts could be justified. All too often it seems as if Adorno takes their status to be self-evident, as if the sheer act of endorsing such a concept would suffice to qualify it as a valid standard for critical practice. We are told, for instance, "Emphatic thinking [*Emphatisches*

Denken]" demands "the courage to stand by one's convictions," or "civil courage."[71] Emphatic thinking thus implies courage in the face of opposition. If we
can speak of a "power of thinking" it would entail the capacity "not to swim
with the stream" or a capacity of "resistance against what has been thought
before."[72] But this definition can hardly suffice as an explanation for why any
given emphatic concept should be accepted. After all, many individuals feel
that they embody an admirable strength of conviction when they cleave to
false or irrational concepts in the face of overwhelming social opposition, but
the mere depth of their conviction tells us very little as to whether their concepts truly have merit. The idea of an emphatic concept thus raises the specter of self-authorizing irrationality, and it would not be wrong to ask whether
Adorno has introduced an element of decisionism into his philosophy. What
may at least partially redeem Adorno from this charge is his readiness to admit that all emphatic thinking must always remain vulnerable to failure. "The
individual who thinks must take a risk, not exchange or buy anything on
faith—that is the fundamental experience of the doctrine of autonomy. *Without risk, without the imminent possibility of error, there is objectively no truth.*"[73]
Adorno ascribes to Nietzsche the motto that one must learn "to think danger-
ously [*gefährlich denken*]." But we would be mistaken to interpret Adorno as
recommending a Nietzschean posture of Stoic ataraxia or courage in the face
of danger. On the contrary, for Adorno the danger in question is a feature of
self-critical subjectivity and not a feature of the world; it implies a readiness
to admit error. Where such thinking is genuinely *emphatic*, it hardly permits
itself the inflationary ethics of a will to power; it remains "*vulnerable thinking
[ungedecktes Denken].*"[74]

In the preceding portions of this chapter, I laid out a defense of Adorno
as a dialectical thinker who believes that our criticism makes an appeal to
what he calls emphatic concepts. An emphatic concept plays an indispensable
role for the practice of immanent critique insofar as it expresses a normative
demand and thereby serves as a standard against which we can determine to
what degree our current conditions may have either realized that standard or
failed it. Because emphatic concepts impose the expectation that something
"fulfill its own concept," they are much like *promissory notes* on an unfulfilled
norm. In *Negative Dialectics* he even entertains the thought that apologetic
trends in philosophy such as ontology express an "emphatic need [*nachdrückliches Bedürfnis*]" or a legitimate longing for something that is missing. "In
all of its mutually combative schools, which denounce each other as false,
ontology is apologetic. Its influence could not be understood, however, if it
did not meet an *emphatic* need, the index of something omitted, the longing that the Kantian verdict on the knowledge of the absolute ought not to

rest there."[75] Clearly, however, Adorno is too much of a realist to believe that anything in our social world as it currently exists has actually succeeded in satisfying such a need. On the contrary, he believes that our world is one of nearly catastrophic failure. But it is characteristic of Adorno as a dialectician that he does not conclude from such failure that we should simply abandon our fidelity to emphatic concepts altogether. Even when confronted with catastrophe he holds fast to these concepts insofar as they enable us to take the full measure of the damage that lies before us. All the same, Adorno does not believe that such concepts would have any merit whatsoever if we could not point to at least *some* evidence in our current experience as to what the actual fulfillment of the concept would entail.

Happiness and Human Flourishing

These philosophical motives can help us to understand how Adorno orients his immanent-critical practice toward an unrealized concept of human flourishing. To ward off a possible misunderstanding, I should explain that Adorno himself does not use this term. I suggest it here because it is capacious enough to express the broad suite of unfulfilled hopes and expectations that animate his philosophy. Unfortunately, when we turn to his writing, we find that Adorno is not entirely consistent in his own terminology. As was already discussed in the preface, Adorno offers a wide range of terms—such as "happiness," "truth," "peace," "the right life," and "the reconciled condition"—all of which point in a rather general fashion to an idea of species-wide satisfaction. Earlier in this chapter when I examined his introductory remarks on dialectics, we encountered a similar idea in the form of "the emphatic concept of the human being." Adorno offered this concept chiefly to illustrate the logical presuppositions of the Hegelian dialectic, but I would now like to propose that it retains at least a partial validity beyond the Hegelian framework. At issue is the fundamental principle that human beings cannot flourish apart from the wider set of social arrangements and institutions that Hegel called "objective spirit."[76] In the absence of this social context, Hegel believed, no human being can fully realize its concept and find itself truly at home in its surroundings. Adorno shares this same requirement. Like Hegel, he adheres to the principle that we cannot achieve a true and undistorted fulfillment of our own humanity if the world in which we live remains distorted and false. Unlike Hegel, Adorno believes that there is virtually nothing in our present world that fully satisfies this requirement. He does not go so far as to deny that we lack *all* anticipatory signs as what such fulfillment would be. But he thinks that our actual condition as we live it today remains at a great distance from the unrealized condition as it is expressed in the concept of human flourishing. He characterizes this unrealized condition as one of genuine identity or fulfillment. "If humanity should dispense with the compulsion that has been imposed upon it by the form of identification, it would thereby *identify with its own concept*."[77]

To express this idea of human fulfillment Adorno employs a wide assortment of terms. Although he does not refer to "human flourishing," we find in his work frequent and explicit references to human *happiness*. Admittedly, this term may strike us as rather imprecise, and readers may be forgiven for thinking that it is simply too relaxed in its semantic implications to be of much philosophical interest. But I would suggest that it is thanks to this very imprecision that Adorno can invest the concept of happiness with such normative force. Happiness as Adorno understands it is an emphatic concept of the highest order: condensed into this single word is the nearly impossible demand that humanity live up to its own concept. Needless to say, such a concept can hardly be confined to only one dimension of the human condition; it has many facets and many dimensions. It is expansive enough to cover the full range of human experience, from the simplest pleasures of the body to the most sophisticated satisfactions of the mind. Its moral implications have both depth and height: it reaches down into our shared need for animal warmth but upward even into the domain of the aesthetic where no claim of suffering can go unheard. But it is also socially inclusive: like the Hegelian idea of social freedom, it honors the universalist principle that no individual human being can be fully realized unless all others are realized as well. But this implies a radical transformation in *both* our objective social conditions *and* in our subjective constitution as individuals: "Not merely the objective possibility, but also the subjective capacity for happiness can only be achieved in freedom."[78] Adorno's concept of happiness is therefore nothing less than a comprehensive idea of human flourishing.[79]

One might raise the objection that such a concept is altogether too demanding and raises expectations that could not possibly be met. But this objection misses the point. Adorno uses happiness as a normative concept *for* our experience and not as an evidentiary concept that can be valid only if it matches up with a corresponding and complete intuition *in* our experience. In this respect the concept of happiness resembles a Kantian postulate: it serves as a guide for the practice of criticism; it does not refer to an object of possible knowledge. In fact, it is possible that it could remain more or less counterfactual. To invoke happiness as an emphatic concept Adorno does not need to know that it has been fully realized in the past, nor does he need to know with absolute certainty that it will be *fully* realized in the future. He only needs to point to particular experiences in the present that have the right kind of anticipatory character. These experiences do not wholly fulfill the emphatic concept, nor should we expect them to. In fact, they do not really *describe* at all; they merely *promise*: "All happiness to this day promises, what has not yet been, and the belief in its immediacy gets in the way of its coming to be."[80] We must take care to note, however, that Adorno never indulges in hyperbolic skepticism: he does not *deny* that our particular experiences in the present truly *are* instances of happiness. If he were to dismiss all such experiences as mere illusion he would have little reason for seeing them as actual "breaks" in the otherwise seamless facade of our everyday experience. His point is quite simply that none of these particular instances fill out the concept of happiness in a wholly satisfactory way. The only experiences we have of happiness are partial and uncertain. They are partial chiefly because they evoke a condition of plenitude where happiness would extend to all of humanity. What Adorno calls "the teleological concept of the happiness of humanity [*den teleologischen Begriff eines Glücks der Menschheit*]" necessarily signifies more than merely the happiness of discrete individuals.[81] As long as happiness is construed only as the satisfaction of individual desires this teleological concept remains unfulfilled. "The fixation on one's own needs and one's own longing disfigures the idea of a happiness which would only arise, when the category of the individual no longer sealed itself off within itself."[82]

The universality that is implicit in the emphatic concept of happiness does not wholly nullify the importance of our particular experiences, but it does introduce a kind of distortion into those experiences that renders them all the less reliable even as *promises*. "Whatever happiness is intermittently tolerated or granted by the existing whole, bears from the start the marks of its own particularity."[83] But these promises are also uncertain because no teleological structure in human history can provide us with an absolute guarantee that this condition will ever be realized in the future. Promises, after all, can simply be annulled: "However void every trace of otherness in it, however much all happiness is marred by revocability: in the breaks that belie identity, that which exists is still pervaded by the ever-broken promises of that otherness. All happiness is but a fragment of the complete happiness that humanity is denied and that they also deny themselves."[84] Our present experiences of happiness are therefore incomplete; they are mere "fragments" of a universal condition. But what they promise remains insecure, and they cannot be relied on as fully legible signposts to a future that is already written.

Such considerations can help us appreciate why Adorno sees all experiences of happiness as *simultaneously* experiences of its uncertainty. He goes so far as to entertain the thought that in a society that is characterized by great distress, any experience we have of happiness must also carry within itself an unflinching recognition of a danger we have barely escaped. He illustrates this thought in what surely ranks among the more amusing if also chilling passages in *Minima Moralia*, where he recalls a childhood song about two rabbits who are frolicking in the grass. When they are shot down by a hunter they fall to the ground as if they were dead. But on realizing that they are in fact still alive, they collect themselves and quickly run off. Adorno interprets this tale as a commentary on the intermingling of happiness and fear. Because the world as it now exists is threatened with destruction, so too is our experience. What Adorno calls our unrestricted "openness to experience" leaves us in a state of total vulnerability that verges on "self-abandonment," yet it is only in this condition that "the vanquished rediscovers himself."[85] From this Adorno draws the conclusion that one can survive the world's madness only by seeking to stand apart from it. If one remains apart or eccentric to the dominant order one can then recognize "the unreality of despair" and take to heart the fact, "not only that one is still living, but rather *that there is still life [daß noch Leben ist]*."[86] The rabbit's powerless cunning can thereby serve as a sign not only for its own particular survival; it also carries the universal promise of redemption for all concerned, not excluding even the hunter himself. It seems self-evident that in this passage Adorno encrypted his personal experience as a refugee from European persecution. But this makes his interpretation all the more striking. For even while he insists on the promise of redemption he does not allow such a counterfactual possibility to vanquish the memory of the disaster he has survived. Indeed, no survivor is exempted from the grim knowledge that happiness and suffering remain intertwined. "For what would happiness be," he asks, "if it were not measured by the immeasurable grief at what is?"[87]

Although it would be easy to fault this concept of happiness for its excessive generality or imprecision, I wish to argue that what may seem like vagueness is better understood as the expression of a maximalist demand. Adorno's criticism of the world is ruthless and unrelenting because he refuses to accept any conception of human fulfillment that would impose constraints on its satisfaction. His idea of happiness is *comprehensive* in the sense that it envisions a state of affairs that would satisfy all human needs and desires at once. To be sure, we may find it difficult to imagine what such a comprehensive happiness would be like, but Adorno was convinced that even in our distorted condition we can identify certain instances that serve as models or promissory notes for this kind of fulfillment.

A helpful illustration of what he has in mind is found in "Kultur and Culture," a lecture that he delivered no less than eighteen times between 1956 and

1965. The extraordinary frequency of its presentation might alert us to its significance for the author, since it provides an especially moving and expansive account of human happiness. The concept of culture, Adorno explains, should be understood not as the taming or domination of nature but rather the "conserving of something for its own sake." The word *culture*, derived from the Latin *colere*, means "care," and it therefore implies "that what human beings acquire or subject to their rule should not be radically broken or eradicated but rather simultaneously preserved in its own being."[88] Later in my discussion (chapter 3) I elaborate on this idea of culture as a nondominating ethic of responsiveness to the world. For the time being, however, I simply wish to underscore the fact that Adorno's idea of culture covers a wide range of human experiences: it refers both to artifacts of formal culture (in the aesthetic sense) and to the somatic dimension of everyday experience (in what we might call the anthropological sense). In Shakespeare's *Romeo and Juliet*, for example, he discovers an expression of the human longing for "utopian fulfillment."

> Were its motif not the fulfillment, the boundless fulfillment [*die schrankenlose Erfüllung*] of love, the full erotic love between these people, the overwhelming power of this play would hardly exist. If this play did not exhibit—maybe not as a tendency but certainly as a source of power that gives life to everything [*die Kraftquelle, aus der all das lebt*]—the demand, *there should be happiness* [*es soll Glück sein*], for the freedom to give joy to one another, for fulfillment and for the absence of restrictions, then even the poem about the nightingale and the lark—one of the greatest poems that anyone has ever written in a European language—would not be a work of art, the spiritual work that it is.[89]

This is a striking confirmation of the philosophical importance that Adorno ascribes to happiness as a normative demand. Such examples, however, have also left some readers with the unfortunate impression that Adorno was an aesthetic conservative who relished only the most traditional artifacts of "high" and exclusively European culture. But this impression is immediately corrected once we read his admiring (if admittedly rather sentimental) account of the happiness that American children derive from the simple experience of consuming ice cream: "The way in which every American child can devour an ice cream cone and thereby at any moment find a fulfillment of childhood bliss—something to which our [European] children once vainly craned their necks—is truly part of the fulfilled utopia [*ein Stück der erfüllten Utopie*]."[90] Notwithstanding the apparent sentimentalism of such an example, the key insight that Adorno wishes to convey is that our own life is already punctuated by special experiences that are expressive of a normative demand, namely, the demand that "there should be happiness [*es soll Glück sein*]." This demand is hardly confined to experiences of traditional art; rather, it manifests itself in an astonishing variety of human experiences each one of which might be seen as a "source of energy." Most important of all, this demand for fulfillment, or *Erfüllung*, is truly boundless and unrestricted. In the passage quoted above about the love between Romeo and Juliet, Adorno characterizes this demand for fulfillment in maximalist terms. Notwithstanding his reputation as the architect of a "melancholy science," Adorno seems unwilling to place any constraints on his conception of happiness or human flourishing. "Culture" becomes synonymous with the fulfillment of human life itself.

Happiness and the Limits of Formalism

I have explained above how Adorno understands happiness in a truly comprehensive sense as a condition of human flourishing. But I further explained that no actual experience of happiness that is available to us in our current world fully lives up to its emphatic concept. Here it may be relevant to note that Kant long ago anticipated the objection that happiness cannot serve as a reliable concept of moral deliberation because it is simply too casual a term and too capacious in its meaning. "All people," he observes, "have already . . . the strongest and deepest inclination to happiness because it is just in this idea that *all inclinations unite in one sum*." But it turns out that such a unified conception of happiness is internally contradictory: "The precept of happiness is often so constituted that it greatly infringes on some inclinations," from which it follows that if some inclinations are to be satisfied others must be excluded. A man who is stricken with gout (to take Kant's example) might feel moved to satisfy his particular need for culinary enjoyment even though this satisfaction can only compromise his no less legitimate need for health. Kant also believes that various individuals have differing conceptions as to what would make them happy, which means that it cannot serve as a universal criterion for moral philosophy. He concludes that "one can form no determinate and sure concept of the sum of satisfaction of all inclinations under the name of happiness."[91]

In his own reflections on moral philosophy, Adorno frequently refers to Kant's conception of happiness. But he does not consider Kant's objections to happiness altogether persuasive. On the contrary, Adorno seems to believe that a sufficiently rich conception of happiness would entail a condition that somehow satisfied all of our needs at once without contradiction or exclusion. This assumption is only possible because he thinks of happiness not in the restricted sense as the particular satisfaction of individual needs or desires but in a truly expansive sense as a comprehensive ideal of human flourishing in conditions of social freedom. Happiness, for Adorno, requires a total transformation of the human being along with a total transformation of its social context. To the suggestion that certain individuals might not flourish in a transformed society, Adorno's response is that they still suffer from the afflictions of the damaged one. "In a state of freedom even the sharpest critic would be a different person, like the ones he wants to change. The chances are that every citizen of the wrong world would find the right one unbearable; he would be too impaired for it."[92]

The disagreement between Adorno and Kant concerning the role that happiness should play in our moral deliberations merits closer inspection. For Kant, we can conceive of ourselves as moral agents only if we act on the basis of a maxim that takes the form of universal law. In this conception of freedom nothing that we happen to desire as empirical beings can be permitted to enter into our moral reflections. The Kantian will must remain unresponsive to all objects in the empirical world, and our own natural inclinations fall under this very same prohibition. To be sure, Kant allows that all human beings will be concerned with their own happiness: "To be happy is necessarily the demand of every rational but finite being and therefore an unavoidable determining ground of its faculty of desire." Kant is ready to make this concession because he recognizes that human beings in their finitude have worldly needs that are not already satisfied in advance: "For, satisfaction with one's whole existence is not, as it were, an original possession and a beatitude, which would presuppose a consciousness of one's independent self-sufficiency, but is instead a problem imposed on him by his finite nature itself, because he is needy and this need is directed to the matter of his faculty of desire."[93]

For Kant, this concession to our finite nature as worldly beings has only limited significance: it does not and cannot disturb the universalist conception of morality as duty to the moral law. Our natural desires are merely subjective, and so too are the feelings of pleasure or displeasure that are aroused when we seek to satisfy those desires. "For, although the concept of happiness *everywhere* underlies the practical relation of *objects* to the faculty of desire, it is still only the general name for subjective determining grounds." Happiness, in other words, does not signify a universal principle since what it demands can only be known by referring to the individual feelings of particular subjects. Even for a single individual, these feelings are variable, and they can never be more than "*subjectively necessary*"; that is, they can never amount to more than a mere "law of nature." Moreover, such feelings will also vary for different subjects. Kant's conclusion is that these feelings "can never yield a law because, in the desire for happiness, it is not the form of lawfulness that counts but simply the matter."[94]

Notwithstanding these objections, Kant does not entirely deny that happiness has some rightful place in considerations of practical reason. He permits it to enter into moral philosophy, not as an a priori principle of the free will, but as an indispensable component in the idea of the *summum bonum*, or highest good.[95] In our moral conduct we obey only what takes the form of a universal law, and the morality of an action cannot depend on its end. But even if we do not commit ourselves to moral conduct for the sake of a particular end, nevertheless we want to know about the ultimate consequences of our actions. This is true in the most comprehensive sense insofar as we conceive of the sum of all our actions as directed toward the highest good. The highest good is the idea of a condition in which our happiness would be proportional to our virtue. It follows that although happiness does not and cannot enter directly into our deliberations concerning the requirements of morality, the highest good nonetheless expresses our rational hope that what morality demands will also (eventually) coincide with our happiness. But this hope is something more than merely wishful thinking; we can commit ourselves to the highest good only if we conceive of it as *possible*. "Now, inasmuch as virtue and happiness together constitute possession of the highest good in a person, and happiness distributed in exact proportion to morality . . . constitutes the *highest good* of a possible world, the latter means the whole, the complete good." But Kant hastens to explain that virtue, unlike happiness, imposes its demands without further conditions. This is not the case for happiness, since "happiness . . . is not of itself absolute and in all respects good but always presupposes morally lawful conduct as its condition."[96] We are deserving of happiness only if we are morally virtuous. Unfortunately, however, human life is finite, and we cannot be guaranteed of obtaining complete happiness or the moral perfection that would warrant such happiness. To conceive of the highest good as a possibility therefore requires both that we conceive of ourselves as immortal (in order to attain moral perfection) and that we conceive of a benevolent God (who ensures the happiness we deserve). Immortality and God are therefore *postulates* of practical reason that are necessary to our concept of the highest good.[97]

I have more to say in the following chapter about Adorno's discussion of the postulates. For my present purposes, however, I wish to focus on Adorno's response to the Kantian view that the concept of a moral action sensu stricto cannot be made conditional on the happiness it may bring.[98] As noted above, the categorical imperative wholly *excludes* any such conditions. For Adorno, however, the well-known dissociation between freedom and happiness in

Kant's philosophy is a further symptom of its "sublime sobriety."[99] This is not intended as praise. Kant elevates the will into an autonomous realm in which all concerns for our material existence can have no moral relevance: he denies that our present happiness can be a legitimate factor in our moral reasoning not least because he regards all facts of human feeling as variable or inconsistent. Adorno explicitly rejects this explanation. "Happiness is not invariant [*Glück ist keine Invariante*]," he writes. "Only unhappiness is an invariant that has its essence in the ever-sameness."[100] All that is human is marked by transience, and no philosophy that ignores this constitutive fact of our human nature can assist us in our reflections on human flourishing. This is Kant's fatal error. Because he denies the transient for the sake of pure reason, his moral philosophy has no grip on our actual experience. By asserting the primacy of the rational will above natural inclination, the concept of happiness is expelled from its rightful place in human life. But this expulsion does an injustice to both reason and human nature. Although Kant wishes to pay "honor" to freedom by cleansing it of all imperfection, his efforts misfire: he "simultaneously condemns the person to unfreedom."[101] The drive to purity results in a distorted concept of the human being that even Kant himself may not have found wholly credible. In Kant's own argumentation Adorno detects signs of ambivalence:

> If, in some passages, as in the magnificent Note Two to the Second Theorem from the Principles of Practical Reason, Kant inclined to happiness after all, this was a case where his humanity broke through [*durchbrach*] the norm of consistency. It may have dawned on him that without such relenting [*Erbittlichkeit*] the moral law would be impossible to live by—that the pure rational principle of personality must converge with the principle of personal self-preservation, with the totality of a man's "interests," which include his happiness.[102]

For Adorno, then, the concession to happiness that appears within the bounds of Kant's own philosophy becomes a symptom of a fuller humanity that cannot be wholly effaced. Kant's stance on happiness is therefore "no less ambivalent than the bourgeois spirit as a whole," since it would guarantee "the pursuit of happiness" to the individual, yet would also forbid it in deference to "the moral necessities of labor."[103]

Adorno believes that the constraints imposed on happiness in Kant's moral philosophy are illustrative of a more general difficulty, namely, the limited role that is assigned to happiness in the modern (liberal) understanding of freedom. It is not insignificant that in the original German text of *Negative*

Dialectics Adorno quotes the phrase, "the pursuit of happiness," in the English, since he sees this idea as a paradigm of the capitalist work ethic that predominates in modern society, especially (though not exclusively) in Great Britain and North America. Freedom in bourgeois society becomes merely freedom *for* the market. The result is an antinomy in the modern idea of freedom: it is defined as freedom for the *pursuit* of happiness even while modern liberal ideology construes it as freedom *from* happiness. This idea is not only restrictive; it is *repressive*. The "absolute autonomy of the will" implies nothing less than the "absolute domination over inner nature [*absolute Herrschaft über die inner Natur*]."[104] The Kantian idea of the absolutely free will thus become for Adorno yet another sign of reason's will to mastery. The "formal logic of pure consistency" becomes "the highest moral authority"; it subordinates "every impulse to [the] logical unity," and it asserts "its [own] primacy over what is diffuse in nature, indeed over all diversity of the non-identical."[105] If we draw back from the details of this argument, we can see how it provides us with yet another illustration of Adorno's commitment to the practice of immanent critique. The uncertain status of happiness in Kant's philosophy illustrates the general uncertainty of happiness in modern experience itself. Distorted and disdained, happiness is the non-identical as it appears under the ban of bourgeois morality.

Adorno seeks to redeem happiness from this ban. In a society that is characterized by widespread despair, the promise of happiness can only manifest itself as the non-identical; in the rifts and fissures that expose the world's claim to identity as an illusion. Yet happiness, as I argue in this chapter, remains an *emphatic* concept in the sense that it serves as a standard by which Adorno can take the measure of how our society has failed its own promise. It is crucial to note, however, that for Adorno happiness itself is not *merely* a standard or concept. Rather, it is the name by which he refers to a capacious *experience* of human flourishing that we glimpse only on the rarest occasions. This condition is one that exceeds the bounds of mere conceptuality, since Adorno believes that our concepts are always insufficient in relation to the world they would describe. Happiness is surely the best illustration of this insufficiency since it is the *other* to reason but also an *intrinsic part* of reason's own idea of the highest good. For Adorno, this antinomy is not specific to Kant; it is characteristic of all conventional philosophy that has not escaped from the magic circle of idealism. In our moral reflection as in our claims to knowledge, the subject reaches out beyond its own formal categories toward a nonconceptual world only to defeat its purposes by mistaking the concept for the object itself. Human flourishing, for Adorno, breaks through all such formalism, and it has an *irreducibly materialist meaning*, insofar as it implies the full satisfaction of our objective desires and needs. "All happiness," he writes, "aims at sensual fulfillment and gains its objectivity in that fulfillment."[106] This fact can help us understand why Adorno rarely confines happiness to definitions. He prefers to *describe* or merely point to marginal experiences that can illustrate, however imperfectly, what true happiness would be. I will have more to say on this materialist meaning in the chapter that follows.

3

Materialism and Nature

In the previous chapter I argued that Adorno appeals to happiness as an emphatic concept of human flourishing. This concept is comprehensive in the sense that it entails the fulfillment of the human being in all its dimensions, from the most basic needs to the highest intellectual and aesthetic pleasures. Because Adorno cannot conceive of happiness without this multidimensional fulfillment, his criticism of the present world confronts it with a maximalist demand that would involve a far-reaching transformation, not only in the objective conditions of society, but also in our subjective capacity to find our satisfaction in those conditions. In this chapter I want to develop this claim in greater depth by exploring the fuller implications of what I will call Adorno's *materialism*. My claim is that Adorno can be understood as a materialist in a broad and nondoctrinal sense insofar as his philosophy identifies our this-worldly and sensuous being as the locus of all human fulfillment. In this respect his philosophy draws inspiration from the Marxian principle that we cannot conceive of our satisfaction as human beings apart from our "relationship to the sensuous external world [*das Verhältnis zur sinnlichen Außenwelt*]."[1]

To be sure, Marxism is hardly the unique resource for Adorno's materialism.[2] In his 1965 lectures on metaphysics, Adorno goes so far as to entertain certain affinities between his own materialism and earlier materialist philosophers such as Leucippus and Democritus. He suggests that because these materialists understand matter as the "ultimate ground of being" they do not wholly surrender their bond with the logic of metaphysical explanation, and one might even categorize them as "*metaphysical* materialists."[3] Such comparisons, however, do not suffice to capture what is most distinctive in Adorno's own materialist commitments. Materialism as Adorno understands it also suggests a certain kind of philosophical anthropology that fills out the idea of our sensuous being as a mimetic relationship between external nature and human nature. This relationship is not an idealistic abstraction; it is implicit in all of human experience, from the most innocent to the most elevated, and it obtains even in those moments of worldly fulfillment that Adorno characterizes as "metaphysical experience." He readily admits that in current conditions this vital component of our experience is threatened with extinction. But he does not believe that it has yet been fully destroyed. Indeed, if he could not identify at least small traces of this enduring mimetic bond in our sensuous experience he would lack all evidence for the normative sources his philosophy requires.[4] Needless to say, such a concept of human fulfillment can be described as materialist only in the most expansive sense; but only such an ambitious concept would be broad enough to satisfy the far-reaching demand that underwrites Adorno's social criticism.

The Critical Appropriation of Marxian Themes

Any sincere reader of Adorno should be prepared to admit that he was not a Marxist in the doctrinal sense of that term. If pressed to list the particular points at which Adorno separates himself from Marxist doctrine we might specify three claims.

First, Adorno had little confidence in the revolutionary ambitions of a class-conscious proletariat. The empirical working class as it appeared in Western and Central Europe in the aftermath of the First World War and the Bolshevik Revolution could no longer serve as the singular embodiment of hope for a radical transformation of society, for the simple reason that it had largely integrated itself into the institutional frameworks of bourgeois democracy although it still did not enjoy an equal share of its material wealth. This loss of confidence in a united and revolutionary working class is a distinguishing feature of Frankfurt School critical theory in general. In the initial stages of planning in the early 1920s, the Institute for Social Research was called the Institute for Marxism (Institut für Marxismus), and long afterward students continued to refer to it affectionately as the "café Marx." Under the early leadership of Carl Grünberg, the Institute was dedicated primarily to the task of empirical research into the history of the working class. But already by the end of the decade, the Institute had diverged from this Marxist agenda, and once Max Horkheimer assumed its directorship at the beginning of the 1930s, the separation was complete.[5] For Adorno and his affiliates in the Institute, this loss of confidence in the proletariat became the point of departure for a dramatic revision in the interpretation of Marxist principles that would culminate in critical theory.

Second, Adorno also distinguished himself from Marxist doctrine insofar as he felt little enthusiasm for the anonymous development of technology as the precondition for historical progress. His skepticism regarding advances in technology was surely due (at least in part) to the biographical fact that he came to maturity during the cataclysm of the First World War when so much of human technical ingenuity was turned back in violence upon human civilization itself. His resistance to technological optimism found additional support in Walter Benjamin's essay on the concept of history, where the technological evolutionism of Bernsteinian revisionism is condemned together with "vulgar Marxism," both of which are seen as anticipating the fascist idea of historical progress as a relentless advance in the "mastery of nature [*Naturbeherrschung*]."[6]

Third and most generally, Adorno could see little warrant for sustaining the Marxist interpretation of history as an open field for the self-assertion of the human species. By the mid-twentieth century it became altogether self-evident that the secularized teleology in Marxism was a bad inheritance of the Enlightenment that had lost much of its credibility. Marxist orthodoxy itself was therefore hardly immune to the bad dialectic between enlightenment and barbarism. As a consequence, Adorno could feel little confidence in any of the inherited (liberal or historicist) teleologies of progress, even though his justified skepticism in the older, ideologically tainted concepts of progress did not move him wholly to abandon the aspiration for a species-wide improvement in socioeconomic conditions.

Materialism as Adorno understood it therefore shares little in common with the reductive species of Eastern bloc ideology that he saw as locked within a "materialistic world-view."[7] In *Philosophische Terminologie*, he goes so far as to warn that a materialistic ideology can be "extremely repressive" because "the idea of the materiality [*Stoffhaftigkeit*] of human beings" turns them into "pure objects of domination."[8] A reductive materialism of this kind fails to recognize the crucial fact of dialectical mediation; it sees right through human consciousness as if it were a mere epiphenomenon of a material base. But any philosophy that refuses to recognize at least the relative autonomy of consciousness cannot serve as the foundation for an emancipatory philosophy because it denies from the very beginning the freedom it is supposed to promote. Historical materialism thereby loses its normative commitment to a still-unrealized ideal of freedom; it becomes not a theory aiming for utopia but an affirmation of *dystopia*. As a critique of bourgeois society in particular Marxism correctly locates the secret of social reproduction in the fact of exploited labor. But as a theory of *all* human society Marxism eternalizes this exploitation, with the ironic consequence that it ends by affirming the illusion of social necessity that it had promised to dismantle. For if consciousness is purely epiphenomenal to a naturalistic base, then there can no longer be any sense in protesting against the causal mechanism. Marxism in this reductive form carries the ideological taint of its bourgeois origins: it expresses a meta-physics of compulsion. This is the true meaning behind Adorno's well-known remark that "Marx wanted to turn to the world into a giant workhouse."[9]

Implicit in this complaint is the philosophical concern that the Marxist emphasis on our material conditions will lapse into mere determinism and encourage our uncritical submission to the given. Adorno was acutely aware of the problem that in an affirmative society the dominant schools in philoso-phy can also serve as instruments of affirmation. This apologetic tendency, he believed, was evident in the school of phenomenology, which, in obedience to the Husserlian dictum that one must return "to the things themselves [*zur Sachen selbst*]," had become not just a methodological orientation, but an ide-ology of adaptation. The possibility of surrender to given conditions became abundantly clear in Heidegger's existential ontology, in which philosophy had betrayed its critical moment and had become (in Adorno's words) little more than a pseudo-religious exercise that "sanctifies [the] everyday world [*seinen Alltag heiligt*]."[10] Mere facticity thereby takes on the unimpeachable authority of the normative and criticism loses its grip. A similar risk of apologetics is also evident in Marxism itself, especially when it hardens into an unreflective ideology and, in the guise of a so-called dialectical materialism, degenerates into a species of positivism. Marxist theory is thus vulnerable to two types of distortion: "On the one hand, the theory is defamed—in the West—on the other hand, it is fetishized—in the East. In the East, the theory is placed under a taboo; in the West, it is considered a cardinal sin to concern oneself with it."[11] Here Adorno raises a crucial question: How we can properly distinguish between materialism in the critical-philosophical sense and its own degraded form as an affirmative and positivistic ideology?

In the 1962 summer semester seminar, "Marx and the Basic Concepts of Sociological Theory," Adorno seeks to address this question. His answer is that Marx's materialist insights can be of value for critical theory only if we appropriate them by means of an immanent critique. Marxist theory is "bur-dened with a whole string of questions," he explains, and our philosophi-cal problem today is due chiefly to the fact that "these aspects are not de-veloped further but instead criticized from outside *without confronting the theory with its own immanent difficulties*."[12] An immanent critique can pro-ceed only if it addresses the problem of material conditioning from the inside. More precisely, this means that consciousness cannot be simply bypassed as if it were a mere epiphenomenon to matter. Instead, the reality of material conditions must first be discovered *within consciousness itself* by exploring the subject's experience of dependency on what lies beyond its own domain. The experiential and interior dimension of the subject thereby becomes the irreducible point of departure for a dialectical turn toward the object.

The Priority of the Object

The turn to the object is evident not only in Adorno's philosophical interpretation of Marxism; it is the common theme in his approach to virtually all of the dominant philosophies of the modern era, including those that confine their attention chiefly to the interiority of subjective consciousness.[13] I already mentioned the 1924 thesis, "The Transcendence of the Thing and the Noematic in Husserl's Phenomenology," in which Adorno identifies the dialectical bond that obtains between "Being as consciousness" and "Being as Reality."[14] The aporia that appears at the heart of Husserlian idealism is only one instance of a more general problem that afflicts idealism in all its forms, namely, that it cannot dissociate itself from the "thing-world [*Dingwelt*]" that transcends the mental sphere.[15] In his 1927 study of the unconscious Adorno once again pursues this very same problematic: through immanent critique he discovers a materialist motif in psychoanalysis. Mental phenomena are not purely individual in etiology, nor can they claim independence from the external world. Rather, they are the internal deposit of social contents even if this social origin is disavowed.[16]

Both of these early studies can be understood as exercises in immanent criticism. In psychoanalysis as in phenomenology, Adorno believes that we must first look *inward* in order to then move *outward*. By exploring the interiority of consciousness he thereby discloses the exteriority of the mind-transcendent world. In these two studies we can already discern the defining insight of Adorno's later philosophy: the individual subject is neither self-identical nor self-sufficient, and it does not enjoy the metaphysical primacy it wishes to claim for itself. This insight, however, is not gained by a simple act of turning away from the subject; it is achieved only by first burrowing *into* the subject to discover its suppressed dependency. This insight, in other words, is distinctively dialectical. Adorno does not wish to quit the terrain of idealism entirely; he means to challenge its authority from *within* by compelling it to acknowledge its reliance on materialism as its prior condition. He takes this route chiefly because he believes that the human dependency on external conditions is best revealed by examining the internal antinomies of subjective experience itself. But this means that idealism is not simply dismissed; it is sublated into a new species of materialism in which its truth moment still survives.

By the time he wrote *Negative Dialectics*, Adorno could look back at his entire philosophical career as a set of variations on a single theme. "Ever since the author has trusted in his own intellectual impulses, he sensed that it was his task *to break through the delusion of constitutive subjectivity by means of the power of the subject* [*mit der Kraft des Subjekts den Trug konstituver Subjektivität zu durchbrechen*]."[17] This is the mature statement of the dialectical turn to materialism that was already evident in the works of the younger scholar. Despite certain differences in formulation, we can identify Adorno's enduring commitment to the basic claim: materialism is best discovered not by simply abandoning the subject, but rather by interrogating the subject's ownmost domain in order to shatter the illusion of its authority. "Theory, insofar as it is dialectical—just as thoroughly as the Marxist one—*must be immanent*, even when it finally negates the entire sphere in which it moves."[18] Adorno insists on this point not least because he wishes to draw a sharp distinction between his own philosophical understanding of materialism and materialism in the "vulgar-metaphysical" sense. The difference between them is pronounced. Materialism in the vulgar sense is simply the name that we assign to a reductive but freestanding metaphysics that has no connection whatsoever with the idealism to which it is opposed. Materialism in the genuinely dialectical sense, however, only emerges once it has first absorbed the lessons of idealism itself. "Materialism," Adorno explains, "is no longer a counter-position to be assumed by will." Rather, it is "the intrinsic concept [or epitome; *Inbegriff*] of the critique of idealism."[19]

This distinction is especially instructive insofar as Adorno wants to explain how his own materialism avoids the error of mindless positivism. His explanation once again involves the dialectical gesture of moving *through* the presuppositions of idealism itself. After all, it is idealism that is most consumed with a fear of the mind's surrender. The anxiety that consciousness would be brought to a halt and forced to submit to the "immediately given" is chiefly a fiction that consciousness itself has largely invented so as to ensure its continued primacy.[20] Idealism misunderstands materialism as positivism in order to rob materialism of its validity. But this rejection of materialism is premature. "Materialism," Adorno explains, "is not the dogma which its canny opponents accuse it of, but rather the dissolution of something which for its part is seen through as dogmatic; hence its justification in critical philosophy."[21] If Adorno wishes to combat the error of a positivistic materialism and recuperate its truth for critical theory, he can do so, however, not by a mere shift of terrain but only by dismantling the idealistic dogma of the mind's sovereignty from the inside.

In his mature work this turn to materialism announces itself as "the priority of the object [*der Vorrang des Objekts*]."[22] Adorno chooses this phrase with some care as it implies ranking rather than absolute sovereignty; he does not misunderstand priority as an exclusive claim to metaphysical reality. He recognizes, in other words, that *both* subject *and* object must still play an indispensable role in philosophy; neither can be wholly absorbed into the other. Nor does he wish to contest the primacy of the subject by a crude act of inversion. Rather, he accepts the primacy of the subject even as he seeks to move beyond it. This is chiefly because the subject's claim to primacy represents an initial but necessary moment in its bid to free itself from its own thing-like inertia. "The turn to the subject . . . does not simply disappear with its revision; this revision occurs not least of all in the subjective interest in freedom."[23] But Adorno also accepts the primacy of the subject for purely epistemological reasons insofar as he recognizes the element of truth in Kant's so-called Copernican Revolution. The objective world is known *through* subjectivity, and the subject's mediating role in knowledge cannot be eliminated without undoing the well-ordered structure of objective reality.

In claiming the object's primacy, Adorno wishes to convey the idea that the dialectical relationship between subject and object is not fully symmetrical. "The primacy of the object means . . . that subject for its part is object in a qualitatively different, more radical sense than object . . . is also subject."[24] Although it is a trivial truth that the object cannot be known except through consciousness, the object is nonetheless more than our knowledge of it. "What is known through consciousness must be a something." Adorno readily accepts the lesson of the Copernican turn, namely, that the subject plays a necessary and mediating role in the constitution of objects. But he insists on a further implication, that "mediation applies to something mediated [*Vermittlung geht auf Vermitteltes*]."[25] It would no doubt be tempting to construe even this argument as little more than a restatement of Kant's transcendental idealism, in which the thing-in-itself is conceived as a quasi-metaphysical if unknowable aspect of reality that lies beyond all possible experience. Adorno, however, warns off this interpretation. If the primacy of the object can be affirmed at all, then it must be somehow *determinable*. In other words, it must be "more than the Kantian thing-in-itself as the unknown cause of appearance."[26] As I will explain momentarily, this claim has far-reaching consequences for Adorno's understanding of the non-identical as a something that appears *within* and not beyond the bounds of possible experience.

The stark asymmetry between subject and object becomes truly apparent once Adorno raises the rather striking claim that the subject is also object.

The subject must *be something* rather than nothing, and this suggests that it has an "irreducibly objective moment [*irreduzibel objektives Moment*]." Indeed, the subject could hardly be expected to play a decisive role in the constitution of the objective world if it did not also rank as "an existent being [*ein Seiendes*]." Although we may prefer to think of the subject as an *actus purus*, or pure gesture of thought, we must nonetheless refer to the subject as "something that acts." The subject's own objectivity is therefore not something that can be "conjured away."[27] (Indeed, this theme of objectivity plays a crucial role in Adorno's interpretation of the subject as a material, sensuous being, as I explain further on.) The corollary, however, does not hold true. For the object to be an object, it is not the case that it *also* needs to be a subject. Admittedly, the object is also *mediated*: it must submit to the subject's own constitutive conditions if it is to become an object of possible experience. But the fact of its mediation through the subject's constitutive conditions for the sake of knowledge does not require any such mediation for the mere fact of its being. Hence the asymmetry:

> By means of the inequality in the concept of mediation, the subject falls to the object totally differently than the latter to the former. The object can only be thought through the subject, but always preserves itself in contrast to this as an other; the subject is, however, according to its own constitution, already an object in advance. The object is not to be thought out of existence from the subject, even as an idea; but the subject, from the object. In the meaning of subjectivity is also the reckoning of being an object; but not so in the meaning of objectivity, to be a subject.[28]

At issue, then, is a question of asymmetrical dependency. Whereas idealism sees the object as dependent on the subject, Adorno sees the subject as dependent on the object. Admittedly, the object too is mediated subjectively and socially. But "according to its own concept it is not so thoroughly dependent upon subject as subject is dependent upon objectivity."[29] This dependency, however, can also be understood in a more mundane sense. As a materialist, Adorno refuses to assign the subject a privileged status beyond the material world. Because the human being is an object no less than the material objects that surround it, its dependency on such objects is a matter of sheer survival. To lose one's status as an object would be to lose oneself entirely. This materialist insight into the radical dependency of the human being would seem to be the deeper meaning behind Adorno's claim that the subject is also an object. Given this basic asymmetry Adorno concludes that priority should be assigned not to the subject but to the object.

In an ingenious (if perhaps rather counterintuitive) interpretation of *Critique of Pure Reason*, Adorno argues that even in Kant's philosophy we can detect an acknowledgment of primacy of the object. Despite its well-known assertion regarding the spontaneity of the mind, the Kantian doctrine is divided between activity and passivity, because it can secure genuine knowledge only insofar as it accepts its dependency (*Abhängigkeit*) on what is given in experience. Kant situates the thing-in-itself beyond all possible experience, but he recognizes that it is also the condition *for* experience: "No objectivity of thinking as an act would be possible at all if thinking in itself, according to its own form, *were not bound to what is not itself properly thinking*."[30] This means that all thinking must involve not only activity but also a deeper and even more insistent passivity. For experience to be possible at all demands a *capacity* for passivity that is comparable to what is called object cathexis in psychoanalysis:

> Where thinking is truly productive, where it creates, it is also always a reacting. Passivity lies at the heart of the active moment. . . . This is thinking's passivity. Its efforts coincide with its capacity [*Fähigkeit*] for such passivity. Psychology calls this "object-relation" or "object cathexis." However, it extends far beyond the psychological dimension of the thought process. Objectivity, the truth of thoughts, depends on their relation to the matter at hand [*zur Sache*].[31]

Notwithstanding the doctrine of object constitution, Adorno believes that this "cathexis with the object [*Objektbesetzung*]" is a condition for any and all experience. "Thinking as a subjective act must initially surrender itself to the matter at hand," he argues, "even when, as Kant and the Idealists taught, thinking constitutes or indeed even produces its matter at hand."[32] Adorno conceives of this cathexis with the object as something of far greater significance than mere epistemology. What he calls the "the fragile primacy of the object" becomes a feature of our experience as embodied beings whose need for animal warmth binds us to the world. In one of his more striking phrases, Adorno declares that "*thinking must snuggle up to an object* [*Denken einem Objekt sich anschmiegen muß*]."[33] The theme of the primacy of the object thus alerts us to a category of singular importance in Adorno's philosophy: the category of *experience*.[34]

The Turn to Experience

In the previous chapter, I introduced the theme of happiness or human flourishing, and I specified that Adorno conceives of happiness in a comprehensive

sense that includes the fullest recognition of our material life. In this chapter
I have sought to elaborate on the claim that Adorno should be understood
as a materialist, and I have provided what I take to be a more or less faithful reconstruction of his argument concerning the priority of the object. It
is important, however, that we do not misunderstand the meaning of this
priority. The turning of philosophical attention toward the object should not
be misconstrued as a mere regression to subjectless immediacy. Rather, it
requires what Adorno calls "the second reflection of the Copernican turn."[35]
Philosophy must fully acknowledge the constitutive power of the subject, but
it must *also* challenge that power from within. It is therefore up to the subject
in a state of critical awareness to attain a better recognition concerning the
limits of its authority. "*Only through subjective reflection*, and that upon the
subject, is primacy of the object attainable [*Einzig subjektiver Reflexion, und
der aufs Subjekt, is der Vorrang des Objekts erreichbar*]."[36] This claim bears a
close resemblance to its Kantian model. The Copernican Revolution as Kant
understood it meant that reason would establish both the extent and the limits of its knowledge, and this twofold insight could be reached only through
reason's act of critical self-reflection. In his call for a *second* Copernican turn,
Adorno does not mean to turn reason back 180 degrees to its starting point
as if the first stage of self-criticism had never been achieved. Rather, he sees
his own philosophical effort as a dialectical overcoming of its Kantian model.

Adorno embraces the Kantian idea that we can only establish the legitimacy of our claims to knowledge through an act of self-criticism. But he believes that this gesture did not go far enough, because it conceived of a *limit*
only as a fixed boundary for all possible experience and it failed to incorporate
the experience of that limitation *within* experience itself. A genuine turning
toward the object would mean that we move beyond the principle that the
subject enjoys full sovereignty over its proper domain; instead, it would mean
that the subject adopt a posture of epistemic humility even within its own
experiential domain. From its Kantian predecessor it would retain the most
crucial insight, namely, that our experience already contains within itself a
moment of non-identity that calls into question the mind's constitutive power:

> Even after the second reflection of the Copernican turn, there still remains some
> truth to Kant's most contestable thesis: the distinction between the transcen-
> dental thing-in-itself and the constituted, concretely objective thing. For then
> object would finally be the non-identical liberated from the subjective spell and
> comprehensible through its own self-critique [*das Nichtidentische, befreit vom
> subjektiven Bann und zu greifen durch dessen Selbstkritik hindurch*].[37]

Adorno believes that Kant was right to conceive of the thing-in-itself as that which is non-identical to the subject. He even glimpsed the further implications of this idea, namely, that this non-identity breaks the "spell" of the subject's pretense to authority over its own experience. But Kant could not fully accept these implications. He persisted in his "unshakable faith" in the primacy of subjectivity.[38] This meant that he could only think of the non-identical as the sublime other to cognition. What Kant failed to acknowledge, however, was that the non-identical does not lie *beyond* all possible experience as an unknown and unknowable *Ding-an-sich*. Rather, the non-identical appears as a moment of resistance or otherness that is constitutive of worldly experience itself.

For Adorno the turn toward the object thus culminates in a new theory of experience. He is painfully aware of the fact that the concept of experience in modern philosophy is afflicted with ambivalence and controversy.[39] It can be used as a license for mindless empiricism but also as a warrant for flights into boundless enthusiasm where rational criticism completely loses its bearings. But he is especially aware that under modern conditions of social conformity the possibility that we might still open ourselves to experience has grown ever more unlikely. The traditional concept of ideology that once seemed sufficient as an explanation for our voluntary submission to socially oppressive institutions is no longer adequate for the conditions of late-modern capitalism. We now find that even our innermost needs and desires are shaped in such a way as to produce the illusion of a harmonistic fit between consciousness and society. To explain this illusion, Adorno and Horkheimer introduced the theory of the culture industry. Far more than a theory of mass-media forms (such as popular film and advertising), the culture industry is understood as the late-modern extension of ideology that functions like a Kantian schematism in the preformation of individual experience. Our personal convictions and public commitments are not born from an unstructured encounter with our surroundings; they are given to us in a stereotyped form only once they have already passed through the standardizing processes of the culture industry.[40] These processes acknowledge only the imperative of instrumental reason that everything submit to the principle of exchange. An instrumentalist imperative governs nearly all our conduct, not only in our encounter with other subjects, but even in our encounter with the everyday objects as well. Indeed, it has compromised our experiential capacities to such a degree that we must now fear a "dying out" or "withering of experience [*Absterben der Erfahrung*]" to the point where the subject would be entirely imprisoned within itself.[41]

Openness and Vulnerability

To avoid misunderstanding, we must take care to note that Adorno sustains an important distinction between emphatic (or normatively rich) experience and experience in the conventional (or normatively impoverished) sense.[42] Indeed, it is crucial to the overall success of Adorno's critical project that he does not go so far as to declare that our capacity for emphatic experience has already died out entirely. He acknowledges that emphatic experience is now endangered or in the *process* of dying out (*Absterben*), but he resists the hyperbolic conclusion that it is no longer possible at all. More often than not, he is content to report in a despairing tone on "those seamless and streamlined categorical forms that are *increasingly coming to prevail today* [*den in sich bruchlosen, stromlinienförmigen, kategorialen Formen, die heute zu den vorwaltenden werden*]."[43] The "withering of experience" is thus a tendency rather than an already realized condition. Although it is indisputable that he sees our capacity for experience as ever more compromised by the culture industry and the prevailing trend toward social uniformity, he still believes that moments of experience in the higher sense remain at least a possibility, even if this possibility is growing vanishingly small.

We have now arrived at one of the more enigmatic themes in Adorno's philosophy. Experiences that still qualify as true or emphatic have the quality of material epiphanies. They are "moments where living experience or living cognition breaks through the crust of reified and pre-formed conventionalized concepts and perceptions."[44] Experiences of this kind are distinctive in that they offer us a glimpse of things in their singularity and not merely as reproductions of what has been preformed for us in advance. This is where "we really come to know something, where our thinking is fulfilled, instead of simply feeding off the already given and socially approved view of the object."[45] Adorno describes such an experience as "a kind of collision [*Zusammenstoß*]" or "explosion" from which there springs the "sudden and illuminating character of what is called intuition [*das Jähe und Aufleuchtende des sogenannten Intuitiven*]."[46] Adorno is careful to add that no such experience is wholly without precedent. For no experience of this kind could be possible were it not for the "whole fabric of experiences [*jenes ganze Geflecht der Erfahrungen*]" that "only transpires in a really living way where we are not compelled to think in a purely controlled manner, where we still preserve something resembling our freedom of consciousness, where our thinking is not already simply directed by the norms which it is supposed to observe."[47]

In such moments of emphatic experience we are afforded a glimpse of the non-identical. As I discussed in the previous chapter, an emphatic experience is comparable to an emphatic concept insofar as it plays the role of a normative standard against which we can measure the distortion of our experience in the everyday sense. Such a standard is higher than the purely conventional norms that typically constrain us in everyday experience. If Adorno did not believe in the possibility of this kind of special or emphatic experience, he could not point to any available standard against which he could judge conventional experience to be a distortion or failure. To be sure, experiences of this kind are hardly common, since our social conditioning is sufficiently powerful that we are typically inhibited as human beings from developing the various capacities that would be required for us to recognize them as such. Nearly everything in our social order is designed to leave these capacities in a state of atrophy, even if they have not shut down entirely. All the same, Adorno clearly believes that emphatic experience remains at least a marginal possibility, and it is only thanks to this special kind of experience that we occasionally succeed in breaking through conventionalized schema so as to encounter the non-identical in its irreducible particularity.

The subjective disposition that makes such an experience possible involves a certain posture of openness and anticipation. "All theory," Adorno tells us, "is open [*jede Theorie offen ist*]" and must remain just as open as experience itself.[48] Like the "open" dialectic that he adopts for philosophy in contrast to the "closed" dialectic of the German Idealists, Adorno also believes that in our lived conduct we should not approach the world as if we were armed against it with the full arsenal of our concepts and categories. Rather, we should sustain ourselves in a posture of openness to what our experience may bring. His characterization of this posture merits close inspection:

> Knowledge of the object is brought closer by the act of the subject rending the veil it weaves about the object. It can do this only when, passive, without anxiety, it entrusts itself to its own *experience* [*Fähig dazu ist es nur wo es in angstloser Passivität der eigenen Erfahrung sich anvertraut*]. In the places where subjective reason senses subjective contingency, the priority of the object shimmers through: that in the object which is not a subjective addition.[49]

These lines may rank among the more intriguing sentences that Adorno ever wrote, and it is perhaps not insignificant that during his lifetime they remained unpublished. Their tone is too unguarded, much like the attitude they recommend. Although their lesson remains undeveloped, they adumbrate what we might call *an ethics of vulnerability*. The human being can realize its humanity only if, in full awareness and without naïveté, it willingly lays down its intellectual armaments and entrusts itself to the world.[50] Adorno characterizes this posture as our "openness [*Offenheit*]" to experience, a posture that exhibits a peculiar affinity to *empiricism*. In the concluding hour of the 1965 lectures on metaphysics, he notes that the concept of openness brings with it "the possibility of disappointment [*jene Möglichkeit des Entäuschtwerdens*]."[51] Openness thus implies vulnerability and even the risk of suffering.[52] This is the deeper and *ethical* significance in Adorno's philosophical turn toward the object. With the completion of this turn, worldly experience becomes the site in which the human subject first discovers the limits of its own subjectivity and is confronted with the possibility of suffering *and* happiness.[53]

The Nature in Human Nature

In the preceding discussion I suggested that Adorno's ethic of vulnerability is already implicit in his concept of experience; we will become truly human only when we permit ourselves to become responsive to the world. I now wish to elaborate further on this concept of experience by exploring the various ways in which experience becomes for Adorno the locus of normative insight. Before developing this claim, however, it is important to ward off a possible objection. Although no reader would wish to accuse him of advocating regression, his turn to experience may still invite the suspicion that, despite all his protests to the contrary, what Adorno actually longs for would appear to be a state of mindless communion where all the cognitive and practical achievements of human reason could be simply set aside. If this suspicion were correct, then the "second turn" of the Copernican Revolution would be little more than a regressive return to a precritical and dogmatic point of origin, where the subject would play no role whatsoever in the constitution of its experience. This objection is obviously mistaken but hardly unsurprising, since it is yet another instance of the broader interpretive tendency to see Adorno as a philosopher who has given up on the promises of enlightenment. To see how this interpretation is mistaken, it would be helpful to take a brief detour through the "philosophical fragments" that Adorno cowrote with Horkheimer.

   Dialectic of Enlightenment may very well be the "blackest book" in critical theory.[54] But it cannot be construed as a totalizing indictment of reason. Although its pages are devoted chiefly to a critical genealogy of the historical complicity between reason and power, its driving purpose (as already announced in the original coauthored preface) is "to prepare a *positive* concept of enlightenment which liberates it from its entanglement in blind domination."[55] This positive concept is *emphatic* insofar as it serves as the indispensable norm by which the self-betrayal of the enlightenment can first be identified at all. For such a self-critique to be possible, in other words, the enlightenment must be understood as having *failed its very own concept*. Only this can explain why the authors feel they are justified in proclaiming, "Enlightenment is more than enlightenment [*Aufklärung ist mehr als Aufklärung*]."[56] The non-identity within the concept permits them to believe, despite all historical evidence to the contrary, that "enlightenment is opposed in principle to domination [*ist Aufklärung der Herrschaft überhaupt entgegengesetzt*]."[57] So long as they keep this non-identity in view, the thesis that "enlightenment reverts to myth" cannot be construed as a one-sided and totalizing indictment of reason; rather, it is meant as a reminder that reason still retains its unrealized promise: "Each advance of civilization has renewed not only mastery but also the prospect of its alleviation."[58] This promise cannot be realized if reason simply rejects its own achievements. Rather, what is urgently needed is "the self-reflection of thought."[59] Enlightenment in this self-reflective sense could not simply mean the subject's regression to its prerational condition. Rather, it would mean "the remembrance of nature within the subject [*Engedenken der Natur im Subject*]."[60]

From the detour above we can derive the important lesson that Adorno does not yearn for a mere return to prerational experience. The opening of the subject toward the object does not involve an act of regression but an act of *remembrance* and *recognition* that must be undertaken from the standpoint of its maturity. It is only from this retrospective vantage of a subject that has wrested itself free from an all-consuming nature that the subject can then recall the nature it has suppressed. Remembrance, then, should not be mistaken for the restoration of a lost paradise, nor does it signify a mindless arcadia where sheep may safely graze. From the plateau of its rational self-reflection the subject does not abandon the cognitive and practical advantages that it has gained over the course of its enlightenment. The idea of the human being realizes its own truth only in its flowering: "No progress is to be assumed that would imply that humanity in general already existed and therefore could progress. Rather progress would be the very establishment of humanity in the first place."[61] The emphatic concept of humanity is therefore teleological, not descriptive. This is surely the meaning behind Adorno's claim, "The human being is a result, not an *eidos* [*Der Mensch ist Resultat, kein εἶδος*]." Adorno remains faithful to this result insofar as it serves as the anticipatory standard by which to judge all of the various ways in which the historical Enlightenment has so far failed its concept. All of these considerations are gathered together into the thought that the human being can truly flourish qua human, only if, as a fully enlightened subject, it *also* succeeds in opening itself to its own experience. This experience, however, must be of a certain kind. Namely, it must be such as to permit the human being a recollective acknowledgment of the *nature* that is part of its own inherent nature but from which it has simultaneously split itself off in its struggle to gain its freedom.

We must therefore address the question as to what Adorno understands by human nature.[62] An important clue is to be found in his idea that it belongs to the very essence of human being that we are material beings whose flourishing is predicated on the satisfaction of our material desires and needs. This idea bears an obvious debt to the ideal of human freedom as it was conceived by Marx: "The overcoming of private property is thus the complete *emancipation of all human senses*; but it is this emancipation precisely because these senses and attributes have become, subjectively and objectively, *human*."[63] This passage from the *Paris Manuscripts* exemplifies the early and more humanist phase in the career of the younger Marx, when he was not embarrassed to express his conception of freedom in terms of a philosophical anthropology.[64] The human being is defined teleologically as a being who comes into its own or flourishes only insofar as social conditions allow. Under conditions of private property its nature as a this-worldly and sensuous being cannot be realized, and it is only with the abolition of private property that its senses can *become* genuinely human for the first time. The emancipation of the human being in the emphatic sense is therefore nothing less than the emancipation of its sensuous being.

Adorno shares with Marx the basic idea that the human being is a sensuous being whose self-realization as human cannot be dissociated from its full satisfaction as nature. But he also shares with Marx a certain reluctance to interpret this idea in a one-sided or reductive manner, as if it warranted the claim that the human being can be wholly understood in terms of its most rudimentary needs. The satisfaction of human need is a necessary but not a sufficient condition for being human.[65] He insists on this point chiefly because he understands that our experience of purely material gratification underwent a grave distortion as we gradually became civilized. The process of "historical sublimation" has brought us to the point where we now draw a sharp distinction between sensory and spiritual happiness. But this distinction itself is a bad consequence of the dialectic of enlightenment. We should not conceive of our "literal, sensory happiness" as if it were something better or more fundamental to our humanity than "the forbidden happiness of spirit," because with this distinction we forget that "the split-off, sensory happiness [*das abgespaltene sinnliche Glück*] assumes the appearance of something regressive, much as the relationship of children to food will offend the adults."[66] True freedom would avoid this sensuous regression; it would unite the sensuous with the spiritual in a comprehensive experience of human flourishing that would harmonize enlightenment with sensuality, reason with nature. In what follows I would like to illustrate this claim by exploring three instructive passages from Adorno's work.

Three Illustrations

1. THE LOTUS EATERS

An important warning against sensuous regression can be found in *Dialectic of Enlightenment*, where Adorno and Horkheimer turn their attention to the episode of the Lotus Eaters from Homer's *Odyssey*. The sailors who eat of the honeyed fruit succumb to a state of blissful oblivion: "As soon as each had eaten the honeyed fruit of the plant, all thoughts of reporting to us or escaping were banished from his mind. All they now wished for was to stay where they were with the Lotus-eaters, to browse on the lotus, and to forget that they had a home to return to."[67] Adorno and Horkheimer interpret this tale as a further symptom of the enlightenment's dialectic of progress and regression. From the perspective of an advanced civilization, happiness can appear only in the distorted counter-image of a mindless and sensuous regression that human beings in modern society are typically forbidden. "Self-preserving reason cannot permit such an idyll—reminiscent of the happiness induced by narcotics, by which subordinate classes have been made capable of enduring the unendurable in ossified social orders—among its own people." But the dream of happiness without any rational labor whatsoever is little more than an idyll that is projected backward upon the nature we have escaped. "It is the mere *illusion* of happiness [*der bloße Schein von Glück*], a dull aimless vegetating, as impoverished as the life of animals."[68] Adorno and Horkheimer are certain that this episode does not present us with a true image of human happiness; at best it portrays only "an absence of the awareness of unhappiness [*die Absenz des Bewußtseins von Unglück*]." Our efforts must be directed *forward* to a condition that would be far more than regression. "Happiness . . . contains truth *within itself*."[69] The ideal of our actual fulfillment could not mean condemning us to blissful ignorance, because happiness is "in essence a result." The happiness that beckons to humanity at the endpoint of our development would therefore *include* our sensuous fulfillment as a necessary but not sufficient condition; it would involve the fullest realization of our humanity.

2. SOMATIC PLEASURE

In all of his work Adorno's antipathy to naturalistic regression is self-evident. But this antipathy does not prevent him from also trying to redeem the purely sensuous element in human experience from the repressive social norms that have disfigured our idea of human happiness. Although he is careful to say that our happiness would involve more than a mere communion with nature, he is no less committed to the principle that happiness must entail a full acknowledgment of the body and its sensuous desires. This principle receives special emphasis in his critical remarks on the ambivalent status of pleasure in psychoanalysis. In the reflection from *Minima Moralia* that is titled, "This Side of the Pleasure Principle," Adorno criticizes Freud for his "unenlightened enlightenment [*unaufgeklärte Aufklärung*]."[70] Once again we confront the implicit logic that identifies the Enlightenment's failure against its emphatic concept. The repression that Freud considers necessary for enlightened civilization turns reason into a mere superstructure [*ein bloßer Überbau*] because it is seen as little more than a rational apparatus for the management of irrational drives. But this theory of repression likewise distorts the pleasure that is repressed; Freud conceives of pleasure only in a very limited sense, as an instrument for the preservation of the species. He draws too sharp a line between reason and pleasure and thereby distorts both, allowing pleasure to survive only as prerational instinct. He fails to acknowledge "that moment in pleasure which transcends subservience to nature [*das Moment daran benannt wäre, das über den Kreis der Naturverfallenheit hinausgeht*]."

Adorno believes that this merely instrumentalist and naturalistic understanding of pleasure is a sign of the general hostility that psychoanalysis directs against all utopian ideals. The shuddering tone with which Freud damns all of the "perverse practices [*die perversen Praktiken*]" of modern culture is not unrelated to the dismissive tone that he adopts in *Future of an Illusion* when he cites the verdict of the "commercial traveller" that heaven should be left to "the angels and the sparrows." These two attitudes may strike us as wholly dissimilar: the first condemns this-worldly hedonism, while the second heaps scorn on otherworldly fantasy. But Adorno sees them as symptoms of the very same reductionism that recognizes in the human being only what can be cashed out in purely instrumentalist terms. "Those who feel equal revulsion for pleasure and paradise are indeed best suited to serve as objects." This is why patients who successfully pass through analysis exhibit characteristics of "the empty and the mechanized." Because it would reduce the human being to a manageable object, psychoanalysis is at once a cure *and* an affirmation of an underlying social pathology. Adorno wishes to save pleasure from its psychoanalytic disfigurement, and he elevates it into the realm of utopian truth that was once reserved for religion. "He alone who could situate utopia [*die Utopie*] in blind somatic pleasure [*in der blinden somatischen Lust*] . . . has a stable and valid idea of truth [*einer Idee von Wahrheit fähig, die standhielte*]."[71]

Although Adorno is often reticent about his normative commitments, in the above remarks on psychoanalysis he states without embarrassment that we must not dissociate the utopia of human flourishing from bodily satisfaction. He accuses Freud of betraying this utopian ideal. As a contradictory formation in bourgeois culture, psychoanalysis thus appears "Janus-faced." It offers both a diagnosis of repression and a justification as to why that repression is necessary. At least in this respect Freud is truly a child of his time, since he is caught between "desire for the open emancipation of the oppressed" and "apology for open oppression." He resolves this ambivalence by capitulating to bourgeois imperatives and violating his own emancipatory aims. In turning against pleasure, however, Freud dishonors what Adorno calls the "critical standard [*kritische Maßstab*]" that inheres in psychoanalysis itself: the utopia of an undistorted happiness. Here, then, is an instructive specimen of immanent-critical method: Adorno does not merely dismiss psychoanalysis as a thoroughly ideological formation. Rather, he discerns the moment of contradiction in psychoanalysis that might be liberated from its ideological constraints. But this is something more than a critique of psychoanalysis in particular. Adorno clearly means to redeem happiness as the normative standard for his own philosophy.

3. THE GIFT

The attempt to redeem the sensuous aspect of our natural being for a comprehensive ideal of human flourishing also stands out as the key theme in yet another passage from *Minima Moralia*, in which Adorno uses his micrological glance to analyze the cultural practice of gift exchange. His interpretation bears a striking resemblance to the insights found in the 1924 ethnographic study of the gift by Marcel Mauss.[72] In his comments on the potlatch, Mauss had argued that the practice of exchanging gifts cannot be understood in isolation from the surrounding culture because its meaning is truly *pluridimensional* and extends into every value sphere of life—juridical, economic, religious, and aesthetic. It is nothing less than a *fait social totale*. His key discovery was that for those who take gift exchange seriously, it signifies far more than a mere transfer of things. Rather, "to make a gift of something to someone is to make a present of some part of oneself." Mauss pursued this insight with the critical and openly socialist intent of reviving the half-dormant practice of gift exchange for the benefit of modern society. "A considerable part of our morality and our lives themselves are still permeated with this same atmosphere of the gift, where obligation and liberty intermingle. Fortunately, everything is still not wholly categorized in terms of buying and selling. Things still have a sentimental as well as venal value, assuming values merely of this kind exist. We possess more than a tradesman morality."[73]

In *Minima Moralia* Adorno pursues a similar line of analysis. Like Mauss, he believes that the giving of a gift is incompatible with mere exchange; it is the fulfillment of a species of happiness in and through our common bond as human beings, since in the act of giving and receiving we experience a mimetic responsiveness to those around us. "Real giving has its happiness in imagining the happiness of the receiver. It means choosing, expending time, going out of one's way, thinking of the other as a subject."[74] Also like Mauss, Adorno pursues this claim with the critical intent of someone who sees through the mystifications of capitalism. His specific target is the logic of commodity fetishism that Marx had diagnosed as "the definite social relation between human beings which assumes here, for them, the fantastical form of a relation between things." Because the gift signifies an alternative to the commodity, in capitalist society the practice of gift exchange can too easily take on the false allure of sentimental atavism. But Adorno insists that it is not an instance of mere sentimentality; rather, it remains a promising (albeit embattled and marginalized) ideal that holds out to us a model for a better society. The difficulty, however, is that this ideal is now threatened with extinction. Displaced by the institutional system of administrative benevolence, the selfless act of giving a gift is becoming as rare and endangered as humanity itself: "In its organized operations, basic human impulse no longer has any room." The entire habit of selfless generosity is now suffering decay: "People are unlearning how to give [*Die Menschen verlernen das Schenken*]."[75]

For Adorno the decay of the gift is not incidental to, nor is it a mere distraction from, the more serious problems that afflict modern society. He refuses to see it in isolation from the totality of our social experience. Here too he follows the example of Mauss: in its embattled status the gift is a *total social fact* in which all the difficulties of the social world find their expression. But it is crucial to note that nowhere in this analysis does Adorno permit himself the hyperbolic and implausible statement that gift giving has altogether vanished. He recognizes that the principles of capitalist exchange have penetrated into nearly every facet of human experience, but he also clings to the fact that at the interstices of our experience we can still glimpse alternative practices that contest the prevailing logic. Although the market is a unified system, it is nonetheless shot through with contradictions. Without such contradictions he would have to characterize the entirety of our social world as uniformly false, and the gift would not be a total social fact but only an inexplicable anomaly. But in that case he could not invest any significance in the fact of its unlikely survival. What is truly striking about his analysis, however, is that he sees the gift *not* as simply anomalous but as a sign of particular human qualities that persist even in the midst of generalized social distortion. "There is no-one today," he insists, "for whom imagination would not discover what would make him thoroughly happy."[76] Although the actual practice may be in decline, the gift is nonetheless the manifestation of what Adorno calls "irreplaceable capacities [*unersetzlichen Fähigkeiten*]."[77] He understands these capacities as essential to our sensuous nature as human beings, and he warns that such capacities "cannot flourish in the isolated cell of pure interiority" and can survive "only in live contact with the warmth of things [*nur in Fühlung mit der Warme der Dinge*]."[78] Although the gift may seem a marginal and insignificant social practice, it turns out be an essential mark of our natural being. "Every undistorted relationship, indeed perhaps the conciliation that is part of organic life itself, is a gift [*Alle nicht entstellte Beziehung, ja vielleicht das Versöhnende am organischen Leben selber, ist ein Schenken*]."[79] He fears that if we were to lose this capacity entirely, we would lose all responsiveness to the world. In such a circumstance, however, a "coldness [*Kälte*]" would descend on all our experience, and we would lose touch with our own humanity. The practice of giving a gift is therefore more than cultural; it marks our transitional status as organic beings at the boundary between culture and nature.

The Redemption of Human Nature

All three of the cases discussed above help illustrate what I have called Adorno's materialism, and they underscore his distinctive view that the human being can flourish as human only if it holds itself open and unguarded to the sensuous world. Human flourishing thus involves the flourishing of our own natural being. In a conversation with Horkheimer, Adorno once observed, "Philosophy exists in order to redeem what you see in the look of the animal."[80] To be sure, the human being too is an animal among animals, though modern civilization has exerted much effort in seeking to distinguish itself from its own animal condition. But if philosophy ignores the natural side of human nature, it imprisons itself within the purely cognitive subject and loses contact with sensuous experience. But this would be tantamount to a betrayal of philosophy's mission. This is the redemptive purpose that motivates Adorno's turn toward the primacy of the object. If the prospect for human flourishing is in jeopardy today this is chiefly because our social order is constituted in such a way as to weaken our capacity for experience. From this analysis it should therefore be clear that even in his immanent critique of bourgeois experience Adorno has not lost sight of the objective world. He continues to believe that the ultimate source of our difficulties is to be found not in the disabilities of individual subjects but in the objective features of our society. The bond between subject and object is not yet entirely broken. Like Marx, however, Adorno believes that only a total transformation in social relations would be sufficient to bring about the emancipation of the senses and the redemption of human nature.

4

From Metaphysics to Morality

In the previous chapter I suggested that Adorno can be broadly understood as a materialist who sees the human being as a sensuous creature whose flourishing depends on (though is not limited to) the full satisfaction of its material needs. The concept of a human "need" is of course a topic of great controversy not only in the thought of Adorno, but in the wider tradition of emancipatory social criticism to which he contributed.[1] One of the more controversial questions is whether the very idea of human need implies a transhistorical constant that can be ascribed to human nature itself or whether human need should instead be understood as historically variable. In the analysis above, I examined Adorno's unusual claim that human beings can realize their humanity only if they sustain their "live contact with the warmth of things." This suggests a readiness to entertain an idea of a human need that is not only historical, but constitutive of our being human as such. On this question Adorno finds himself in a difficult position. He does not wish to issue any dogmatic pronouncements regarding an invariant human nature, but neither does he wish to give up entirely on the materialist view that human beings have certain biological needs that simply must be met. His attempt to resolve this philosophical difficulty is instructive not least because it helps us appreciate how much his critique of modern society is directed toward an emphatic concept of human flourishing.

In this chapter I wish to unite the concept of human flourishing (as presented in chapter 2) with the concept of materialism (as presented in chapter 3) in order to explain what I will call Adorno's *materialist conception of morality*. My aim is to demonstrate that Adorno's materialism culminates in a new conception of normative obligation, or what he calls the "Thou shalt." This obligation inheres in our common experiences as sensuous beings who are vulnerable to suffering but oriented teleologically toward happiness. To motivate this argument, however, I want to start by deepening and elaborating on the general claim (as introduced in the previous chapters) that Adorno is committed to an ideal of happiness or human flourishing. I have argued that this ideal is comprehensive insofar as it spans the full range of human experience, from the satisfaction of our most basic bodily needs and desires to the most sophisticated forms of aesthetic and even "metaphysical" fulfillment. We can appreciate how this comprehensive ideal unites the various facets of Adorno's philosophy if we begin with the rudimentary fact of everyday need, then pursue his line of argument as he progresses from the somatic and the mimetic in the realm of metaphysical experience. Finally, we shall see how the argument for human flourishing culminates in a broadly materialist conception of morality that he calls "the demand for the right life [*Forderung nach dem richtigen Leben*]."[2]

Need and Desire

In his 1942 "Theses on Need," Adorno seeks to answer the question as to whether critical theory must commit itself to the category of an entirely natural or historically invariant need. He recognizes, of course, that a distinction between what is natural and what is social can be hard to sustain, especially if one takes seriously the perspective of historical materialism according to which human nature itself is not pregiven or anterior to history but is something that emerges only historically. It follows that "need" too must be a historical category. The real difficulty arises, however, once we seek to draw a simple distinction between needs and desires, where the first refers to natural requirements that impinge on the human being from the outside as a matter of brute necessity and the second refers to socially acquired investments that we fulfill only insofar as they are expressive of our freedom. Adorno rejects this distinction chiefly because he thinks it is a bad inference from our present life. "Needs," he argues, "are not static. That needs appear static today, that they seem fixated on the reproduction of perennial sameness, is just a reflection of material production, which assumes a stationary character with the elimination of the free market and competition, along with the simultaneous perpetuation of class domination. When needs no longer appear static, they will take on a completely different aspect."[3] Under conditions of scarcity and structural inequality, we wrongly project backward into the human past a crude and ahistorical division between what human beings require as a matter of brute necessity and what they merely want but could do without. But such a division is erroneous. The distinction between freedom and necessity is not anterior to human history; it is a distinction produced *by* history.[4]

It follows that were historical conditions different, we would construe even the category of brute necessity in a fundamentally different manner. "*If production were immediately, unconditionally, and unrestrictedly reorganized according to the satisfaction of needs—even and especially those produced by capitalism—then the needs themselves would be decisively transformed.* The opacity of [the distinction between] genuine and false needs belongs essentially to class domination. Within the latter context, the reproduction of life and its oppression form a unity."[5] Adorno is therefore moved to reject the question of what people *truly* need as a piece of ideology. The attempt to specify true needs is philosophically suspicious on several counts, not least because it implies a transhistorical and quasi-naturalistic standard that conflicts with our recognition of human nature as constituted through society and history. But the notion of true needs is also suspicious because it can easily serve as a warrant for reducing the ascribed needs of people who live elsewhere on the globe to an absolute minimum:

> The question of the immediate satisfaction of need is not to be posed in terms of social and natural, primary and secondary, correct and false; rather, it coincides with the question of the *suffering* [*Leiden*] of the vast majority of all human beings on the planet. If we produced that which *all* human beings most urgently need here and now, then we would be relieved of inflated social-psychological concerns about the legitimacy of their needs.[6]

In rejecting the question of whether a need is social or natural, Adorno anticipates a still-unrealized condition when human beings would no longer conceive of need as a necessity that has been imposed on us by nature. In such a condition freedom itself would undergo a dramatic transformation.

Two features of this argument deserve special notice. First, it seems that Adorno is committed to a condition that is far more than minimalist, since he sees the idea that we must satisfy only a minimal satisfaction of need as a piece of bourgeois ideology, and he urges us to accept an ideal of human flourishing that would dramatically exceed the satisfaction of minimal standards. Second, his rejection of merely minimalist need also points toward a different relationship between humanity and nature. For once humanity has been emancipated from the laws of quasi-naturalistic necessity, we would no longer understand ourselves as subjects who are essentially split off from the natural world and see it as an array of objects that have meaning for us only in terms of their possible utility. "Productivity in its genuine, undisfigured sense will, for the first time, have a real effect on need: not by assuaging unsatisfied need with useless things, but rather because satisfied need will make it possible to

relate to the world without knocking it into shape through universal usefulness." Only with the genuine satisfaction of need will we be in a position to
adopt a mode of conduct that will finally enable us to glimpse the "reconciliation with nature [*die Versöhnung mit der Natur*]."[7]

Mimesis and Materialism

Adorno's reflections on desire and need merit greater elaboration than I can
provide here. I have considered this problem only because it sheds light on
the question of how Adorno understands the human being's enduring bond
with nature. He assigns enormous philosophical importance to this bond as
a deep or even "archaic" feature of human experience that is anterior to all
considerations of utility. Well before the human being took up an instrumentalist stance toward its surroundings and began to subordinate the world to
its own chosen ends, it already exhibited a special capacity for responsiveness to nature that cannot be construed in merely instrumentalist terms. This
capacity involves mimicry or resemblance. In his discussion of this mimetic
capacity, Adorno describes a distinctive "mode of conduct [*Verhalten*]" by
which we hold ourselves open in a state of responsiveness to nature. Rather
than signifying our dissociation from nature, the so-called mimetic capacity
expresses the fundamental *similarity* that already obtains between the human
being and nature, simply in virtue of the fact that the human being itself is a
natural being. In the 1965 lectures on history and freedom, Adorno explains
that mimetic conduct is neither voluntary nor causal: it belongs to a stratum
in human experience that is therefore deeper than the distinction between
desire and need. Mimesis is "not causally determined by objective factors";
rather, it involves "an *involuntary* adjustment to something extra-mental."[8]
Although Adorno sees this adjustment as in some sense irrational, he nonetheless understands it as intrinsic to "the definition of freedom."[9]

In developing the concept of mimesis, Adorno borrows freely from Walter Benjamin, who in his 1933 essay defines mimesis as nature's "capacity for
producing similarities [*Fähigkeit im Produzieren von Ähnlichkeiten*]" or to
"become similar and conduct oneself in similarity [*ähnlich zu werden und
sich zu verhalten*]." Benjamin goes so far as to suggest that there is perhaps
no higher function in the human being in which "the mimetic faculty [*das
mimetische Vermögen*]" does not play a decisive role.[10] Adorno owes a further
debt to Roger Callois on the role of mimesis in nature, and also to Mauss and
Hubert who, in their *General Theory of Magic*, define mimesis as a relation
of "sympathie."[11] The concept of mimesis assumes an especially prominent

role in *Dialectic of Enlightenment*, where Horkheimer and Adorno characterize it as our "organic adaptation to otherness."[12] Their argument takes the
form of a speculative anthropology.[13] At the dawn of its development the
human animal demonstrates an unwilled responsiveness to its natural surroundings. Danger could make its hair stand on end or even bring the heart
to a stop.[14] Such responsiveness is beyond our subjective control, and it is a
constitutive feature of human biology. "The self which experiences itself in
such reactions—rigidity of the skin, muscles, and limbs—is not quite master of them. For a few moments they mimic the motionlessness of nature."[15]
Our capacity to respond mimetically to nature belongs to the earliest phase
of human history when instrumentalism did not yet mean domination. The
human being wished to gain some control over nature even in the most innocent acts of primitive domestication such as taming fire or harvesting crops.
But with the advance of instrumental reason the mimetic element undergoes
repression and begins to atrophy. The ego gradually hardens itself against its
surroundings, and instead of responding sympathetically to nature it seeks
only to dominate it. Natural differentiation is subsumed under sameness, and
"bodily adaptation to nature is replaced by [in Kant's phrase] 'recognition in
a concept.'"[16]

Notwithstanding the gradual atrophy of our mimetic capacities, however,
Adorno and Horkheimer take care to note that these capacities have not yet
been wholly vanquished. It is a crucial premise of the argument in *Dialectic
of Enlightenment* that mimesis still survives even where it has suffered serious distortion. The progress of reason intensifies not only the necessity of
repression but also the longing to release what has been repressed; the cul-
tivated subject turns in vengeance against whatever has not fully submitted
to the imperatives of civilization. This is why civilized humanity reacts with
revulsion against gestures of suppressed natural immediacy: "touching, nes-
tling, soothing, coaxing [*Berühren, Anschmiegen, Beschwichtigen, Zureden*]."[17]
Hostility is directed most of all against anyone who betrays signs of disinhibi-
tion or who is imagined to be closer to nature. For Adorno and Horkheimer,
the modern taboo on mimesis is therefore crucial to the emergence of anti-
Semitism.[18] Hatred of the racialized other is an external manifestation of the
hatred with which the ego turns against its own natural drives. Fascism capi-
talizes on this hatred. It does not actually dismantle the structures of modern
civilization but offers to the mob merely a *simulation* of regression: it is not a
genuine return to nature but only a "mimesis of mimesis."[19]

The concept of genuine mimesis plays a key role in Adorno's turn to the
object. Indeed, we might even say that mimesis is simply the noninstrumental

relation in which the subject opens itself to the object and entrusts itself to its own sensuous experience.[20] More surprising, however, is Adorno's claim that mimesis has a rightful place in our understanding of freedom. Because our mimetic behavior has an involuntary and irrational character, its importance in theories of freedom is seldom acknowledged.[21] We tend to see it as an atavistic and regressive impulse that must be wholly expunged if we wish to conceive of ourselves as autonomous beings. The imperatives of civilization have made it all the more difficult for us to acknowledge its survival. However, according to Adorno, its presence is a necessary component of freedom itself, without which our experience of freedom would be fatally compromised. "The more the ego obtains control over itself and over nature, the more it learns to master itself and the more questionable it finds its own freedom. . . . We might almost go so far as to say that while something like freedom becomes possible only through the development of consciousness, *at the same time* this very same development of consciousness effectively ensures that freedom is pushed back into the realm of archaic, mimetic impulse that is so essential to it."[22] Freedom and mimesis are therefore not opposed; they are complementary and necessary moments in our emphatic concept of the human being. "The concept of freedom," Adorno argues, "could not be formulated in the absence of recourse to something prior to the ego, to an impulse that is in a sense a bodily impulse that has not yet been subjected to the centralizing authority of consciousness."[23] This argument is not as counterintuitive as it may seem. As I have suggested in this book, Adorno subscribes to a truly comprehensive idea of human flourishing that seeks to reconcile the sensual and the intellectual facets of our experience. Seen in this light, there is nothing surprising in his suggestion that genuine freedom would also involve the satisfaction of material impulses that lie below the threshold of the conscious mind.

Metaphysical Experience

In the previous chapter I argued that Adorno subscribes to a materialist conception of human flourishing. Although this idea is not Marxist in the narrow sense, he borrows from Marx the general view that the human being has an irreducibly sensuous character that no social criticism can afford to ignore. True freedom would entail the emancipation of our sensuous and material nature from repressive social conditions that permit us to recognize only those features of our being that can have value within the constraints of a market economy. The theme of a turn toward the object is the philosophical analogue to this emancipatory task. Concepts permit the subject to gain control over nature by subsuming the particular under the universal; material difference is reduced to a uniform or homogeneous mass. This reduction transforms not only the world but also human life into material that is susceptible to exchange. Concept formation is thereby understood as an initial and preparatory moment in the prehistory of capitalism. By turning from the subject to the object, Adorno announces a protest against the dominance of the exchange principle. He wishes to set free the object in all of its difference and particularity. But our senses are fully opened to the world only when our capacity for mimesis is at last permitted to flourish. Commodity exchange has stunted this capacity, and it thereby endangers the very possibility of experience itself.

This brings me to a question that is vital to the success of Adorno's critical efforts. I have argued that the practice of immanent social critique as Adorno understands it can proceed only if he can point to concrete instances in our current experience that have the right sort of normative and anticipatory character such that they afford us a glimpse of what true fulfillment would be. But if experience *as such* were no longer possible, then no instances of this kind would be available and Adorno's project would collapse. It is therefore imperative to his argument that he sustain at least some minimal confidence in the enduring possibility of experience. Mimesis plays an important role in this argument because it is only in virtue of our mimetic capacity that we remain open to our experience and are afforded an encounter with the irreducible plenitude and particularity of the material world. Adorno recognizes, of course, that the mimetic capacity has atrophied, but he does not believe it has been wholly extinguished. Immanent social critique is possible if and only if mimetic experience is possible.

As discussed in chapter 1, Adorno provides us with a poignant illustration of this argument in his brief commentary on children's games.[24] It is worth recalling his basic claims. In a market economy all of human experience is in danger of reduction to what Marx called the "equivalent form." Adorno quotes this idea from *Capital* but offers an intriguing elaboration: the imperative of life-maintenance turns all human activities into "mere means" and "reduces them to interchangeable, abstract labor-time." The result is that the "quality of things ceases to be their essence and becomes the accidental appearance of their value." The principle of equivalence, however, is not only an objective feature of the economy; it also "disfigures all perceptions." When the world is transformed into an array of mere commodities the human sensorium itself undergoes a kind of disenchantment. Hence the significance of children's games. "In his purposeless activity the child, by a subterfuge, sides with use-value against exchange value. Precisely because he deprives the things with which he plays of their mediated usefulness he seeks to rescue in them what is benign toward people, and not what subserves the exchange relation that equally deforms both humanity and things."[25] In children's games Adorno discerns the survival of a redemptive principle that is otherwise in danger of extinction. Without theoretical comprehension the child brings to life in its toys a moment of resistance against the commodity form. "[Children] remain true to their destiny by not performing, not participating in the process of abstraction that levels down that destiny, but instead abide as allegories of what they specifically are." To be sure, children's games are marginal to the logic of the market. They are "scattered" but not "ensnared" in the prevailing order. Due to their marginality, however, they embody an alternative to the current world. "They are unconscious exercises for the right life [*bewußtlose Übungen zum richten Leben*]."[26]

I already discussed Adorno's remarks on games earlier in this book. I have recalled the remarks here because they underscore the special importance that Adorno ascribes to experiences of nonfungible particularity. If he places a premium on scenes from childhood, this is chiefly because he thinks that such moments do not typically suffer from the near-fatal distortion that is introduced into experience once the individual assumes its role in the adult world of commodity exchange. This may also explain why even adults may find it pleasing to observe children at play; in their innocence we can discern the encrypted promise of a better life. The child retains the mimetic capacity that tends to weaken in the adult, which may further explain why the child exhibits a special fascination for animals, whose own names seem to embody their particularity and are "utterly impossible to exchange."[27] Such experiences of what resists the equivalence form are of vital importance for Adorno chiefly because he believes that they afford us an anticipatory glimpse of a better world, in which all things would at last be permitted to stand out in their irreducible difference and particularity. "The reconciled condition [*Der versöhnte Zustand*] would not annex the alien by means of a philosophical imperialism, but would find its happiness [*Glück*] in the fact that the latter remains what is distant and divergent in the given nearness, as far beyond the heterogenous as what is its own."[28]

In revisiting these reflections, I do not mean to suggest that Adorno conceives of such experiences as a special privilege that is reserved only for the enchanted world of childhood. The happiness that we find in the nonfungible particularity of things is also available to us in the enigmatic phenomenon that he calls "metaphysical experience."[29] The affinity between games and metaphysical experience is not as surprising as it may seem. The experience that Adorno characterizes as "metaphysical" does not lie in a supersensible realm of pure ideas or forms; rather, it has the very same qualities of materiality and particularity that Adorno locates in childhood experience. Adorno seems to have first introduced the category of metaphysical experience in his 1965–66 lectures on negative dialectics, where he speculates on the possibility of "intellectual experience [*geistige Erfahrung*]."[30] In the published text *Negative Dialectics*, he modifies his terminology and now refers to such experiences as "metaphysical." The change is not insignificant. The idea of metaphysical experience surely ranks among the most perplexing themes in his writing, not least because the term itself suggests a willful transgression against the philosophical tradition. For Kant, metaphysics designates that which surpasses the bounds of all possible experience.[31] To suggest that our experience could still have a genuinely metaphysical dimension or could even yield a species of metaphysical knowledge would seem to represent a violation of received terminology.

Adorno is nonetheless fascinated by the question of whether something like a "metaphysical experience" would be possible in the modern era, when experience as such is now threatened with extinction.[32] Metaphysical experience as he understands it would be in some respects analogous to those "primal experiences [*Urerlebnisse*]" that have a religious character, except it would be possible within a wholly concrete, particular, and worldly location for those who have forsworn religion. It is perhaps best captured by Proust, who invokes "the happiness invoked by the names of villages such as Otterbach, Watterbach, Reuenthal, Monbrunn."[33] Following Proust's example, Adorno believes that place-names signify the very paradigm of true experience. This is so especially (though not exclusively) for children:

> To the child it is obvious that what delights it about its favorite little town is to be found *there and only there*, and nowhere else; it errs, but its error constitutes the model of experience, that of a concept, which ultimately would be that of the thing itself, not the poverty of that which is shorn away from things.[34]

The crucial mark of such an experience is its *singularity*, namely, that it attaches to a particular place and time. It follows that for every individual the experience in question would be entirely different. Adorno himself seems to have felt a special attachment to the village of Amorbach, where he and his parents would often take their vacation.[35] The experience arises "uniquely in view of what is absolutely, indissolubly individualized," and it involves the hope that by approaching that particular site one would be afforded an experience of ultimate satisfaction or happiness. One would find oneself "enraptured at that one spot, without squinting at the generality."[36] Adorno describes this as an experience of near-total fusion, as if one could at last *inhabit* a singular location. "One believes, that if one goes there one would be *within* the fulfilled [*in dem Erfüllten*], as if it were there."[37] In such a condition the experiential gap between subject and object would finally be closed; or (in Adorno's rather puzzling phrase) "the concept of the concept" would be fulfilled. In metaphysical experience the subject seems to achieve the paradoxical condition for which it has always yearned: its complete identification with the non-identical.

Metaphysical experience would therefore signify nothing less than "the promise of happiness [*am Versprechen des Glücks*]."[38] Although his remarks on this enigmatic concept may invite the charge of naive romanticism, we must not neglect to note that Adorno *denies* that such an experience can ever be fully realized, not least, perhaps, because the surrounding unhappiness of the world will always impinge on this moment of apparent bliss. The ideal of subject-object fusion may beckon on the horizon, but even if one were finally to arrive at the particular location one could never achieve the fulfillment one has sought. "If one is actually there, that which has been promised recedes like a rainbow [*Ist man wirklich dort, so weicht das Versprochene zurück wie der Regenbogen*]."[39] Nevertheless, Adorno suggests that even while the experience remains incomplete, one is not seized with disappointment. Rather, "one feels that one is too close, and that this is why one does not see it."[40] Metaphysical experience is therefore a concept that points toward a species of total fulfillment or happiness that we have not yet truly achieved. The concept itself appears to be self-contradictory: As Adorno tells us, it is "antinomical [*antinomisch*]," if not in the Kantian sense, because it alerts us to a possibility of an experience for the subject that would surpass the subject's control:

> What is announced in what is metaphysical without recourse to the experience of the subject, without its immediate being-present [*Dabeisein*], is helpless before the desire of the autonomous subject, to permit nothing to be foisted on it, which would not be comprehensible to it.[41]

The antinomical quality that Adorno ascribes to metaphysical experience is therefore a constitutive feature of any experience that would seem to hold out the promise of total fulfillment. "*Happiness, the only aspect of metaphysical experience that is more than powerless yearning*, grants the interior of objects as what is simultaneously removed from it."[42]

Notwithstanding these various specifications, the status of metaphysical experience in Adorno's philosophy remains unclear. Before I turn to Adorno's discussion of the relationship between metaphysics and morality, three points merit special emphasis.

1. We should not conflate metaphysical experience with religious experience, though it is no doubt tempting to construe it as a secular analogue to revelation (*Offenbarung*). Adorno seems to have been especially eager to draw a sharp distinction between metaphysical experience and "religious primal experience [*religiöse Urerlebnisse*]," and this may explain why he modified his terminology and called this experience "metaphysical" rather than "spiritual [*geistige*]." The crucial difference would be that metaphysical experience has a thoroughly *this-worldly* character. Although it challenges the self-assurance of the subject, it is nevertheless an encounter with a specific location that lies on *this side* of the objective world; it is not a theophany that opens the subject to a heavenly beyond.[43]

2. Metaphysical experience is an encounter with the material world in all of its irreducible plenitude and particularity. If Adorno seems unusually preoccupied with this idea it is chiefly because it exemplifies his wish to turn our philosophical attention toward the non-identical as that which always surpasses the capacities of the cognitive subject. He is not primarily interested in the question of geographic specificity, but he is nonetheless fascinated by the power of proper names insofar as they refer only to particulars and never to universals.

3. Finally and most importantly, the most relevant feature of metaphysical experience is that it offers a *promise of happiness*. I have argued in this book that to affirm the possibility of human flourishing, Adorno needs to be able to point to at least *some* validation in our experience that our hopes for a better world are not in vain. The category of metaphysical experience is meant to satisfy just this philosophical requirement.[44] Metaphysical experience is *charged with normativity*, but, much like the "metaphysics" that shows up as a light in the prison cell in Beethoven's *Fidelio*, this is a species of normativity that is *fully immanent to the world*. Although such an experience is necessarily partial and incomplete, it points toward the possibility of a total happiness that in current conditions remains unfulfilled.

A Materialist Morality

In both this chapter and the previous one, I have explored the various ways in which Adorno understands materialism. As we have seen, his materialism is so capacious that it even permits him to reconceive ostensibly defunct categories of the metaphysical tradition in materialist terms. This, I argue, is the philosophical intent behind his striking claim that "metaphysics has slipped into material existence."[45] His point is that metaphysical inquiry has not simply vanished, nor has it been stripped of its validity thanks to a logical analysis of language (as logical positivists such as Carnap have claimed).[46] Adorno strongly resists such deflationary gestures. Rather, he argues that metaphysics has been sublated dialectically: its shift in meaning registers a fundamental transformation in human experience and self-understanding.[47] He presents this argument in various iterations but perhaps never with as much force as in the concluding portion of *Negative Dialectics*, "Meditations on Metaphysics." His claim involves a strong interpretation of the historical events subsumed under the place-name "Auschwitz," a term that he uses not only as a metonym for the crimes of the Third Reich but also in a more general sense to signify all comparable atrocities and the consequent rupture in human self-understanding. It was once an essential tenet of the philosophical tradition that our metaphysical ideas were somehow compatible with our worldly experience: we conceived of the immutable realm of Platonic form or Hegelian spirit as manifested within the temporal realm of appearance. This tenet was a secularized expression of the "mystical" or theological teaching that the "innerworldly" is relevant to "transcendence." After Auschwitz, however, such beliefs have lost all credibility. The assertion that we could still find transcendent meaning in worldly catastrophe has become little more than "sanctimonious prattle [*Salbadern*]," and it does a grave injustice to the victims.[48] Adorno's conclusion is that our "capacity for metaphysics" has been "crippled [*gelähmt*]," because "what occurred has smashed the basis of the compatibility between speculative metaphysical thinking with experience."[49]

The atrocities associated with the name "Auschwitz" therefore compel us to rethink the received terms of the metaphysical tradition. In tandem with the catastrophic changes in historical experience, the very categories that once belonged to metaphysical speculation also underwent a dramatic transformation and were compelled to turn away from their otherworldly referents. Adorno is careful to explain, however, that this change did not *entirely* rob these categories of their meaning. The change involved not a simple overcoming (or abstract negation) but a genuinely dialectical sublation (or *Aufhebung*) of metaphysics into the framework of this-worldly experience. Metaphysical ideas survive not as referents to an otherworldly or supersensible sphere but only in the domain of our moral thinking, where they play an important role as postulates for this-worldly and critical practice. As I explain below, Adorno seeks to enlist the Kantian category of the metaphysical ideas for the sake of a new moral philosophy. To understand how this would be possible, however, we must now examine what Adorno calls the Kantian "rescue of the intelligible sphere [*Rettung der intelligiblen Sphäre*]."[50]

The Postulate of the Highest Good

Among the more striking themes in Adorno's philosophy is the claim that although the inherited concepts of the metaphysical tradition have been deflated and are no longer compatible with modern experience, we should nonetheless hold on to these concepts insofar as they may still retain their validity when applied to critical practice. He expresses this claim at many points in his work, most famously in the concluding line of *Negative Dialectics*, where we are told that critical thinking still expresses "solidarity with metaphysics at the moment of its fall [*ist solidarisch mit Metaphysik im Augenblick ihres Sturzes*]."[51]

We can better grasp the significance of this unusual idea if we consider Adorno's remarks on the status of the postulates in Kant's practical philosophy. Consider the following passage:

> The Kant of the Critique of Reason said in the doctrine of ideas, that theory would not be possible without metaphysics. That it, however, is possible, implies that right of metaphysics, to which the same Kant, who smashed it through the effect of his work, held fast. The Kantian rescue of the intelligible sphere is not only, as everyone knows, Protestant apologetics, but would also like to intervene in the dialectic of enlightenment there, where this latter terminates in the abolition of reason.[52]

Here we are presented with a paradigm of dialectical interpretation. Adorno acknowledges that in conventional narratives of philosophy Kant appears as the "all-destroyer [*der Alleszermalmer*]" (Mendelssohn) who brought speculative metaphysics to an end. But Kant is no less known for his attempt in the second *Critique* to restore dignity to the very same metaphysical ideas that in the first *Critique* he had deemed invalid. He did so by transforming the key ideas (God, freedom, and immortality) from categories of metaphysical knowledge into postulates of practical reason. Kant's "rescue" of the intelligible realm should not be dismissed as a specious exercise in religious apologetics (as critics such as Heinrich Heine have long claimed).[53] Rather, it should be understood as an attempt to retain what is truly indispensable in our metaphysical concepts even as he also conspired with the Enlightenment to revoke their right to a legitimate place in empirical experience. The nominalist trend in modern philosophy has gradually evacuated all metaphysical ideas of objective meaning. That Kant could intervene *against* this trend on behalf of the metaphysical ideas was due to the fact that even while he banished them from theoretical philosophy, he nonetheless recognized their vital role in practical philosophy. He directed his efforts especially toward redeeming the religious idea of immortality:

The Kantian desire for the rescue [of the metaphysical ideas] is grounded in something far deeper than solely a pious wish; it is a desire to hold something of the traditional ideas in hand in the midst of, and contrary to, nominalism; and this desire is attested to by the construction of immortality as a postulate of practical reason. It condemns the intolerability of what exists and reinforces the Spirit, which cognizes it.[54]

To appreciate the significance of Adorno's interpretation some background is necessary. In the *Critique of Practical Reason*, Kant introduced the postulate of immortality in order to fill a gap in our moral reasoning. In our moral conduct we act solely on the basis of a rationally derived concept of duty and without any regard for considerations of pleasure or personal satisfaction. Kant understood, however, that such a constrained and wholly impersonal conception of duty leaves us without any confidence that our conduct will eventually produce a condition in which the demands of morality will be united with our personal need for happiness. As I have already explained, practical reason is therefore justified in positing the postulate of *the highest good*. Adorno offers an intriguing if unconventional interpretation of this argument. He sees it as a sign in Kant's thought of an unresolved contest between reason and its own self-imposed constraints. Despite his own pretensions of rationalist limitation, Kant cannot help but imagine a condition of ultimate satisfaction that would necessarily stretch even beyond the bounds of death. "That no innerworldly betterment would suffice to do justice to the dead; that none would touch upon the injustice of death, is what moves Kantian reason to hope against reason. The secret of his philosophy is the unthinkability of despair."[55]

To be sure, Adorno himself cannot countenance the concept of immorality in any literal sense. His own materialism restrains him from endorsing such an extravagant idea.[56] Much like Kant, he rejects as illegitimate the use of the metaphysical ideas within the bounds of possible experience. However, also like Kant, the concept that he has disavowed as an object of possible knowledge nevertheless returns as a postulate of practical reason. Adorno understands the postulate of the highest good as indispensable to the practice of social criticism insofar as it expresses a maximalist demand. We confront the world with a maximalist demand for ultimate happiness, and by this standard the world must be judged a failure. It could very well be that this demand is impossible to meet, but it is nevertheless the animating force of all our criticism without which we would be compelled to accept the world as it is. In appealing to this standard, what distinguishes Adorno from Kant is that Adorno believes that the metaphysically derived concept of the highest good must be reconceived in purely *materialist* terms. This is precisely what he means when he says that "metaphysics has slipped into material existence [*die Metaphysik geschlüpft ist in das materielle Dasein*]."[57]

Adorno invokes the theme of a materialist transformation of metaphysical concepts to develop a new conception of morality. In the series of lectures on metaphysics that he offered in 1965, just a year before the publication of *Negative Dialectics*, he is not ashamed to speak of this new morality as "the demand for the right life."[58] He further argues that this demand is the expression of a *metaphysical* principle in the sense that it "points beyond mere facticity." In the following passage Adorno gathers together these various claims into a robust affirmation of moral materialism:

> If I say to you that the true basis of morality is to be found in bodily feeling, in identification with unbearable pain, I am showing you from a different side something which I earlier tried to indicate in a far more abstract form. It is that morality, that which can be called moral, i.e., *the demand for the right life* [*die Forderung nach dem richtigen Leben*] lives on in openly materialist motifs; that precisely the metaphysical principle of such a "Thou shalt" ["*Du sollst*"]— and this "Thou shalt"—*is indeed a metaphysical principle that points beyond mere facticity*—can find its justification only in the recourse to material reality, to corporeal, physical reality, and not to its opposite pole, the pure thought.[59]

This passage merits close consideration as it offers one of the boldest statements of Adorno's moral materialism. In it we can see how he seeks to redeem the metaphysical ideas for the sake of a materialist conception of morality. In their original form the metaphysical ideas referred to the intelligible world; but following the historical collapse of the metaphysical tradition, this is no longer possible. Nevertheless, Adorno does not believe that with this collapse the metaphysical ideas have altogether lost their relevance. Rather, he believes that they can be redirected away from the purely intelligible sphere and transposed into material reality. But they do not merely affirm reality as it is. Following the model of the Kantian postulates, their function is more prescriptive than descriptive: they carry the normative force of a "thou shalt." Nor is their form merely negative: "thou shalt" signifies something more than "thou shalt not."[60] They impose on us a moral demand that points beyond the current world and toward what Adorno calls "the right life."[61]

Much is at stake in this argument. First, if we take Adorno's phrasing in earnest, it would appear that we cannot characterize Adorno's moral philosophy in purely negative terms, since his critical efforts are oriented not simply away from the bad but toward the good. More striking still, however, we cannot fail to notice that his concept of the good or the "right life" comes freighted with a *maximalist* meaning. The normative demand that it imposes on the world still carries a trace of the metaphysical idea that nothing, not even death, can be permitted to temper our hope for human fulfillment. Although the *summum bonum*, or highest good, survives only as a postulate for critical practice, its demand for ultimate fulfillment remains undiminished. It is in this sense of a truly maximal demand (which Adorno appears to have inherited from the Kantian doctrine of the postulates) that he calls the "unthinkability of despair." Of course, Adorno recognizes that this normative demand is impossibly strong, and no world in which suffering still persists could possibly satisfy such a stringent criterion. "*The smallest trace of senseless suffering* in the experienced world" would suffice to "condemn the whole of identity philosophy . . . as lies."[62] He invokes from Walter Benjamin the remark, "So long as there is even a single beggar, there will be *mythos*."[63] But it is just this demythologized utopia of a world without suffering that provides Adorno with the critical orientation he requires. Because our demands are maximalist, it follows that our criticism of the current world must be ruthless and unrelenting.

Happiness and Suffering

As I bring this chapter to a close, I wish to emphasize the point that Adorno's materialism is not simply a theme in a formal philosophical argument. He clearly believes that materialism is the only suitable framework in which we can grant full recognition to the phenomenon of suffering in human experience. Indeed, the fact that we can suffer at all is quite simply constitutive of our material existence as human beings. This possibility is already implicit in the philosophical idea of the primacy of the object. "Suffering," explains Adorno, "is the objectivity which weighs on the subject."[64] The philosophical argument that we should acknowledge this primacy, however, is also meant to be something *more than an argument*. It describes a moral demand, or "thou shalt," that we feel on a somatic level and that urges us to hold ourselves open and unguarded to the reality of human suffering. We can, of course, try to wall ourselves off from this reality, but this would require that we isolate ourselves from worldly experience altogether. And this is precisely what Adorno thinks the idealist tradition really amounts to: it is a long and futile effort to deny the fact of our own dependency on the world and on the material conditions that make our suffering a constant and truly constitutive possibility of being human.

In the previous chapter I referred to Adorno's ethics of vulnerability. Now we are finally in a position to grasp the true significance of this ethical theme. The conditions of possibility for our happiness are *also* the conditions for the possibility of our suffering; we cannot hope for the one if we are not exposed to the other. Here, then, is the ultimate reason we must forswear idealism and acknowledge the primacy of the object. For we can have no experience of genuine happiness if we do not also leave ourselves vulnerable to the risk of its negation. Happiness, however, also serves as an indispensable and materialist norm without which our criticism could have no traction, and if we did not have at least *some* experience as to what happiness would consist in we could not judge the world to have failed. Recall Adorno's striking phrase (quoted in chapter 2): "Consciousness could not despair at all over what is grey, if it did not harbor the concept of a different color, whose scattered trace is not lacking in the negative whole."[65] To condemn what is wrong in the world already implicates us in a medium of contrastive concepts. If we are not to remain locked in a mere affirmation of the given, we must have some experiential evidence for how the world could be different from how it is.

We can now appreciate why Adorno sees suffering and happiness as bound in a relation of dialectical entailment. To orient ourselves toward happiness is to make explicit the future-directed standard that animates our critical efforts. "Happiness . . . is essentially a result. It unfolds from the dialectical sublation of suffering."[66] This is why Adorno believes that to hold ourselves open to possible suffering is the highest requirement for all morality and all moral criticism.[67] We must fully commit ourselves to remaining open and responsive to suffering if our criticism is to have any grip on the material world. He even suggests that if we truly listen to human suffering, we can already hear in it a kind of protest against the conditions that produced it. "Woe speaks: Go [*Weh spricht: vergeh*]." To be sure, this is true only insofar as we respond to suffering in the proper fashion, by seeking a remedy for those very conditions. Adorno does not mean to say that suffering on its own could somehow suffice as a critical response. What is required would be a species of *recognition* whereby our own responsiveness and vulnerability to the condition of others could serve as the point of departure for ethical and political action. "What is specifically materialistic thereby converges with the critical, with socially transforming praxis."[68] In this argument we can glimpse the germ of an argument that would only come to prominence among later exponents of critical theory, especially Axel Honneth, who has made recognition the central theme of his work.[69] Although Adorno does not fully develop this argument, he understands that any responsiveness to the pain of others must presuppose the subject's openness to experience. For Adorno the stakes of critical theory could not be higher. As Adorno observes, "The need to give voice to suffering is the condition of all truth."[70]

5

6

5

Aesthetic Theory

When the unedited text of Adorno's *Aesthetic Theory* was published post-humously in 1970, the book met with a rather cool reception not least because it extolled a species of high modernism that was already in decline. Especially in the visual arts, the center of gravity had already made a decisive shift in tandem with the changing flow of global capitalism from Paris and Berlin to New York, where, by the 1960s, even the last phase of abstract expressionism typified by the heroic individualism of Jackson Pollock had ceded its author-ity to new fashions such as pop art. Two works by Andy Warhol from 1962, *Campbell's Soup Cans* and *Marilyn Diptych*, became twin icons for the aging of the avant-garde and its displacement by a far more ironic sensibility that playfully transgressed the line between art and commerce, embracing both the fetishism of commodities and the no less decisive fetishism of persons. It should hardly surprise us that in this new aesthetic climate Adorno's attempt to sustain the modernist ideal of autonomous art against the blandishments of the culture industry could strike some readers as hopelessly antiquated. For younger readers in the 1970s who longed for a more *engagé* mode of aes-thetic expression, it was not uncommon to declare that not only Adorno, but the broader institution of Frankfurt School critical theory had capitulated to tradition and that the appeal to high modernism was a further sign of its ob-solescence. Among the many misrepresentations of Adorno that have gained widespread credence in the public imagination, perhaps none is so persistent as the view that he was a man of wealth and privilege who turned away from the debasements of mass culture and found an exalted refuge in a depoliti-cized realm of pure art. This strong verdict against Adorno for his apparent retreat into mere aestheticism was a commonplace even among more sym-pathetic and discerning readers, who felt that in Adorno's work the "eman-cipatory hopes" that had once been directed toward the public domain were "transposed in the aesthetic realm" but were left completely powerless with their promise unfulfilled.[1] For such readers, it seemed self-evident that the imperatives of social and political praxis must assume precedence, while any concern for aesthetics thereby took on the conservative stigma of political helplessness that Walter Benjamin once diagnosed as "left-wing melancholy."[2]

In this chapter I wish to offer at least a partial defense of Adorno against this negative reception. Aesthetics for Adorno does not mean aestheticism. He looks to art not as a retreat from social concerns but as a species of socially invested criticism. He believes that the artwork is and *must* be social all the way through to its innermost structure, and it can serve as an embodiment of truth only if it remains open and responsive to the fact of social suffering. But this does not mean that its purposes are purely negative. As a seismograph of social experience the artwork is at once a transcript of human suffering *and* an anticipation of human flourishing. It acknowledges both of these moments without resolution, and it holds out to us a *promesse du bonheur* only insofar as it also responds to our despair. Indeed, it is only in virtue of its open or unresolved dialectic that the artwork can serve as a sign of freedom in an unfree world.

In the previous chapter I examined how Adorno applies the practice of immanent critique to redeem moments of possibility at the interstices of everyday experience and in the mimetic bond that connects humanity with its own repressed nature. In this chapter I wish to explore his further attempt to disclose anticipatory fragments of unrealized happiness that lie untapped in the artifacts of modern art. Adorno's aesthetic concerns cannot be ignored. No discussion of the sources of normativity in his work can be complete if it does not take into its compass the critical and normative power that inheres in aesthetic experience. To understand this claim we must reckon with a fact that we can easily overlook if we assign Adorno's thought to a conventional canon of social and political philosophy. In his collected works the volumes that address questions of art, chiefly musicological but also literary, comprise a full half of the published corpus. Among these volumes are the music monographs (on Wagner, Mahler, and Berg and the posthumously published notes and sketches on Beethoven), vigorously argued polemics such as *Philosophy of New Music*, and assorted essays that testify to the inspiration Adorno found in the Second Viennese School (Schoenberg, Berg, and Webern). No less noteworthy are the insightful essays on literature (including ones that address Hölderlin, Kafka, and Beckett). At issue, however, is not the sheer number of pages that he devoted to any particular topic but the significance of this topic to his overall philosophical purposes. The aesthetic for Adorno is hardly peripheral, and the notion that it belongs to a distinctive but separate sphere in his philosophy is already misleading. On the contrary; as I shall argue below, the aesthetic occupies a central place in his understanding of what is means to be human.[3] If we shut our eyes to the luminous glow of art we blind ourselves to what was for Adorno among the most enduring redoubts of normativity in the darkening landscape of late capitalist experience.

The Persistence of the Aura

What is most distinctive in Adorno's account of aesthetic experience first becomes clear when it is seen in a comparative light alongside the well-known essay, "The Work of Art in the Age of Its Technical Reproducibility," which was written by his friend and colleague Walter Benjamin in the mid-1930s. Benjamin wishes to tell the history of aesthetics as a necessary chapter in the dialectical narrative of human emancipation. The artwork first emerges in the context of archaic society where aesthetic experience obtained as little more than a single moment within the holistic web of magical and religious practice. The artwork in the distinctively *modern* sense appears only once it undergoes a process of disenchantment and is disembedded from this traditionalist framework: the aesthetic then comes into being as an experience that claimed full autonomy from its surroundings. But it was Benjamin's genius as a cultural critic with Marxist ambitions that he exposed the modern claim to autonomy as a bourgeois illusion. The cult of *l'art pour l'art* remained caught in an inherited spell of quasi-religious ritual that still held the viewer in submission. Ironically, this so-called negative theology of high-bourgeois art was no less a symptom of unfreedom than the feudal aesthetic it had displaced. For the bourgeoisie the veneration of the artwork had become a solitary act of piety that resisted all social entanglements and devoted itself solely to the artwork in a psychological state of concentration: focus meant secular rapture. Benjamin calls for this final illusion to be shattered. Techniques of reproduction in photography and film are supposed to release artworks from the bonds of bourgeois idolatry and plunge them into the volatile realm of collective experience where they are free to multiply and circulate without limit. The "aura" of the artwork is supposed to finally dissolve, with the consequence that the artwork would be robbed of its singular authority. For the first time in history the masses are enlisted into the novel experience of art without illusion. Rather than submit to artworks as objects of worship, they will absorb them in a state of distraction, and in this experience they are to discover a promise of their own political agency.

In the many years since its composition Benjamin's essay has assumed a nearly incontrovertible prestige in debates concerning the status of art in

the late-modern era. With its assault on the traditional idol of aesthetic autonomy, along with its rather more surprising affirmation of "distraction"
over concentration as the psychological mode best suited to modern aesthetic experience, it became for many theorists an early anticipation of the
revolt within-but-against modernism that would come to be defined as *postmodernism*. By 1974, when Peter Bürger (despite his specific disagreements
with Benjamin) criticized the bourgeois concept of aesthetic autonomy in
his *Theory of the Avant-Garde*, it seemed that Benjamin's basic verdict was
now secure: high modernism now belonged to the irrevocable past, and it
was widely assumed among art critics and philosophers alike that only if the
artwork were released from the modernist spell would the "gap between the
aesthetic and the practical sphere" finally be bridged.[4]

Adorno's place in these ongoing debates is by no means simple. We can
appreciate his own contribution to aesthetic theory by charting its emergence
from the ongoing dialectical contest with his colleague. In a remarkable letter
from March 18, 1936, Adorno expresses his discontent with Benjamin's essay
and raises specific doubts as to whether it is right to interpret the decay of the
aura as a necessary step on the linear path toward aesthetic and human freedom. In his letter Adorno contests the essay on two fronts. On the one hand,
he admits that it would be "bourgeois romanticism" to ascribe the artwork's
power to the persistence of traditional categories such as the individual "personality." On the other hand, he warns against the "anarchistic romanticism"
that would place "blind trust in the spontaneous powers of the proletariat."
Neither of these two versions of romanticism is acceptable; they are merely
the "torn halves of an integral freedom" that we cannot hope to restore simply by forcing them back together.[5] Benjamin completely ignores the irony
that he wishes to emancipate the artwork from the context of tradition but
would then confine it within the no less authoritarian milieu of the working
class. In his Brechtian zeal for an ostensibly communist aesthetics, Benjamin
ultimately poses a false choice: he opts for the ideal of the artwork as an instrument of political mass mobilization but fails to see how this mobilization
betrays the very art it hoped to redeem.

More worrisome still, Benjamin is far too sanguine regarding the libera-
tory effect of technological innovation in aesthetics. He misses a crucial fact,
namely, that mechanical reproducibility does not simply free the artwork
from its social bonds but also tightens those bonds by leaving the artwork exposed to its thoroughgoing commodification. Adorno recognizes this irony.
The aura's decay should not be understood as an unambiguous sign of progress; it is a highly ambivalent phenomenon that signifies both emancipation

and reification. Adorno does not see the aura as a residue of bourgeois ideology that clings to the artwork like a misty vapor and inhibits its development. He is willing to admit that the aura signifies the artwork's entanglement in a magical spell, but he insists that this magic cannot be entirely dissolved if we wish the artwork to fulfill its emancipatory promise. "The heart of the autonomous work of art does not itself belong to the dimension of myth," he explains. Rather, the artwork's autonomy is "intrinsically dialectical" because *within it "the magical is crossed with the sign of freedom [daß sie in sich das Magische verschränkt mit dem Zeichen der Freiheit]."*[6]

The tension between Adorno and Benjamin concerning the embattled status of the aura was not confined to a brief episode in their friendship; Adorno unilaterally carried on with their debate well after Benjamin's suicide in 1940. Especially in the pages of the posthumously published *Aesthetic Theory* (1970), Adorno pursues the disagreement with his late friend with such intensity that Benjamin seems to persist as a spectral presence whose claims still command recognition. The explanation for his uncanny survival may be partly biographical. Since their first encounter in Frankfurt in 1923, Adorno had admired Benjamin, his senior by eleven years, as a gifted thinker whose interpretive originality served as a model for his own cultural criticism. Adorno's 1933 *Habilitationsschrift* on Kierkegaard bore such a strong resemblance, not in its subject matter but in its method, to Benjamin's own study of the German *Trauerspiel* that Gershom Scholem confided to Benjamin that he saw Adorno's book as an act of "sublime plagiarism."[7] The fact that Benjamin's study was not accepted for habilitation and he was condemned to a life of intellectual wandering outside the university has left a bitter memory that has refused to fade, not least because Adorno survived the catastrophe that claimed his friend.[8] On the question of Adorno's negative cathexis with Benjamin—his constant attempts to challenge Benjamin's arguments even while he invokes the prestige of Benjamin's name—it may not be entirely inappropriate to speak of something akin to survivor's guilt.

None of these biographical details, however, should deter us from examining the substance of their debate.[9] If art for Adorno is the "sign of freedom" in unfreedom, this is because it is the best analogue we have within the bounds of sensuous life for an experience that is set free from social constraints. Aesthetic autonomy is always only partial since the artwork can never actually transcend the social world that first makes it possible: it enjoys only a *relative* autonomy. But the artwork nonetheless becomes a sign *within* material conditions of the transcendence *from* material conditions that the artwork has inherited from religion. In *Aesthetic Theory* Adorno describes art as "the secularization of transcendence [*Säkularisierung von Transcendenz*]."[10] This statement is especially revealing since it reminds us that Adorno does not entirely disagree with the premises of Benjamin's essay. He shares with Benjamin the essential insight that the bourgeois artwork, in its claims to autonomy, still retains the afterglow of the theological power it must also disavow. Benjamin had argued that artwork's "ritualistic basis," "no matter how mediated it may be," persists "even in the most profane form of worship of beauty" and that we can still detect its archaic remains in "secularized ritual [*säkularisiertes Ritual*]" of a "pure art" where it assumes the minimalist form of a "negative theology." Adorno embraces this insight, but he rejects the further inference that the artwork can only be free if it is completely stripped of these theological residues. The thoroughgoing "disenchantment of art [*Entzauberung der Kunst*]" that Benjamin recommends would not bring about art's freedom but only its self-negation; it would signify "the deaestheticization of art [*die Entkunstung der Kunst*]."[11] Perhaps nowhere else in *Aesthetic Theory* does Adorno express his disagreement with Benjamin with such apodictic force. "Aura," he warns, "is not only—as Benjamin claimed—the here and now of the artwork, it is whatever goes beyond its factual givenness, its content; *one cannot abolish it and still want art*."[12]

The Sign of Freedom

I will not dwell any further on the details of the intellectual debate between Adorno and Benjamin. I simply wish to call attention to Adorno's claim that the autonomous artwork should be understood as a "sign of freedom" that persists even in the midst of unfree conditions.[13] This claim is no doubt controversial, not least because it looks suspiciously like a defense of aesthetic idealism, namely, the view that an "autonomous" artwork is the bearer of a nondependent or intrinsic value that has nothing to do with the social conditions that brought it into being. If Adorno had meant to suggest that the autonomous artwork has intrinsic value in this sense, then we would be justified in faulting him for a serious theoretical error. He would be guilty of what we might call *the fetishism of artworks*, an ideological misunderstanding similar in character to what Marx identified as the *fetishism of commodities*. The analogy is imprecise but nonetheless suggestive. In *Capital* Marx says of the commodity that it is "a very queer thing, abounding in metaphysical subtleties and theological niceties."[14] A fetish in the original or religious sense is an object fashioned by human labor that appears as if it were a deity endowed with independent life. Marx appeals to this analogy to explain how capitalism generates the necessary illusion that a commodity has an inherent value that belongs to it quite apart from the conditions of its production. Adorno's notion of the autonomous artwork would seem to invite this very same accusation insofar as it ascribes inherent value to the artwork, as if that value could obtain in total dissociation from the conditions of its production.

To defend Adorno against this charge, we must first recall that he draws an important distinction between the autonomous artwork and the artwork-as-commodity. The artwork-as-commodity is no different from all other commodities insofar as its value lies chiefly in the fact that it can be exchanged on the market. This is why Adorno prefers to speak of these not as works of art but as products of the culture industry. An autonomous artwork, however, has a more contradictory or conflicted character. It too it is a commodity that can be exchanged as such, but it is also the bearer of a use value that is nonfungible or resistant to exchange. In his 1938 essay, "The Fetish Character in Music and Regression in Hearing," Adorno expresses the fear that exchange value is beginning to overtake use value and may eventually vanquish it entirely: "The more inexorably the principle of exchange-value destroys use-values for human beings, the more deeply does exchange-value disguise itself as the object of enjoyment."[15] Where this occurs, as in the consumption of mass-produced music, the commodity is seen as valuable only insofar as it resembles all other commodities. This explains, for example, why all specimens of so-called light music resemble one another down to their innermost form. What makes a "hit song" a commercial success is the fact that it can hardly be distinguished from all the other hit songs that came before it. Adorno believes that this process of standardization is gradually colonizing our aesthetic experience to the point where some day no artworks will retain their autonomy and all will have submitted to the imperative of thoroughgoing commodification.

The above argument, however, still leaves the key question unanswered. Even if Adorno believed that autonomous artworks were on the verge of disappearing, we might still suspect him of endowing them with the magical quality of nonsocial independence that no artworks can ever truly have. To warn that they are endangered is still to imagine them as possible in principle. What ultimately saves Adorno from this charge is the fact that he understands the distinction between autonomous and commodified art as *qualitative* rather than *typological*. The distinction, in other words, describes a quality that is shared by all artworks rather than sorting them into two types or classes. The quality that he ascribes to autonomous art is potentially to be found in *all* works of art, though in varying degrees (and some works also fail to be art simply for formal reasons that have little to do with their commodification). In this respect he remains faithful to the dialectical spirit of Benjamin's well-known dictum, "There is *no* document of culture which is not *at the same time* a document of barbarism."[16]

This inclusive insight into the dialectical character of all cultural artifacts is easily missed, especially by those who see Adorno as an elitist who prefers only one type of aesthetic objects and disdains the realm of commodities as irrevocably fallen. Adorno himself may be partly to blame for encouraging this impression by indulging in sheer polemic when he writes about the products of the culture industry. But when we read him charitably, we can see through his more exaggerated pronouncements to the underlying principles that merit philosophical consideration. Even in his more lacerating condemnation of the culture industry in *Dialectic of Enlightenment*, it is clear that he understands the distinction between autonomous art and art-as-commodity qualitatively and not typologically. Adorno is prepared to admit that even "light" art can take on subversive features (as is the case, for instance, in the comedic films of the Marx Brothers).[17] And he recognizes that the autonomous artwork too is a commodity; after all, even Beethoven sold his compositions for money.[18] His occasionally polemical style should not distract us from the underlying premise of immanent critique, namely, that our social world is not uniformly false but is shot through with contradiction. And this contradictory status is no less evident in the various artifacts that circulate in our social world as *simultaneously* artworks and commodities. Adorno fully acknowledges the unresolved contradiction that inheres in the artifacts we consume, and this is why he insists (against Benjamin) that the autonomous artwork has an "intrinsically dialectical" character. He does not imagine that any artwork could exist entirely free of imperfection, as if it somehow hovered as a pure form of beauty beyond the contradictions of the capitalist world. On the contrary, the artwork emerges from, and must therefore acknowledge, just those contradictions. This is the true meaning of his otherwise enigmatic remark to Benjamin that in the autonomous artwork "the magical is *crossed with* the sign of freedom."[19]

The Analogy to Play

In the preceding section I have explored some of the reasons Adorno is committed to the category of autonomous art. But the account I have offered thus far could still leave us with the impression that Adorno understands this autonomy in purely negative terms, as if it meant nothing more than the artwork's *resistance* to exchange. This impression is not entirely mistaken, insofar as Adorno sees the autonomous artwork as a site of persistent negativity in a social order that is in other respects growing ever more "affirmative" by foreclosing any awareness of possible alternatives. But I have not yet offered an adequate account as to what this negativity consists in beyond the mere fact of resistance.[20] If autonomous art has some further significance beyond its status as negation, we need to understand what alternative it is meant to embody. In other words, we must pose the question: Resistance on behalf of *what*?

We have already encountered a provisional answer to this question in Adorno's analysis of child's play (*Spiel*). As I explained at some length in the previous chapter, Adorno claims that children's toys preserve the "use value" in objects against their reduction to mere objects for exchange and thereby redeems in them what is "benign toward humanity [*den Menschen gut*]."[21] Children's toys serve as unconscious anticipations of a world set free from "the process of abstraction," where objects would at last be permitted to become "what they specifically are."[22] I now wish to mobilize those insights to suggest an analogy between the autonomous artwork and a child's toy (*Spielzeug*). The analogy is no doubt imperfect, as are all analogies insofar as they alert us to similarities across difference. One noteworthy difference is that most artworks involve a highly deliberate and skillful structuring of material rather than a joyful release of purely unfettered imagination. But the analogy is nonetheless revealing for several reasons. Like a toy, the artwork preserves the embattled use value of the object against the forces that would submerge it into the solvent of universal exchange. A small confusion is dispelled once we note that Adorno refers to "use value" to describe the particularity of an object insofar as it has a distinctive place in human experience; he refers to "exchange value" as the generic quality of an object insofar as it circulates on the market as a commodity. Adorno sees the autonomous artwork much as a child sees its beloved toy: as a singular and particular thing that is quite literally irreplaceable. This quality of uniqueness is what Adorno (following Benjamin) means by "aura." Just as a child invests the toy with all the meaningfulness of its particular world, so too one is drawn to an artwork because one finds in it something that is unique to that artwork alone. Like the use value of a child's toy, the use value of an artwork lies in its nonfungible particularity. To see it as exchangeable for any other artwork would be to miss what distinguishes it as an artwork at all. This is the reasoning behind Adorno's rather striking claim that *one cannot abolish the aura and still want art*.[23]

We might pursue the analogy a step further. A child who cherishes an object in its particularity sees it as the bearer of an intrinsic purpose that is valued for its own sake and not for the sake of additional purposes that lie outside the context of imaginative play.[24] According to Adorno, this may also explain why children are instinctively drawn to animals who seem to exist "without any purpose recognizable to human beings" and whose own names seem to express what is "thoroughly non-exchangeable."[25] We discover an analogous principle in Kantian aesthetics, in which a beautiful artwork is seen as the embodiment of "purposiveness without purpose [*Zweckmäßigkeit ohne Zweck*]."[26] In *Dialectic of Enlightenment* Adorno and Horkheimer warn us that in modern society this principle has now been inverted: the artwork must submit to "purposelessness for purposes dictated by the market [*der Zwecklosigkeit für Zwecke, die der Markt deklariert*]."[27] If art was once seen as the bearer of intrinsic value and even became the object of secular veneration as in the ideal of *l'art pour l'art*, it is now defined primarily by its exchange value, and it is consumed not for its own sake but for purposes of relaxation or prestige.[28]

However, the analogy between art and play can also be misleading. In the paralipomena to *Aesthetic Theory* Adorno accepts the basic view that play survives in art insofar as it signifies the redemptive moment by which art raises itself above the immediacy of instrumental praxis.[29] He nonetheless expresses the concern that play, unlike art, is still marked by regressive features that bind it to childhood and even to the prerational life of animals. The crucial difference, he claims, lies in the fact that "forms of play [*Spielformen*]" are always and without exception forms of "repetition" and therefore still bear the trace of merely "purposive rationality [*Zweckrationalität*]."[30] Adorno therefore rejects Schiller's thesis in the *Letters on the Aesthetic Education of Humankind* that the "play-drive [*Spieltrieb*]" would signify the "freedom-from-purpose [*Zweckfreiheit*]" that distinguishes us as fully human. This thesis simply reflects the basic misunderstanding of bourgeois society that cannot conceive of freedom without compulsion. Against Schiller, Adorno insists that play, unlike art, remains caught in the spell of a repetition compulsion that misconstrues obedience as if it were genuine happiness.[31] Similar considerations also move Adorno to criticize the well-known thesis of *Homo Ludens* (1938) by the Dutch cultural historian Johan Huizinga, who argues that play is the universal and necessary condition for all culture.[32] Adorno faults Huizinga chiefly for his failure to recognize that the element of play is traceable to instrumentalist praxis and has little in common with the genuinely aesthetic category of semblance (*Schein*).

Notwithstanding this criticism, however, Adorno allows for the possibility that play itself contains a moment of semblance or imagination that escapes the logic of instrumental reason.[33] For not all instances of play take the form of a game that requires a repetitive obedience to rules. In his own reflections on the utopian moment in children's play, it is fairly clear that Adorno has in mind not competitive games but children's interaction with toys and their immersion in a landscape of imagination. Due to these imaginative or counterfactual elements, play can also signify the *breaking* of rules or even willful transgression, as is evident, for example, in humor. Adorno therefore praises Huizinga for understanding that all play contains an element of joking or disbelief. "It is in this consciousness of *the untruth of the true*," Adorno concludes, that "all art participates in humor." This humorous dimension of aesthetics becomes especially evident in exemplars of "dark modernism" such as the works of Kafka and Beckett. What Huizinga calls "the unity and indivisibility of belief and unbelief" thereby becomes for Adorno a crucial feature that is valid both for play and "for all art."[34]

I have pursued the analogy between art and play chiefly because it sheds an unfamiliar light on Adorno's aesthetic theory, which many readers would characterize as severe or even dour. This impression is not altogether inaccurate, but I believe it misses a vital theme that motivates Adorno not only in his reflections on art, but throughout his philosophy, namely, that immanent critique is directed toward the discovery of the non-identical as that which resists the dominant order and thereby anticipates reconciliation. Indeed, if Adorno finds a special meaning in metaphysical experience and in the child's experience at play, this is because he understands both of them as instances of non-identity, as experiences that bear within themselves a promise of happiness or human flourishing. This same promise is what animates Adorno in his aesthetic criticism. The severity of his criticism is not a symptom of mere bleakness; it is the shadow side of the exacting and maximalist expectations for human fulfillment that he brings to his encounter with art. The normative demand that is at work in his aesthetic criticism is seldom obvious to the reader chiefly because Adorno often prefers to express it in its negative form as a judgment of failure. But we can hardly make sense of this failure if we do not see it as a mismatch between the emphatic concept and its empirical instantiation. Inherent in the very concept of the artwork is the expectation that it satisfy extraordinarily demanding criteria, so it should hardly surprise us that few examples of art actually fulfill this expectation.[35]

Art and Suffering

We have now arrived at what I take to be the single most important but least appreciated theme in Adorno's aesthetic theory. When we consider the idea of a fully autonomous artwork, it can be tempting to believe that an artwork can only be autonomous if it has the status of a world-transcendent object that has turned its back on the world. This conception is also partly to blame for the widespread view that Adorno as a philosopher was an incorrigible elitist and an aesthete who preferred the pleasures of haut-bourgeois art to the burdens of social responsibility. Much like the portrait of the philosopher, however, this conception of the autonomous artwork is thoroughly mistaken. Adorno believes that an autonomous artwork merits its status *as an artwork* only insofar as it is responsive to the human condition. If an artwork were to close itself off from the world, it might still retain the superficial appearance, in both formal composition and sensuous content, that we have come to expect from artworks when we visit a concert hall or museum. But it would no longer be art. To appreciate the true force of this claim, we need to recognize that the concept of autonomous art in Adorno's philosophy has an irreducibly normative meaning. "The concept of an artwork implies that of its success. Failed artworks are not art."[36] An artwork cannot *succeed* in the relevant sense if it remains indifferent to the problems that besiege us as social beings. On the contrary, an artwork can only succeed, can only *be* an artwork at all, if it opens itself fully to those problems.

If we wish to know how Adorno conceives of art and what role it plays in his overall conception of philosophy, this claim is indispensable. In the preceding chapter I offered some remarks on Adorno's ethics of vulnerability. I noted that his materialist understanding of morality takes as its point of departure the experience of human beings when they hold themselves open and unguarded to the reality of human suffering. In *Negative Dialectics* Adorno goes so far as to claim that "the need to give voice to suffering is the condition of all truth."[37] In his reflections on aesthetics, Adorno honors this very same principle. An artwork that did not give voice to suffering would no longer be truthful; it would be merely a further instance of ideology. In drawing this inference, Adorno appeals implicitly to a premise that he has inherited from the German Idealists and from Marx, namely, that an artwork is a thoroughly human artifact and an embodiment of human labor. It is nothing less than an *objectification* of human subjectivity.[38] If an artwork were to close itself off entirely from the social conditions of its production it would confront us as something alien (or, we might even say, as *alienated labor*). In this regard an artwork is no different from a human being: the very same vulnerability that we expect from human subjects we should also expect of the artworks they create. If an artwork is to have the status of truth it must be responsive to its surroundings and serve as a faithful transcript of human suffering. In *Aesthetic Theory* Adorno entertains the question of whether art without such responsiveness would even be art at all. "For what would art be as the writing of history if it swept aside the memory of accumulated suffering?"[39]

Autonomy and Heteronomy

I have suggested above that Adorno believes that art can only be true if it is responsive to the actual conditions that surround it. Or, stated succinctly, an artwork must be no less damaged than its damaged world. This requirement is not always stated with candor, though it should be clear that Adorno regards it as the guiding principle of his philosophical aesthetics. If he rarely feels obliged to state this principle in a forthright fashion, this is because he is chiefly preoccupied with the question as to how an artwork can nonetheless uphold its *autonomy* even in the midst of the damaged and damaging social conditions to which it responds. I wish to argue that this is the primary question that animates Adorno in his reflections on art. The stakes in this matter are indeed high, since it is not at all obvious how he can sustain his commitment to the autonomy of art while *also* honoring the principle that art remain open and responsive to its surroundings.

An artwork is said to be autonomous insofar as it resists the prevailing logic of social and economic exchange. Our current social order is one that seeks to reduce difference to universal fungibility so as to facilitate the capitalist imperative that all objects become mere instances of the same standard of value. If autonomy means that something obeys rules that it prescribes *to itself*, then aesthetic autonomy designates the quality by which an artwork obeys the rules that it gives to itself rather than the rules that are imposed on it by the social imperatives of the market. Adorno believes that an artwork exhibits this self-prescriptive quality if it resists the rules of social exchange and instead obeys "the law of form [*Formgesetz*]."[40] This criterion is indeed paramount to his definition of art: form, he claims, is *"the central concept"* of aesthetics.[41] In this definition of art we can discern a rough analogy to Kant's moral philosophy. Just as the Kantian moral agent sustains its freedom by following its self-prescribed laws, so too the artwork draws back from its social determination only by means of the laws of its own self-imposed form. To be sure, Adorno recognizes that aesthetic autonomy is no less precarious than moral autonomy. Just as our moral conduct imposes on us the demanding formalism of the categorical imperative, so too an artwork only succeeds in its autonomy if it upholds the laws of self-imposed form against the demands of its surroundings. "The concept of form marks out art's sharp antithesis to an empirical world in which art's right to exist has become uncertain. Art has precisely the same chance of survival as does form, no better."[42]

All the same, Adorno never goes so far as to equate aesthetic autonomy with social transcendence. Works of art always exhibit a "dual nature" insofar as they are "autonomous structures *and* social phenomena."[43] This implies that artworks never succeed in *completely* closing themselves off from their social surroundings. An autonomous artwork is no more a seamless whole than is society itself. Indeed, he explicitly rejects the ideal of a "closed artwork [*geschlossenen Kunstwerk*]" just as he rejects the ideal of a "closed society [*geschlossenen Gesellschaft*]."[44] Both are equally questionable. An artwork is not a closed and perfect thing but is instead the embodiment of unresolved contradiction. It follows that a successful artwork is autonomous *and* heteronomous *at once*. Although this claim may strike us as paradoxical, it is simply a restatement of the cardinal insight of negative dialectics, according to which no instance of human reality can claim to have achieved full reconciliation. In *Aesthetic Theory* Adorno urges us to see that the autonomous and heteronomous moments of the artwork are not only simultaneous; they mutually entail one another even in their antagonism. Of the artwork he writes, "It is for itself, and it is not; it would lack its autonomy without its heterogeneity."[45] Stated differently, this means that an artwork can respond truthfully to the damaged world that lies outside its walls only if it succeeds in drawing back from the world as its negation. If it did not somehow separate itself from the world it would simply be absorbed into it as yet another commodity. Conversely, if it were to sever its bond with the world entirely and take no interest in its damaged condition it would thereby surrender its claims to truth. With its twofold character as simultaneously autonomous *and* heteronomous, the artwork thus resembles a monad. Although it is not reducible to the world, it nonetheless recapitulates the world "windowlessly [*fensterlos*]" within its own aesthetic frame.[46]

Adorno's remarks on the monad-like character of the artwork are conflicted. Artworks have an immanent structuration (*Gefügtheit*) that enhances the illusion of their hermetic isolation, but precisely through the internal organization of their own materials they also reproduce "the intellectual domination of reality [*der geistigen Herrschaft über die Wirklichkeit*]."[47] It is therefore impossible when analyzing an artwork wholly to distinguish between the internal and external, although nothing that is external remains legible as sedimented social content without undergoing an alchemical transformation: "What is transcendent to them is imported into them as that by which they in the first place become an immanent nexus. These categories are, however, so completely modified that only the shadow of bindingness remains."[48] This would seem to suggest that the social content of an artwork should be discovered only through an immanent analysis of the specific work's aesthetic form. But even while he insists that aesthetic interpretation should proceed by means of immanent critique, Adorno also warns that this procedure should not serve further to enhance the illusion of an artwork's hermetic closure. For the artwork's claim to a total independence in its meaning is no less illusory than is the human subject's claim to independence from its social world: "If it is made absolute, immanent analysis falls prey to ideology, against which it struggled when it wanted to devote itself to the artworks internally rather than deducing their worldviews."[49] The artwork's monad-like character must therefore be understood dialectically. "The monadological constitution of artworks in themselves points beyond itself."[50] It follows that the very principle of form by which an artwork is said to secure its autonomy is *also* the principle by which an artwork remains responsive to the society that surrounds it. "The unresolved antagonisms of reality return in artworks as immanent problems of form."[51]

This dialectical interpretation of the monad underwrites Adorno's twofold claim that the artwork is at once autonomous *and* responsive to worldly suffering: "All artworks are a priori polemical" because they "bear witness that the empirical world, their other from which they are emphatically separated, should be other than it is."[52] Needless to say, Adorno warns against the naive thought that in their critical task of "bearing witness" artworks could beckon to us as islands of utopia or total fulfillment. On the contrary, he insists that "there are no perfect works." For if an artwork could stand before us as an image of unblemished perfection, this would imply that "reconciliation would be possible in the midst of the unreconciled."[53] Adorno upholds the distinction between the "emphatic" or normative standard of a successful artwork and its compromised empirical instantiation, but he does not believe that this gap can be fully closed. Because all art is human, it is scored by the wounds and blemishes of the human world from which it is born. In an imperfect world, art too must be imperfect, lest it surrender its truth status and become an ideological affirmation of a false reality. It is in this sense that all successful art must be negative, *not* because it portrays the world as a realm of total despair, but rather because through its internal disunity it also offers us a truthful portrait of our unreconciled condition. This criterion applies even to seemingly "beautiful" and "harmonious" works of art such as the music of Mozart, whose compositions may sound to us as if they were "unpolemical," as if they floated in a "pure sphere of spirit" beyond social contamination.[54] Even Mozart's music, however, is partially negative, since it stages a contest between reconciliation and social reality that we hear as "painful sweetness [*schmerzhafte Süße*]."[55]

Jazz, Suffering, Hope

It should be noted that in his interpretation of popular art forms Adorno was not always consistent, and he did not always honor his own stated principle

that an artwork embodies the dialectical contradictions of society. His interpretation of commodified music is especially unfortunate and has caused a
great deal of confusion, drawing down upon Adorno various accusations, not
only of elitism, but also of racism and cultural reaction. In the secondary literature on Adorno's musicological and cultural criticism, a disproportionate
share of attention has been spent on his essays on jazz. The debates are still
ongoing and have often involved fundamental misunderstandings or factual
errors.[56] I do not intend to enter into these controversies at length here, except
to note that they shed further light on the question of Adorno's alleged negativism. It is worth recalling that the musical form that he called "jazz" was not
what we understand by this term today; it was a mass-marketed form of light
entertainment associated chiefly with big band orchestras such as the one
led by Paul Whiteman, the director of an all-white ensemble who was much
celebrated in the interwar era as the "King of Jazz." This may help explain why
Adorno understands jazz not as a legitimate musical form but as little more
than a commodity that has fully succumbed to the rules of standardization
that facilitate its circulation in the market. Even gestures of apparent freedom
such as improvisation are understood as illusions that merely confirm unfreedom: "the so-called improvisations are actually reduced to the more or
less feeble rehashing of basic formulas in which the schema shines through
at every moment."[57]

However, even if we allow for the historical specificity of Adorno's understanding of jazz as a commodity form, his conclusions are clearly hyperbolic
insofar as they leave no room for the recognition of dialectical contradiction.
As the exemplar of fully commodified music, jazz is condemned in toto as
merely a commodity in which the constitutive tension between freedom and
unfreedom has yielded to a premature reconciliation. But surely such a verdict
should strike us as one-sided. Specifically, it presupposes the possibility of a
music genre that has *completely* surrendered to the commodity form. However, as I have argued above, the distinction between autonomous art and art-
as-commodity is best understood qualitatively rather than typologically. In
his remarks on jazz Adorno adopts the typological distinction and therefore
fails to hear *anything* in jazz that might signify the persistence of an unresolved dialectic. Most striking of all, however, is his failure to recognize the
irrepressible energies of both protest and hope that belong to jazz as a seismograph of African American experience: "The Negro spirituals, antecedents
of the blues, were slave songs and as such combined the lament of unfreedom
with its oppressed confirmation."[58] This sentence may very well rank among
the least discerning in Adorno's entire oeuvre: it ignores the hope for a better
world that resounds throughout a complex musical lineage across its many

centuries. Moreover, it is an interpretation that violates Adorno's own stated principle from *Negative Dialectics*, namely, that all art has its share in truth insofar as it serves as a transcript of human suffering: "Perennial suffering has as much right to express itself as the martyr has to scream."[59] With this principle Adorno rescinds his earlier and frequently misunderstood dictum that poetry after Auschwitz would be barbaric.[60] It is all the more striking and regrettable, then, that Adorno did not extend this same principle to the blues and to jazz.[61] Rather than concede that jazz must be granted the same right to self-expression as all other art forms, he adopts the censorious judgment that jazz is the seamless product of a seamless world: "With jazz, a disenfranchised subjectivity plunges from the commodity world into the commodity world; the system does not allow for a way out."[62] This conclusion is surely hyperbolic. But it should be noted that this thoroughly negative and undialectical verdict on jazz is one instance that appears to validate the negativist interpretation of Adorno's thought in general. Jazz becomes the signature of totalized social falsehood. If we wish to contest this negative verdict, we would also need to reject the totalizing image of a society-without-an-exit that supports it.

A Dialectic of Secularization

In this chapter I have explored Adorno's general claim that artworks are successful if and only if they are responsive to human suffering. But they can satisfy this requirement only if they take up a critical stance toward the world and thematize its contradictions on the level of their own form. This criticism is not only negative, however, because it also holds out a promise of happiness that lies beyond the suffering it transcribes. In this sense a successful artwork is at once transcendent *and* immanent; in other words, it is an instance of "immanent transcendence." This idea of an artwork's dialectical status—as both autonomous and responsive to suffering—remains controversial, not least because in philosophical aesthetics the very notion of autonomy has grown antiquated and is often seen as a desperate bid to retain the illusion of social isolation when it is in fact little more than a mask for social privilege. The will to shatter the illusion of aesthetic autonomy became a major gesture in modern aesthetics especially after Brecht, whose *Verfremdungseffekt* was meant as a strike against bourgeois complacency. It is therefore tempting to accuse Adorno of seeking an extorted reconciliation between two incompatible aesthetic schools—between a school that adhered to the tradition of bourgeois idealism and its concept of aesthetic autonomy and a rebellious school that rejected that idealist inheritance and wished to break through the so-called fourth wall of a merely fictive representation.

To defend Adorno against this accusation, we would have to accept his claim that in a truthful work of art autonomy and social critique are not contradictory but are simply two necessary moments in aesthetic success. No artwork can be responsive to the social world and critical of its imperfection if it simply bends to the world's authority. Once again we can discern Adorno's ongoing dispute with Benjamin: On the one hand, an artwork that surrenders its autonomous character does not become a paradigm of aesthetic engagement; it becomes simply one commodity among others. On the other hand, although an artwork cannot fully consummate its separation from its social surroundings, neither can it completely annul that separation in the interests of political "relevance." If art is to play a genuinely critical role in society by revealing its imperfections, it can do so only if it remains poised on the knife's edge between immanence and transcendence, neither of which would be safe on its own from ideology. Critique presupposes "a standpoint removed, even though by hair's breadth, from the scope of existence, whereas we well know that any possible knowledge must not only be first wrested from what is, if it shall hold good, but is also marked, for this very reason, by the same distortion and indigence which it seeks to escape."[63] Adorno's concept of the artwork is the very embodiment of this critical possibility.

Adorno recognized that the very category of autonomous art was plagued with controversy, and he was hardly sanguine as to whether art itself would endure over the long term. In *Aesthetic Theory*, he writes that it is "thinkable, and not merely an abstract possibility, that great music . . . was possible only during a limited phase of humanity."[64] For Adorno the historical emergence of autonomous art was conditional on the social ascent of the bourgeoisie and its institutional and ideological emancipation from feudal authority. Art became a real possibility only at a rather late date in modern history with the unbinding of aesthetic experience from its sacral origins. But if autonomous art appeared in concert with social rationalization, then the very processes that first made it possible also threatened its survival; the birth of art was also the beginning of its death. Here we are confronted with a phenomenon that we might call *a dialectic of aesthetic secularization*. With the gradual reification of consciousness by the culture industry Adorno warned of "the withering of experience [*die verdorrte Erfahrung*]" in general, and he feared that "art may have entered the age of its decline [*Zeitalter ihres Untergangs*]."[65] For Adorno, we might say, autonomous art was evanescent but essential. Without the promise that still beckoned from aesthetic experience, he could sustain little hope for the redemption of humanity.

6

Aesthetic Experience

In the preceding chapter I argued that Adorno conceived of the artwork as an embodiment of the unresolved dialectic between freedom and unfreedom. Much like the human subject, an artwork is fully realized only insofar as it holds itself open and responsive to the world from which it is born. Earlier in this book I suggested that this posture of responsiveness is the very precondition for morality. It follows that an artwork is only successful or "true" if it sustains this moral stance. It was Adorno's great anxiety that in an era of increasing commodification successful art in this distinctively normative sense was on the verge of disappearing. He feared that once it had vanished humankind would have lost an invaluable resource, because art is a rare if embattled preserve that contains *both* a transcription of our suffering *and* a promise of our happiness.

To pursue this argument in further depth, we must look not just at the philosophical claims *about* art that Adorno explores in his aesthetic theory but also at the substantive exercises in aesthetic analysis, especially musicological analysis, that occupy such a large share of his oeuvre. After all, if we truly wish to appreciate what may still be of value in his reflections on art, we must understand not only his contribution to aesthetic philosophy; we also need to appreciate his insights into the *experiential* dimension of specific artworks themselves. Indeed, it is a key principle in Adorno's philosophy that theory must always remain in an intimate if dialectical proximity to the object it seeks to understand. In the draft introduction to *Aesthetic Theory* Adorno writes that aesthetics can be productive only if it combines critical "distance from the empirical" with a "closeness bordering on embodiment [*leibhaft*]."[1] It must be possible to judge the artwork both from the outside and "from within" so as to seize upon what he calls its "experiential force [*andrängenden Erfahrung*]."[2] In this chapter I wish to honor this claim. What is of paramount significance in art must eventually admit of discursive analysis, but it first becomes available to us in the sensuous particularity of aesthetic experience itself. This emphasis on aesthetic *experience* over aesthetic *theory* accords with Adorno's principled commitment to the priority of the object as such. It is a further expression of his basic view as a materialist that our concepts refer to a moment of non-identity that will always exceed the grasp of mere conceptuality. If art enjoys a distinctive prestige for Adorno, this is because he sees it as a preserve for the nonconceptual and mimetic element in human experience that elsewhere in society is verging on extinction.

This may help explain why the very notion of an aesthetic *theory* for Adorno is riddled with ambivalence. On the one hand, he is not embarrassed to state with apodictic certitude that "the truth content of an artwork requires philosophy."[3] No artwork in his view remains self-identical or purely what it is as if it were a timeless truth. Artworks become what they are because they "summon forth forms of spirit" through the process of "commentary and critique."[4] On the other hand, he also claims that aesthetic theory cannot succeed if it remains external to aesthetic experience, as if it were an array of disembodied claims lacking intrinsic connection to the objects it seeks to interpret. "So long as the work is not entered," Adorno writes (with reference to Goethe), "as a chapel would be entered, all the talk about objectivity in matters of aesthetics . . . remains pure assertion."[5] Any genuine theory of aesthetics that does not collapse back into sterile theoreticism must therefore emerge from the labor of immanent criticism and from an actual encounter with the art object in all its sensuous particularity.

The reflections above now leave us better equipped to understand the normative significance that Adorno ascribes to aesthetic experience. In what follows, I explore four such examples of aesthetic experience. I shall focus on musical experience in particular, not simply because music is the aesthetic medium with which I am most familiar, but, more importantly, because it is the medium that obviously lies at the center of Adorno's own thinking. Indeed, without risk of exaggeration it could well be said that for Adorno music enjoyed a paradigmatic status among all the arts. The explanation for this is partly biographical. From earliest childhood on he seems to have found in music the singular promise of fulfillment or happiness that he characterized as "metaphysical experience." In *Minima Moralia* he recalls the "Cradle Song" by Brahms that he associates with the curtain around his childhood bed that protected him from light and enabled him to sleep "in an unending peace without fear."[6] Such memories surely nourished in him not only a personal love for music but also a principled conviction that the formal and experiential qualities of music could serve as a model for philosophy itself. Early in his life Adorno was confronted with the demand that he make a painful choice between careers. In a 1926 letter, his instructor in composition, Alban Berg, sought to assure his student of his musical talent but also warned him that he could not pursue both music and philosophy. "I have become absolutely convinced," Berg wrote, "that you are qualified to achieve the *highest* by way of profound insight into music . . . and will do so through major philosophical works. Whether in the process your musical works (I mean your compositions), upon which I have set such high hopes, are neglected, is a fear I always have when I think of you. . . . [Y]ou will one day have to choose: Kant *or* Beethoven."[7] Although Adorno held Berg in the highest esteem, he refused to accept that any such choice was necessary. More than twenty years later, in a 1948 letter to Thomas Mann, he offered a belated rejoinder to his teacher: "I studied philosophy and music. Instead of deciding exclusively for one subject or the other, I have always had the feeling that my real vocation was to pursue *one and the same thing in both of these different realms*."[8] In what follows, I want to take this claim seriously by considering the "lessons" for philosophy that Adorno believes might be derived from the experiential texture of music itself. I will limit my discussion to four musical examples, two of which are by Beethoven.

Preliminary Comment on Late Style

Before I proceed to the musical illustrations, it is worth pausing for a moment to consider the special and even privileged place that Beethoven's music occupies in Adorno's aesthetic philosophy.[9] It is well known that Adorno ranked Beethoven's compositions among the greatest artifacts of bourgeois culture. This is readily apparent in the notes and fragments that Adorno left behind for his never-finished study of Beethoven.[10] Written as early as 1938 and extending all the way to 1966, these notes demonstrate that Beethoven's music remained a constant preoccupation for Adorno throughout his career. He was drawn to it not simply as a matter of personal taste, but, more importantly, because he came to believe that it exemplified certain nondiscursive or experiential qualities that made it a suitable analogue to his own philosophy. This was primarily the case of those works that Beethoven had composed during the final decade of his life (roughly, from 1815 to 1837) that exemplified what Adorno called "late style." The first two musical illustrations that I wish to explore below are both instances of late style.

As a preliminary matter, it may prove helpful to revisit the basic contrast between the works of the so-called middle period and those of the composer's later years. Inspired by the famous name that was given to the Third

Symphony in E-flat Major ("the Eroica"), musicologists such as Scott Burn-ham have characterized the works of the middle period as "heroic," though we might just as easily call this style "Promethean."[11] In Greek myth Prometheus defies the gods and enhances the power of humanity by giving the gift of fire. His name seems especially apt when we recall that Beethoven borrowed the main theme of the finale to his 1801 ballet, "The Creatures of Prometheus" (Op. 43), for both the fourth movement of the Third Symphony and for the "Eroica Variations" for piano (Op. 35).[12] The most distinctive feature of the heroic style (and one that is immediately apparent to nearly any listener, even those who have little musical training) is the impression that the music is an embodiment of willful subjectivity. The thematic material is typically bold or self-assured, and as it undergoes elaboration and development the musical subject assumes anthropomorphic qualities to become the chief protagonist in a heroic drama of struggle and self-realization.

For Adorno, the heroic style demonstrates the strong affinity between the works of Beethoven's middle period and the philosophy of Hegel: they both exemplify a logic of dialectical mediation that moves through division and struggle to fulfillment. In the unpublished 1939 text, "Towards a Theory of Beethoven," Adorno writes of the "special relationship between the systems of Beethoven and Hegel," which is evident in the fact that the composer, like the philosopher, seeks to confirm "the unity of the whole." The Beethovenian form, Adorno observes, "is an integral whole, in which each individual mo-ment is determined by its function within the whole only to the extent that these individual moments contradict and cancel each other, yet are preserved on a higher level within the whole."[13] Adorno makes explicit the analogy be-tween the musical material and the individual subject who at first confronts the social world as an obstruction but ultimately succeeds in manifesting its agency in all of its surroundings. "Only the whole provides their identity; as individual elements they are antithetical to each other *as is the individual to the society confronting him.*"[14] In the *Phenomenology of Spirit* Hegel states that "the true is the whole [*Das wahre ist das Ganze*]." The Promethean works of Beethoven's middle period exemplify this very same logic of dialectical ful-fillment insofar as the musical subject is analogous to the Hegelian spirit that passes through difficulty to reconciliation. "Beethoven's music," Adorno con-cludes, is "a means for putting to the test the idea that the whole is the truth."[15]

In the works of the late style this Hegelian idea is exposed as a failure. "Beethoven's music is Hegelian philosophy," Adorno writes, "but at the same time it is *truer than that philosophy.*"[16] Not only does Beethoven reject the aesthetic of self-assertion and fulfillment; he turns against the principle of totality itself. "The key to the very late Beethoven lies in the fact that *in this music the idea of totality as something already achieved had become unbearable*."[17] Although Adorno never explains what individual factors may have been responsible for the composer's shift in style, he clearly believes that the transformation has a supra-personal significance insofar as it correlates with broader historical changes both in philosophy and in social consciousness. The heroic style was premised on a largely fictive identity between the bourgeois subject and the objective world, even if in the early phase of capitalist expansion it was natural for the bourgeoisie to believe in its power to create the world after its own image. In the late style, however, this will to mastery is exposed as an illusion, and the subject is confronted with the limits of its power. Subject and object are broken apart, and the result is a style not of unity but of fragmentation: "The late Beethoven's demand for truth rejects the illusion of that identity of subjective and objective, which is almost the same thing as the classicist idea. A polarization results. Unity is transcended, yielding fragmentariness [*Einheit transcendiert zum Fragmentarischen*]."[18]

Adorno offers a fullest characterization of this idea in the well-known 1937 essay, "Beethoven's Late-Style." The works of the composer's later years are not documents of personal hardship or decline. Rather, they testify to the powerlessness of the human subject as such:

> The force of subjectivity in late works is the irascible gesture with which it leaves them. It bursts them asunder, not in order to express itself but, expressionlessly, to cast off the illusion of art. Of the works it leaves only fragments behind, communicating itself, as if in ciphers, only through the spaces it has violently vacated. Touched by death, the masterly hand sets free the matter it previously formed. The fissures and rifts [*Risse und Sprünge*] within it, bearing witness to the ego's finite impotence before what exists [*Zeugnis der endlichen Ohnmacht des Ichs vorm Seienden*], are its last work.[19]

The above passage can serve as our point of departure as we seek to understand how Adorno derives philosophical lessons from musical experience. It should not escape our attention that in his characterization of Beethoven's late style Adorno introduces themes that also appear in his own philosophy. The works of Beethoven's late style are no longer harmonious but riven by "tears and fissures [*Risse und Sprünge*]" that are left behind by an artist who no longer strives for total mastery of his material.[20] This metaphorical language anticipates the famous conclusion to *Minima Moralia* where we are told that philosophy too must adopt a perspective on the world that will reveal its "rifts and crevices [*Risse und Schründe*]."[21] In such remarks we can see Adorno groping toward the critique of idealist totalization that would come to fruition in *Negative Dialectics*. Beethoven's late style thereby becomes something more than an aesthetic preference; it becomes a methodological model for what philosophy itself should be. In a fragment from 1953, Adorno compresses this lesson into a bold aphorism: "One can no longer compose like Beethoven, but one must *think* as he composed."[22]

First Musical Example: Beethoven, Symphony no. 9 in D Minor (Op. 125)

Let us now consider the first musical example, Beethoven's Symphony no. 9 in D Minor (Op. 125); specifically, the concluding portion in the first movement (*Allegro ma non troppo, un poco maestoso*) when the thematic subject makes its reprise. The passage in question begins a little beyond the halfway point of the movement at bar 301. As the tympani begin to roll, the strings return to the opening theme, a spare statement of a falling fifth from the dominant to the tonic, which is then followed by a falling fourth from the tonic to the lower dominant, which then descends one final time to the tonic an octave below. In musical grammar this ranks as one of the simplest statements possible: it is little more than a blocklike descent that lacks melodic shape and recalls the tentative phrases by the violins with which the movement began. But in the reprise the phrases are now played *fortissimo*; backed by the thunderous tympani, they sound far more decisive or even harsh.[23] Meanwhile, the key has shifted, from D minor to D major, with the major third (F-sharp) now heard in the bass, a highly unstable first inversion. Although it has been said that the entire symphony consists in a tonal "quest for D major," this early shift brings little consolation or tonal definition.[24] On the contrary, the effect is so devastating that the listener may feel thrown off balance. The sense of harmonic disorientation only grows more intense as the musical subject leaves its tonal home, and the intrusion of a diminished fifth opens the way toward the recapitulation.

In *Aesthetic Theory* Adorno interprets this passage as a paradigmatic moment in which the subject undergoes the experience of "being shaken [*Erschütterung*]." The auditor "loses the ground beneath his feet" and "the possibility of truth, embodied in the aesthetic image, becomes tangible."[25] More significant still, Adorno describes it as a moment that cannot be contained within the categorial structures of merely subjective experience (*Erlebnis*). Rather, it is "the moment in which the recipient forgets himself and disappears into the work." The feeling of being shaken is therefore less an individual experience than it is a mimetic response to the immediacy of the musical event: "The experience of art as its truth or untruth is more than subjective

EXAMPLE 1. Ludwig van Beethoven, Symphony no. 9 in D Minor, Op. 125. Arranged for piano by Percy Goetschius. Analytic Symphony Series. (Oliver Ditson: Bryn Mawr, PA, 1937). Mvt. 1, Allegro ma non troppo, un poco maestoso, mm. 301–32.

experience: it is the breakthrough of objectivity in subjective consciousness [*Durchbruch von Objektivität im subjektiven Bewußtsein*]." Adorno interprets this breakthrough as signifying both the liquidation of the subject and the primacy of the object, but he hastens to add that the subject can experience this primacy only if it avoids all regression and remains in a state of concentration:

> Being-shaken [*Erschütterung*], radically opposed to the conventional idea of experience [*Erlebnis*], provides no particular satisfaction for the I; it bears no similarity to desire. Rather, it is a memento of the liquidation of the I, which, shaken, perceives its own limitedness and finitude. This experience [*Erfahrung*] is contrary to the weakening of the I that the culture industry manipulates. . . . To catch even the slightest glimpse beyond the prison [*Gefängnis*] that it itself is, the I requires not distraction [*Zerstreuung*] but rather the utmost tension; that preserves the shudder, an involuntary comportment [*Verhalten*], incidentally, from becoming regression.[26]

With this interpretation Adorno seeks to capture through quasi-phenomenological description what he means by the priority of the object. The musical experience of *Erschütterung* (which might be better translated as "shattering" or even "devastation") tests the integrity of the subject nearly to the point of annihilation and thereby serves as "a memento of the liquidation of the I" who becomes aware of its own "limitedness and finitude."[27] It is crucial here to note that Adorno interprets this experience not as a trauma but as *a promise of emancipation*. "For a few moments, the I becomes aware, in real terms, of the possibility of letting self-preservation fall away," though of course this event is confined to the realm of aesthetic semblance and the self "does not actually succeed in realizing this possibility."[28] In the recapitulation, the I catches a glimpse beyond the "prison" of the well-armored self. For Adorno, this is a vision of freedom as it was promised even in the earlier, "heroic" works such as *Fidelio*, where it appeared only as a dim light within the prison's walls. In Beethoven's late style, this promise becomes an experiential revelation: the subject is confronted with its own limits.[29]

At this point it may be worth noting that Adorno's interpretation stands in stark contrast to the feminist interpretation of the Ninth Symphony by the musicologist Susan McClary, who described the very same moment in the recapitulation as "one of the most horrifyingly violent episodes in the history of music." For McClary, this passage thematizes not the finitude of the self but instead the identification of pleasure with "thrusting desire" and "murderous rage."[30] Among musicologists, this controversial interpretation has gained much notoriety and has inspired a great deal of intriguing commentary that

I cannot begin to summarize here.[31] I would only note that McClary's in-terpretation seems to presuppose an identity between the musical material and a personal (ostensibly male) agent, whose actions are transcribed expres-sively into the texture of the music itself.[32] But Adorno calls into question this identity: he sees it as a symptom of the subject's unwarranted confidence in its own world-shaping power. Because he assigns primacy not to the subject but the object, he is more attuned to the possibility that the listening subject would feel shaken rather than confirmed by its disorienting encounter with the musical material. If we were to pursue this interpretation a step further, we might arrive at the feminist conclusion (pace McClary) that the music does not enhance but actually *undermines* the subject's presumably male authority. Adorno makes this conclusion explicit when he observes that in the reprise the subject comes to recognize not its power but its limitation. In Beethoven's music he hears an aesthetic refutation of all claims to subject-object identity. "The Ninth Symphony," he concludes, "puts less faith in identity than does Hegel's philosophy."[33] Where identity is shattered, the non-identical shines through: within the prison of the modern subject we catch a glimpse of a hap-piness without domination.

Second Musical Example: Beethoven, String Quartet no. 13 in B-flat Major (Op. 130)

In a 1966 address on Norddeutscher Rundfunk, Adorno returned to the ques-tion of "late style" with a commentary on the String Quartet no. 13 in B-flat Major (Op. 130). He concluded with remarks on the fifth movement, the Ca-vatina, a lilting slow movement in E-flat major that comes with the directive, *adagio molto espressivo*. The written text from the 1966 radio address informs us that Adorno ended his remarks with a brief recording of an excerpt from the Cavatina (bars 23 to 30). Before I explore these remarks, it may be relevant to note that Beethoven himself ranked the Cavatina among his personal favorites. To Karl Holz, the second violinist in the Schuppanzigh Quartet, he confessed that the Cavatina "was composed in the very tears of misery, and that never had one of his own pieces moved him so deeply."[34] To be sure, not all audi-tors have responded to the movement so favorably. Stravinsky, for example, summarily dismissed the Cavatina as "pedestrian" (a term he also applied to many of the late quartets).[35] More typical, however, is the opinion mentioned by Joseph Kerman, who quotes an unnamed source who said of the Cavatina that its emotions "are so intimate that it hardly seems right to be allowed to witness them."[36] The impression that the music testifies to inaccessibly private feeling may strike us as ironic since the Cavatina would gain not only public, but potentially cosmic fame when, in 1977, it was sent into space on the two Voyager spacecrafts as the very last musical selection on the "Golden Record."[37]

Adorno naturally knew nothing of this later history. In his own remarks on the Cavatina, he is chiefly concerned to challenge the view that it is a transcript of private emotion. Rather, he interprets it as the highest specimen of late style insofar as it registers the *weakening* of subjectivity and thereby participates in "the process of musical demythologization."[38] Beethoven's works in the heroic style still honored the incontestable authority of the principle of harmony, by which Adorno means "harmony in the sense of aesthetic harmony, or balance, roundedness." Harmony had once signified the "identity of the composing subject with his language." In the late works, however, this identity is exposed as a myth. Late works such as Opus 130 represent not the pinnacle of subjective expression but rather the unraveling of the subject's power. "The dying hand," Adorno writes, ". . . releases what it had previously clutched fast, shaped, controlled, so that what is released becomes its higher truth." The Cavatina thereby exemplifies "the abandonment of the illusion of harmony." In the final moments of the radio address, Adorno hastens to explain that this attenuation of the subject should not be construed in a merely negative sense as a loss of power or as renunciation. Rather, we should understand it as "an expression of *hope*."[39]

It would be mistaken to believe that any work of music could hold out to us an unqualified promise of hope. Ever since Hesiod related the ambivalent story of hope (ἐλπίς) as the last evil that was not released from Pandora's jar, hope has remained a concept riven with contradiction.[40] Either it is something preserved for humanity to buttress our faith in the future or it is a danger that is kept from humanity for our own protection. In the Cavatina this uncertainty becomes thematic. At bar 42, when the tonality undergoes an abrupt shift to a very remote key, Beethoven adds the performance instruction, "Beklemmt" (oppressed, or stifled).[41] For a few brief moments the accompaniment is reduced to a simple pulse while the first violin that once carried the movement's main melody seems unable to sing: it is reduced to a series of tentative, faltering gestures that seem to have lost their rhythmic footing. Among the sketches for his Beethoven book, Adorno remarks on this moment of oppression in the Cavatina: he characterizes it as a "shadow," or as the sound of a voice that "hardly dares to stir" and "holds its breath."[42] Few other moments in Beethoven's music better illustrate the aesthetic of vulnerability that Adorno endorses as a model for human experience. The voice of the violin is the voice of the human being who knows it must carry on but feels no assurance of closure. If it can still hope at all, it is only the "stifled hope [*beklemmte Hoffnung*]" of a subject who feels itself oppressed or caught

EXAMPLE 2. Ludwig van Beethoven, String Quartet no. 13, Op. 130. Mvt. 5, Cavatina, mm. 42–50.

in the shadows of overwhelming social powers and who recognizes that the prospect for happiness has grown ever more unlikely.[43] It is the sound of a happiness disfigured by its prohibition.

Before we leave the musical world of Beethoven and move on to the third example, I wish to emphasize the point that Adorno does not reserve the term "late style" only for Beethoven's final compositions. The characteristic features of late style were elevated into criteria with a general validity across differences of history. This may strike us as counterintuitive, since we commonly think of Adorno as a historicist not only in his social philosophy but also in his aesthetics. If for Hegel "philosophy is its own age comprehended in thought," we are naturally tempted to say that for Adorno too a great work of art would also be "its own age" as embodied in the particularity of its sensuous material. Much to our surprise, however, Adorno rejects this historicist principle as a criterion of aesthetic success. Late style becomes not one style among many but rather a *style that resists style*. This is because for Adorno the moment of hope in a work of art is the moment that permits us a glimpse beyond domination.

In *Dialectic of Enlightenment* we are told, "The great artists were never those whose works embodied style in its least fractured." This was true already in the "classical" style of Mozart whose works "contain objective tendencies which resist the style they incarnate." And it remained the case "up to Schönberg and Picasso," since "great artists have been mistrustful of style."[44] If I understand him correctly here, Adorno means to say that the very notion of "style" implies a kind of schematism that imposes not only intelligibility, but unity and regularity on the experiential manifold. But such regularity corresponds to social conformity, since it would mean that nothing could show itself within the bounds of our experience that did not affirm the eternal repetition of the same. If a work of art is to serve as an expression of hope, it must therefore transgress this mythic repetition and rescind from the rules that are embodied both in the artwork and in society. This is why "late style" becomes for Adorno a generalized category of aesthetic appraisal even if the specific modalities of aesthetic transgression change over time. Even the works of Richard Wagner, whose aesthetic style of mythic heroism and self-assertion Adorno criticizes at length in his 1964 monograph, are interpreted by Adorno as containing within themselves a dialectical moment of protest against their own values: not Siegfried but Mime becomes the *antihero* of Wagner's *Ring* cycle: in his very weakness he embodies the critique of domination. The implicit protest against muscular heroism comes to the fore especially in Wagner's late work. Especially in *Parsifal*, Adorno detects a style that falls into the orbit of decadence and portrays its key protagonist not as powerful but as suffering a mortal wound.[45] In the pages of *Aesthetic Theory* (a study that is more typically seen as confining its discussion to high modernism) the historical scope of analysis extends far wider than is often acknowledged, and Adorno does not hesitate to speak of late style as a characteristic that is shared by much earlier artists such as Michelangelo and Rembrandt.[46] Those who wish to read Adorno only as a theorist of modernism often neglect to note that "late style" is not merely the name for what he calls "an alleged historical temperament." Rather, he declares that it has "exemplary force" that extends "far beyond any individual oeuvre."[47] This point should be kept in mind as we leave the world of Beethoven and turn our attention to later specimens of musical modernism.

Third Musical Example: Gustav Mahler, Symphony no. 3 in D Minor

Among all of Adorno's musicological monographs, it is perhaps the 1960 study of Mahler that confirms late style as the only aesthetic suitable to the modern age. It may be relevant to note that at the time of the book's initial publication, the unfinished Tenth Symphony had still not seen its 1964 London world premiere in the well-known version by Deryck Cooke. In the preface to his book's second edition in 1963, Adorno feels he must explain why he has omitted any discussion of the Tenth, even though he explicitly identifies it as a definitive specimen of Mahler's "late style." While it is customary to divide the composer's works into three periods, it would not be implausible to apply the term more liberally to all of the mature works, at least after the so-called first period that ends with *Des Knaben Wunderhorn* in 1901. Much like the music of the later Beethoven, Mahler's later compositions abandon the will to completion. Their "experiential core" is "brokenness [*Gebrochenheit*]."[48] Ironically, then, the excluded Tenth Symphony would have been the culminating illustration of Adorno's argument.

The Mahler book bears an intriguing subtitle: *A Musical Physiognomy*. The intent, however, is to move not inward but outward: Adorno does not wish to infer the composer's inner psychology from the outer form of his works. Rather, he means to discover in the specific form of Mahler's music the general contours of modern society. *His book is a physiognomy of modernity by means of its music.* Adorno calls upon all of his formidable literary skills for the sake of a musical description that is also *more than* musical. In fact, it is nothing less than a portrait of Adorno's own critical method. Not unlike Adorno himself, Mahler the outsider is able to discern in his broken surroundings small fragments of compromised beauty. "Free as only one can be who has not himself been entirely swallowed by culture, in his musical vagrancy he picks up the broken glass by the roadside and holds it up to the sun so that all the colors are refracted."[49] In this remarkable passage Mahler's compositional method becomes an analogue to Adorno's manner of social criticism: the smallest fragments of non-identity are gathered together to reveal not only darkness but also small glimpses of light.

For Adorno, what signifies fulfillment in Mahler's music lies not in the rare gesture of total closure (as in the grandiose choral finale to the Second

Symphony, with its literal promise of "resurrection") but rather in the more characteristic emphasis on exclusion and fragmentation. By allying itself with those who are dispatched to the margins of society, the music announces a protest against domination and exclusion.[50] Thematic materials such as Ländler, or folk tunes, and even bits of Eastern European Jewish klezmer are all gathered up as a "shabby residue" that "accuses the triumphant."[51] But Adorno does not interpret this aesthetic as merely negative. If the composer turns his attention to the fragment, this is because he finds in it a hope that is stronger than the whole from which it has been expelled. *"In the debased and vilified materials of music he scratches for forbidden happiness [Im erniedrigten und beleidigten Musikstoff schürft er nach unerlaubtem Glück]."*[52]

Perhaps nowhere else in Mahler's music does the promise of an unfulfilled happiness become more pronounced than in the Third Symphony. Adorno takes special interest in the passage from the trio in the scherzo (the third movement) when the posthorn makes its "scandalously audacious" entrance and then, the second time, is joined by the violins. Mahler's score gives them the direction, "wie nachhorchend" (as if listening), which suggests to Adorno that they will not turn their backs on the posthorn's suffering even if the solo bears a resemblance to kitsch.[53] Their music "incorporates the fractures without which the whole world would disintegrate *[So wird noch das Brüchige eingebaut, ohne daß das Ganze zerbräche]."* The violins thereby move beyond mere negation; they *"affirm the possible, the promise, without which not a second's breath could be drawn [bejahen sie die Möglichkeit, das Versprechen, ohne das keine Sekunde sich atmen ließe]."*[54] This interpretation is illustrative of the homology between musical and social form. The violins express the persistence of human breath and the demand for emancipation; but what they promise is no more certain than the *stifled* (*beklemmt*) breath of the violin from Beethoven's Cavatina.

Adorno is especially drawn to Mahler's Third Symphony because he hears it as the repository of embattled nature. It is well known that the composer conferred overtly programmatic titles on each of its movements. The second movement carries the name, "What the Flowers in the Meadow Tell Me," and the third movement has the name, "What the Animals of the Forest Tell Me."[55] The prominence of this creaturely symbolism bespeaks both a longing for a return to nature and the melancholy awareness that the way back to paradise is blocked. "Through animals humanity becomes aware of itself as impeded nature."[56] Mahler constantly expresses the yearning for a breakthrough from the closed course of the world even while he acknowledges that this breakthrough has been thwarted. Once again, however, we should not interpret the effect as merely negative. In *Aesthetic Theory* Adorno tells

EXAMPLE 3. Gustav Mahler, Symphony no. 3 in D Minor. Mvt. 3, Comodo (Scherzando), mm. 490–504.

us that the artwork, though purely θέσει (human artifice), is nonetheless the representative of φύσει (nature). It stands for that which is not merely for the subject, or, in Kantian terms, for what would be the thing-in-itself.[57] In his Mahler book Adorno anticipates this same conclusion. Culture both withdraws from nature and seeks to rescue that which in nature has been silenced. Mahler's music thereby becomes mimetic. It wishes to comport itself "like animals," and it thereby "confers utterance on the speechless by imitating their ways in sound."[58] As in Kafka's fables, in Mahler's music "the animal realm is the human world as it would appear from the standpoint of redemption [*Standpunkt der Erlösung*]."[59]

By aligning itself with the nature that civilization has repressed, Mahler's music helps sustain our own attenuated capacity for mimesis. It thereby helps preserve our responsiveness to human suffering: "The artwork, chained to culture, seeks to burst the chain and show compassion for the derelict residue."[60] Himself an outcast, Mahler records in his music the pains of all those who have been outcast, "the lost outpost," and those who have "fallen from the ranks." However, those who are "wholly unfree" do not remain mere ciphers of their own unhappiness; rather, they also "*embody freedom*."[61] Such considerations lend further support for the claim that Adorno hears Mahler's music not merely as a song of lamentation but also as an expression of hope. Much like Beethoven does in the Cavatina from Opus 130, Mahler inscribes this hope into his music negatively as "fractures [*Brüche*]" that bear witness to human suffering even while he refuses to succumb to total despair. The fractures in the music are like legible signs that point beyond the current world and anticipate its transformation. They are "the script of truth [*die Schrift von Wahrheit*]."[62]

Just three years after the appearance of his book on Mahler (second edition, 1963), Adorno published his *Negative Dialectics*. Although the two works could hardly be more dissimilar in form, their manifold thematic affinities are so pronounced that one is tempted to say that Mahler's music became for Adorno an aesthetic template for his philosophy. Key insights from the earlier book reappear nearly verbatim in the later one. Especially relevant are the remarks on happiness, a theme to which Adorno assigns great importance as the standard of human flourishing. In the Mahler book, we read that "the music of the mature Mahler *knows happiness only as something revocable* [*kennt Glück nur noch als widerrufliches*]"[63] In *Negative Dialectics* we reencounter the very same lesson. "All happiness," Adorno writes, "is distorted by its revocability [*alles Glück durch seine Widerruflichkeit entstellt ist*]."[64] In the scherzo to the Third Symphony, Adorno hears in the violins a "promise [*Versprechen*]" that the discarded fragment will at last find its recognition. This

musical promise is later recapitulated as the defining principle of Adorno's
own philosophy:

> As untenable as the traces of the Other are in it; as much as *all happiness is*
> *distorted by its revocability* [*Widerruflichkeit*], the existent is nevertheless shot
> through, in the gaps that stamp identity as a lie, with the promises, constantly
> broken, of that Other. Every happiness is a fragment of the total happiness,
> which human beings are denied and which they deny themselves. [*Jegliches*
> *Glück ist Fragment des ganzen Glücks, das den Menschen sich versagt und das*
> *sie sich versagen*].[65]

Fourth Musical Example: The Second Viennese School
(Kranichstein Lecture, 1957)

Adorno observed that the "painful element" that became so pronounced especially in Mahler's later works was already an anticipation of the avant-garde.
Mahler's "tonal, predominantly consonant music" points forward to "the climate of absolute dissonance, the blackness of the new Music."[66] Adorno was
not alone in recognizing the strong stream of inspiration that flows from the
later works of Mahler into the "emancipated" dissonances that characterized
the works of the so-called Second Viennese School. In music history this affinity is common knowledge.[67] Although Mahler himself never made the decisive leap into atonality, he nonetheless expressed great admiration for the
younger Arnold Schoenberg, despite their enormous differences in musical
and personal temperament. Mahler even mentored Schoenberg in composition, and Schoenberg in turn revered Mahler as a "saint."[68]

Adorno's esteem for the achievements of Schoenberg and his circle is
thoroughly documented and requires little emphasis here.[69] Especially after his years of musical apprenticeship with Alban Berg, Adorno became a
kind of impresario for the entire circle, and in the 1949 *Philosophie der neuen*
Musik Adorno presented himself as the champion of the Schoenbergian
aesthetic, which he compared favorably (if rather too polemically) to the
"archaism" and "regression" he found in the music of Stravinsky.[70] Adorno,
however, also harbored serious reservations regarding what he considered
the "mechanical" application of the twelve-tone method of composition in
Schoenberg's later work. He feared that with all its manifold constraints the
twelve-tone method risked becoming an unreflective technique that would
petrify into "an objective image of repressive society."[71] He warned that
Schoenberg's legacy would only survive if its method served as a support for
"free composition."[72]

The lines of inspiration, both aesthetic and philosophical, that connect Adorno to the Second Viennese School are so numerous it may seem misleading to isolate a single work for extended analysis.[73] Berg's Chamber Concerto for Piano and Violin with 13 Wind Instruments (completed in 1925) is a powerful example, not least because in the first movement the composer introduces a theme that pays homage to his two colleagues by spelling out their names in German notation: Schoenberg, Webern, Berg. Among the more dramatic moments is the first variation, played by the solo piano.

Rather than fasten my attention here on only one composition, however, for the fourth example I wish instead to draw together the various themes of the preceding discussion by examining a rather more comprehensive statement. At the 1957 meeting of the annual Ferienkurse in Darmstadt, Adorno delivered the Kranichstein lecture, "Criteria of New Music," which formed the basis for the eponymous essay that was published in *Klangfiguren* two years later. Adorno ascribed such importance to this lecture that he explicitly recommended it to students in his lectures on aesthetics as a paradigm for his own philosophical method.[74] The 1957 lecture is especially instructive insofar as it offers a corrective to the superficial and erroneous impression that "advanced music has no other truth than that it is as full of atrocities as the world in which it is written."[75] From this impression its opponents can easily draw the verdict that there is no need for the new music at all since it merely duplicates the world with all its manifold horrors.

In the Kranichstein lecture, Adorno seeks to defend the new music against this claim. Adorno begins by recalling the traditional criteria of aesthetic judgment as they were canonized by Kant in the third *Critique*. In his well-known remarks on the dynamical sublime, Kant had detailed the feelings that are aroused in us when we are confronted with the overpowering events of nature. These events include "bold, overhanging, and, as it were, threatening rocks, thunderclouds piled up to the vault of heaven, borne along with flashes and peals, volcanoes in all their violence of destruction, hurricanes leaving desolation in their track, the boundless ocean rising with rebellious force, the high waterfall of some mighty river [and so forth]."[76] According to Kant, such experiences leave us with the impression that our own powers of resistance may be no match for the forces of nature. But Kant then adds an important qualification: we find the sight of nature's sublimity attractive only so long as we observe it from a position of relative safety. "We gladly call these objects sublime," Kant writes, "because they elevate the strength of our soul above its usual level, and allow us to discover within ourselves a capacity for resistance of quite another kind, which gives us the courage to measure ourselves

EXAMPLE 4. Alban Berg, Chamber Concerto for Piano and Violin with 13 Wind Instruments. Mvt. 1, I. Thema scherzoso con variazioni, mm. 31–45.

against the apparent all-powerfulness of nature."[77] Confronted with the irresistibility of nature's power, we come to recognize not only our physical powerlessness but also our "capacity for judging ourselves as independent of it." Our experience of the sublime thus awakens in us a feeling of our essential superiority over those incidental factors of our material life (worldly goods, health, and life itself) on which we had imagined ourselves to depend. For Kant the lesson of the sublime is therefore twofold: although the human being must submit (outwardly) to nature's dominion, "the humanity in our person remains undemeaned."[78]

Adorno argues that in the late-modern era this classical interpretation of the sublime now demands serious revision.[79] For Kant it was still plausible to believe that we could discover in sublime experience a validation of the human spirit. Adorno rejects this belief. Now that our experience of the sublime has migrated from nature to society, we are confronted with the fact of a social world that has hardened into a second nature.[80] The natural terror of the Lisbon earthquake was both realized and outstripped by the purely human terror of Auschwitz. But this shift of terrain—from natural to social catastrophe—has also transformed our understanding of the sublime. We must now confront the sublime without any trust in our own security: we have been robbed of "the illusion that some absolute is guaranteed in spirit's standing its ground."[81] The modern experience of terror is no longer the feeling of a human subject that remains fully confident of its distance from what it observes. Terror has become objective.

This transformation has far-reaching implications for Adorno's theory of modern art. To grasp why this would be the case, we should note that Adorno harkens back to the human capacity for mimesis, which he characterizes as a "reflex-like imitation [*reflexhafte Nachahmung*]" of our natural surroundings. It is this mimetic capacity that permits the human spirit to gain some separation from nature without immediately turning nature into an object for domination. This separation can only be partial, however, since the human spirit cannot fully consummate its withdrawal from nature without separating itself from its own natural being. But the separation is nonetheless necessary insofar as "spirit" signifies something that is "other than existing reality [*was anders ist als das Seiende*]."[82] Mimesis, we might say, is the earliest manifestation of our special capacity as human beings to take up a second-order or reflective stance on sensual conditions as they are given. Mimesis is therefore nothing else than our own critical reason but *within* nature: it is a species of rationality that we practiced before reification began to take hold and reason sought to effect a total break from nature. Mimesis, in other words, is nature's capacity to gain some reflective distance upon itself.[83] But in the modern era this capacity verges on collapse. Art therefore stands as a refuge for an embattled mimesis that can still be heard in the new music:

> At the end of the bourgeois epoch spirit recalls the mimesis of prehistoric times, the reflex-like imitation, the futile impulse from which the spirit, the thing that was different from existing reality, once arose. Overwhelmed by the power of things, it took refuge in the rudimentary minimum to which the world of things had forced it to regress. *In the new music, however, this precarious happiness is as fully present as despair* [*Dies prekäre Glück indessen ist in der exponierten neuen Musik so gegenwärtig wie die Verzweiflung*].[84]

This argument is stated with great compression and calls out for a more expansive restatement: as the world of things in its sheer facticity has grown ever more overwhelming and demands our uncritical assent, the human spirit has gone into retreat. It has been compelled to hide itself in the "rudimentary minimum" of an aesthetic experience that still retains at least some traces of the mimetic capacity that is elsewhere marginalized or repressed. Now, it is art perhaps most of all that preserves the memory of suppressed mimesis. Autonomous art is therefore an instance of our own capacity for reflection on nature. Even as it thematizes the modern separation between nature and spirit it also bears witness to their enduring bond. It is this dialectic—the *simultaneous* separation and connection between nature and spirit—that makes modern music an occasion for what Adorno calls a *precarious happiness* (*prekäres Glück*).

In the concluding lines of the Kranichstein lecture, Adorno reminds his readers that even the most dissonant chords can express not only pain (*Schmerz*) but also pleasure (*Lust*). "The manifold sonorities do not just hurt, but rather were, in their cutting brokenness, always at the same time also beautiful."[85] He further recalls that Alban Berg once expressed a yearning "one day to hear a chord consisting of eight different notes on eight brass instruments playing *fortissimo*."[86] Such a desire speaks to the mimetic impulse that survives not only in music but also in rare moments of everyday experience and childhood bliss. Among "the most powerful aesthetic impulses," Adorno writes, is what "a child feels when he leaves a footprint in freshly fallen snow."[87] For Adorno such somatic experiences are not unrelated to our experiences of the musical avant-garde. The composer of the new music does not turn it into a mere seismograph of social horror, because the critique of our present condition must also sustain some grasp of the beauty that lies beyond it. "The threshold that separates the advanced composer from the stifling atmosphere of the so-called intact world is . . . crossed when *he commits himself to this beauty without reservation*."[88] Even the new music is therefore more than a mirror of social catastrophe; it also bears witness to a normative promise of universal happiness whose complete fulfillment lies beyond our current suffering.

Une promesse du bonheur

In this chapter I have explored the various ways in which Adorno looked to aesthetic experience as a resource for philosophical insight. That he ascribed great importance to the question of aesthetics is altogether obvious, as even a brief glance at his teaching schedule will confirm. Between 1950 and 1968, during his final two decades as a professor of philosophy in Frankfurt, he offered a lecture course in aesthetics on no less than six separate occasions. It would be wrong, of course, to infer that was drawn to aesthetics *only* as a resource of philosophical insight or that he was primarily interested in the *lessons* that could be derived from the encounter with autonomous art. This understanding of art would degrade it to little more than a kind of raw material that is intended for human purposes much as coal is mined as a source of energy. In his interpretations of Hölderlin's poetry and Beckett's *Endgame*, Adorno expressed great hostility to the interpretive strategy (associated with Heidegger and others) that art be understood as a mere repository of philosophical "meaning" that can be drawn from its aesthetic context and made available for nonaesthetic needs.[89] All the same, he clearly believed that if autonomous art is to continue to play any role in modern experience, this will be due chiefly to the fact that it holds out to us a promise of happiness or human flourishing that is everywhere threatened with extinction. In the 1958–59 course on aesthetics, he addressed this question with unusual candor. "Works of art are not divine manifestations but the work of humans, and this gives them both their limits and their connection to human matters."[90] If we can ascribe importance to aesthetic experience, this is chiefly due to "the happiness emanating from works of art [*das Glück, das von den Kunstwerken ausgeht*]." Adorno regards such happiness as an indispensable feature of aesthetic experience without which art would have no significant place in our lives. "*[If] indeed [it] no longer has any connection to happiness why should I be compelled to have any dealings with works of art?*"[91]

The claim that art holds out to us a *promesse du bonheur*, a "promise of happiness [*Versprechen des Glücks*]," is a familiar conceit that recurs with some frequency in Adorno's philosophy, though the original dictum as expressed by Stendhal ("la beauté n'est que la promesse du bonheur") appears in a slightly modified form: Stendhal wrote of beauty, not art.[92] Variations on this theme can be found already in the 1938 essay, "On the Fetish-Character in Music," where we are told that "the *promesse du bonheur*, once the definition of art, can no longer be found except where the mark has been torn from the countenance of false happiness."[93] The phrase appears some time later in *Minima Moralia*, and it assumes even greater prominence both in *Negative Dialectics* and in *Aesthetic Theory*, where Adorno cites Stendhal's phrase almost as if it were an authoritative definition. But in this last version Adorno immediately qualifies the statement with a characteristic gesture of negation: "Art is the promise of happiness that is broken [*Kunst ist das Versprechen des Glücks, das gebrochen wird*]."[94] And in the paralimpomena to *Aesthetic Theory* Adorno takes this remark a step further and adds the more paradoxical thought that art must break its promise *precisely so as to remain faithful to it*:

> Stendhal's dictum of art as the *promesse du bonheur* implies that art does its part for existence by accentuating what in it prefigures utopia. But this utopic element is constantly decreasing, while existence increasingly becomes merely self-equivalent. For this reason art is ever less able to make itself like existence. Because all happiness found in the status quo is an ersatz and false, art must break its promise in order to stay true to it [*Weil alles Glück am Bestehenden und in ihm Ersatz und falsch ist, muß sie das Versprechen brechen, um ihm die Treue zu halten*].[95]

Although it would be easy to construe the above claim as a flat-out denial that art offers *any* promise of happiness, if we read it with care we can see that Adorno really means to suggest that the promissory (or "utopian") moment in art is now endangered or is about to disappear, *not* that it has wholly disappeared already. The culture industry seeks to satisfy us by planning for and exploiting "the need for happiness [*das Glücksbedürfnis*]." Here we confront once again the problem of the false exit. Because he is concerned to protect the genuinely promissory element in art against the risk of its sabotage for purposes of ideological adjustment, he insists that art must explicitly thematize its own status as semblance (*Schein*). Art can remain faithful to the genuine promise of happiness only because it does not misrepresent the happiness it proffers as more than illusion. "Art is magic delivered from the lie of being truth."[96]

In this section, I wish to examine the significance of Adorno's claim that art is a "promise of happiness." To pursue this claim further I take my initial cue from the excellent paper by Gordon Finlayson on Adorno's idea of art as a *promesse du bonheur*.[97] Finlayson notes that the concept of a promise should not be understood in the illocutionary sense of a subject who commits itself to fulfilling an obligation. By promise, Adorno has in mind the objective sense, as for example when one observes that "Teddie promises to be a good composer" or "the weather looks promising." This is a crucial distinction not least because it helps defend Adorno against the charge that he has illicitly anthropomorphized art by transforming it into an agent who is capable of making or discharging obligations. The distinction is also helpful, however, because it helps us see how the concept of art's promise remains interlaced with uncertainty. The claim that art holds out to us a *promise* of happiness is significant chiefly because a promise has an intermediary modal status: it is stronger than mere yearning but weaker than a guarantee. To say that something is a promise is hardly the same as saying that the future condition it names is certain to occur. After all, it belongs to the very concept of a promise that it can be broken. When Adorno says that art is a *promise* of happiness, he means that happiness belongs to the experience of art only as an anticipation but with the added force of a normative expectation: it tells us something about what our life is *not yet* but *should* be, though it affords us no absolute confirmation that our life is destined to be that way in the future.

I believe that this is what Adorno has in mind when he suggests that in the new music we are offered an experience that intermingles happiness with despair. To say that the music affords us the promise of a happiness that is *precarious* is just to say that given the damaged condition of our current world all we can hope to discover in the music is an anticipation of happiness that is likewise uncertain. In the preceding section, I showed how Adorno seeks to interpret aesthetic experience, specifically musical experience, as holding out to us an essential insight into our nature as human beings. The general lesson that emerged from the cases described above can be summarized in the claim that our happiness is precarious, or, stated differently, that our flourishing is far from guaranteed. At this point the reader may feel moved to object that Adorno's aesthetic theory is far too austere to permit even this rather modest acknowledgment of a promised happiness to stand uncontested.[98] The general thrust of my argument is that this objection is mistaken. If Adorno is not an "austere negativist" (in Finlayson's phrase), this is because he believes that our experience of art affords us something far more dialectical and conflictual than thoroughgoing negativity. Just as he rejects any harmonistic image of social reality as ideological, so too he insists that an artwork exhibits "manifoldness [*Mannigfaltigkeit*]," or, in other words, that any true work of art is "in itself antagonistic and divided [*antagonistisch und gespalten*]."[99] Nor is this the case exclusively for contemporary art. Adorno speculates that such division may very well be a defining feature of artwork as such. Even when it is merely "latent" we can ascribe this inner antagonism "to *all art overall*."[100]

At this point those who wish to defend the thesis of austere negativism might raise the further objection that in Adorno's writing the theme of happiness seldom receives sustained philosophical attention. To this objection one can respond that even the smallest concession to happiness as a genuine possibility would suffice to prove that the thesis of totalizing negativity cannot be entirely accurate. If Adorno seldom permits himself utopian flights of speculation as to what true happiness would consist in, this is not because he believes it lacks all significance but only because he fears that any attempt to elaborate on its meaning will fall prey to falsification. In an unguarded moment during the 1958–59 lectures on aesthetics he offers the bold and rather uncharacteristic declaration that inherent in the idea of a work of art is the promise of "utopia" or "absolute fulfillment [*die absolute Erfüllung*]."[101] At the same, however, we must protect ourselves against the thought that such fulfillment is wholly available to us "as something already here and now." We can easily succumb to this illusion of present immediacy if we "smooth over the antagonisms and the suffering" that "are to blame for this utopia remaining unfulfilled in reality."[102] In chapter 1, I referred to this as the problem of the "false exit." The culture industry seeks to fulfill our longing for true happiness with false promises that only bind us more decisively to the administered world. As the culture industry becomes ever more powerful, the risk of the false exit only grows more pronounced. For this reason we must resist the facile satisfactions of a happiness that makes no further demands on our social surroundings. In a damaged world any experience of happiness we may find in art must also be damaged and incomplete. But we should not conclude that the experience of happiness is altogether lacking. All artworks are internally divided or they no longer qualify as artworks. An artwork must therefore contain negativity if it is to serve as a truthful embodiment of our untrue world; so it follows that an artwork bears within itself a "*simultaneously critical and utopian intention*."[103] The negative and the utopian remain in a state of tension that cannot be resolved without the artwork collapsing into ideology. Our experience of an artwork is "always something wounding [*ein Verletzendes ist*]," and "where it no longer hurts anyone but rather, blends completely into the closed surface of experience, it essentially ceases to be a living work of art at all."[104]

In the previous chapter, I argued that the distinction between the autonomous artwork and the artwork-as-commodity should be understood in a qualitative sense and not as a distinction between two separable classes of objects. Adorno confirms this point in his claim that even in the autonomous artwork the ideological moment cannot be wholly expelled: "The spirit which speaks from a work of art, once that spirit is truly objectified, is always *both the spirit of society and the spirit of a critique of society* [*immer der Geist der Gesellschaft und zugleich der Geist einer Kritik an der Gesellschaft ist*]."[105] The simultaneity of ideology and its critique is a characteristic of all artwork, and we experience this as the simultaneity of happiness and pain, though we should take care to note that these moments cannot be sharply distinguished, since happiness bespeaks a genuine promise that is irreducible to ideology.

The example of dissonance in music provides us with a helpful illustration of this general principle. In dissonance we discover

> not only this aspect of an expression of negativity, of this suffering, but always at the same time *the happiness of giving nature its voice [sondern immer zugleich auch das Glück, der Natur ihre Stimme zu geben]*, finding something not yet taken, drawing something into the work that . . . has not yet been domesticated, something akin to fresh snow, which thus reminds us of something other than the ever-same machinery of bourgeois society in which we are all trapped. . . . [T]he dissonating aspect is *pain and happiness at once [Schmerz und Glück in eins]*.[106]

Although the experience of dissonance in music is his preferred example, Adorno also claims that the very same simultaneity of negativity *and* happiness can also be in found in literature and in the visual arts. Toward the conclusion of his 1958–59 lectures on aesthetics he offers similar comments on our experience of color in Manet's paintings. These colors "express something threatening, frightening, and evil through the harshness and sharpness of their contrasts, but are simultaneously experienced very directly as stimulating, *as something positive like happiness or exhilaration [ja, als ein Positives, als etwas wie Glück oder wie Rausch erfahren werden]*."[107] Whether we are listening to the music of Alban Berg or captivated by a painting by Manet, we discover what Adorno calls an "interplay [*Ineinanderspielen*]" between "negativity on the one hand and the experience of happiness or utopia on the other [*der Negativität auf der einen Seite und der Erfahrung des Glücks oder der Utopie auf der anderen*]."[108]

It is a frequent theme of Adorno's aesthetic theory that the unresolved tension in art is always in danger of premature resolution. Our experience of an artwork constantly threatens to collapse into either the illusory consolations of ideology or the no less facile comforts of pleasure. But as Adorno never ceases to remind us, this precarity inheres in the very concept of the autonomous artwork itself. The notion that we could discover something that even approximates untroubled beauty in a troubled world is simply not credible, since it presupposes a readiness to forgo the easier satisfactions that lie immediately to hand. "The sublimation which characterizes the realm of beauty is a very precarious one [*eine sehr prekäre ist*]."[109] And in fact this sublimation "never fully succeeds," since the realm of beauty "can pass at any time."[110]

In the 1958–59 lectures Adorno admonishes his auditors with this same idea on several different occasions. He insists that "the establishment of the aesthetic sphere as one lying beyond desire is *always precarious*."[111] He further explains, "You should not take something like the idea that the aesthetic realm is removed from empirical reality as an absolute definition, rather, you must also take it as an aspect that is subject to historical dialectic and is precarious— precarious in the same way I told you in one of the previous sessions that so- called disinterested pleasure is a precarious thing."[112] The frequency with which he returns to this same idea is due to the fact that he understands the emer- gence of the autonomous artwork as merely one moment within the larger dialectic of enlightenment: the artwork is constantly in danger of betraying its true purposes by submitting to the imperatives of instrumental reason. Aesthetic experience is only possible if it distances itself from the realm of merely purposive rationality, but to do so it must draw back from the happi- ness of immediate gratification. Much like Odysseus, who must bind himself in order to experience the Siren's song as mere pleasure without purpose, so too our cultural ideal of aesthetic autonomy exemplifies both happiness and unfreedom at once.[113] It follows that "*the potential for collapse is inherent in the idea of beauty itself*."[114]

The above considerations shed further light on the idea that art is a *prom- ise of happiness*. Notice that the claim that an artwork *promises* happiness is not the same as the claim that an artwork alone can actually *fulfill* what it has promised. This distinction is crucial to Adorno's conception of aesthetic ex- perience as something that occurs only within social conditions that impose sharp limits on experience in general and thereby inhibit us from enjoying anything like pure satisfaction or bliss. Plato, by contrast, seems to believe that the experience of beauty (as he describes it in the *Symposium*) can draw the mind out of its material constraints and ultimately afford us a glimpse of the eternally beautiful itself. But Adorno insists that our transient and mate- rial world is the domain within which we can experience anything like beauty at all; aesthetic experience is never decontextualized but is governed by the material conditions in which it occurs. Only if these material conditions were dramatically transformed could the happiness that art merely promises find its ultimate realization. At the same time, however, Adorno believes that in our encounter with a truly powerful artwork something happens to us that is far more momentous than the experience of receiving a promise. We undergo an actual transformation. As Adorno explains in the paralipomena to his *Aes- thetic Theory*, "The feelings provoked by artworks are real and to this extent extra-aesthetic [*real und insofern außerästhetisch*]."[115] Perhaps nowhere else in Adorno's writings on art does he express a principle that so directly counters the accusation of mere aestheticism. The category of aesthetic experience is altogether too narrow to capture the significance of this transformation. Perhaps ironically, his account of this transformation is not unlike the experience he ascribes to Plato. The encounter with a beautiful artwork would consist in "true aesthetic enthusiasm," or "Platonic ἐνθουσιασμός." In such a state of enthusiasm one might feel moved to exclaim in sheer astonishment, "How beautiful, how beautiful, how beautiful," even while one "dissolved into the intuition of the matter itself."[116]

The comparison to Plato may strike us as surprising, especially if we have grown accustomed to the view that Adorno condemns all experiences of beauty as illusory or inauthentic. We can make better sense of the comparison once we understand why he describes such experiences as "real." Clearly he does not mean that in our encounter with art we feel ourselves somehow magnified or endowed with a more expansive sense of self. The notion of aesthetic experience as spiritual uplift is utterly foreign to his manner of thinking. On the contrary, he claims that art *"eludes any attempt to make it like ourselves and like the subject."*[117] Rather, the encounter with art *calls the subject into question* and affords it an experience of freedom beyond the confinement of its own subjectivity. In the lecture on aesthetics (January 8, 1959) Adorno describes this as a "breakthrough [*Durchbruch*]":

> What I mean by breakthrough is that there are moments . . . in which that feeling of being lifted out, that feeling, if you will, of transcending mere existence, is intensely concentrated and actualizes itself, and in which it seems to us as if the absolutely mediated, namely that idea of being freed, is something immediate after all, where we think we can directly touch it [*jene Idee des Befreitseins, doch ein Unmittelbares wäre, wo wir glauben, sie unmittelbar greifen zu können*].[118]

Adorno believes that such moments are most likely "the highest and the most decisive which artistic experience can achieve."[119] Indeed, he describes them as moments of happiness that are equal in their power to the highest moments that are possible in life. All the same, he specifies that in these moments the subject does not achieve confirmation of itself *as* a subject. Rather, its happiness consists in "being overwhelmed [*Überwältigtwerden*]," of "forgetting oneself [*Selbstvergessenheit*]," even to the point where it may seem that the subject experiences something like its "annihilation [*Auslöschung*]."[120]

> It is then as if, in that moment—one could call them moments of weeping— the subject were collapsing, inwardly shaken [*das Subjekt in sich erschüttert zusammenstürtzen würde*]. [They are] really moments in which the subject annihilates itself and experiences happiness at this annihilation [*sein Glück*

hat an dieser Auslöschung]—and not happiness at being granted something
as a subject.[121]

The encounter with art is significant for Adorno precisely because it affords us
an experience of a happiness that would lie beyond the confines of subjectivity.
He recognizes, of course, that this claim may strike us as rather puzzling, since
it can be difficult to make sense of the idea of "experience without subjectivity."
But he does not mean to deny the reality of the subject altogether. He means
only that aesthetic experience can provide us with an important insight into
the limits of our subjective power and a deepened awareness of our precarity as human beings. In the paralipomena to *Aesthetic Theory* he insists that
"the subject shaken by art has real experiences [*Das von Kunst erschütterte
Subjekt macht reale Erfahrungen*]."[122] The happiness that we experience in our
encounter with art thereby assists us in breaking through the petrifaction that
is gradually overtaking us in modern society. Adorno regards this transformation as the highest and most important consequences of aesthetic experience.
"It rescues subjectivity, even subjective aesthetics, through its negation."[123]

Aesthetic Experience and Social Critique

From the preceding discussion it should now be apparent that Adorno does
not believe that aesthetic experience alone could suffice to effect a radical
transformation in human life. He recognizes that aesthetic experience cannot
be understood apart from the broader network of human relationships and
institutions in which it is embedded, and he knows that it would therefore be
naive to imagine that art alone could serve as a remedy for the manifold de-
ficiencies of modern society. All the same, he ascribes enormous importance
to art and he refuses to see it as a mere distraction or retreat from the more
serious business of social critique. In this chapter I have tried to make sense
of his rather striking idea that art appears as a promise of happiness or a "sign
of freedom" in an unfree world. But Adorno is no less aware of the fact that
the happiness that we discover in aesthetic experience must remain only a
promise so long as it stands in starkest contradiction to its surroundings. This
may explain why we are told in *Aesthetic Theory* that not just some art, but
all art is endowed with sadness. It conveys a melancholy sigh, "Oh, were it
only so [*O wär es doch*]," a sigh that interlaces the true promise of happiness
with the grim recognition that in our current social conditions this promise
remains unfulfilled.[124]

    For Adorno, then, the central questions of aesthetics could not be di-
vorced from the questions of human purpose that animate critical thinking

across all boundaries of disciplinary specialization. His commitment to the "autonomy" of art does not contradict this holistic principle: art is both social and antisocial: it is only through its withdrawal into the immanent laws of its own form that art can sustain a critical function toward its own social conditions. But the emphasis on criticism should not tempt us into losing sight of the deeper normative promise that inheres in aesthetic experience. It is at this point that we can discern the reprisal of the materialist motif concerning the "primacy of the object." If Adorno cleaves passionately to the survival of art, this is chiefly because he sees it as a promise of a material happiness that society denies. Despite all of the distortions of the human being, we still possess a capacity to respond in art to an experience of beauty that used to be given to us in the experience of nature. Natural beauty, Adorno tells us, is given to us through a sensual receptivity beyond all domination: it "points to the primacy of the object in subjective experience."[125] But Adorno does not think that nature in itself still persists with the independence it would need to sustain this responsiveness. If this power has withered in most precincts of life, it still survives in art like a final bequest from a nature that has long since fallen into ruin.

I have argued in this book that Adorno looks to material experience as a source of insight that can furnish social criticism with the normative orientation it needs if it is to point beyond current conditions toward an unrealized future. This is why art remains of great relevance to his critical project. In the winter semester (1958–59) course on aesthetics we are told that "art is an attempt to do justice to all that falls victim to [the] ongoing concept of control over nature." If the dialectic of enlightenment is an ongoing process of increased domination that distances us both from one another and from the nonhuman environment, then art "has the task of revoking this process."[126] Art is the "memory of the suppressed"; namely, it sustains for us "the memory of all those internal powers which are destroyed by the process of progressive human rationalization."[127] To be sure, art remains confined to the realm of semblance (*Schein*): it cannot overcome its mediated relationship to sensuous nature. Adorno is hardly blind to the fact that an artwork cannot achieve the happiness it promises if this promise were confined to its aesthetic frame alone. He does not repeat the utopian fantasy (once articulated by Schiller) that humanity could find its ultimate fulfillment in aesthetic experience alone. But he nonetheless insists on the status of art as "anticipated reconciliation [*antezipierte Versöhnung*]."[128] The artwork occurs *within* semblance but also points *beyond* semblance to genuine peace.

Social Criticism Today

In this book I have tried to shed light on the question of normativity in Adorno's critical philosophy. My inquiry has taken as a starting premise that any answer to this question would have to be comprehensive, in the sense that it would have to apply across the full range of Adorno's philosophical interests. The question cannot be properly understood if we isolate only one dimension of his thought in deference to received conventions of academic inquiry. Over the course of his life he explored an astonishing variety of themes, and he never took up a permanent residence in any single academic discipline: he contributed to sociology as well as musicology, philosophy as well as literary criticism. Toward all of these fields, however, he assumed the posture of an outsider and a critic who made the experience of extraterritoriality into an essential motif for his thought. "Today," he observed, "it is part of morality not to be at home in one's home."[1] This remark, I believe, should also serve as a desideratum for our interpretation of his philosophical legacy. To speak of his aesthetics or his practical philosophy as separable domains may send us down a false path where we imagine his thought as conforming to the customary distinctions that now predominate in the modern research university. His principled resistance to these distinctions is recorded in the very first aphorism in *Minima Moralia*: "The occupation with things of the mind has by now itself become 'practical,' a business with strict division of labor, departments and restricted entry."[2] Adorno knew that any thinker who chose to reject such divisions would likely be dismissed as unprofessional or a mere dilettante. Yet he had little respect for conventions of disciplinary identity, and he developed his thinking in a spirit of freedom that willfully flouted their authority.

In this study I have followed the philosopher's example by assuming that the normative standard that animates his criticism must be sufficiently

comprehensive as to retain its relevance across all of his work, from his contributions to sociology to his speculations on metaphysics and from his lectures on moral philosophy to his writings on matters of musical and literary aesthetics. I have characterized this standard as happiness, or "human
flourishing," a concept that has the advantage of situating his thought within
a specific philosophical tradition but is still broad enough to express his idea
of total fulfillment in all domains of life. I have further suggested that this
standard appears in his work in the form of an "emphatic concept," a term
of art that he uses to designate the higher norm against which we can judge
particular instances of failure. But this immediately raises the suspicion as to
whether I may have betrayed the spirit of his philosophy by insisting that this
question must have a single answer. After all, Adorno was not embarrassed
to say that his thinking had a fragmentary and antisystemic character. Already in his 1931 inaugural lecture as a professor in Frankfurt, he announced
that philosophy must reject the illusion of an "absolute beginning." This anti-
foundationalist orientation was to remain a constant of his philosophy to the
very end of his career. In the 1969 lecture "Resignation" (from which I quoted
in the preface), Adorno confirmed that thinking "is not secured, not by the
existing conditions, nor by ends yet to be achieved, nor by any kind of battalions."[3] It may therefore appear contrarian of me to insist that we identify a
single and unifying normative impulse that runs through all his social criticism. For those who are inclined to skepticism regarding the place of normative commitments in social theory, I wish to offer some remarks in these
concluding pages as to why this exercise still merits our consideration.

Normativity in Social Theory

The practice of social criticism takes as its point of departure the basic insight that the present world is not as it should be. But one cannot stay fixed
at this rudimentary claim. It is not enough simply to announce that one finds
social reality objectionable as if one were a child objecting to the food that is
placed before him. The stark view that the world can be neatly divided into
two opposed camps of "friend" and "foe" is a symptom of infantile regression and not a sign of existential depth as its proponents might believe.[4] The
social critic needs to move beyond such a primitive sense of dissatisfaction
to specify in what respects social reality is deficient and what expectations it
has failed. But this is only possible if the critic somehow withdraws her con-
sent from conditions as they are given. Adorno describes this gesture as "self-
detachment from the weight of the factual [*von der Schwere des Fakischen*

sich Loslösen]."[5] In effecting such a withdrawal, however, the critic cannot imagine that she could ever *fully* unbind herself from the social world she inhabits, since there is no alternative world of pure thinking or ideals to which she can retreat. What self-detachment really amounts to is little more than a critical judgment that the surrounding world has failed to realize its own internal ideals. Social critique must therefore be immanent critique or it is not critique at all.

Social criticism is therefore immediately drawn into the task of identifying alternative sources of insight or normative demands that are immanent to our own social reality. The skeptic who wishes to object that no such alternative sources are available would be forced to conclude that no meaningful objections can be raised against conditions as they are. But this would be tantamount to surrendering the task of social criticism altogether. Adorno is not a skeptic in this sense. To be sure, he recognizes that the self-detachment at issue cannot involve world-transcendence, and he is therefore ready to admit that the skeptic is partly right to call it "the utterly impossible, because it presupposes a standpoint removed, even though by a hair's breadth, from the scope of existence."[6] But he is nonetheless committed to the task of looking *within* the world for alternative sources of normativity that point beyond the world as it is given and furnish an anticipatory glimpse of its unrealized possibilities. In this respect he remains faithful to the Marxist idea (an inheritance from Hegel) that the path of criticism must be immanent and that "we shall develop for the world new principles *from the existing principles of the world*."[7] It is here, however, that Adorno confronts a more serious challenge. Given the overwhelming "weight of the factual," it may seem nearly impossible to understand how we could ever hope to discover such principles and use them as points of critical leverage against the surrounding world. The skeptic will say the world as we found it is simply too powerful and that even if we could identify principles that conflict with the current order, they would be far too weak to serve as reliable guides.

It has been a major task of this book to show that Adorno recognizes the force of this objection. He is ready to admit that in a damaged world, the sources of normativity that are available to us for the practice of social criticism are likewise damaged and uncertain. For "any possible knowledge must not only be first wrested from what is, if it shall hold binding, but is also marked, for this very reason, by the same distortion and indigence which it seeks to escape."[8] We must therefore admit that we possess no knowledge of the *absolutely* good (and this is the meaning of Adorno's remark in his lectures on moral philosophy, where we are told in no uncertain terms that we lack any such "absolute" knowledge). The philosophical challenge for Adorno, however, is that he does not wish to permit the absence of absolute or undamaged standards to serve as a warrant for thoroughgoing skepticism. He holds fast to the promise of happiness even if nothing in our experience can possibly equip us with the absolute certainty that this promise can be realized.

Throughout this book I have called attention to some of the ways in which Adorno sustained his philosophical affinities with the Left-Hegelian or Marxist tradition, even if he never paid fealty to Marxism as a settled doctrine. The insight that I have just outlined above regarding the damaged condition of our normative standards is a further illustration of this enduring affinity. Marx himself was cognizant of the fact that bourgeois society has made itself into a normative authority for the world as it is given; and it has erected formidable obstructions, both ideological and institutional, that inhibit us from seeing how the world could ever be otherwise than it is. The proletariat too is caught up in this very same authoritative network, even though according to Marx it is the primary if not exclusive victim of the system's functioning. But the proletariat is *also* the embodiment of possibility: it carries within itself the latent anticipation of a condition that has not yet come into being. Because he was allergic to utopianism, however, Marx recognized that in an imperfect society it would be naive to look upon the working class as a paradigm of perfection. In their hunger and misery, he saw not just degradation but also a protest against the conditions that caused that misery. They became the damaged embodiment of an unrealized ideal. Adorno inherits from Marx this dialectical understanding of a damaged normativity: he believes that we should look to our social surroundings to discover the norms we require for the task of social criticism even while he recognizes that those very norms will bear all the wounds and imperfections of the world from which they are born. The Marxist theory of immiseration is applied to normativity itself.

Anti-Foundationalism and Precarity

The arguments sketched above permit us to draw an important distinction between precarity and total skepticism. Adorno recognized that the standard of human flourishing that sustains his social criticism is lacking in secure foundations since it can only appear to us in a partial and uncertain form. We may experience fleeting moments of happiness, but these moments too will be compromised by the general suffering that both surrounds them and even pervades them to their innermost core. In a striking passage from *Minima Moralia* he portrays the social critic as striving for moral insight but cognizant of its uncertainty: "While he gropingly forms his own life in the frail image of a right [*richtigen*] existence, he should never forget its frailty, nor how

little the image is a substitute for *the right life* [*das richtige Leben*]."⁹ All the
same, Adorno did not see the frailty of our moral insight as a license for resignation. Although he granted that our knowledge of the good is uncertain,
he did not wish to deny that it remains available to us in some fashion, however precarious and partial it may be. Hence his remark that the "emphatic
concept of thinking [*emphatischer Begriff vom Denken*]" remains "open" to
experience and "holds fast to possibility [*hält es die Möglichkeit fest*]," even
though it is "not secured" or grounded in any conditions in the present or
the future.¹⁰

Adorno saw anti-foundationalism as the general predicament of all modern philosophy. In a lecture on aesthetics he once remarked that "the secure
foundation" of all the philosophical disciplines had grown "somewhat precarious."¹¹ But he did not see such anti-foundationalism as an affliction to be
cured. Rather, he saw it as an unavoidable and even constitutive feature of the
modern condition itself. Once we have reckoned honestly with the full implications of modern history, we must accept the fundamental truth that there can
be no going back to the naive teachings of the premodern age, when we felt
ourselves to be in peaceful communion with nature and we took comfort in
the belief that our moral precepts are somehow inscribed into the very structure of the cosmos. For Adorno the breakdown of this holistic picture is not
something that can be undone, nor should we seek to do so. The disenchantment of the world is not merely a process of loss, it is a path we must travel
if we wish to arrive at any kind of genuine knowledge of both the world and
ourselves. In this condition of generalized precarity, anti-foundationalism
becomes the only stance that is suitable for modern philosophy. But what it
offers is something more than metaphysical insight; it can also be seen as the
point of departure for a new understanding of morality as well. The precarity
of philosophy alerts us to a certain precarity that is constitutive of human life
itself. Pursuing this line of thought, I have argued that Adorno endorses what
I have called an *ethics of vulnerability*. Below I wish to draw out some of the
further implications of this idea, with special attention to how it may bear on
the problem of modern political pathologies.

Fascism and Vulnerability

Anti-foundationalism in ethics begins with the simple claim that the human
being cannot find a wholly secure basis for morality in either the objective
facts of nature or the intersubjectively valid principles of human reason itself.
Adorno accepts this negative claim but interprets it in a novel way; he sees
it as leading not to a disabling moral skepticism but rather to an altogether

different species of moral conduct. For Adorno, to be moral is precisely to forgo the quest for total security in moral knowledge. Indeed, he wishes to abandon the project of securing absolute foundations for moral philosophy, even while he still seeks to imagine what truly moral conduct would be like. Rather than seek the guidance of moral argumentation, he locates the origins of morality in a certain kind of *moral disposition*. This disposition or moral posture is what I have called Adorno's ethics of vulnerability.

Such an ethics would involve a readiness to accept the fact of our precarity by holding ourselves open and unguarded to experience such that we remain fully responsive to others and to their suffering. This suggests that morality consists in something like a comportment (*Verhalten*) or moral disposition rather than a set of discursive principles. As I noted in the introduction Adorno seems to regard the attempt to articulate the requirements of morality through rational argumentation as misguided. In his study of Adorno's practical philosophy, Fabian Freyenhagen offers an excellent explanation as to why Adorno rejects this rationalist approach. My disagreement with Freyenhagen chiefly concerns the question of whether Adorno has anything more compelling to offer in its place. I wish to argue that Adorno offers something more substantial than a negative ethics of living less wrongly; rather, he provides us with a portrait of the *morally responsive personality*.

At this point it may be worth pausing to defend against a certain misunderstanding. Adorno's idea of a "disposition" does not mean that he is content to endorse an individualist model of moral character such as the kind that we associate with virtue ethics. Notwithstanding his interest in the psychological or characterological aspect of ethical life, Adorno never retreats from political and institutional life in a self-sufficient moral philosophy that is founded on individual conduct alone. In the late essay, "Marginalia to Theory and Practice," he notes that Kant developed his intuitions regarding the nature of moral conduct with reference to "the sphere of business and private life." Kant offered "the concept of an ethics based on conviction [*Gesinnungsethik*], whose subject must be the individuated singular person."[12] Adorno recognizes that such an individualist morality that is grounded in the privacy of the will ignores the social and institutional frameworks that are necessary if human beings are to gain their full self-realization. The insufficiencies in Kantian moral philosophy must therefore be remedied by appealing to the Hegelian model of social freedom. "Kant's moral philosophy and Hegel's philosophy of right represent two dialectical stages in the bourgeois self-consciousness of praxis." But Adorno also fears that the Hegelian model is no less one-sided than the Kantian model for which it offers a necessary corrective. Although it is supposed to lend social objectivity to the concept of the moral, Hegel's concept of *Sittlichkeit* actually "dissolves" the concept of the moral into the political. "Polarized according to the dichotomy of the particular and the universal that tears apart this consciousness both philosophies are false."[13]

Adorno seeks to mediate between Kant and Hegel. Whereas Kant's moral philosophy carries the risk of ontological self-isolation, Hegel's ideal of social freedom carries the no less serious risk that the individual could be lost in the bureaucratic collective. A political philosophy that places the highest emphasis on public and institutional life can too easily degenerate into a warrant for mere instrumentalism that also introduces a serious distortion into the human being, who then hardens into the cold and purely practical persona that modern society requires: "Whereas praxis promises to lead people out of their self-isolation, praxis itself has always been isolated; for this reason practical people are *unresponsive* [*unansprechbar*] and the relation of praxis to its object is a priori undermined. Indeed, one could ask whether in its indifference toward its object [*Indifferenz gegens Objekt*] all nature-dominating praxis up to the present day is not in fact praxis in name only."[14] If Adorno warns against the premature leap into praxis, this is not because he abjures all social action. Rather, he is anxious to ensure that society serve as a suitable theater for the flourishing of the human being in all its manifold dimensions.

We can gain a better sense of what Adorno thinks such a moral disposition might be like by consulting *The Authoritarian Personality* (1950), the landmark study in social psychology that Adorno conducted with a small research team in Berkeley, California.[15] I have written at some length about the premises and purposes of this study elsewhere, and for my present needs I will confine myself to only a brief summary.[16] The book starts from the assumption that those who are most susceptible to fascist propaganda exhibit certain psychological tendencies that can be first identified by means of quantitative and qualitative empirical studies (involving both mass-distributed questionnaires and personal interviews). These are then mapped on a scale: those individuals who score high on the "F-scale" are said to display the strongest inclination toward fascism. Needless to say, the understanding of fascism that underwrites this study is remarkably broad: the researchers were not so provincial or lacking in imagination to rest content with the belief that fascism is a uniquely European political phenomenon that cannot recur in different guises or at other places and times. They understood it as the modern manifestation of tendencies that are at least latent in *all* of human civilization; it is a dialectic between domination and submission that inheres in our collective history and that we have never yet managed to overcome. Notwithstanding this capacious definition, however, they never imply that fascism itself has its origins in psychopathology alone. They insist that they were concerned with purely *subjective* (psychological) rather than *objective* (political and socio-economic) factors. Their task was to understand not the *causes* of fascism but why so many individuals feel drawn to it.

Their conclusion is striking. An individual who scores highest on the F-scale and is therefore identified as most susceptible to fascism need not be someone who consciously endorses the full suite of explicitly fascist principles. Rather, it is an individual who exhibits a generalized psychological *disposition*. This disposition is not a distinctive type; rather, it is a syndrome of tendencies that afflict all individuals, though in varying degrees. These include but are not limited to conventionalism, fear of conspiracy, hostility to outsiders or foreigners, "tough-mindedness," and stereotypy, or rigidity in thinking. In his preface to the book, Max Horkheimer (who served as editor for Studies in Prejudice, the series in which the study appeared) even suggests that the research team has identified a new " 'anthropological' species."[17] Although this may be an exaggeration, it expresses the basic intuition of the study, namely, that the inclination toward fascism is due to holistic features of overall social-psychological disposition and not specific defects of the individual psyche. In the concluding pages of their study the authors claim that the authoritarian personality reflects a far more basic problem that they diagnose as the "*inability to have experience.*"[18] The susceptibility to fascist propaganda could be redressed only if there were "an increase in people's capacity to see themselves and to be themselves." The authors are ambivalent as to whether such an inability to have experience is something that could be remedied on a purely individual basis. On the one hand, they suggest that the remedy lies in early childhood experience. "All that is really essential," they write, "is that children be genuinely loved and treated as individual humans."[19] On the other hand, they believe that the inability to have experience reflects "the total organization of society" and can be changed "only as that society is changed."[20]

This holistic diagnosis of fascism raises many questions. The ambivalence that runs through the book regarding possible remedies to authoritarianism is a sign of an unresolved problem in its social-psychological method: Does society furnish the shaping conditions for the individual's psychology, or do factors of individual psychology explain why society has assumed its present form? The authors insist that society must always come first in the causal chain, but the total change in objective social conditions that they recommend can have little effect if the subjective conditions remain as they were. In his unpublished critical "Remarks" on the authoritarianism study Adorno tries to resolve this problem by historicizing its psychoanalytic instruments.[21] The study relies on a psychoanalytic model of the stable and well-integrated ego that under modern social conditions has now begun to dissolve. As the modern self loses its structural integrity, it will become little more than a "bundle of reactions" that will have lost the capacity for genuine experience and will thereby become even more susceptible to external manipulation. This criticism only enhances Adorno's doubt as to whether fascism's enduring appeal can be remedied on a purely individual basis. In this line of reasoning, however, we can also discern the thematic key to Adorno's moral philosophy.

I suggested above that in his thoughts on the prerequisites for moral conduct, Adorno sketches the outlines of the moral disposition or personality. The contrast with the authoritarian personality can bring this alternative into sharper relief. The individual subject who qualifies as "authoritarian" is one who makes a fetish of "hardness [*Härte*]."[22] In its longing for security and invulnerability, it closes itself off from everything it regards as a threat, and it therefore suffers from a fatal deficiency: the inability to have experience. Unlike its counterpart, the potentially moral subject is willing to admit its vulnerability. Passive but without anxiety, it holds itself open to the world and can respond to the suffering of others insofar as "it entrusts itself to its own experience [*in angstloser Passivität der eigenen Erfahrung sich anvertraut*]."[23] The contrast between these two psychological portraits is hardly coincidental. After all, Adorno's social criticism was originally forged in the historical crucible of emergent fascism. So it should not surprise us that his moral philosophy would emerge chiefly as a response to this very same world-historical danger. But this immediately raises the related question as to whether Adorno believed that the threat of a reemergent fascism could be effectively diminished by cultivating a properly moral disposition. It seems doubtful that he was so naive. As noted above, he recognized that the moral personality structure that would prove most resistant to fascism was becoming increasingly rare. The general trend of society was toward the "withering of experience" together with the decline in the conditions that made it possible to be a subject at all. It followed that the conditions conducive to fascism were likely to grow only more pronounced. In his 1959 lecture on the collective task of working through the past, Adorno offered a sober confession: "I consider the survival of National Socialism *within* democracy to be potentially more menacing than the survival of fascist tendencies *against* democracy."[24] Adorno's moral philosophy was hardly naive; it is forged in the context of an altogether realistic forecast concerning the future of civilized humanity.

Never Again Auschwitz

At the beginning of this book, I referred to the remarks from the 1959 lectures on Kant's theoretical philosophy, in which Adorno encouraged his auditors to read the first *Critique* without appealing to reified and conventional interpretations that might obscure its true meaning. Throughout my discussion, I have tried to honor this suggestion by taking note of the philosophical affinities between Adorno and Kant wherever these might prove illuminating. The affinities are as strong as the differences. Through immanent critique, Adorno believed he could discover lessons in Kant's philosophy that might be turned in a materialist direction and mobilized for his own work. As we have seen, Adorno was especially interested in the Kantian doctrine of the thing-in-itself as a signpost marking the limits of subjective reason. Transformed into the language of materialism, the thing-in-itself became in Adorno's philosophy a model for the non-identical, the worldly objectivity that resists subjectivistic reduction. In this philosophical inheritance we can already discern the outlines of a new moral attitude: the doctrine of the thing-in-itself, once dialectically reconfigured, can serve as a lesson in epistemic humility.[25]

But Adorno also took a strong interest in Kant's practical philosophy. The metaphysical ideas that Kant reinterpreted as postulates of practical reason were transformed by Adorno into the materialist motif of happiness as the *summum bonum* that animates all social-critical practice.[26] Perhaps the most striking affinity, however, is the one that appears only in the concluding pages of *Negative Dialectics*, where Adorno announces the urgent need for a "new categorical imperative." Here too Adorno believes that he can mobilize a theme from Kant's philosophy even while he translates it into the language of materialism: "Hitler has imposed *a new categorical imperative* upon humanity in the state of their unfreedom: to arrange their thinking and conduct [*ihr Denken und Handeln*], so that Auschwitz never repeats itself, so that nothing similar may happen again."[27]

Adorno pays homage to Kant's original idea of a moral obligation in insisting that the new imperative must retain the form of genuine universalism: the negative injunction is imposed not on discrete individuals but on *all human beings*. This universality is possible only because "Auschwitz" becomes far more than the name of a single event: for Adorno, it comprehends all similar atrocities, none of which can claim for itself the dark prestige of incomparability. But he refuses to accept Kant's further premise that the moral imperative can be secured only if it assumes a rational-conceptual form. The new imperative is too "unruly [*widerspenstig*]" for any such "grounding [*Begründung*]." Adorno goes so far as to suggest that we should resist the demand for rational grounding altogether. He believes that to treat the imperative discursively would already be "heinous [*Frevel*]": it would presuppose a sharp division between justification and sensuous experience, as if the brute fact of human suffering were not already sufficient to arouse our moral outrage. Adorno rejects this rationalist requirement; he insists that the impulse to morality first announces itself as something nondiscursive and even "bodily [*leibhaft*]." It originates as "abhorrence to unbearable physical pain [*Abscheu vor dem unerträglichen physischen Schmerz*]." Adorno thereby translates Kant's discursive formula of universal morality into the language of materialism. For once rational "grounding [*Begründung*]" has lost its legitimacy the brute fact of material experience is all that remains: "Only in the unvarnished materialistic motive does morality survive [*Nur im ungeschminkt materialistischen Motiv überlebt Moral*]."[28]

The specific problem of "grounding" in considerations of moral philosophy alerts us to the more general question: Does modern philosophy still allow for the possibility of grounding at all? It is surely tempting to categorize Adorno alongside other thinkers in the modern era who embrace the lesson, inherited from Nietzsche, that philosophy has been set free from all foundationalist certitudes. As I have suggested above, it is plausible to see Adorno as an anti-foundationalist thinker at least in certain respects: he sees metaphysics as a philosophical tradition that placed unwarranted confidence in the unity and intelligibility of the world, and he believes that historical catastrophe has now left this tradition in ruins. But if we wish to identify what is truly distinctive in his thinking the label of anti-foundationalism is far too capacious to be of much value. At the very least we must draw a distinction between anti-foundationalism and anti-humanism. Although Adorno shares with other anti-foundationalists of the modern era a general skepticism regarding the attempt to secure our claims to knowledge and morality in an invariant or metaphysical ground, this skepticism does not extinguish his belief in the humanist subject. It is true that he wishes to deny the humanist subject its illusion of self-grounding; he reconceives of the subject not as a ground but as an opening upon a non-identity that exceeds its power. But he never wholly leaves the terrain of the human subject. Rather, he mobilizes the energies of critical subjectivity to challenge its authority from the inside.

In this respect Adorno must be sharply distinguished from Heidegger, who especially after the Second World War distanced himself from humanism and looked upon it as little more than a final chapter in the history of metaphysical error. Heidegger drew from anti-foundationalism the wrong lessons: in his earlier works of existential ontology, the discovery that Dasein has no ground (*Grund*) other than an abyss (*Abgrund*) is an occasion for a transformative anxiety that motivates the human being to seize upon the finitude of its own existence with even greater resolve (*Entschlossenheit*). The philosophy of anti-foundationalism that might have awakened the human being to an experience of greater openness (*Offenheit*) and responsiveness to the suffering of others only hardens itself against the world, and it ends up in a vacuous ethic of self-affirmation. The early Heidegger ascribes the highest normative significance to *Sein-zum-Tode* as the individuating, or "non-relational," anticipation of death. It is this category before all others that promises to disclose Dasein in its ineluctable finitude when it is "held out into the nothing," as if this were the essential condition of a being who lacks all essence. But a death that undergoes such a transfiguration becomes hygienic, a mere device for ontological insight that shares little in common with the experience it purports to name. Although he has a great deal to say about the significance of death, Heidegger almost never mentions the fact of our material suffering. Instead of recognizing our *vulnerability*, he extols the revelatory truth of Dasein's being-toward-death that will throw the human being back into the "hardness of its fate [*die Härte seines Schicksals*]."[29]

In his later works Heidegger tries to circumvent the anthropocentric theme of Dasein altogether; he adopts the mournful posture of a sage who can do little more than document the way stations along Being's path of error, or *Irrweg*. He assures us that the attempt to overcome metaphysical humanism does not imply inhumanity; but the philosopher of Being is left with few resources to comprehend the true significance of the crimes against humanity he never explicitly condemned. Instead of acknowledging the magnitude of his own error, he goes so far as to blame the victims; he redescribes their murder as "self-annihilation [*Selbstvernichtung*]."[30] Adorno, by contrast, interprets the atrocities of the war as the centerpiece of a new moral philosophy in which material suffering becomes the negative standard against which all possible happiness must find its measure. The new categorical imperative can be understood, in part, as a rejoinder to Heidegger. Dialectics displaces ontology, and "thinking [*Denken*]" loses its pseudo-theological prestige as an abstract practice of meditating on the revelations of Being. Instead, we are asked to arrange not only our thinking but also our conduct so that similar atrocities will never again occur.

The particular question of "ethics after Auschwitz" raises a more general philosophical concern that I felt would be best to leave for the conclusion. Throughout this book I have sought to defend the view that Adorno upholds a maximalist standard of happiness or human flourishing, and I have further suggested that this standard is necessary as a postulate for his social criticism. But one can easily imagine an interlocutor who would raise the following objection: "You want to say that Adorno appeals, however obliquely, to some implicit and largely counterfactual vision of the good life, the right life, the reconciled condition, and so forth. (His language when he alludes to this condition is remarkably vague, as you admit; but let's leave that problem aside.)

The more general philosophical worry is that the ethical standard 'never again Auschwitz' is far too thin to do the work that would be required to get us to a condition as rich as human flourishing. In fact, Adorno's 'new categorical imperative' looks as if it has *no positive content whatsoever*. It may tell us what *not* to do, but it provides us with no substantive prescriptions as to what we *should* do. Even if one were to try with all one's might to twist it around into some kind of positive statement, it still seems fairly obvious that it can equip us with little more than an absolute *minimum* or mere baseline for our ethical conduct. But surely this minimum falls far short of any conception of the good or right life, does it not? After all, once this baseline has been met, a post-Auschwitz ethics falls silent, and it can offer no further guidance as to how our life should be arranged. Ultimately, despite all of your efforts to draw out a thick standard of the good from Adorno's philosophy, doesn't the ethical injunction 'never again Auschwitz' still look remarkably impoverished? And why isn't this ethical injunction a perfect illustration of the negativist interpretation? To state the problem clearly: How could such a minimalist morality inform the maximalist standard of human flourishing?"

At first glance this surely looks like a compelling objection, so it is important that I explain precisely why my imaginary interlocutor is mistaken. If the objection is right, then we should be able to distinguish between two ethical tasks. The first task would be to satisfy the "baseline" or minimalist requirement to arrange our world so as to prevent any future events like Auschwitz. The second task would be to transform the world in a far more dramatic and radical fashion so as to realize the condition of human flourishing. Now, the objection presupposes that these two ethical tasks are distinct; it assumes that the prospect of human flourishing brings with it substantive and distinctive moral and political requirements that reach well beyond the rudimentary minimum of preventing catastrophe.

But this is an assumption that Adorno flatly rejects. On the contrary, he discerns an essential *continuity* between the everyday conditions of modern civilization and the extreme conditions that first made Auschwitz possible.[31] He believes that bourgeois society already contains a "latent violence" that could at any moment break free of its fragile constraints and lapse into overt barbarism.[32] It is this belief in the strong continuity between "normal" bourgeois society and fascist catastrophe that can help us appreciate Adorno's more extraordinary claims about the fascism that inheres in our everyday conduct, the claim, for instance, that even the simplest mechanisms that we use in order to open windows and doors already betray "violent, hard-hitting, unresting jerkiness of fascist maltreatment."[33] Adorno is therefore unimpressed with self-satisfied ideologists of liberal democracy who console themselves with the thought that fascism can be understood as a mere anomaly or a deviation from the path of history. Unlike theorists of the "Sonderweg," he insists on the mutual complicities between fascism and ostensibly "normal" bourgeois modernity. "That fascism lives on," he observed, "is due to the fact that the objective conditions of society that degenerated into fascism continue to exist."[34] It is therefore mistaken to ascribe to Adorno the consoling thought that one can draw a strong distinction between the conditions for fascism and the conditions for bourgeois modernity. On the contrary, Adorno understands them as mutually imbricated; and we might say that this is only one instance of the more general thesis (as elaborated in *Dialectic of Enlightenment* and elsewhere) that the conditions for civilizational catastrophe and barbarism already inhere in bourgeois modernity itself.

Once we accept the thesis of mutual imbrication, it becomes far more difficult to imagine how we could satisfy the baseline conditions that would rule out catastrophe without effecting a complete transformation in the general conditions of bourgeois society. For Adorno, "Auschwitz" is quite simply the name for a *constitutive possibility* that belongs to bourgeois modernity as it is. To eliminate the conditions that made Auschwitz possible would thus require that we *also* address the basic features of bourgeois society that first made it susceptible to such barbaric consequences. The objection of my imaginary interlocutor (as presented above) therefore rests on a mistaken assumption about Adorno's interpretation of what we might call "normal" society. For it turns out that the injunction, "Never again Auschwitz," suggests something far more substantive than a minimalist standard for moral conduct. If we are morally bound "to arrange their thinking and conduct" such that nothing like Auschwitz ever again recur, then such a moral obligation is hardly minimal at all. Rather, it imposes on us extraordinarily stringent demands, with maximalist implications for the ways in which we organize our lives both individual and collective. And the only kind of society that would be truly immune to the threat of renewed barbarism would be the society in which we are at last permitted to flourish as fully human.

Anti-Humanism and Genealogy

The polemical term "anti-humanism" appears all too often in the context of politically charged debates concerning the inheritance of Nietzschean and Heideggerian motifs in modern French philosophy. In these controversies Adorno played only the most marginal role, since he developed the major themes of his negative dialectic in a German cultural and philosophical climate that was still relatively immune to the *nouvelle vague* of anti-humanist philosophy that would become especially prominent in postwar France. It is nonetheless permissible to ask whether we can learn any lessons from the comparison between Adorno and Foucault. As I bring this book to a conclusion, I want to offer a brief comment as to why this comparison strikes me as philosophically misleading. Although these remarks may seem ill suited here, it is my hope that the comparison might shed additional light on what is truly distinctive in Adorno's philosophy.[35] My specific motivation is to underscore an important difference regarding the problem of normativity.

Adorno died in 1969, Foucault in 1984. During the half century since the death of his German contemporary, Foucault's reputation has soared not least because he helped clear the way toward a genuinely emancipatory style of thought that inherited the best insights from both Nietzsche and Heidegger without recapitulating their errors. Unlike his predecessors, Foucault is interested in neither the heroism of ungrounded existence nor the retrieval of a half-forgotten *Seinsverständnis*. Suspicious of all metaphysical or naturalizing claims, the early Foucault puts historicism to work in the service of "archaeology," exposing the historical volatility and contingency of all epistemological and institutional regimes. In *Les mots et les choses* (1966) he goes so far as to historicize even the humanist subject that has served in the modern era as the transcendental ground for all knowledge, and he forecasts a new era when the human being might vanish "like a face drawn in sand at the edge of the sea."[36] (The puzzling question as to how the phenomenon of a meaning framework is supposed to obtain at all if it is torn free from its own conditions of possibility receives no satisfactory answer.)

This historicist dismantling of transcendental humanism persists well into the later phase of his career when Foucault effects the turn from archaeology to genealogy.[37] The new method defamiliarizes conventional impulses of humanitarian world improvement, and it forces us to confront the ongoing complicity between knowledge and power. In classic works such as *Surveiller et punir* (1975), he redescribes the project of the Enlightenment from the disenchanted perspective of a genealogist who recognizes that norms of liberation are also strategies of discipline and surveillance.[38] Prison reform becomes yet another instance in this ironic narrative: what may have seemed only a benevolent attempt to impose limits on social discipline is shown to be a ruse for extending its anonymous power. In late works such as *The History of Sexuality* (1984), Foucault applies this genealogical method to genocide itself. State campaigns to manage or exterminate entire populations are no longer seen as catastrophic ruptures in civilization; they are redescribed as instances of a "bio-politics" that inheres in all modern societies as part of their ostensibly normal operation.[39]

Foucault is at his best when he puts his historicism to work for the purposes of a defamiliarizing historical description that unmasks normativity as power. He therefore disavows all explicitly normative commitments insofar as they would surely be vulnerable to the very same strategy of unmasking. He nevertheless borrows from Nietzsche an implicit standard of anarchistic freedom even while he sees all remaining standards as mere constraints that would only inhibit the human subject from the practice of endless experimentation and self-invention. Although even this last standard could also be exposed as power—a self-reflexive gesture that Nietzsche welcomed—Foucault largely rescinds from the task of explaining why self-invention would serve as the better alternative (though it is fairly clear that he finds it preferable). The question of self-reflexivity remains unanswered. He performs his genealogies in a spirit of emancipation but refuses to say where he is situated in the world he describes: this is a question (in his words) that should be left to "the bureaucrats and the police."[40] But surely this is not an adequate response. A social theory that can give no account of its own critical purposes must run into serious philosophical difficulties if it asks us to see the whole of the social world as analogous to a prison where all available light is merely an instrument of ongoing surveillance. If genealogical description is to serve as a *critical* strategy, then it must at least be possible for the critic to appeal to some norm of freedom (even if only a counterfactual one) that would not count as merely another instance of "the carceral society." But Foucault offers no such norm.[41] Instead he insists that power is pervasive and creative: social discipline is not a mere technique of domination; it also brings its objects into being. By blurring the line between power and ontology, Foucault draws the extravagant conclusion that social discipline actually *constitutes* the human subjects that are the primary objects of its gaze.[42] This leaves him in a paradoxical position where he can no longer explain why any particular form of social discipline should be more objectionable than another. The instruments of social description have no moment of truth that could even partially transcend the field of their operation. Beneath the networks of power we cannot identify a preexisting subject of desire and suffering who cries out to be set free from their unwanted control. The subject who was first brought into being through social discipline would simply vanish at the instant of its liberation.

Adorno is immune to this paradox. On the one hand, he is vigorously opposed to the inflationary concept of the subject as a will to power. On the other hand, he is never tempted by the crypto-metaphysical claim that the human subject as such is fully constituted by social forms of disciplinary knowledge. Nowhere in his work is he tempted by the thought that the subject depends for its very existence on strategies of social knowledge as if it were little more than the fragile filament in a spider's web spun by anonymous powers. Unlike Foucault, Adorno does not wish to *overcome* the humanist subject or expose it as merely a metaphysical illusion; he only wishes to challenge its primacy, its domination over the material world. But he performs this critical task from *within* the experiential horizon of the human being without calling its fundamental reality into question. Since the beginning of his philosophical career, he had assigned himself a single task: "to break through the delusion of constitutive subjectivity with the power of the subject."[43] If he succeeds in this effort, it is because he holds fast to the reality of the human subject even while he contests its claims to world mastery. This is what I have called Adorno's philosophical anthropology. The human being as Adorno conceives it has both materiality and inner depth: its suffering is no less real than its longing for happiness.

Here, then, is the crucial point of disagreement: unlike Adorno, Foucault pursues the project of genealogical dismantling to its antirealist conclusion where any faith in the subject as a natural being is held in suspension. Created rather than born, the subject as Foucault conceives it is pure *nomos* without *physis*. But this thesis of total social constitution offers nothing more compelling than a poststructuralist reprisal of a precritical idealism. Bishop Berkeley believed he could secure God's reality with the infamous dictum, *esse est percipi*. Foucault erases God but retains the idea of constitution in the omniscient power of the social gaze. He believes that he has thereby dissolved the reality of the human subject: to be seen is to be.[44] Adorno resists this idealist turn. As a materialist who still acknowledges the embattled and vulnerable moment of nature in human nature, he recognizes that the world retains its nonidentity and is not dependent on the schemes by which it is known. Insisting on the dialectical distinction between subject and object, he refuses to see either of them as a mere precipitate of the other.[45] To underscore what is truly at stake in the philosophical disagreement between Adorno and Foucault, it may suffice to consider their rather different conceptions of the prison. In Foucault's carceral society, it makes little sense to ask whether we can locate an immanent source of normativity: the light that appears within the walls of the prison serves only as a pervasive medium for the power that first constitutes the subject as an object of disciplinary surveillance. Adorno follows a different path. In the prison from *Fidelio*, he interprets social immanence not as a seamless and harmonistic whole but as a contradictory formation that is shot through with fleeting moments of normative promise. Although the idea of freedom has grown dim and virtually "powerless," it nevertheless makes an appearance as *"the glimmer of light which falls into the prison itself."*[46]

Proust's Theological Idea

In this book I have argued that Adorno's philosophy exemplifies the practice of immanent critique. It looks upon present society not as a seamless and fallen realm that lacks all normative possibility but as a space of fragmentation and contradiction that bears within itself critical resources that point toward both its overcoming and its completion. Adorno pursues this immanent-critical strategy of interpretation across all regions of social and individual experience. From morality to sociology and from politics to aesthetics, his micrological glance exposes the "rifts and fissures" in everything it sees, and it leaves us with a vision of the world not as final or fixed in its meaning but as forever open to alternatives. His dialectic is defined not by closure but possibility. No doubt this interpretive method can induce in some readers a sense of vertigo insofar as Adorno seldom permits any element in our social experience to remain wholly as it was or to harden into something determinate and secure. What is volatile is always available for further criticism. Perhaps no other topic better illustrates both the difficulties and the promises of Adorno's immanent-critical method than theology, a topic I have written about elsewhere but have mentioned here only in passing.[47] The role of theological (or religious) concepts in Adorno's philosophy is much contested and merits further comment below.

When addressing the question of Adorno and theology the great temptation would be to assign his work to only one of two mutually exclusive camps: *either* atheism *or* religion. Some would describe him as unsympathetic to religion, while others believe that he is an essentially religious thinker. To both interpretive parties in this struggle the dialectical answer is obvious: Adorno resists the dualistic requirement that we should be forced to choose. Rather, he insists on the *dialectical* possibility of recuperating the insights of religious tradition even while turning them toward nonreligious ends. Michael Theunissen identifies this gesture as the *sublation (Aufhebung)* of metaphysics, the dialectical alternative to Heidegger's task of metaphysical *overcoming (Überwindung)*.[48] Adorno characterizes it as "the transmutation of metaphysics into history [*die Transmutation von Metaphysik in Geschichte*]."[49] Transmutation signifies more than a mere transfer or a shift of terrain: when the concepts of

traditional metaphysics undergo what Adorno calls a "migration into the profane [*Einwanderung ins Profane*]" they do not and *cannot* remain as they once
were. Their historical transformation "secularizes metaphysics [*säkularisiert
Metaphysik*] into the secular category pure and simple, that of decay."[50] Philosophy no longer fastens its attention on eternity; rather, it looks for redemption
in "that which is smallest" in "the fragments struck loose by decay" that even in
their transience nonetheless appear to "bear objective meanings."[51] But insofar
as all claims to objective meaning have grown precarious, Adorno insists that
history compels us to find the promise of our fulfillment not in a metaphysical
beyond but only in that which is most fleeting or evanescent: "No meditation
on transcendence is possible any more except by virtue of transience; eternity
appears not as such but as shot through with what is most transient."[52]

    In a 1945 lecture, "Art and Religion Today," Adorno expresses his admira-
tion for Proust's *À la recherche du temps perdu*, a masterpiece of literature that
illustrates what he calls a "truly theological idea." To be sure, Proust is hardly
a theologian in any traditional sense since he takes no interest in eternity;
rather, he surrenders himself without restraint to "what is most futile, the
most insignificant, the most fugitive traces of memory."[53] But this emphasis
on "the concrete and the individual" becomes so saturated with the promise
of happiness that it assumes the redemptive meaning that was once ascribed
to religion. Proust saves life from death, not by invoking the otherworldly
metaphysics of religious tradition, but rather by entrusting himself entirely
to the transience and particularity of worldly experience. In this interpretation we see once again how Adorno pursues a strategy of immanent critique:
he finds anticipations of human flourishing in the most insignificant details
of material life. The smallest fragment of this-worldly happiness becomes
charged with a maximalist demand for the world's transformation.

    Adorno's remarks on Proust shed a helpful light on the question of how
the religiously derived concept of a species-wide redemption can persist in
negative dialectics without compromising its materialist premise. In the idea
of the *fragment* Adorno pays homage to an implicitly Kantian principle of
universalization: a fragment is the broken piece of a missing whole. It follows
that there can be no happiness for the individual that does not already include
a demand for the happiness of all humankind. I have argued in this book that
the concept of happiness serves a critical function in Adorno's philosophy not
unlike the Kantian concept of the *summum bonum*: it is a postulate that one
must presuppose for the practice of social criticism even if from the vantage
of theoretical reason it would seem to lack objective validity. Unlike Kant,
however, no sooner has Adorno introduced the theme of happiness than he
retracts it as a scandal, since the fact of unhappiness contests its validity from

all sides. Given the enormous pressures of social conformity and social repression, Adorno doubts that even the individual could ever be fully happy:
"Every happiness is a fragment of the total happiness, which human beings
are denied and which they deny themselves."[54]

Notwithstanding this doubt, however, Adorno does not permit himself
the simplicity of total despair. He grants a legitimate place in his thinking
for fleeting instances of happiness even while he admits that there is nothing in our experience that would count as instances of *total* happiness without qualification. This distinction is indispensable to his moral philosophy,
which we might otherwise be inclined to categorize as a species of thoroughgoing moral skepticism. Recall my argument that, for Adorno, an imperfect x
still counts as an x. Although he asserts in his lectures on problems in moral
philosophy that we have no knowledge of the "absolute good," this does not
deter him from nevertheless claiming that we possess knowledge of the good
as it appears in a partial and damaged form.[55] The key thought here is that to
claim knowledge of a fragmentary happiness (or fragmentary good) we are
not thereby required to claim knowledge of happiness (or the good) in its
seamless perfection. In his philosophy the concept of happiness remains no
less riven with contradiction than social reality itself.

As I have argued, Adorno's concept of happiness is modeled after the Kantian attempt to salvage the metaphysical ideas for the sake of practical reason.
This naturally raises the question as to whether Adorno has illicitly retained
a concept that should have lost all objective meaning with the collapse of
metaphysics. Is the demand for universal happiness merely the illegitimate
trace of theological expectations that Adorno should have disavowed? Does
he hold fast, despite his skepticism, to a species of religious philosophy? The
answer to this question is by no means obvious, not least because (as noted
above) with his principled commitment to dialectical thinking Adorno refuses the crude dualism between atheism and religion. All the same, it should
be readily apparent that his philosophy hardly amounts to anything as definitive as a crypto-theology; even to characterize it as a "minimal theology"
may be excessive.[56] Readers who seek in Adorno's philosophy an unqualified
affirmation of religious consciousness are bound to feel disappointment because it makes no allowances whatsoever for the reality of the divine. On the
contrary; from theology Adorno borrows only the counterfactual idea of a
"messianic" perspective that sheds light on the brokenness of the world. This
counterfactual method does not warrant the name "theology," not even "negative theology," since it borrows from theology nothing more than a postulate for the practice of criticism.[57] The unsatisfied (and possibly unsatisfiable)
idea of redemption may be implicit in the "demand" that criticism imposes

on the world. But in the final sentence of *Minima Moralia* Adorno explicitly denies that by invoking the idea of redemption for the sake of critical practice he has somehow committed himself to positive theological knowledge: "Beyond the demand that is placed on our thinking, however, the question regarding the reality or unreality of redemption itself is a matter of near total indifference."[58]

With this agnostic conclusion Adorno makes it clear that he is unmoved by the claims of religious faith. He sees in theology an important archive from which he can borrow the conceptual resources for the practice of critique, but he insists that these resources will retain their validity only if they undergo an immanent-critical appropriation, or a "migration into the profane [*Einwanderung ins Profane*]."[59] In the Lurianic Kabbalah, as it was introduced to him via Gershom Scholem, Adorno had discovered the concept of the "shells [*Schalen*]" or fragments of divine light that have been scattered throughout creation. According to Isaac Luria, humanity must share in the responsibility of seeking out these fragments in order to restore unity to the divine. At the end of *Negative Dialectics* Adorno makes use of this mystical motif to describe his own immanent-critical practice: what he calls the "micrological glance" aims to rescue the particular from the "shells [*Schalen*]" in which it has been hidden. Like Proust, however, he pursues this task not for the sake of an otherworldly referent but only for the sake of this-worldly perfection. The language of theology remains available to him only because it expresses a maximalist demand: "the smallest innerworldly markings would be of relevance to the absolute." Such thinking is therefore no longer explicitly theological, but it is nevertheless "solidaristic with metaphysics at the moment of its fall."[60]

In this concluding sentence Adorno conveys the twofold thought that although he rejects metaphysics in the traditional sense, he can sustain fidelity to a vanishing metaphysics through the very practice of immanent critique. This claim is remarkable not least because it seems simultaneously both to affirm and to deny the relevance of theology for the sake of secular criticism. But this concept of secularization is dialectical insofar as it registers both moments at once. The ultimate lesson of Adorno's philosophical masterpiece would seem to be that negative dialectics seeks to uphold the truth in theology but only insofar as the latter has passed through the trial of a relentless secularization. Not unlike Benjamin, Adorno believes that "the idea of happiness [*Vorstellung des Glücks*]" is "indissociably connected with that of redemption [*Erlösung*]."[61] And yet Adorno will not permit redemption to survive without metaphysical compromise. Within the bounds of a materialist philosophy, happiness is the only valid form in which the theological concept remains at all intelligible. The concept of redemption can no longer claim the prestige of transcendence or invariance: it has grown as fragile and evanescent as human life itself.[62] The smallest moments of happiness, such as those transcribed by Proust, serve as present anticipations of the highest good. Even the happiness of a child is "a fragment of fulfilled utopia [*ein Stück der erfüllten Utopie*]," which signifies "the peacefulness, the absence of fear and threat that one pictures to oneself as the chiliastic kingdom."[63]

Sources and Justifications

As I bring this book to a close, it should be noted that I have not laid out a philosophical argument as to how Adorno secures a final and incontestable grounding for his normative commitments. At this point, however, I hope that it is now clear why Adorno abjures any such requirement. Without succumbing to thoroughgoing skepticism, he acknowledges that our knowledge of the good can never be "absolute," and he accepts the precarity of our normative insight as a constitutive feature of the modern condition. Permit me to recall once again the February 1969 radio address with which I began this book, when Adorno sought to defend himself against student activists who had accused him of political quietism. His only defense was to insist on the intrinsic force of critical thinking: stronger than any mode of merely strategic theory that already bends to instrumental application, "open thinking" would already be "transformative praxis." Adorno admits that what he calls "the emphatic concept of thinking" is "not secured" by "existing conditions," or by "ends yet to be achieved," or by "any kind of battalions."[64]

What should intrigue us in these remarks is Adorno's strong resistance to the suggestion that our normative commitments can be valid only if they submit to the test of rational argument and emerge in the form of thoroughly certain knowledge. To grasp what is at stake in this matter it may be helpful to draw a distinction between *sources* and *justifications*. The sources of normativity would be the various phenomena that we experience *as* normative, namely, as phenomena that awaken us to a certain kind of moral response. Adorno identifies such phenomena with a range of experiences, with brute somatic pleasure but also with higher modes of aesthetic fulfillment, and with many instances of "mimesis" that exemplify our openness and responsiveness both to nature and to others. Such experiences are what Adorno characterizes in *Negative Dialectics* as the "fragments" of a total happiness that the world in general denies. These fragments are not constructs of reason; rather, they are given to us in worldly experience. Moreover, Adorno denies that such experiences can provide us with unfailing standards of normativity. The fact that they are given does not suffice to warrant a return to the premodern belief that morality is built into the objective structure of the nonhuman world. Adorno knows that our normative experiences have lost the luster of unshakable truth, and whatever guidance they may have once provided has now grown precarious and uncertain. This precarity is chiefly due to what Adorno calls the "withering of experience." The dialectic of social rationalization has compromised not only common frameworks of political freedom; it has also damaged us as human beings, leaving us ever colder and less responsive to the suffering of others.

Here we must confront what may be the most enigmatic and controversial problems in Adorno's thought. Adorno often describes these sources of normativity as if they were *self-certifying*, as if such experiences were *intrinsically* normative and bore their moral truth inscribed on their foreheads. But such a premise seems to rely on *the myth of the normatively given*. The sources of normativity as Adorno understands them do not appear to us with the full-dress prestige of rational justification, and in fact he seems resistant to the suggestion that any rational justification would be necessary. Such sources are more like phenomenological models that do not *argue* but only *show*.[65] Their role is to illustrate, with all their fragility, other ways of being human. They exemplify the bare outlines of a right life in the midst of the wrong one.

However, problems that afflict any such conception of the normatively given are well known. It is all too easy for Adorno to imply that experiences of moral insight simply announce their own validity and require no further proof, and, when confronted with the challenge as to how he can know that the sources convey those normative truths, he can do little more than insist on the authority of his own interpretation. If he wishes to avoid the intuitionist and irrationalist implications of this response, he must at least leave his interpretations open to further revision. I believe we must therefore resist the suggestion that any sources of normativity speak for themselves or carry their own justification. Rather, we must allow a distinctive space for justification as a second-order, discursive exercise in which all sources of normativity enter into an ongoing contest of rival interpretations and all participants accept some intersubjective standards of validation.[66] Whether Adorno would have been willing to acknowledge the importance of such a practice remains unclear. Running through his work is a pronounced suspicion regarding the task of philosophical justification as such; he fears that in appealing to concepts we tend to lose sight of the sources that lie beyond the space of reasons in material experience. We are therefore confronted with a crucial question: Can we retain what is best in Adorno's theory of normative sources even while we bring it into alignment with a theory of intersubjective justification? Can the appeal to experience be harmonized with the demand for validation? Such a task would involve the ongoing work of reconciling the two major currents of thought that have run through the history of critical theory over the past one hundred years. But this is a task that lies well beyond the purview of this book.

Thinking and Happiness

In this book I have sought to defend the claim that Adorno appeals to fragmentary experiences of happiness as sources of normativity that animate his own critical practice. To this I have added the important proviso that Adorno sees such experiences as no less damaged than the world in which they are found. He recognizes that today all sources of normativity have suffered a marked decline, and he feels little confidence in the power of philosophy to reawaken those primary experiences once they have lost their authority. Critical thinking, he tells us, has grown no less precarious than happiness itself. "Whatever has once been thought" can be "suppressed," it can be "forgotten," or it can even "vanish" altogether.[67] When reading Adorno such warnings must be kept in mind since they serve as cautionary notes against any premature or utopian faith in the certainty of a better life to come. In the introduction to this book it was suggested that Adorno saw Gnosticism as a "temptation" that he did not always manage to resist. I must now add a crucial qualification, namely, that Gnosticism is not an *unwanted* temptation but a *necessary* one, since it confronts our normative claims with a skeptical test they must survive. If Adorno was fascinated by Gnosticism, this is because he understood that if the practice of social criticism is to remain free from dogmatism it must dwell in the uncertainty of a historical condition where our ethical and political commitments remain forever open to contestation and revision. This is the key difference between Adorno's open dialectic and the Hegelian dialectic of closure or "absolute knowing."

Adorno's moral materialism does not strive for a definitive or determinate negation of Gnosticism; rather, it remains *within* the gnostic world even while it seeks for immanent signs of freedom that point beyond its walls. Such considerations would suggest that we cannot overcome a certain antinomy in our conception of morality and freedom. In his 1963 lectures on the topic "Problems of Moral Philosophy," he insists on this point:

> Something like the right life [*ein richtiges Leben*] is not conceivable unless you hold fast to both conscience and responsibility. At this point then we find

> ourselves really and truly in an antinomical situation. *We need to hold fast to*
> *the normative [an dem Normativen], to self-criticism, to the question of right*
> *and wrong, and at the same time to a sense of the fallibility of the authority that*
> *has the confidence to undertake such self-criticism.*[68]

If Adorno does not seek a resolution to this antinomy, it is because he sees
it as constitutive of our current social condition. We must face up to the challenge of the negativist interpretation even while we also "hold fast to the normative," and thereby sustain our hope for a life that would finally be worth
living.

All the same, Adorno remained confident that a certain normative commitment already inheres in the sheer act of critical thinking itself. This normativity is grounded in something deeper than mere reason alone, and it
reaches well beyond the satisfactions of the philosopher who strives for intellectual beatitude in the isolation of his study. If Adorno doubted that philosophy could furnish our normative commitments with justifications that are
rational in character, this is because he felt that reason in its current form has
lost contact with the material experiences that animate human life and make
it worthwhile. What I have called Adorno's materialist morality is the philosophical name for an attempt to restore this contact, to call philosophy back
from its conceptual flights so that it can entrust itself to experience and take
instruction from the manifold experiences that beckon to us from the realm
of the non-identical. Such "open thinking" is not an invitation to irrational-
ism, though it is suspicious of seeking a final and rational justification for
our normative commitments. It finds its highest warrant not in philosophical argument but in an experience of universal happiness that belongs to the
human species as its unrealized promise. But this was a happiness that he
associated with his own experience of *thinking*. "The happiness that dawns
in the eye of the thinking person," Adorno once observed, "is the happiness
of humanity."[69] More than half a century since his death, when the promise
of happiness is too often betrayed, these words can perhaps stand as both his
epitaph and an enduring testament to his memory.

Acknowledgments

This book has its origins in a series of three lectures that were delivered in June 2019 at the Wolfgang von Goethe Universität, Frankfurt, to commemorate Theodor W. Adorno on the occasion of the fiftieth anniversary of his death. The Adorno-Vorlesungen, sponsored by the Institute for Social Research (IfS) in cooperation with Suhrkamp Verlag, are a distinguished lecture series that has been ongoing for many years, and in the past its speakers have addressed a wide variety of themes. To mark the half century since Adorno's passing, however, it was considered appropriate that the lectures should address the philosophical legacy of the thinker for whom the series is named. I was deeply honored to receive this special invitation, and I wish to acknowledge all of the individuals who made the lectures possible and who assisted me in revising them for publication.

I am especially grateful to Axel Honneth, who was director of the IfS, and whose own philosophical labors have done so much to demonstrate the enduring power of the Frankfurt School tradition of critical theory. I was also gratified to receive a warm welcome from other members of the faculty at the Institute, especially Ferdinand Sutterlüty, who served as the Institute's director after Axel Honneth stepped down from the post. I was also grateful for discerning comments and criticism from members of the audience during my presentations. I would especially like to mention Rainer Forst, Rahel Jaeggi, and Martin Saar. But there are a great many more who were in attendance. Unfortunately, in the heat of the moment I did not take care to record the names of all those who responded to my presentations, and I hope I will be forgiven for failing to list them all here.

During my 2019 visit in Frankfurt, I was greeted with exceptional warmth by members of the Institute's staff and fellows, and I would especially like to mention Sidonia Blättler, who assured that my visit would run smoothly. A number of other students, administrators, and affiliates of the IfS served as hosts during my stay, and a small group of them even took me on an informal walking tour of the neighborhood where Adorno had lived during the post-war era. The lectures, after all, were offered as a modest testimony to the philosopher's enduring importance, and I would like to imagine that Adorno's spirit (if such an antiquated word is still permissible) continues to haunt the streets around Frankfurt's Westend. In the Institute itself, of course, one can still detect his continued presence, and I was grateful for permission to play a few tentative notes on his old piano.

Of the original three lectures that I delivered in June 2019, very little now stands as it was then. Except for a few transitional passages and quotations, the text is entirely new. Although the basic thrust of my argument remains largely unchanged, it has been much extended but also refined and, I hope, improved. During the period of writing the book, I was fortunate to have the opportunity to present my arguments to various audiences on several occasions. A compressed version of my main argument was first presented as a paper in a graduate seminar on critical theory in Berlin hosted by Rahel Jaeggi (Humboldt Universität) and Robin Celikates (Freie Universität), who invited me there in December 2019. Their kindness during my visit has left an indelible memory. I presented the paper once again to colleagues in the Department of German at the University of Michigan, where I was invited to give the Grilk Lecture in February 2020; a similar paper was later presented to the Anne Tanenbaum Centre for Jewish Studies at the University of Toronto in March 2021; and I offered a revised version of the paper a final time in the Program for Critical Theory at the University of California, Berkeley, in late March 2021. On all these occasions I was the beneficiary of spirited and insightful comments, and I hope that the present book serves as evidence of my gratitude.

I should also take care to mention the many scholars whose work has served as an inspiration for the arguments presented here. These include but are by no means limited to Seyla Benhabib, J. M. Bernstein, Maeve Cooke, James Gordon Finlayson, Espen Hammer, Axel Honneth, Rahel Jaeggi, Martin Jay, Iain Macdonald, Brian O'Connor, Max Pensky, and Michael Rosen.

Four scholars deserve special mention. First, I am grateful to Fabian Freyenhagen, whose 2013 book, *Adorno's Practical Philosophy*, ranks among the very best contributions to the field, and whose arguments helped inspire my own. Although I have come to rather different conclusions, my disagreements hardly diminish my admiration for his exemplary scholarship. Second, I am grateful to Rainer Forst, who presented his thoughts on the philosophical foundations of contemporary critical theory in a lecture at Harvard University in September 2019. His distinctive interest in the problem of justification and his discerning remarks on the connection between Kant and Marx have helped me a great deal as I have tried to develop my understanding of Adorno's place in the philosophical tradition. Third, I wish to mention my philosophical debts to Axel Honneth, whose arguments concerning the central role of recognition in social theory have inspired some of my own reflections on the significance of mimesis and responsiveness to human suffering. Fourth and finally, I would like to register my special gratitude to Jürgen Habermas, whose contributions to critical theory continue to inspire my thinking in countless ways, even if the arguments presented in this book reflect an ongoing if modest disagreement between us. Habermas himself has helped us appreciate how philosophical insight emerges from the ongoing practice of rational contestation, and I trust that my efforts here may serve as further evidence for that principle. By sheer coincidence, less than two weeks after I presented the Adorno-Vorlesungen, Professor Habermas celebrated his ninetieth birthday, an occasion that was marked with a public lecture at the Goethe-Universität Frankfurt. Attended by a vast audience of students and colleagues, his lecture not only confirmed, but deepened my admiration for all he has achieved in the many years since he first presented himself to Adorno as a young man. The Institute for Social Research was founded in Frankfurt a hundred years ago, in 1923, and if critical theory continues to flourish in all the diversity of its voices a century later, there can be no doubt that we owe the greatest debt of gratitude to Jürgen Habermas himself.

No book should go to press without the benefit of discerning criticism. For their critical comments on drafts of the book manuscript, I would also like to express my warm gratitude to James Gordon Finlayson, Martin Jay, Iain Macdonald, and Max Pensky. All four are scholars of great erudition and philosophical acumen, and the book in its current form incorporates their suggestions, though of course all flaws are entirely my own responsibility. My Harvard colleague and friend Alex Rehding also offered excellent comments on the entire manuscript and provided special guidance on matters of musicology. Finally, I owe a special, heartfelt thanks to my dear friend John Schott, the musician and composer, both for his particular insights on the passages about music and for his scrupulous work in proofreading the full manuscript.

No scholar can learn, let alone breathe, in an airless room. I have had the great fortune of learning from some of the best scholars in the field, some in person but others only through their publications. But I have also learned from the many students who have participated in numerous seminars on Adorno and social theory over the past several years. I offered one such seminar, on the topic of Adorno's aesthetic theory, at the School of Criticism and Theory (SCT) at Cornell University in 2018. I am grateful to the many students in that seminar for their many insights and to the then director of the SCT, Hent de Vries, for the invitation to spend the summer in Ithaca as a visiting professor.

In undertaking the revisions for this book, I was assisted by Michael Mango, a doctoral student at Harvard whose discernment and diligent research is evident on every page. He has helped me immeasurably. Musical examples were transcribed by Alexander W. Cowan.

Finally, I am also grateful to my publishers in Germany and North America. At Suhrkamp Verlag, I am especially grateful to my editor, Eva Gilmer, whose confidence in this project has not diminished during the years that it took for me to revise and expand the lectures into a more respectable (if nevertheless still-flawed) book. Suhrkamp Verlag stands for the highest ideals in philosophical scholarship, and it is an honor to publish the German-language version of my book with such an esteemed publisher. I am equally grateful to Kyle Wagner at the University of Chicago Press and to the two anonymous readers whose discerning comments prompted me to refine and clarify many points of confusion in my arguments. The English-language version of the manuscript was edited with great care by Sheila Berg. The index was prepared by Derek Gottlieb.

On a more personal note, many friends have offered their insights and support while I pursued the arguments presented here. They know of the challenges that life has brought my way in recent years, and I am grateful for their friendship. Among them I wish to mention my beloved wife, who has shown great tolerance for the unlikely epiphanies of insight that come upon me usually during dinner. But, more importantly, she has demonstrated her superb philosophical acumen at every turn. It is hardly an exaggeration to say that she is responsible for nearly all of the best thoughts that I have only transcribed here. To share one's life with a person of such astonishing intelligence can be rather humbling, but it also ranks among the greatest gifts that one could wish for.

It would be wrong to conclude these acknowledgments without mentioning the sobering fact that this book was completed during the long and difficult period of the world pandemic caused by the novel coronavirus. Although it is perhaps a truism, it is nonetheless a truth worth stating that the disease has revealed in the most dramatic way the precarity of human life. But this is true not only in the natural sense, insofar as we share with all organisms a vulnerability to illness and death; it is also true in the social sense, since the pandemic has magnified already stark inequalities of wealth both within each society and between the various countries across the globe. I share with others of my social standing in North America the wholly undeserved good fortune that I survived the pandemic without great personal loss. But I have come through the experience with an enhanced understanding of the precarity of the human condition. Suffering comes in an infinity of forms for which no happiness, no matter how great, can offer a sufficient remedy. For readers who may have experienced such suffering in their own lives, it will not be hard to detect its traces in the pages of this book.

Frankfurt am Main, 2019
Cape Cod, Massachusetts, 2022

Abbreviations

This book refers to the standard edition of Adorno's *Gesammelte Schriften*, edited by Rolf Tiedemann with assistance from Gretel Adorno, Susan Buck-Morss, and Klaus Schultz (Frankfurt am Main: Suhrkamp, 1970). The individual volumes are cited as GS, followed by the appropriate volume number and page.

GS 1: *Philosophische Frühschriften*. 3. Aufl., 1996.

GS 2: *Kierkegaard. Konstruktion des Ästhetischen*. 2. Aufl., 1990.

GS 3: *Max Horkheimer und Theodor W. Adorno*, Dialektik der Aufklärung. Philosophische Fragmente. 3. Aufl., 1996.

GS 4: *Minima Moralia. Reflexionen aus dem beschädigten Leben*. 2. Aufl., 1996.

GS 5: *Zur Metakritik der Erkenntnistheorie / Drei Studien zu Hegel*. 5. [recte: 4.] Aufl., 1996.

GS 6: *Negative Dialektik / Jargon der Eigentlichkeit*. 5. Aufl., 1996.

GS 7: *Ästhetische Theorie*. 6. Aufl., 1996.

GS 8: *Soziologische Schriften* I. 4. Aufl., 1996.

GS 9.1: *Soziologische Schriften* II. Erste Hälfte. 3. Aufl., 1997.

GS 9.2: *Soziologische Schriften* II. Zweite Hälfte. 3. Aufl., 1997.

GS 10.1: *Kulturkritik und Gesellschaft* I. Prismen / Ohne Leitbild. 2. Aufl., 1996.

GS 10.2: *Kulturkritik und Gesellschaft* II. Eingriffe / Stichworte / Anhang. 2. Aufl., 1996.

GS 11: *Noten zur Literatur*. 4. Aufl., 1996.

GS 12: *Philosophie der neuen Musik*. 2. Aufl., 1990.

GS 13: *Die musikalischen Monographien: Wagner, Mahler, Berg*. 4. Aufl., 1996.

GS 14:   *Dissonanzen. Einleitung in die Musiksoziologie.* 4. Aufl., 1996.

GS 15:   Theodor W. Adorno und Hanns Eisler, *Komposition für den Film:*
         Der getreue Korrepetitor. 2. Aufl., 1996.

GS 16:   *Musikalische Schriften I: Klangfiguren.* II: *Quasi una fantasia: Musi-*
         kalische Schriften III. 2. Aufl., 1990.

GS 17:   *Musikalische Schriften IV: Moments musicaux: Impromptus.* 1982.

GS 18:   *Musikalische Schriften V.* 1984.

GS 19:   *Musikalische Schriften VI.* 1984.

GS 20.1: *Vermischte Schriften I.* 1986.

GS 20.2: *Vermischte Schriften II.* 1986.

Individual volumes of the published versions from Adorno's *Nachgelassene*
Schriften und Briefe (Frankfurt am Main: Suhrkamp, 2021) are cited as NGS,
followed by the section number (Abt.), volume number, and page.

Abteilung I: Fragment gebliebene Schriften

NGS, Abt. 1: Band 1   *Beethoven: Philosophie der Musik* (1994).

NGS, Abt. 1: Band 2   *Zu einer Theorie der musikalischen Reproduktion*
                       (2001).

NGS, Abt. 1: Band 3   *Current of Music: Elements of a Radio Theory*
                       (2006).

Abteilung II: Philosophische Notizen (ca. 5 Bände).

Abteilung III: Poetische Versuche (1 Band).

Abteilung IV: Vorlesungen.

NGS, Abt. IV: Band 1   *Erkenntnistheorie* (1957/58), 2018.

NGS, Abt. IV: Band 2   *Einführung in die Dialektik* (1958), 2010.

NGS, Abt. IV: Band 3   *Ästhetik* (1958/59), 2009.

NGS, Abt. IV: Band 4   *Kants "Kritik der reinen Vernunft"* (1959), 1995.

NGS, Abt. IV: Band 5   *Einleitung in die Philosophie* (1959/60).

NGS, Abt. IV: Band 6   *Philosophie und Soziologie* (1960), 2011.

NGS, Abt. IV: Band 7   *Ontologie und Dialektik* (1960/61), 2002.

NGS, Abt. IV: Band 8   *Ästhetik* (1961/62), gepl für 2022.

NGS, Abt. IV: Band 9   *Philosophische Terminologie* (1962/63), 2016.

NGS, Abt. IV: Band 10   *Probleme der Moralphilosophie* (1963), 1996.

NGS, Abt. IV: Band 11   *Fragen der Dialektik* (1963/64), 2021.

NGS, Abt. IV: Band 12   *Philosophische Elemente einer Theorie der Gesell-*
                        schaft (1964/65), 2008.

NGS, Abt. IV: Band 13 *Zur Lehre von der Geschichte und der Freiheit*
(1964/65), 2001.

NGS, Abt. IV: Band 14 *Metaphysik. Begriff und Probleme* (1965), 1998.

NGS, Abt. IV: Band 15 *Einleitung in die Soziologie* (1968), 1993.

NGS, Abt. IV: Band 16 *Vorlesung über Negative Dialektik*, 2003.

NGS, Abt. IV: Band 17 *Kranichsteiner Vorlesungen* (with DVD), 2014.

NGS, Abt. IV: Band 18 *Stichworte und Stenogramm-Fragmente zu nicht
erhaltenen Vorlesungen.*

Abteilung V: Vorträge und Gespräche

NGS, Abt. V: Band 1   *Vorträge 1949–1968*, 2019.

Abbreviations for Frequently Cited Works by Adorno

AE   *Aesthetik* (1958/59). Frankfurt am Main: Suhrkamp, 2009. In English as *Aesthetics 1958/59*. Ed. Eberhard Ortland. Trans. Wieland
Hoban Cambridge: Polity, 2018.

AR   *The Adorno Reader*. Ed. Brian O'Connor. Oxford: Blackwell,
2000.

AT   *Aesthetic Theory*. Trans. Robert Hullot-Kentor. Minneapolis:
University of Minnesota Press, 1997. In German as *Ästhetische
Theorie*, in GS 7. Frankfurt am Main: Suhrkamp, 1970.

AP   Theodor W. Adorno et al., *The Authoritarian Personality*. Orig.
1950; repr. London: Verso Press, 2019.

BO   "Bourgeois Opera," in *Sound Figures*. Stanford: Stanford University
Press, 1999. 15–28; "Bürgerliche Oper," in *Klangfiguren*. Darm-
städter Gespräche, 1955; Frankfurt am Main: Suhrkamp, 1959.
Reprinted in GS 16, 31.

BPM   *Beethoven: The Philosophy of Music*. Ed. Rolf Tiedemann. Trans.
Edmund Jephcott. Stanford: Stanford University Press, 1998. In
German as *Beethoven: Philosophie der Musik*. NGS, Abt. 1, I.

CCS   "Cultural Criticism and Society." In PRSM, 17–34; GS 10:1, 11–30.

CM   *Critical Models: Interventions and Catchwords*. Trans. Henry
Pickford. New York: Columbia University Press, 2005.

DE   Theodor W. Adorno and Max Horkheimer, *Dialectic of Enlightenment: Philosophical Fragments*. Trans. Edmund Jephcott Stanford:
Stanford University Press, 2007.

ID   *Einführung in die Dialektik*. Frankfurt am Main: Suhrkamp,
2010. In English as *An Introduction to Dialectics*. Ed. Christoph

Ziermann. Trans. Nicholas Walker. Cambridge: Polity, 2017. English edition also abbreviated ID.

ES   *Einleitung in die Soziologie.* Frankfurt am Main: Suhrkamp, 1993. In English as *Introduction to Sociology*. Trans. Edmund Jephcott. Stanford: Stanford University Press, 2000.

HF   *History and Freedom: Lectures 1964–1965.* Ed. Rolf Tiedemann. Trans. Rodney Livingstone. Cambridge: Polity, 2006.

KC   "*Kultur* and Culture," trans. Mark Kalbus. *Social Text 99* 27, no. 2 (Summer 2009): 145–58. In German, "Kultur und Culture." In Adorno, *Vorträge 1949–1968*. Frankfurt am Main: Suhrkamp, 2019. 156–76.

KKV   *Kants "Kritik der reinen Vernunft."* Frankfurt am Main: Suhrkamp, 1995. In English as *Kant's "Critique of Pure Reason."* Trans. Rodney Livingstone. Stanford: Stanford University Press, 2001.

KNM   "Criteria of New Music," in *Sound Figures*. Trans. Rodney Livingstone. Stanford: Stanford University Press, 1999. In German as "Kriterien der neuen Musik," in GS 16, 227.

MCP   *Metaphysics: Concepts and Problems.* Trans. Edmund Jephcott. Stanford: Stanford University Press, 2000.

MM   *Minima Moralia: Reflections from Damaged Life.* Trans. E. F. N. Jephcott. London: New Left Books, 1974.

MMP   *Mahler: A Musical Physiognomy.* Trans. Edmund Jephcott. Chicago: University of Chicago Press, 1992.

MTP   "Marginalia to Theory and Practice," in CM, 259–78; in German as "Marginalien zu Theorie und Praxis," in GS 10.2, 759–82.

ND   *Negative Dialektik*, in GS 6. Frankfurt am Main: Suhrkamp, 1966. For the English, I have consulted the version by Dennis Redmond (2001), with my own modifications where indicated.

NPT   "Notes on Philosophical Thinking," in CM, 127–34. In German as "Anmerkungen zum philosophischen Denken," in GS 10.2, 599–607.

PEG   Adorno, *Philosophical Elements of a Theory of Society*. Lectures 1964. Cambridge: Polity, 2019. In German as *Philosophische Elemente einer Theorie der Gesellschaft*. Frankfurt am Main: Suhrkamp, 2008.

PMP   *Probleme der Moralphilosophie.* Frankfurt am Main: Suhrkamp, 1996. In English as *Problems of Moral Philosophy*. Trans. Rodney Livingstone. Malden: Polity, 2000.

PNM   *Philosophy of New Music.* Trans. Robert Hullot-Kentor. Minneapolis: University of Minnesota Press, 2019.

PRSM   *Prisms.* Trans. Samuel and Shierry Weber. Cambridge, MA: MIT Press, 1981.

PS   *Philosophy and Sociology.* Ed. Dirk Braunstein. Trans. Nicholas
        Walker. Cambridge: Polity, 2022. In German in NGS, Abt. IV:
        Band 6, *Philosophie und Soziologie* (1960), 2011.
RSGN   "Resignation," in CM, 289–93; in German in GS 10.2, 794–99.
SO   "Subject and Object," in CM, 245–58. In German in GS 10.2, 741–58.
TN   "Theses on Need," trans. Iain Macdonald and Martin Shuster, in
        Theodor Adorno and Max Horkheimer, *Towards a New Manifesto.*
        London: Verso, 2019, 79–90; "Thesen über Bedürfnis" (1942),
        in GS 8, 392–96.

Other Frequently Cited Works

BC   Peter E. Gordon, Espen Hammer, and Max Pensky, eds., *The
        Blackwell Companion to Adorno.* London: Blackwell, 2020.
CC   Fred Rush, ed., *The Cambridge Companion to Adorno.* Cambridge:
        Cambridge University Press, 2004.
FF   Fabian Freyenhagen, *Adorno's Practical Philosophy: Living Less
        Wrongly.* Cambridge: Cambridge University Press, 2013.
MER   *The Marx-Engels Reader*, 2nd ed. Ed. Robert C. Tucker. New York:
        Norton, 1978.
PDM   Jürgen Habermas, *The Philosophical Discourse of Modernity: Twelve
        Lectures.* Trans. Frederick G. Lawrence. Cambridge, MA: MIT
        Press, 1987.
RFS   Peter E. Gordon, Espen Hammer, and Axel Honneth, *The Routledge
        Companion to the Frankfurt School.* London: Routledge, 2019.

Notes

Preface

1. "Too fragmented are World and Life! I will take myself to see a German professor!" Heinrich Heine, "Zu fragmentarisch ist Welt und Leben!," LVIII, in "Die Heimkehr," *Buch der Lieder* (Hamburg: Hoffmann und Campe, 1827).

2. For a summary of this troubled encounter, see Hans Kundnani, "The Frankfurt School and the West German Student Movement," in RFS, 221–34.

3. RSGN, 393; GS 10.2, 798.

4. RSGN, 292–93; GS 10.2, 798.

5. "Denken ist nicht die geistige Reproduktion dessen, was ohnehin ist. Solange es nicht abbricht, hält es die *Möglichkeit* fest. Sein Unstillbares, der Widerwille dagegen, sich abspeisen zu lassen, verweigert sich der törichten Weisheit von Resignation. In ihm ist das utopische Moment desto stärker, je weniger es—auch das eine Form des Rückfalls—zur Utopie sich vergegenständlicht und dadurch deren Verwirklichung sabotiert. Offenes Denken weist über sich hinaus." *Kritische Modelle*, GS 10.2, 798. My emphasis. For an important clarification of the "real possibilities" that are implicit in Adorno's concept of "realization [*Verwirklichung*]," see Iain Macdonald, *What Would Be Different: Figures of Possibility in Adorno* (Stanford: Stanford University Press, 2019).

6. "Wie kritisches Denken selber zu rechtfertigen sei." Habermas, "Adorno, Urgeschichte der Subjektivität und verwilderte Selbstbehauptung" (1969), in *Philosophische-Politische Profile* (Frankfurt am Main: Suhrkamp, 1987).

7. See, e.g., *Minima Moralia*, §6, where Adorno acknowledges "die Absenz einer jeden objektiv verbindlichen Sitte." As Iain Macdonald has observed, this skepticism suggests that, like Hegel, Adorno does not wish to appeal to a "moral law" but rather a valid form of *ethical life*, or *Sittlichkeit*. GS 4, 28. My thanks to Iain Macdonald for alerting me to this passage and its philosophical significance.

8. See, e.g., the conversation with Ernst Bloch, "Something's Missing: A Discussion between Ernst Bloch and Theodor W. Adorno on the Contradictions of Utopian Longing," in Ernst Bloch, *The Utopian Function of Art and Literature: Selected Essays*, trans. Jack Zipes and Frank Mecklenburg (Cambridge, MA: MIT Press, 1989), 1–17.

9. Quoted from Adorno, "Heine the Wound," in *Notes to Literature, Volume One*, trans. Shierry Weber Nicholsen (New York: Columbia University Press, 1991), 80–85. In German as

"Die Wunde Heine," in GS 11, 95–100. My emphasis. I am grateful to Iain Macdonald for alerting me to this passage.

10. Adorno and Bloch, "Something's Missing," 7. My emphasis on "categories"; the other emphases are in the original.

11. KC, 145–58; quote from 149; translation modified. NGS, Abt. V: Band 1: 156–76. My emphasis. To the reader who remains skeptical about my use of the term "human flourishing," it may be worth considering just how frequently Adorno appeals to a utopian condition such as "boundless fulfillment" as the counterfactual norm that guides his criticism.

12. Unlike the Greek idea of *eudaimonia*, however, Adorno considers the hedonic or sensual satisfaction of the human being as essential to our fulfillment and not subordinate to reason. For a careful reconstruction of happiness in Aristotle and the importance of the *Eudemian Ethics* alongside the (better-known) *Nicomachean Ethics*, see, e.g., Anthony Kenny, *Aristotle on the Perfect Life* (Oxford: Oxford University Press, 1992).

13. KC, in NGS, Abt. V: Band 1: 156–76.

14. "Thus I would say that what is essential about the concept of utopia is that it does not consist of a certain, single selected category that changes itself and from which everything constitutes itself, for example, in that one assumes that the category of happiness alone is the key to utopia." Adorno and Bloch, "Something's Missing," 7.

15. "bezieht sich auf einen Bereich, der für undenkliche Zeiten als der eigentliche der Philosophie galt, seit deren Verwandlung in Methode aber der intellektuellen Nichtachtung, der sententiösen Willkür und am Ende der Vergessenheit verfiel: *die Lehre vom richtigen Leben*." Dedication (to Max Horkheimer), in MM, 13, translation modified. "Zueignung" (to Max Horkheimer). GS 4, 13. My emphasis.

Introduction

1. "Lassen Sie mich mit der Fiktion beginnen, daß Sie von der 'Kritik der reinen Vernunft' noch nichts wissen. Diese Fiktion ist legitim und illegitim zugleich: sie ist illegitim insofern, als ein Werk von der Art der erkenntnistheoretischen Hauptschrift Kants natürlich selbst heute noch eine solche Autorität ausstrahlt, daß jeder irgend etwas davon gehört hat; sie ist aber in einem tieferen Sinn, glaube ich, gar nicht sof iktiv, wie sie sich anhört. Zunächst könnte man ja sagen, daß das, was man so irgendwie von einer Philosophie hat läuten hören, imallgemeinen eher dazu beiträgt, ihren eigentlichen Gehalt zu verdunkeln, als ihn klarzulegen. Die üblichen Formeln, auf die man die Philosophien zu bringen pflegt, tendieren dazu, die Werke zu verdinglichen, zu verhärten und eine genuine Beziehung zu ihnen eigentlich zu erschweren." KKR, English (Lecture 1: May 12, 1959), 1. NGS, Abt. IV: Band 4: 9.

2. MM (§18), 39; GS 4, 43.

3. MM ("Dedication"), 15, translation modified. GS 4, 13.

4. It is one of the purposes of this book to qualify the one-sided and frequently repeated caricature of Adorno as simply an opponent of happiness. For a thought-provoking account of happiness that places an important emphasis on its potentially ideological and oppressive features, see Sara Ahmed, *The Promise of Happiness* (Durham, NC: Duke University Press, 2010).

5. J. W. von Goethe, *Faust, Eine Tragödie* (Munich: Bremer Presse, 1925), 70.

6. Hegel offers a more precise account in his *Logic*: "The Speculative stage, or stage of Positive Reason, apprehends the unity of terms (propositions) in their opposition—the affirmative,

which is involved in their disintegration and in their transition." Hegel, *The Science of Logik: Encyclopedia of the Philosophical Sciences*, §82. See also the "Remark" on the meaning of *Aufhebung* in ch. 1, §21. My thanks to Gordon Finlayson for alerting me to this.

7. See Hans Mayer, *Thomas Mann: Werk und Entwicklung* (Berlin: Verlag Volk und Welt, 1950), 370. For the exchange between Mann and Adorno regarding Mayer's apparent "discovery," see Theodor Adorno and Thomas Mann, *Briefwechsel, 1943–1955*, ed. Christoph Gödde and Thomas Sprecher (Frankfurt am Main: Suhrkamp, 2002). Adorno's letter is dated July 6, 1950; Mann's response is dated July 11, 1950. The identity of Mann's Mephistopheles as Adorno is repeated in Jean-François Lyotard, "Adorno as the Devil," *Telos* (Spring 1974): 127–37.

8. For a summary of this affair, see Michael Maar, "Teddy and Tommy: The Masks of Doctor Faustus," *New Left Review* (March–April 2003): 113–30.

9. For a classic statement of the negativist interpretation, see Michael Theunissen, "Negativität bei Adorno," in *Adorno-Konferenz 1983*, ed. Ludwig von Friedeburg and Jürgen Habermas (Frankfurt am Main: Suhrkamp, 1983), 41–66.

10. PMP, 175. NGS, Abt. IV: Band 10: 261.

11. NGS, Abt. IV: Band 10: 261.

12. "Jedes Menschenbild ist Ideologie außer dem negative." "Zum Verhältnis von Soziologie und Psychologie," *Frankfurter Beiträge zur Soziologie*, Festschrift für Max Horkheimer (Europäische Verlagsanstalt, 1955), Band I. Republished in GS, 8: 42–45. In English as Adorno, "Sociology and Psychology" (Part II), *New Left Review* 47 (1968): 84.

13. PMP, 175. NGS, Abt. IV: Band 10: 261.

14. "Kein Spalt im Fels des Bestehenden, an dem der Griff des Ironikers sich zu halten vermöchte." Adorno, MM (§134), 211. GS 4, 241.

15. For a reading of Adorno as a gnostic, see Michael Pauen, *Dithyrambiker des Untergangs: Gnostizismus in Ästhetik und Philosophie der Moderne* (Berlin: Akademie Verlag, 1994). My thanks to Gordon Finlayson for alerting me to Pauen's book.

16. Georg Lukács, *Die Zerstörung der Vernunft* (Neuwied am Rhein: Luchterhand, 1962), 219.

17. PDM, Lecture 2; English, 43; German, 57.

18. "Modernity can and will no longer borrow the criteria by which it takes its orientation from the models supplied by another epoch; *it has to create its normativity out of itself*." PDM, Lecture I, 7; German, 16. Emphasis in original.

19. PDM, English, Lecture II, 40; German, 53.

20. PDM, English, Lecture II, 42; German, 56.

21. For a different account of the relationship between critical theory and poststructuralism, see Martin Saar, "Critical Theory and Poststructuralism," in RFS, 323–35.

22. PDM, English, Lecture V, 106. German, 130.

23. PDM, English, Lecture V, 119. German, 144; emphasis in original.

24. Max Horkheimer und Theodor W. Adorno, "Rettung der Aufklärung: Diskussion über eine geplante Schrift zur Dialektik" (1946), in Horkheimer, *Gesammelte Schriften*, Band 12 (Frankfurt am Main: S. Fischer, 1985), 594.

25. See, e.g., "Editor's Afterword," in DE, English edition, 217–47.

26. PDM, Lecture V: English, 118. German, 143.

27. PDM, Lecture V: English, 119. German, 144.

28. PDM, Lecture V: English, 119. German, 144. On this theme, see Martin Jay, "The Debate over the Performative Contradiction: Habermas versus the Poststructuralists," in *Philosophical*

Interventions in the Unfinished Project of Enlightenment, ed. Axel Honneth, Thomas McCarthy, Claus Offe, and Albrecht Wellmer (Cambridge, MA: MIT Press, 1992), 261–79.

29. PDM, Lecture V: English, 127. German, 154.

30. "I do not share the basic premise of Critical Theory, as it took shape during the early 1940s, the premise that instrumental reason has gained such dominance that there is really no way out of a total system of delusion [*Verblendungszusammenhang*], in which insight is achieved only in flashes by isolated individuals." Quoted from Jürgen Habermas, "Political Experience and the Renewal of Marxist Theory" (interview with Dietlef Horster and Willem van Reijen), in Peter Dews, *Autonomy and Solidarity: Interviews with Jürgen Habermas* (London: Verso, 1986), 78.

31. "Anyone who abides in a paradox on the very spot once occupied by philosophy with its ultimate groundings is not just taking up an uncomfortable position; one can only hold that place if one makes it at least minimally plausible that there is *no way out*." PDM, English, 128. German, 155. Emphasis in original.

32. For a superb discussion of this charge, see James Gordon Finlayson, "Morality and Critical Theory: On the Normative Problem of Frankfurt School Critical Theory," *Telos* 146 (2009): 7–42.

33. On the idea of self-authorization, see Peter E. Gordon, "Self-Authorizing Modernity" (Review of Terry Pinkard, *German Philosophy, 1760–1860*, and Frederick Beiser, *German Idealism: The Struggle against Subjectivism, 1781–1801*), *History and Theory* 44, no. 1 (February 2005): 121–37.

34. On the theme of a "normative deficit of modernity," see Peter E. Gordon, "Contesting Secularization: Remarks on the Normative Deficit of Modernity after Weber," in *Formation of Belief: Historical Approaches to Religion and the Secular*, ed. Katja Guenther, Philip Nord, and Max Weiss (Princeton, NJ: Princeton University Press, 2019), 184–201. See also Peter E. Gordon, "Critical Theory between the Sacred and the Profane," *Constellations* 23, no. 4 (May 2016): 466–81. In German as Gordon, "Kritische Theorie zwischen Sakralen und Profane," *WestEnd: Neue Zeitschrift für Sozialforschung* 1 (2016): 3–34.

35. Axel Honneth, *Disrespect: The Normative Foundations of Critical Theory* (Cambridge: Polity, 2007), 65–67.

36. Honneth, *Disrespect*, 65. My emphasis.

37. Honneth, *Disrespect*, 65. My emphasis on "closed."

38. Honneth, *Disrespect*, 66.

39. Honneth, *Disrespect*, 66.

40. Honneth, *Disrespect*, 65.

41. Axel Honneth, "A Physiognomy of the Capitalist Form of Life: A Sketch of Adorno's Social Theory," *Constellations* 12, no. 1 (2005): 60.

42. Honneth, "A Physiognomy," 60.

43. Honneth, "A Physiognomy," 60.

44. Honneth, "A Physiognomy," 61.

45. Honneth, "A Physiognomy," 61.

46. GS 6, 203. As quoted by Honneth, "A Physiognomy," 61.

47. Honneth, "A Physiognomy," 61.

48. Honneth, "A Physiognomy," 61.

49. Honneth, "A Physiognomy," 61.

50. For a different account of the differences between Honneth and Adorno, see Naveh Frumer, "Negative Freedom or Integrated Domination? Adorno versus Honneth," *European Journal of Philosophy* 28 (March 2020): 126–41.

51. What Adorno calls the "right life" bears a close resemblance to the normatively rich concept of the "good." This concept distinguishes Adorno from the tradition of liberal political theory, in which relatively thin conceptions of justice as fairness have largely displaced the attempt to uphold a universal ideal of human flourishing. Adorno's commitment to this ideal places him in closer proximity to neo-Aristotelian and Hegelian traditions than to political liberalism. In this respect at least, Adorno also shares much in common with the philosophy developed by Axel Honneth. Specifically, Adorno anticipates Honneth's claim that when we criticize what is wrong in society we must have in mind some ideal of "the conditions which constitute a necessary presupposition for the good life." Honneth's diagnosis of social *pathology* is not intelligible without this normatively thick concept of condition that would allow for human flourishing. On the notion of social pathology, see Honneth, *Disrespect*, esp. ch. 1, "Pathologies of the Social: The Past and Present of Social Philosophy," 3–48. I have quoted here from ch. 2, "A Disclosing Critique of Society," 56.

52. The arguments offered in this book might also contribute in a different way to Honneth's philosophical project. Honneth suggests that critical theory can proceed only if it takes as its point of departure the pre-theoretical and normatively rich phenomenon of intersubjective *recognition*. Because social reality is constituted through the ongoing activity of mutual recognition between human subjects, it is possible to ground our common interest in emancipatory social praxis in this basic and constitutive feature of our shared sociality. But this already suggests that the theory of recognition is not self-standing. To claim that recognition is essential to our social being we need some prior account as to what human beings are like such that such recognition would be possible. What is required is a species of philosophical anthropology, or an account of the common *capacity* for recognition that belongs to us simply in virtue of our being human. One of my purposes in this book is to offer some insights into this pre-theoretical capacity or disposition, which I will refer to as *responsiveness*. Clues to this capacity, I will argue, can be found in Adorno's philosophical writings. Honneth himself has noted the link between his theory of recognition and Adorno's idea of mimesis. See, e.g., the remarks in Axel Honneth, *Reification: A New Look at an Old Idea*, Berkeley Tanner Lectures (Oxford: Oxford University Press, 2008), esp. 44–45.

53. J. M. Bernstein, *Adorno: Disenchantment and Ethics* (Cambridge: Cambridge University Press, 2001), quotes from 443 and 447.

54. FF. For full publication information, see my list of abbreviations.

55. FF, 7.

56. FF, 22.

57. FF, 20.

58. FF, 10.

59. FF, 239; my emphasis.

60. FF, 243; my emphasis.

61. GS 6, 358–65. For the full reconstruction, see FF, ch. 5, "A New Categorical Imperative," 133–61.

62. For a discussion, see FF, 156–57.

63. FF, 221.

64. FF, 246.

65. FF, 247.

66. FF, 253.

67. FF, 239.

68. Adorno, "The Actuality of Philosophy," in AR, 31; in GS 1, 334.

69. "Man könnte, wenn man ein ganz böser und abgefeimter Mensch ist, sogar auf die Idee kommen, daß bereits in der szientifischen Forderung eines bruchlosen Kontinuums der soziologischen Erkenntnis, wie es etwa dem großen System von Talcott Parsons zu Grunde liegt, bereits etwas wie eine harmonistische Tendenz steckt; daß also die Bruchlosigkeit der Darstellungsform, der Systematisierung der sozialen Phänomene dabei—unbewußt natürlich, es ist der objektive Geist hier am Werk—die Tendenz in sich hat, die konstitutiven tragenden Widersprüche der Gesellschaft ein bißchen aus der Welt zu erklären." ES, 7. NGS, Abt. IV: Band 15: 18.

70. "this philosophy is indeed an attempt to construe or construct reality, but precisely not as a seamless process. It attempts to do so in the breaks and fractures, and by virtue of the breaks and fractures harbored within reality itself." ID, 38 (Lecture 5, 3 June 1958). NGS, Abt. IV: Band 15: 59.

71. MM (§153), 247. GS 4, 283.

72. AT, 319. GS 7, 473.

73. DE, 115. GS 3, 166–67.

74. DE, 115. GS 3, 167.

75. "Und dadurch kommt dann wirklich jene grauenvolle Parodie einer Identität des objektiv herrschenden Zustands oder der objektiv den Menschen aufgezwungenen Bedingungen und ihre eigenen Bewußtseins zutage, wie sie etwa in dem Buch 'Brave New World' von Aldous Huxley vor nun 34 Jahren zum ersten Mal entworfen worden ist. Ich möchte damit schließen, daß ich sagen möchte, das Argument, das hier erhobenwerden könnte, daß nämlich, wenn eine solche Identität herrsche, ganz gleich, wie sie zustande gekommen sei und ganz gleich, was für einen Inhalt sie habe, 'everyone is happy nowadays' wie es in jenem Roman von Huxley heißt, daß mir dieses Argument sophistisch und deshalb untriftig erscheint, weil eben doch an unzähligen Stellen diese falsche Identität sich als brüchig erweist, und weil sie sofort mit Neurose, mit Leiden, mit allen möglichen Verstümmelungsphänomenen bezahlt wird, sobald man nur ein bißchen unter die Oberfläche des glücklichen Einverständnisses [blickt]." PEG, 113.

76. ES, 11. NGS, Abt. IV: Band 15: 25. My emphasis.

77. "diese Konzeption von Soziologie, die ihre erste und, wenn Sie so wollen, radikale Ausprägung durch Vilfredo Pareto erfahren hat, von Grund auf falsch erscheint, zunächst einmal aus dem ganz einfachen Grund, weil durch die Negation des Begriffs der Wahrheit, die in dieser Vorstellung vom total ideologischen Charakter alles gesellschaftlich bezogenen Bewußtseins besteht, die Unterscheidung von wahr und falsch überhaupt unmöglich gemacht wird; und weil man von falschem Bewußtsein überhaupt gar nicht reden kann, wenn nicht die Möglichkeit eines richtigen Bewußtseins doch auch besteht." In English: "I should like to tell you that this conception of sociology, which was given its first and, perhaps, its most radical formulation by Vifredo Pareto, seems to me to be fundamentally false. It is false, first of all, for the very simple reason that the negation of the idea of truth, which is implicit in this notion of the wholly ideological character of all society-related consciousness, makes it impossible to distinguish between true and false. Secondly, *one cannot talk of false consciousness unless the possibility of a true consciousness also exists.*" ES, 11. NGS, Abt IV: Band 15: 25. My emphasis.

78. Some passages in the following explanation are borrowed from Peter E. Gordon, "Realism and Utopia in *The Authoritarian Personality*," Polity 54, no. 1 (January 2022): 8–28.

79. Marx and Engels, *Manifesto of the Communist Party*, in MER, 481.

80. Max Horkheimer, "Traditional and Critical Theory," in *Critical Theory: Selected Essays* (London: Continuum, 1975), 188–243.

81. CCS, in PRSM, 34. GS 10.1, 29.

82. "Irony's medium, the difference between ideology and reality, has disappeared. The former resigns itself to confirmation of reality by its mere duplication. Irony used to say; such it claims to be, but such it is; today, however, the world, even in its most radical lie, falls back on the argument that things are like this, a simple finding which coincides, for it, with the good [*Ihr Medium, die Differenz zwischen Ideologie und Wirklichkeit, ist geschwunden. Jene resigniert zur Bestätigung der Wirklichkeit durch deren bloße Verdoppelung. Ironie drückte aus: das behauptet es zu sein, so aber ist es; heute jedoch beruft die Welt noch in der radikalen Lüge sich darauf, daß es eben so seit, und solcher einfache Befund koinzidiert ihr mit dem Guten*]." Adorno, MM (§134), 211. GS 4, 241.

83. "Alle Phänomene starren wie Hoheitszeichen absoluter Herrschaft dessen was ist." CCS, in PRSM, 34. GS 10.1, 29.

84. A possible solution would be to say that suffering already amounts to an implicit criticism of the conditions that caused that suffering. The difficulty with this solution is that even the concept of implicit criticism already suggests some awareness of who or what is to blame. Unfortunately, in socioeconomic arrangements of stark inequality, many people believe that their failure or suffering is deserved or is their own fault. If their suffering were sufficient to count as implicit social criticism, they would at least need to be disabused of this false belief.

85. J. M. Bernstein expresses this claim with great clarity: "Adorno must think otherness can be found in experience or else he would be committed to the belief that the guilt context of the living is absolute and all. Not everything can be shaped by the negative whole without making even the statement of that fact unintelligible." Bernstein, *Adorno: Ethics and Disenchantment*, 437. See also Simon Jarvis, *Adorno: A Critical Introduction* (Malden, MA: Polity, 1998): 211–16.

86. Adorno, *Erziehung zur Mündigkeit: Vorträge und Gespräche mit Hellmut Becker, 1959–1969* (Frankfurt am Main: Suhrkamp, 2017).

87. Adorno, *Erziehung zur Mündigkeit*, 133.

88. See, e.g., the essay "Engagement" (translated as "Commitment"), in *Notes to Literature*, vol. 2, trans. Shierry Weber Nicholsen (New York: Columbia University Press, 1992), 76–94. In GS 11, 409–30. Also see "Marginalia to Theory and Praxis," in CM, 259–78; GS 10.2, 759–82.

89. Adorno, *Erziehung zur Mündigkeit. Vorträge und Gespräche mit Hellmut Becker, 1959–1969* (Frankfurt am Main: Suhrkamp, 2017).

90. Espen Hammer has suggested that Adorno conceives of political education chiefly in negative terms. Pedagogy does not aim toward what is best; rather, Adorno sees it as "a means to avoid the worst." This is not altogether accurate insofar as Adorno explicitly endorses (in Hammer's own words) "the values of critique and *Selbstdenken*," where the latter might be translated as "thinking for oneself." That these values signify a positive normative orientation strikes me as rather uncontroversial. Notwithstanding this disagreement, Hammer's discussion of this matter is illuminating. See Espen Hammer, *Adorno and the Political* (New York: Routledge, 2005), 70 passim.

91. On this theme, see Volker Heins, "Saying Things That Hurt: Adorno as Educator," *Thesis Eleven* 110, no. 1 (2012): 68–72; quote from 74. For other important reflections on Adorno's role as a public intellectual, see Max Pensky, "Beyond the Message in a Bottle: The Other Critical Theory," *Constellations* 10, no. 1: (2003): 135–44; and Stefan Müller-Doohm, "Theodor W. Adorno and Jürgen Habermas—Two Ways of Being a Public Intellectual," *European Journal of Social Theory* 8, no. 3 (2005): 269–80.

92. For an example of this twofold portrait, see Jürgen Habermas, "Grossherzige Remigranten: Über jüdische Philosophen in der frühen Bundesrepublik. Eine persönliche Erinnerung," *Neue Zürcher Zeitung* (July 2, 2011).

93. Heins, "Saying Things That Hurt," 77.

94. For more on this problem, see Fabian Freyenhagen, "Adorno's Politics: Theory and Praxis in Germany's 1960s," *Philosophy & Social Criticism* 40, no. 9 (2014): 867–93.

95. "eben die Intelligenz, die frei zu schweben vorgibt, in dem gleichen Sein gründlich verwurzelt ist, das es zu verändern gilt." Adorno, "The Sociology of Knowledge and Its Consciousness," in PRSM, 35–50; quote from 48; GS 10.1, 45. See Karl Mannheim, *Ideology and Utopia: An Introduction to the Sociology of Knowledge*, trans. Louis Wirth and Edward Shils (San Diego: Harcourt Brace Jovanovich, 1985; orig. *Ideologie und Utopie*, 1936).

96. For a related argument, see Macdonald, *What Would Be Different*.

97. See Rahel Jaeggi, "'No Individual Can Resist': *Minima Moralia* as Critique of Forms of Life," *Constellations* 12, no. 1 (2005): 65–82; quotes from 77, 80.

98. For Freyenhagen on immanent critique, see FF, 13.

99. Seyla Benhabib, *Critique, Norm, and Utopia: A Study of the Foundations of Critical Theory* (New York: Columbia University Press, 1987), 181. My emphasis.

100. For another attempt to defend the "positive" in Adorno, see Yvonne Sherratt, *Adorno's Positive Dialectic* (Cambridge: Cambridge University Press, 2007).

101. For the well-known critique of Foucault's "crypto-normativity," see Habermas, PDM (English), chs. IX and X. For an important analysis, see David Ingram, "Foucault and Habermas," in *The Cambridge Companion to Foucault*, 2nd rev. ed., ed. Gary Gutting (Cambridge: Cambridge University Press, 2005), 240–83.

102. "Tatsächlich ist es *keineswegs stets möglich*, der Kritik der unmittelbare praktisch Empfehlung des Besseren beizugeben, *obwohl vielfach Kritik derart verfahren kann, indem sie Wirklichkeiten mit den Normen konfrontiert, auf welche jene Wirklichkeiten sich berufen.*" Adorno, "Critique," in CM (Pickford trans.), 287; in GS 10.2, 785–93; quote from 792. My emphasis.

103. Adorno, "Critique," in CM, 287. GS 10.2, 785–93, quote from 793. My emphasis.

104. "Critique," in CM, 288. GS 10.2, 793. My emphasis.

105. "An der Psychoanalyse ist nichts wahr als ihre Übertreibungen." MM (§29), 49. GS 4, 54.

106. "nur die Übertreibung ist wahr." DE, 92. GS 3, 139.

107. "den geheimen Sinn, die Utopia aus ihrer Hülle zu befreien, die wie im kantischen Vernunftbegriff in jener großen Philosophie enthalten ist: die einer Menschheit, die, selbst nicht mehr enstellt, der Entstellung nicht länger bedarf." DE, 93. GS 3, 140.

108. See especially Bert van den Brink, "Gesellschaftstheorie und Übertreibungskunst. Für eine alternative Lesart der Dialektik der Aufklärung," *Neue Rundschau* 1 (1997): 37–59. For an opposing view, see Alexander García Düttmann, "Thinking as Gesture: A Note on Dialectic of Enlightenment," *New German Critique* 81 (Autumn 2000): 143–52.

109. "Alles Denken ist Übertreibung, insofern als jeder Gedanke, der überhaupt einer ist, über seine Einlösung durch gegebene Tatsache hinausschließt." Adorno, "Open Delusion Society," in CM, 108; GS 10.2, 577.

110. "*das Düstere übertreiben, der Maxime folgend, daß heute überhaupt nur Übertreibung das Medium der Wahrheit sei.*" Quoted from "Was bedeutet: Aufarbeitung der Vergangenheit," in GS 10.2, 567.

111. "Aldous Huxley and Utopia," in PRSM, 95–118; GS 10.1, 97–122.

112. Quoted from "Appendix 1: Discussion of Professor Adorno's Lecture, 'The Meaning of Working through the Past,'" in CM (Pickford trans.), 295–306, quote from 305–6; my emphasis.

113. "die Thematic einer jeden tiefergreifenden Besinnung auf moralische oder ethische Fragen ausmachen sollte nämlich die Frage, ob die Kultur und das, wozu diese sogenannte Kulture

geworden ist, überhaupt so etwas wie richtiges Leben zuläßt oder ob sie ein Zusammenhang von Institutionen ist, der *in zunehmendem Maß* ein *solches richtiges Leben geradezu verhindert.*" PMP, English, 14. NGS, Abt. IV: Band 10: 28. My emphasis.

114. Axel Honneth has proposed a different and intriguing way of understanding Adorno's art of exaggeration. For Honneth, Adorno uses exaggeration for the purposes of a "disclosing critique of society." According to Honneth, a disclosing critique is one that no longer has confidence in immanent social norms as the basis for articulating objections to the current order. This is so because the current order is seen as comprehensively false or (in Honneth's terms) "pathological." When a given society is pathological in this comprehensive or totalizing sense, an immanent critique that appeals to available norms is no longer feasible, and instead one must rely on the rhetorical force of redescription. Such a technique "evokes a new and unfamiliar perspective on our social world without at the same time providing social-theoretical evidence that things actually are that way." It is interesting to note that Honneth does not seek to generalize these observations to Adorno's broader philosophy; rather, he suggests only that disclosing critique is the shared strategy in the coauthored *Dialectic of Enlightenment*. See Honneth, "The Possibility of a Disclosing Critique of Society: The *Dialectic of Enlightenment* in Light of Current Debates in Social Criticism," in Honneth, *Disrespect*, 49–62; quotes from 60–61. For reasons advanced elsewhere in this book, I do not believe that the often hyperbolic claims of *Dialectic of Enlightenment* admit of generalization to Adorno's own work. Nor do I believe that *Dialectic of Enlightenment* abandons the appeal to immanent sources of normativity. The category of mimesis in particular suggests just this kind of immanent resource, and it furnishes a counterconcept to what may appear to be the book's otherwise quite pessimistic conclusions.

115. On Adorno and the theme of immanent contradiction in relation to Western Marxism, see Martin Jay, *Marxism and Totality: Adventures of a Concept from Lukács to Habermas* (Berkeley: University of California Press, 1984), esp. ch. 8, 241–75. For a rather more skeptical verdict on Adorno and Marxism, see Perry Anderson, *Considerations on Western Marxism* (London: Verso, 1976).

116. Perhaps it is relevant to note that this principle marks a decisive difference between Adorno and his colleague Walter Benjamin. As I have explained elsewhere, in his late philosophy of history Benjamin appeals to an extrahistorical power that intrudes on the historical continuum as if from the outside. This appeal to a transcendent or "messianic" irruption violates the principle of dialectical immanence, and it therefore raises serious doubts as to whether Benjamin sustains any real bond with historical materialism. See Peter E. Gordon, *Migrants in the Profane: Critical Theory and the Question of Secularization* (New Haven, CT: Yale University Press, 2020).

117. Hegel, *Die Phänomenologie des Geistes*, ed. Hans-Friedrich Wessels and Heinrich Clairmont (Hamburg: Meiner Verlag, 1988), 26; English from Hegel, Preface to *The Phenomenology of Spirit*, trans. Terry Pinkard (Cambridge: Cambridge University Press, 2018), 21.

118. For a more conciliatory view of Marx's attitude toward utopianism, see Steven Lukes, "Marxism and Utopianism," in *Utopias*, ed. P. Alexander and R. Gill (London: Duckworth, 1984), 153–67; for a reconstruction of Marx as a critic of utopianism, see Shlomo Avineri, "Marx's Vision of Future Society and the Problem of Utopianism," *Dissent* (Summer 1973): 323–31, where he writes, "To Marx the main trouble with the utopians is ultimately epistemological. It is not that their schemes are unrealizable, impractical. or rooted in never-never land. It is because the utopians concoct systems at all that they are wrong."

119. Engels, "Socialism: Utopian and Scientific," Part I: "The Development of Utopian Socialism."

120. MER, 517; my emphasis.

121. For a full discussion of this passage in relation to Hegel, see G. A. Cohen, *Marx's Theory of History: A Defence* (Princeton, NJ: Princeton University Press, 1979), 27.

122. Karl Marx and Friedrich Engels, *On the Paris Commune* (Moscow: Progress, 1980), 76.

123. Georg Lohmann, "Marx's Capital and the Question of Normative Standards," *Praxis International* 6, no. 3 (1986): 354–72.

124. "Der Kritiker kann also an jede Form des theoretischen und praktischen Bewusstseins anknüpfen und aus den *eigenen* Formen der existierenden Wirklichkeit die wahre Wirklichkeit als ihr Sollen und ihren Endzweck entwickeln." Karl Marx to Arnold Ruge (Letter, Kreuznach, September 1843), in MER, 12–15; quote from 14. Emphasis in original. In German in Karl Marx, *Der Historische Materialismus: Die Frühschriften*, ed. Siegfried Landshut and Jacob Peter Mayer (Leipzig, 1932), Band I, S. 225.

125. A classic statement of this theme of immanent normativity can be found in the young Marx's letter to his father (10 November 1837): "Setting out from idealism—which, let me say in passing, I had compared to and nourished with that of Kant and Fichte—I hit upon seeking the Idea in the real itself. *If formerly the gods had dwelt above the world, they had now become its center.*" Quoted from *The First Writings of Karl Marx*, ed. Paul M. Schafer (Brooklyn, NY: IG Publishing, 2006), 71–83; quote from 78. My emphasis. In German in *Karl Marx in seinen Briefen*, ed. Saul K. Padover (Munich: C. H. Beck, 1981).

126. "Wir entwickeln der Welt aus den Prinzipien der Welt neue Prinzipien." Marx, as quoted in MER, 14; my emphasis.

127. See, e.g., Shlomo Avineri, "Marx and Jewish Emancipation," *Journal of the History of Ideas.* 25, no. 3 (July–September 1964): 445–50.

128. One of the better- known instances can be found in Marx's critique of the Gotha Program, which contains the line. "Right can never be higher than the economic structure of society and its cultural development conditioned thereby." Marx, "Critique of the Gotha Program," in MER, 525–41; quote at 531. Taking such statements as definitive, though unwarranted, has nonetheless helped to inspire an interesting body of scholarship on Marxism and normativity. See, e.g., Allen W. Wood, "The Marxian Critique of Justice," *Philosophy and Public Affairs* 1, no. 3 (Spring 1972): 244–82; and Richard W. Miller, *Analyzing Marx: Morality, Power, and History* (Princeton, NJ: Princeton University Press, 1984).

129. "The Holy Family," 149; *Werke*, II, 117. Quoted in Avineri, "Marx and Jewish Emancipation," 450. Emphasis in original.

130. "Alles Glück bis heute verspricht, was noch nicht war, und der Glaube an seine Unmittelbarkeit ist dem in Wege, daß es werde." GS 6, 345–46.

131. MM (§146), 227–28. GS 4, 147.

132. Hans-Jürgen Krahl, "The Political Contradictions in Adorno's Critical Theory," *Sociological Review* 23, no. 4 (1975): 307–10; quote at 831.

133. This dialectical principle was given a classic formulation by Jürgen Habermas in his analysis of the concept of publicity (whose phrase I have adapted here). "As long as the presuppositions enumerated above could be assumed as given, as long as publicity existed as a sphere and functioned as a principle, what the public itself believed to be and to be doing *was ideology and simultaneously more than mere ideology*. On the basis of the continuing domination of one class over another, the dominant class nevertheless developed political institutions which credibly embodied as their objective *meaning the idea of their own abolition*. . . . If ideologies are not only manifestations of the socially necessary consciousness in its essential falsity, if there is an

aspect to them that can lay a claim to truth inasmuch as it transcends the status quo in utopian fashion, even if only for purposes of justification, then ideology exists at all only from this period on." Quoted from Habermas, *The Structural Transformation of the Public Sphere*; my emphasis.

134. On this phrase, see the analysis by James Gordon Finlayson, "The Artwork and the Promesse du Bonheur in Adorno," *European Journal of Philosophy* 23, no. 3 (2015): 392–419. I offer a related discussion of this phrase in ch. 6, below.

135. Marx: "Aber die Schwierigkeit liegt nicht darin zu verstehn, daß griechische Kunst und Epos an gewisse gesellschaftliche Entwicklungsformen geknüpft sind. Die Schwierigkeit ist, daß sie uns noch Kunstgenuß gewähren und in gewisser Beziehung *als Norm und unerreichbare* Muster gelten." Marx, *Grundrisse: Foundations of the Critique of Political Economy (Rough Draft)*, trans. Martin Nicolaus (New York: Penguin Books, 1993), 111. Marx, "Einleitung," *Grundrisse der Kritik der politischen Ökonomie* (1857–58), in Karl Marx and Friedrich Engels, *Werke*, Band 13 (Berlin, 1971): 615–42, quoted from 641. My emphasis.

136. "Ein Mann kann nicht wieder zum Kind werden, oder er wird kindisch. *Aber freut ihn die Naivetät des Kindes nicht, und muß er nicht selbst wieder auf einer höhern Stufe streben, seine Wahrheit zu reproduzieren?*" Marx, *Grundrisse: Foundations of the Critique of Political Economy (Rough Draft)*, 111. Marx, "Einleitung," 641. My emphasis.

137. Macdonald, *What Would Be Different*.

138. HF, 148, English. NGS, Abt. IV: Band 13: 209. My emphasis.

139. HF, 149, English. NGS, Abt .IV: Band 13: 210. My emphasis. For a dissenting view of progress as inimical to critical theory, see Amy Allen, *The End of Progress: Decolonizing Critical Theory* (New York: Columbia University Press, 2016).

140. Adorno, Letter to Hans Jonas (October 12, 1959); as quoted in Adorno, MCP (English ed.), 150, editor's note 4.

141. GS 6, 373.

142. "Gnostisch ist ihm die geschaffene Welt die radikal böse und ihre Verneinung die Möglichkeit einer anderen, noch nicht seienden. Solange die Welt ist, wie sie ist, ähneln alle Bilder von Versöhnung, Frieden und Ruhe dem des Todes. Die kleinste Differenz zwischen dem Nichts und dem zur Ruhe Gelangten wäre die Zuflucht der Hoffnung." GS 6, 374.

143. For a related argument concerning Adorno's differences from Beckett's "gnostic predicament," see Espen Hammer, *Adorno's Modernism: Art, Experience, and Catastrophe* (Cambridge: Cambridge University Press, 2015), 147.

144. GS 6, 373.

145. See, e.g., the arguments in Hammer, *Adorno's Modernism*, 154–55.

146. To motivate the arguments in this book, it may prove helpful to consider the ways in which Adorno's social criticism avoids the twin errors of the gnostic *and* the Mephisthophelean. As I have explained above, the gnostic sees society as wholly false and therefore has no other choice than to appeal to world-transcendent standards of the true (much as a gnostic might appeal to the true god who lies elsewhere than our fallen world). As compared to the gnostic, the Mephisthophelean has at least one advantage, in that he sees society not as simply false, but as contradictory; he therefore has the option of seizing on moments of world-immanent contradiction for the purposes of negation. He is "the spirit who always negates [*der Geist der stets verneint*]," yet in willing the bad he serves the good. Here too, however, we find that Adorno pursues a distinctive path. Although he too sees society as fractured rather than seamless, he is not a spirit of relentless negation. Unlike the Mephisthophelean, he is alive to the possibility of finding the good even in the midst of the bad.

147. See, e.g., the programmatic statement by Max Horkheimer, who connects the critique of present society to the normative ideal of a better one. "Unless there is continued theoretical effort, *in the interest of a rationally organized future society*, to shed critical light on present society and to interpret it in the light of traditional theories elaborated in the special sciences, the ground is taken from *the hope of radically improving human existence.*" Max Horkheimer, "Traditional and Critical Theory," in *The Essential Frankfurt School Reader*, ed. Andrew Arato and Eike Gebhardt (London: Bloomsbury, 1978), 188–243; quote from 233. My emphasis.

148. ID, 69. NGS, Abt. IV: Band 2: 103.

Chapter One

1. "Noch die unerbittliche Strenge, mit der sie die Wahrheit übers unwahre Bewußtsein spricht, belibt festgehalten im Bannkreis des Bekämpften, auf dessen Manifestationen sie starrt." CCS, in PRSM, 20; GS 10.1, 12.

2. BO, GS 16, 31.

3. BPM, 160. NGS, Abt. 1, Band 1: 231. Emphasis in original.

4. BO, 21–22. GS 16, 31.

5. "Diese Verschränkung von Mythos und Aufklärung: die der Gefangenschaft in einem blinden und seiner selbst unbewußte System mit der Idee der Freiheit, welche in dessen Mitte aufgeht, definiert das bürgerliche Wesen der Oper." BO, 21. GS 16, 31. My emphasis.

6. "Metaphysik ist überhaupt nicht ein Bereich von Invarianz, dessen man habhaft würde, wenn man durch die vergitterten Fenster des Geschichtlichen hinausblickt; sie ist der sei es auch ohnmächtige Schein des Lichts, der ins Gefängnis selber fällt." BO, 21–22. GS 16, 31. My emphasis.

7. "Diese Verschränkung von Mythos und Aufklärung: die der Gefangenschaft in einem blinden und seiner selbst unbewußte System mit der Idee der Freiheit, welche in dessen Mitte aufgeht, definiert das bürgerliche Wesen der Oper. Von diesem Gesellschaftlichen ist ihre Metaphysik nicht etwa abzuheben. Metaphysik ist überhaupt nicht ein Bereich von Invarianz, dessen man habhaft würde, wenn man durch die vergitterten Fenster des Geschichtlichen hinausblickt; sie ist der sei es auch ohnmächtige Schein des Lichts, der ins Gefängnis selber fällt, um so mächtiger je tiefer ihre Ideen in Geschichte sich einsenken, um so ideologischer, je abstrakter sie ihr gegenübertritt." Adorno, "Bürgerliche Oper," GS 16, 24–39; quote from 31.

8. CCS, in PRSM, 34. GS 10.1, 29.

9. "der mikrologische Blick zertrümmert die Schalen des nach dem Maß des subsumierenden Oberbegriffs hilflos Verenzelten und sprengt seine Identität, den Trug, es wäre bloß Exemplar." GS 6, 400.

10. "Die kleinsten innerweltlichen Züge hätten Relevanz furs Absolute." GS 6, 600.

11. On the themes of reality and possibility in Adorno, see Macdonald, *What Would Be Different*.

12. "Metaphysik im Augenblick ihres Strurzes." GS 6, 400.

13. HF, 91. NGS, Abt. IV: Band 13: 134.

14. G. W. F. Hegel, *The Difference between Fichte's and Schelling's System of Philosophy*, ed. H. S. Harris and Walter Cerf. (Albany: SUNY Press, 1988).

15. "Indem seine Vollendung darin besteht, das, was er ist, seine Substanz, vollkommen zu wissen, so ist dies Wissen sein In-sich-gehen, in welchem er sein Dasein verläßt und seine

Gestalt der Erinnerung übergibt." Hegel, *Die Phänomenologie des Geistes*, in *Werke*, Band III (Frankfurt am Main: Suhrkamp, 1979), §808; quote from 592.

16. Following Redmond's translation of *Salbadern*. GS 6, 354.

17. GS 6, 354.

18. GS 6, 396.

19. "Résumé der Dissertation." GS 1, 376.

20. In his "Résumé der Dissertation" Adorno refers to the "*schlechthingen Transcendenz der Dingwelt.*" GS 1, 376.

21. GS 1, 325; in English as "The Actuality of Philosophy," in AR, 24.

22. GS 1, 325; in English as "The Actuality of Philosophy," in AR, 24.

23. GS 1, 343; in English as "The Actuality of Philosophy," in AR, 38.

24. ID, 21. In German NGS, Abt. IV: Band 2: 36.

25. Habermas, PDM, "the paradoxical concept of the non-identical." 129.

26. For the defense against the "two-worlds" theory, see especially the rejoinder to Locke in Kant, *Prolegomena to Any Future Metaphysics*, ed. Gary Hatfield, Cambridge Texts in the History of Philosophy (Cambridge: Cambridge University Press, 1997), 40.

27. Rae Langton, *Kantian Humility: Our Ignorance of Things in Themselves* (Oxford: Oxford University Press, 1998).

28. KKV, English, 234. NGS, Abt. IV: Band 4: 353.

29. KKV, English, 234. NGS, Abt. IV: Band 4: 353. Emphasis in original.

30. KKV, English, 234. NGS, Abt. IV: Band 4: 353.

31. "in der neueren Zeit den ersten großen Versuch dar—oder vieleicht auch den letzten une einen zum Scheitern verurteilten—, das, was im bloßen Begriff sich nicht bewältigen läßt, durch den bloßen Begriff doch *zu bewältigen.*" KKV, English, 234. NGS, Abt. IV: Band 4: 354. My emphasis.

32. KKV, English, 234. NGS, Abt. IV: Band 4: 354; emphasis in original.

33. Adorno is, of course, highly critical of Kant in other respects. For a discussion, see J. M. Bernstein, "Concept and Object: Adorno's Critique of Kant," in BC, 487–502.

34. HF, English, 92. NGS, Abt. IV: Band 13: 139.

35. For Adorno's critique of authenticity, see Peter E. Gordon, *Adorno and Existence* (Cambridge, MA: Harvard University Press, 2016), 84–119.

36. Elsewhere I have characterized this thought as a "Christological" motif. See Gordon, *Adorno and Existence*, 179.

37. HF, English, 97. NGS, Abt. IV: Band 13: 142. My emphasis.

38. HF, English, 97. NGS, Abt. IV: Band 13: 143.

39. HF, English, 97. NGS, Abt. IV: Band 13: 143.

40. HF, English, 97. My emphasis. NGS, Abt. IV: Band 13: 144.

41. HF, English, 98. NGS, Abt IV: Band 13: 144.

42. HF, English, 98. My emphasis. NGS, Abt IV: Band 13 144.

43. I want to thank Gordon Finlayson (pers. comm.) for suggesting the term "contrastive," which strikes me as remarkably apt.

44. "das Falsche, einmal bestimmt erkannt und präzisiert, bereits Index des Richten, Besseren ist." GS 10.2, 793. Adorno, "Critique," English, Pickford trans., 288.

45. On the mutual implication of the negative and positive, see the helpful discussion in Theunissen, "Negativität bei Adorno." For a further treatment of negation in Adorno and its

ethical implications, also see Martin Shuster, "Adorno and Negative Theology," *Graduate Faculty Philosophy Journal*. 37, no. 1 (2016): 97–130.

46. GS 6, 152. My emphasis.

47. In introducing his negativist interpretation, Freyenhagen offers a thoughtful disclaimer that deserves notice. He acknowledges that he might be charged with "downplaying or even denying the utopian dimension of Adorno's thought." He objects to this charge. He does not deny that Adorno is a utopian "in the sense that he holds on to the possibility *that* things could be different." Rather, what Freyenhagen means to deny is that Adorno "can tell us *how* things would then be—what utopia would consist in positively speaking." FF, 20. Although this is an important distinction, it still goes too far in rejecting the anticipatory instances of the good in the midst of the bad. To state the matter succinctly, Adorno is more alive to the internally contradictory or dialectical nature of social structure and individual experience than the negativist interpretation allows.

48. MM (§146), 227–28. GS 4, 259–61.

49. MM (§146), 227. GS 4, 259.

50. MM (§146), 227. GS 4, 260; translation modified.

51. MM (§146), 228. GS 4, 260.

52. MM (§146), 228. GS 4, 260.

53. MM (§146), 228; translation modified. GS 4, 260–61.

54. The English-language translation by Jephcott translates "Übungen" as "rehearsals." This is an elegant term but perhaps not as suitable as the plainer "exercises." I suspect that Adorno, a trained pianist, preferred this term for its subtle allusion to the kinds of finger exercises developed by Czerny, exercises that were well known to most young piano students (though, admittedly, such finger exercises are anything but innocent or enjoyable games).

55. MM (Frontispiece to Part I), 19. GS 4,20.

56. For a comprehensive account of the meaning of immanent critique, see Titus Stahl, *Immanente Kritik: Elemente einer Theorie sozialer Praktiken* (Frankfurt am Main: Campus Verlag, 2013); for a summary of his arguments, see Titus Stahl, "What Is Immanent Critique," *SSRN Working Paper*, http://ssrn.com/abstract=2357957, doi: 10.2139/xxrn.2357957. In addition to laying out a defense of his own idea of immanent critique, Stahl traces the historical genesis of immanent critique from Hegel through Marx to Frankfurt School critical theory. For a dissenting view that calls into question the strong continuities from Hegel and Marx to Adorno, see the excellent paper by James Gordon Finlayson, "Hegel, Adorno, and the Origins of Immanent Criticism," *British Journal for the History of Philosophy* 22, no. 6 (2014): 1142–66. For further discussion of the historical continuity extending back to Hegel, see Andrew Buchwalter, "Hegel, Marx, and the Concept of Immanent Critique," *Journal of the History of Philosophy*, 29, no. 2 (1991): 253–79; Robert J. Antonio, "Immanent Critique as the Core of Critical Theory: Its Origins and Developments in Hegel, Marx and Contemporary Thought," *British Journal of Sociology* 32, no. 3 (1981): 330–45; and Karin de Boer, "Hegel's Conception of Immanent Critique: Its Sources, Extent, and Limit," in *Conceptions of Critique in Modern and Contemporary Philosophy*, ed. Ruth Sonderegger and Karin de Boer (London: Palgrave Macmillan, 2012), 83–101.

57. CCS, 31. GS 10.1, 26. My emphasis.

58. CCS, 31. GS 10.1, 26. My emphasis.

59. Notice that Adorno does not say that the world is actually a unified whole; its unity is only an ideologically confirmed appearance. CCS, 31. GS 10.1, 26. My emphasis.

60. "Die Wahl eines ihrem Bann entzogenen Standpunkts ist so fiktiv wie nur je die Konstruktion abstracter Utopien." CCS, 31. GS 10.1, 26.

61. CCS, 31. GS 10.1, 26. My emphasis.

62. "Es nimmt das Prinzip ernst, nicht die Ideologie an sich sei unwahr, sonder ihre Prätention, mit der Wirklichkeit übereinzustimmen." CCS, 31. GS 10.1, 27.

63. CCS, 31. GS 10.1, 27.

64. CCS, 31. GS 10.1, 27. My emphasis.

65. Adorno, "Why Still Philosophy," in CM, Pickford trans., 12. My emphasis.

66. MM (§19), 40; GS 4, 44.

67. Finlayson, "Hegel, Adorno, and the Origins of Immanent Criticism," 1157.

68. Finlayson, "Hegel, Adorno, and the Origins of Immanent Criticism," 1158.

69. Finlayson, "Hegel, Adorno, and the Origins of Immanent Criticism," 1158.

70. GS 1, 334; "The Actuality of Philosophy," in AR, 31.

71. GS 6, 370.

72. James Gordon Finlayson, "Adorno's Metaphysics of Moral Solidarity in the Moment of Its Fall," in BC, 615–30.

73. Finlayson, "Adorno's Metaphysics of Moral Solidarity in the Moment of Its Fall," quote from 618.

74. See, e.g., "Fragment des ganzen Glücks," GS 6, 396; "versprengte Spur," in GS 6, 370; and "zerbrochenen Glas," in MMP, 36; GS 13, 184.

75. Michael Theunissen associates this logic of the trace with the metaphysical and theological figure of *prolepsis*, an anticipation of a still-unrealized future condition of unity. See the illuminating discussion in Theunissen, "Negativität bei Adorno."

76. Stahl, "What Is Immanent Critique," 19. Emphasis in original.

77. "Tugendspiegel," in MM (§119), 184–87. GS 4, 210–13; quote from 212.

78. Marx, "Contribution to the Critique of Hegel's *Philosophy of Right*: Introduction," in MER, 53–65; quotes from 54. Emphasis in original.

79. "Hoheitszeichen absoluter Herrschaft dessen was ist." CCS, in PRSM, 34. GS 10.1, 29.

80. "Die Alternative, Kultur ingesamt von außen, unter dem Oberbegriff der Ideologie in Frage zu stellen, oder sie mit den Normen zu konfrontieren, die sie selbst auskristallierite, kann die kritische Theorie nicht anerkennen. Auf der Entscheidung: immanent oder transzendent zu bestehen, ist ein Rückfall in die traditionelle Logik, der Hegels Polemik gegen Kant galt." CCS, in PRSM, 31. GS 10.1, 25–26.

81. For a related discussion, see Brian O'Connor, *Adorno* (New York: Routledge, 2013), 49–50.

82. Jürgen Habermas, "Transcendence from Within, Transcendence in This World," in Habermas, *Religion and Rationality: Essays on Reason, God, and Modernity*, ed. Eduardo Mendieta (Cambridge: Polity, 2002), 67–94. See also Axel Honneth's discussion of "intramundane transcendence," in Nancy Fraser and Axel Honneth, *Redistribution or Recognition? A Political-Philosophical Exchange* (London: Verso, 2003), 238 passim. For an elucidation of this idea, see Christopher Zurn, *Axel Honneth* (Cambridge: Polity, 2015), esp. 150–52.

83. Honneth, *Redistribution or Recognition?*, 238.

84. On this idea, also see my critique of Cambridge School historicizing contextualism, in "Contextualism and Criticism in the History of Ideas," in *Rethinking Modern Intellectual History: Reappraisals and New Perspectives for the Twenty-First Century*, ed. Darrin McMahon and Samuel Moyn (Oxford: Oxford University Press, 2013).

85. For an illustration of this problem, see, e.g., the discussion of psychoanalysis and the dialectical character of its critical standards. Adorno sees Freudian psychoanalysis as torn between two aims, the overcoming of repression and its affirmation. Ultimately the affirmative or ideological aspect is the more powerful, but even this betrayal does not wholly invalidate the "utopian" element that inheres in the psychoanalytic idea of pleasure. See the discussion in MM, "Diesseits des Lustprinzips" (§37), 60–61. GS 4, 37–38.

86. "Nicht anders läßt das Bestehende sich überschreiten als vermöge des Allgemeinen, das dem Bestehenden selbst entlehnt ist. Das Allegemeine triumphiert übers Bestehende durch dessen eigenen Begriff, und darum droht in solchem Triumph die Macht des bloß Seienden stets sich wiederherzustellen aus der gleichen Gewalt, die sie brach." MM (§98), 150. GS 4, 171–72.

87. I therefore fully agree with the succinct statement by Brian O'Connor: "Adorno does not believe that society is absolutely lost, i.e., that no trace of a wholesome notion of human and communal flourishing can be found within it." O'Connor, *Adorno*, 50.

88. In the relevant chapter, Jaeggi uses the term "criticism" instead of "critique." I will use her language here in order to avoid any confusion when quoting from her book.

89. Rahel Jaeggi, *Critique of Forms of Life*, trans Ciaran Cronin (Cambridge, MA: Harvard University Press, 2018), 190.

90. For a summary, see Jaeggi, *Critique of Forms of Life*, 205–6.

91. Jaeggi, *Critique of Forms of Life*, 208.

92. Jaeggi, *Critique of Forms of Life*, 209–10. My emphasis.

93. In the ongoing debate over the question of immanent critique in Adorno's philosophy, one of the more illuminating arguments is that defended by Rahel Jaeggi. In an essay that focuses chiefly on *Minima Moralia*, she suggests that Adorno practiced an unusual kind of immanent critique. We are accustomed to thinking of immanent critique as a dialectical exercise that locates the norms for criticism of society within society. In Jaeggi's words, "The great attractiveness of this method for Hegel's successors from Marx to contemporary critical theory has been that we seem to be able to escape the problem of the 'empty ought' and ineffectual moralism, since what is demanded is already built into reality and not at a utopian distance from it." But, as Jaeggi notes, this method must presuppose that "there is a normativity embedded in reality that is to provide the criteria for its critique." The reality that we wish to criticize must be (in Jaeggi's apt phrase) "normatively charged." According to Jaeggi, however, Adorno does not endorse this presupposition. Although he is committed to immanent critique, he has lost confidence in the presence of any "inner normativity" that could be mobilized for his critical purposes. He thus finds himself in the unusual position of criticizing our current form of life without appealing to any available standards that could serve as critical leverage against it. He must sustain what Jaeggi calls a "balancing act" between "standardlessness" and critique. Jaeggi argues that in *Minima Moralia* Adorno is able to sustain this balance by convincing us "phenomenally" (i.e., through experiential evidence and concrete analysis) of what Jaeggi calls the "discrepancy between social reality and possibility" (80). Jaeggi believes that this kind of discrepancy equips Adorno with an internal critical standard that is sufficient for his critical practice, even while such a *discrepancy* is not strong enough to count as a straightforward *contradiction* (as it would have for Hegel, Marx, and others in the tradition of immanent critique). See Rahel Jaeggi, "'No Individual Can Resist': *Minima Moralia* as Critique of Forms of Life," *Constellations* 12, no. 1 (2005): 65–82; quote above from 80. This is an exceptionally instructive argument, although I disagree with Jaeggi that Adorno conducts immanent critique in a paradoxical mode of "standardlessness." But I

agree with her that he pursues his criticism primarily by alerting us to phenomenological (or "phenomenal") instances of normativity in the lived texture of everyday experience.

94. MM (§78), 121–22. GS 4, 138. My thanks to Iain Macdonald for reminding me of this passage.

95. MM (§78), 121–22. GS 4, 138. My thanks to Iain Macdonald for reminding me of this passage.

Chapter Two

1. On the idea of human flourishing, see Martha Nussbaum, "Human Functioning and Social Justice: In Defense of Aristotelian Essentialism," *Political Theory* 20, no. 2 (1992): 202–46; and Rosalind Hursthouse, *On Virtue Ethics* (Oxford: Oxford University Press, 1999).

2. David Leopold, *The Young Karl Marx: Modern Politics, German Philosophy, and Human Flourishing* (Cambridge: Cambridge University Press, 2007).

3. I am by no means the only commentator to discern affinities between Adorno and Cavell on moral perfectionism. Among the most perspicuous is the essay by Martin Shuster, "Nothing to Know: The Epistemology of Moral Perfectionism in Adorno and Cavell," *Idealistic Studies* 44, no. 1 (2014): 1–29. Shuster's argument draws some inspiration from the opening line of J. M. Bernstein's preface, where it is remarked, "Readers of Adorno are inevitably struck by how everything he wrote was infused with a stringent and commanding ethical intensity." Quoted from Bernstein, *Adorno: Disenchantment and Ethics*, xi; see also the note on Cavell and moral perfectionism in Bernstein at 336. An illuminating paper on the topic is by Alice Crary (who offers a rejoinder to Paul Guyer's Kantian take on moral perfectionism), "A Radical Perfectionist: Revisiting Cavell in the Light of Kant," *Journal of Aesthetic Education* 48, no. 3 (2014): 87–98. For a lucid summary of Cavell on moral perfectionism, see Espen Hammer, *Stanley Cavell: Skepticism, Subjectivity, and the Ordinary* (Cambridge: Polity, 2002), 128–42. Hammer summarizes the comparison with Adorno as follows: "It seems to me that Adorno's ethical views do contain perfectionist elements. Rather than a search for principles, he is looking for ways to bring the self into the ethical equation, emphasizing forms of responsiveness that at times may challenge widespread assumptions (and break with conformity) but that, ultimately, seek to articulate something universal. Some form of self-transformation seems involved in what he takes ethical experience to be" (Espen Hammer; quoted from a personal communication). Also see Hammer's further remarks on Adorno and ethical and political perfectionism, in Espen Hammer, *Adorno and the Political* (London: Routledge, 2005), 9 passim.

4. Adorno, "The Problem of a New Type of Human Being" (Appendix G), in *Currents of Music*, trans. Robert Hullot-Kentor (Cambridge: Polity, 2009), 461–68; quote from 468. My emphasis. NGS, Abt. 1: 660.

5. Adorno's ideal of happiness has received some critical attention already. For an excellent discussion, see Britta Scholze, "Adorno und das Glück," in *Adorno Handbuch: Leben, Werk, Wirkung*, ed. Richard Klein, Johann Kreuzer, and Stefan Müller-Doohm (Berlin: J. B. Metzler Verlag, 2019), 454–62.

6. "Alles Glück auf sinnliche Erfüllung abzielt und an ihr seine Objektivität gewinnt. Ist dem Glück jeglicher Aspekt darauf verstellt, so ist es keines." GS 6, 202.

7. ID 67. In German NGS, Abt. IV: Band 2: 100.

8. ID 67. In German NGS, Abt. IV: Band 2: 100.

9. ID 67. In German NGS, Abt. IV: Band 2: 100. "Organon" emphasis in original; "of truth" my emphasis.

10. "der allgemeinbegriffliche Umfang besteht eigentlich überhaupt in dem Leben des darunter befaßten Besonderen, er erfüllt sich durch das Besondere, und er umfängt es nicht bloß, sondern er entspringt in dem Besonderen und hat sein Leben daran." ID 68. In German NGS, Abt. IV: Band 2: 101.

11. ID 68. In German NGS, Abt. IV: Band 2: 101.

12. ID, 69. In German NGS, Abt. IV: Band 2: 103.

13. "[Hegel] würde sich also nicht mit einer primitiven biologischen Definition Mensch begnügen, sondern würde sagen, wenn wir in der lebendig vollzogenen Erkenntnis von Mensch überhaupt reden, dann denken wir dabei mit Kategorien wie Freiheit wie Individuation, Autonomie, Vernunftbestimmtheit, wie eine ganze Menge anderer Dinge, die in dem Begriff Mensch schon allesamt implizit als dessen objektive Bestimmung enthalten sind." ID, 69. In German NGS, Abt. IV: Band 2: 102-3.

14. ID, 69. In German NGS, Abt. IV: Band 2: 103.

15. "denn dieses Emphatische, das darin gesetzt ist, ohne daß es implicit bereits hervorzutreten brauchte, dieses Emphatische ist ja jetzt und hier in irgend einem besonderen Wesen noch gar nicht verwirklicht." ID, 69. In German NGS, Abt. IV: Band 2: 103.

16. "man könnte beineihe sagen, daß so etwas wie Mensch noch gar nicht gibt, so wie der Begriff der Menschen es von sich aus, objektiv eigentlich begreift." ID, 69. In German NGS, Abt. IV: Band 2: 103.

17. "Mit anderen Worten: Der Satz 'X ist ein Mensch' ist richtig, wie ich es Ihnen gesagt habe, und ist falsch zugleich." ID, 69. In German NGS, Abt. IV: Band 2: 103.

18. "Ich glaube, man brauchte nur einmal wirklich und in allem Ernst diesen Satz auf irgendeinen Menschen anzuwenden, daß der Betreffende ein Mensch sei, und man wird sogleich dieser Differenz innewerden, daß er eigentlich dem Begriff des Menschen im emphatischen Sinn, also dem Begriff des Menschen im Sinn der absoluten Wahrheit, noch gar nicht gerecht wird." ID, 69. In German NGS, Abt. IV: Band 2: 103. My emphasis.

19. See Frederick Neuhouser, "Hegel's Social Philosophy," in *The Cambridge Companion to Hegel*, ed. Frederick C. Beiser (Cambridge: Cambridge University Press, 1993), 204-29.

20. "Und ich glaube, man brauchte nur einmal wirklich und in allem Ernst diesen Satz auf irgendeinen Menschen aufzuwenden, daß der Betreffende eine Mensch sei, und man wird sogleich dieser Differenz innewerden, daß er eigentlich dem Begriff des Menschen im emphatischen Sinn, also dem Begriff des Menschen im Sinn der absoluten Wahrheit, noch gar nicht gerecht wird, war nur freilich vorausssetzt, daß man einen solchen emphatischen Begriff des Menschen, schließlich einen Begriff des richtigen Menschen, schließlich einen Begriff überhaupt der richtigen Organisation der Welt in sich trägt." ID, 69. In German NGS, Abt. IV: Band 2: 103. My emphasis.

21. ID, 73. In German NGS, Abt. IV: Band 2: 108.

22. ID, 73. In German NGS, Abt. IV: Band 2: 108.

23. "Dieser Charakter, daß die Entwicklung, das Treibende schließlich aber auch das, was auf Versöhnung abzielt, etwas ist, was selbst in der Zerrissenheit, in dem Negativen, in dem Leiden der Welt eigentlich steckt, das ist genauso also Erfahrung von der Wirklichkeit ein tragendes Motiv der Hegelschen Dialektik." ID, 73-74. In German NGS, Abt. IV: Band 2: 108.

24. "da mir daran gelegen ist, Ihnen einen Begriff von Dialektik zu geben, der gleichzeitig ein strenger Begriff von Dialektik ist, der auf der anderen Seite aber doch sich innerhalb der problematisch gewordenen idealistischen These nicht erschöpft." ID, 76. In German NGS, Abt. IV: Band 2: 112. My emphasis.

25. ID, 74. In German NGS, Abt. IV: Band 2: 109.

26. On the difference between an *open* and a *closed* dialectic, see Adorno, ID, 21. In German NGS, Abt. IV: Band 2: 36l.

27. "Dialektisch denken heißt also nicht etwa, einem Satz irgendwelcher Art von außen eine andere Meinung entgegenzusetzen, sondern den Gedanken an die Stellen zu treiben, an der [er] gewissermaßen seiner eigenen Endlichkeit, seiner eigenen Falschheit innewird *und dadurch über sich hinaustreibt.*" In German ID, 30. NGS, Abt. IV: Band 2: 48. My emphasis in the English and the German.

28. ID, 30. NGS, Abt. IV: Band 2: 48.

29. ID, 73–74. NGS, Abt. IV: Band 2: 108.

30. ID, 217. NGS, Abt. IV: Band 2: 306.

31. ID, 217. NGS, Abt. IV: Band 2: 306. My emphasis.

32. "Eine Dialektik, die nicht ebenso strikt an jede einzelne Erkenntnis das Maß der Wahrheit so lange anlegt, bis diese einzelne Erkenntnis eben darüber zergeht, wäre von vornherein gewissermaßen der Kraft bar, ohne die ein dialektischer Prozeß überhaupt gar nicht gefaßt werden kann. Und in der Einsicht in das Unwahre, also in dem kritischen Motiv, das ja das eigentlich entscheidende der Dialektik ist, steckt, als ihre notwendige Bedingung, die Idee der Wahrheit drin." In German ID, 189. Translation modified. NGS, Abt. IV: Band 2: 268. My emphasis.

33. "in diesem Moment der Kritik, in dem Moment des weitertreibenden Denkens, unabweisbar und unabdingbar das Motiv der Wahrheit gesetzt und gemeint ist." In German ID, 189. NGS, Abt. IV: Band 2: 268.

34. ID, 189. NGS, Abt. IV: Band 2: 268.

35. ID, 189–90. NGS, Abt. IV: Band 2: 268. My emphasis. Also see his remark from the introductory lectures on dialectics: "I have already said that the relevant criterion [or standard], or the only possibility which dialectical thought acknowledges as such, must be *immanent in character* [Ich hatte Ihnen gesagt, daß der Maßstab, oder daß die einzige Möglichkeit, die die Dialektik dafür sieht, eben die immanente ist]." In German ID, 192. NGS, Abt. IV: Band 2: 272. My emphasis.

36. MM (§153), 247. GS 4, 283.

37. GS 6, 370. My emphasis.

38. In *Negative Dialectics* the necessity of such a standard is condensed into a memorable principle: "Consciousness could not despair at all over what is grey, if it did not harbor the concept of a different color, whose scattered trace is not lacking in the negative whole [*Bewußtsein könnte gar nicht über das Grau verzweifeln, hegte es nicht den Begriff von einer verschiedenen Farbe, deren versprengte Spur im negativen Ganzen nicht fehlt*]." GS 6, 370. I offer some comments on this principle later in the book.

39. I owe this insight to Martin Jay, who notes that Plato seems to have borrowed his initial inspiration for this idea from Democritus. For discussions of the meaning of "emphasis" in Democritus, see Kurt von Fritz, "Democritus' Theory of Vision," in *Science, Medicine and History: Essays on the Evolution of Scientific Thought and Medical Practice*, ed. Edgar Ashworth Underwood (New York: Oxford University Press, 1953), 93–95; and David Lindberg, *Theories of Vision from Al-Kindi to Kepler* (Chicago: University of Chicago Press, 1976), 2–3.

40. Jill Frank, *Poetic Justice: Rereading Plato's "Republic"* (Chicago: University of Chicago Press, 2018), 182–83. My emphasis. My sincere thanks to Jill Frank for assisting me in understanding how Plato makes use of the theme of appearance.

41. For an exemplary statement that contrasts the ideal (or emphatic concept) of art with its empirical instantiation, see Adorno's claim in *Aesthetic Theory*: "Art must turn against itself, in opposition to its own concept." AT, 2. "Sie [die Kunst] muß gegen sich wenden, was ihren eigenen Begriff ausmacht." GS 7, 10. For a similar statement regarding the legitimacy of "the emphatic concept of knowledge [*emphatische Erkenntnis*]," see GS 6, 161, fn. For "emphatic concept of truth [*dem emphatischen Begriff der Wahrheit*]," see ID, 70; in German NGS, Abt. IV: Band 2: 107. And for the general concept "emphatic philosophy [*nachdrücklichen Philosophie*]," see the remarkable discussion of John Dewey's pragmatism, where Adorno insists that philosophy may fail but nonetheless aims toward a certain success: "In principle [philosophy] can always go astray; solely for that reason, achieve something. Skepticism and pragmatism, latest of all Dewey's strikingly humane versions of the latter, recognized this; this is however to be added into the ferment of an emphatic philosophy, not renounced in advance for the sake of its test of validity [Prinzipiell kann sie stets fehlgehen; allein darum etwas gewinnen. Skepsis und Pragmatismus, zuletzt noch dessen überaus humane Version, die Deweysche, haben das einbekannt; es wäre aber als Ferment einer nachdrücklichen Philosophie nachzuführen, nicht auf diese zugunsten ihrere Bewährungsprobe vorweg zu verzichten]." GS 6, 25.

42. On the difference between conventional and emphatic concepts, Hulatt offers a superb and succinct distinction: "Conventional concepts seek to model the presented properties of objects as they exist presently. Emphatic concepts, by contrast, aim at *future* states—they have a normative core to them. Emphatic concepts do not match up with objects as we find them; and this is precisely what allows emphatic concepts to ground criticism of the world as we find it." See Owen Hulatt, "The Place of Mimesis in *Dialectic of Enlightenment*," in RFS, 351–64: quote from 361. Emphasis in original.

43. "Das Urteil, jemand sei ein freier Mann, bezieht sich, *emphatisch gedacht*, auf den Begriff der Freiheit. Der ist jedoch seinerseits evensowohl mehr, als was von jenem Mann prädizert wird, wie jener Mann, durch andere Bestimmungen, mehr ist denn der Begriff seiner Freiheit. Ihr Begriff sagt nicht nur, daß er auf alle einzelnen, als frei definierten Männer angewandt werden könne. Ihn nährt die Idee eines Zustands, in welchem die Einzelnen Qualtiäten hätten, die heut und hier keinem zuzusprechen wären." GS 6, 153–54. My emphasis.

44. "to this day art in the emphatic sense has only existed as bourgeois art [*daß es Kunst emphatischen Anspruchs bis heute nur als bürgerliche gegeben hat*]." AT, 68. GS 7, 251.

45. "Der Begriff des Kunstwerks impliziert den des Gelingens. Mißlungene Kunstwerke sind keine." AT, English, 188. GS 7, 280.

46. "als eine noch partielle, *also nicht aufgefklärt genug*." ID, 188. NGS, Abt. IV: Band 2: 266. My emphasis.

47. "daß nur dadurch, daß man ihr Prinzip konsequent weiterverfolgt, diese Wunden vielleicht geheilt werden können." ID, 188. NGS, Abt. IV: Band 2: 266. My emphasis.

48. For a discussion of this topic, see Martin Shuster, "The Critique of the Enlightenment," in BC, 251–70.

49. Allen, *The End of Progress*.

50. MM (Frontispiece to Part I), 19. GS 4, 20.

51. Hegel, Preface to *Elements of the Philosophy of Right*, ed. Allen W. Wood, trans. H. B. Nisbet, Cambridge Texts in the History of Political Thought (Cambridge: Cambridge University Press, 1991), 23. A similar thought is expressed in the 1819–20 lectures on the philosophy of right, where we read, "The age has at present *nothing to do except to cognize what is at hand*, and thus

to make it accord with thought." Hegel, *Philosophie des Rechts: Die Vorlesung von 1819/1820*, ed. Dieter Henrich (Frankfurt am Main: Suhrkamp, 1983), 290. As quoted in *Elements*, 392 n. 30.

    52. GS 6, 370.

    53. Quoted from Timo Jütten, "Adorno on Hope," *Philosophy and Social Criticism* 45, no. 3 (2019): 284–306; 300.

    54. Jütten, "Adorno on Hope," 300; my emphasis.

    55. MM (§119), 187. GS 4, 212.

    56. PS, quoted from the English, 199–200. NGS, Abt. IV: Band 6: 281.

    57. PS, quoted from the English, 200. NGS, Abt. IV: Band 6: 282.

    58. PS, 198. NGS, Abt. IV: Band 6: 280.

    59. PS, 199. NGS, Abt. IV: Band 6: 280.

    60. PS, 201. NGS, Abt. IV: Band 6: 284.

    61. PS, 202. NGS, Abt. IV: Band 6: 285.

    62. PS, 203. NGS, Abt. IV: Band 6: 286.

    63. PS, 200. NGS, Abt. IV: Band 6: 281.

    64. Nietzsche thus accepts that genealogy itself is an expression of "faith in science" that is based on a "metaphysical faith." And he urges his readers to understand that "even we knowers of today, we godless anti-metaphysicians, still take *our* fire from the blaze set alight by a faith thousands of years old, that faith of the Christians, which was also Plato's faith, that God is truth, that truth is *divine*" (original emphasis). To be sure, Nietzsche does not rest content with this admission of his own commitments to the metaphysics of scientific truth. Rather, he asks, "What if precisely this becomes more and more unbelievable, when nothing any longer turns out to be divine except for error, blindness, and lies—and what if God himself turned out to be our oldest lie?" Nietzsche, *On the Genealogy of Morality and Other Writings*, ed. Keith Ansell Pearson, trans. Carol Diethe, Cambridge Texts in the History of Political Thought (New York: Cambridge University Press, 2007), 163. With this final twist of the screw, Nietzsche can no longer explain why his own genealogical discoveries would qualify as true—and in this respect he parts company from Adorno, who remains fully committed to the norm of truth in sociological research and critique.

    65. PS, 206. NGS, Abt. IV: Band 6: 282.

    66. PS, 206. NGS, Abt. IV: Band 6: 290. My emphasis.

    67. PS, 206. NGS, Abt IV: Band 6: 291.

    68. PS, 206. NGS, Abt IV: Band 6: 291.

    69. "daß man deshalb, weil die Kultur mißlungen ist, weil sie also das nicht gehalten hat, *was sie verspricht*; weil sie Freiheit, weil sie Individualität, weil sie wahre Allgemeinheit den Menschen vorenthalten hat; weil sie also *ihrem eigenen Begriff nicht benügt hat*, daß sie deshalb nun zum alten Eisen zu werden und frisch-fröhlich durch die zynische Herstellung der Menschenverhältnisse unmittelbar zu ersetzen seit. Es ist einer der gefährlichsten Irrtümer, würde ich sagen, die im kollektiven Unbewußten heute bereit sind—und das Wort Irrtum ist dafür viel zu schwach und zu intellektualistisch, anzunehmen, daß etwas deshalb, weil es *nicht das ist, was es verspricht, weil es nicht sein eigener Begriff ist*, auch schlechter sei als das Gegenteil der puren Unmittelbarkeit, das es zerstört." MCP, German, 200. MCP, Jephcott trans., quote at 127–28. My emphasis throughout. NGS, Abt. IV: Band 14: 200.

    70. For a similar claim about the concept of publicity, see Jürgen Habermas, *The Structural Transformation of the Public Sphere: An Inquiry into a Category of Bourgeois Society*, trans. Frederick Lawrence (Cambridge, MA: MIT Press, 1991), 88.

71. NPT, in CM, 132. In German in *Stichworte*, GS 10.2, 604.

72. NPT, in CM, 132. German in *Stichworte*, GS 10.2, 604.

73. "Der einzelne Denkende muß es riskieren, darf nichts unbesehen eintauschen oder abkaufen; das ist der Erfahrungskern der Lehre von der Autonomie. Ohne Risiko, ohne die präsente Möglichkeit von Irrtum, ist objektiv keine Wahrheit." NPT, in CM, 132. German in *Stichworte*, GS 10.2, 605. My emphasis.

74. NPT, in CM, 132. German in *Stichworte*, GS 10.2, 605. My emphasis.

75. "In all ihren einander sich befehlenden und sich gegenseitig als falsche Version ausschließenden Richtungen ist Ontologie apologetisch. Ihre Wirkung wäre aber nicht zu verstehen, käme ihr kein *nachdrückliches* Bedürfnis entgegen, Index eines Versäumten, die Sehnsucht, beim Kantischen Verdikt übers Wissen des Absoluten solle es nicht sein Bewenden haben." GS 6, 69. My emphasis on the English word "emphatic" (here translating the German *nachdrückliches*). Needless to say, Adorno varies his terminology; here he uses *nachdrücklich* as more or less equivalent in meaning to *emphatisch*.

76. On the concept "objective spirit," see Jean-François Kervegan, *The Rational and the Actual: Hegel and Objective Spirit*, trans. Daniela Ginsburg and Martin Shuster (Chicago: University of Chicago Press, 2018).

77. "Soll die Menscheit des Zwangs sich entledigen, der in Gestalt von Identifikation real ihr angetan wird, *so muß sie zugleich die Identität mit ihrem Begriff erlangen*." GS 6, 149. My emphasis.

78. "Nicht bloß die objective Möglichkeit—auch die subjektive Fähigkeit zum Glück gehört erst der Freiheit an." MM (§55), 91. GS 4, 102.

79. Mine is by no means the only interpretation of Adorno's philosophy to make this claim. In her superb essay on this topic, Britta Scholze argues that happiness is "the pivot-point of his thought [*Dreh- und Angelpunkt seines Denkens*]." Although he is seldom willing to expatiate on his idea of happiness in much depth or precision, Adorno sees happiness (in Scholze's words) as "the standard and goal of a successful orientation of humanity [*für ihen das Glück Maßstab und Ziel einer gelingenden Einrichtung der Menschheit*]." Scholze, "Adorno und das Glück," 454.

80. "Alles Glück bis heute verspricht, was noch nicht war, und der Glaube an seine Unmittelbarkeit ist dem in Wege, daß es werde." GS 6, 345–47.

81. GS 6, 345.

82. "die Fixierung des eigenen Bedürfnisses und der eigenen Sehnsucht verunstaltet die Idee eines Glücks, das erst aufginge, wo die Kategorie des Einzelnen nicht länger sich in sich verschlösse." GS 6, 345–46.

83. GS 6, 345–47.

84. "So hinfällig in ihm alle Spuren des Anderen sind; so sehr alles Glück durch seine Widerruflichkeit entstellt ist, das Seiende wird doch in den Brüchen, welche die Identität Lügen strafen, durchsetzt von den stets wieder gebrochenen Versprechungen jenes Anderen. Jegliches Glück ist Fragment des ganzen Glücks, das den Menschen sich versagt und das sie sich versagen." GS 6, 396.

85. MM (§128), 200. GS 4, 227–8l.

86. MM (§128), 200. GS 4, 228. My emphasis.

87. "Was wäre Glück, das sich nicht mäße an der unmeßbaren Trauer dessen was ist." MM (§128), 200. GS 4, 227–28.

88. KC, English, 145–58. In German, "Kultur und Culture," in Adorno, *Vorträge 1949–1968*, 156–76.

89. KC, in English, 145–58; quote from 149; translation modified. My emphasis. In German in Adorno, *Vorträge 1949–1968*, 156–76.

90. KC, in English, 145–58; quote from 150. German in Adorno, *Vorträge 1949–1968*, 156–76.

91. Immanuel Kant, *Groundwork of the Metaphysics of Morals*, ed. and trans. Mary Gregor, Cambridge Texts in the History of Philosophy (Cambridge: Cambridge University Press, 1997), 12; quoted from 4:399. My emphasis.

92. GS 6, 345–47.

93. Kant, *Critique of Practical Reason*, "The Analytic of Pure Practical Reason," ch. 1, "On the Principles of Pure Practical Reason," Remark II (5:25–5:26), in Kant, *Practical Philosophy*, ed and trans. Mary Gregor, *The Cambridge Edition of the Works of Immanuel Kant* (Cambridge: Cambridge University Press, 1996), 159.

94. Kant, "Remark II," 159; emphasis in original. It seems relevant to note that Jürgen Habermas is more or less in agreement with Kant that happiness cannot serve as the primary norm in our moral deliberations because it does not admit of *reasons*.

In a November 1984 interview with Perry Anderson and Peter Dews, Habermas entertains the question of whether a morality of enlightenment can avoid a concept of happiness. In his response, Habermas echoes Kant's objection that happiness is not a determinate concept that applies universally to all individuals: "Morality has certainly to do with justice and also with the wellbeing of others, even with the promotion of the general welfare. But happiness cannot be brought about intentionally, and can only be promoted very indirectly. I prefer a relatively narrow concept of morality. Morality refers to practical questions which can be decided with reasons—to conflicts of action which can be resolved through consensus. Only those questions are moral in a strict sense which can be answered in a meaningful way from the Kantian standpoint of universalization—of what *all* could wish for. At the same time, I prefer a weak concept of moral theory. We have already touched on this: it should explain and justify the moral point of view, and nothing more. Deontic, cognitive and universal moral theories in the Kantian tradition are theories of justice, which must leave the question of the good life unanswered." Quoted from "A Philosophico-Political Profile," interview with Perry Anderson and Peter Dews, conducted November 1984; first published in *New Left Review* (May–June 1985): 75–105. Reprinted as *Autonomy and Solidarity: Interviews with Jürgen Habermas*, rev. ed., ed. Peter Dews (London: Verso, 1986), quoted from 167.

95. See Thomas Höwing, ed., *The Highest Good in Kant's Philosophy* (Berlin: De Gruyter, 2016).

96. Kant, *Critique of Practical Reason*, 229 (5:111). Emphasis in original.

97. The literature on the highest good and the postulates is extensive. For my discussion here I have consulted most of all Christine Korsgaard, *Creating the Kingdom of Ends* (Cambridge: Cambridge University Press, 1996), esp. 27 ff.; Allen Wood, *Kant's Moral Religion* (Ithaca, NY: Cornell University Press, 1970); Stephen Engstrom, "The Concept of the Highest Good in Kant's Moral Theory," *Philosophy and Phenomenological Research* 52, no. 4 (December 1992): 747–80; John Silber, "Kant's Conception of the Highest Good as Immanent and Transcendent," *Philosophical Review* 68 (October 1959): 469–92; and Klaus Düsing, "Das Problem des höchsten Gutes in Kants praktischen Philosophie," *Kant-Studien* 62 (1971): 5–42.

98. For another interpretation of Kant's idea of the highest good in relation to Adorno, see Martin Shuster, *Autonomy after Auschwitz: Adorno, German Idealism, and Modernity* (Chicago: University of Chicago, 2014), esp. 54 ff.

99. GS 6, 255.

100. "nur das Unglück ist es, das sein Wesen hat an der Immergleichheit." GS 6, 345–47.

101. "Aber die Ehre, welche Kant der Freiheit angedeihen läßt, indem er sie von allem sie Beeinträchtigenden reinigen möchte, verurteilt zugleich prinzipiell die Person zur Unfreiheit."

102. GS 6, 253–54.

103. "Zu diesem steht Kant so ambivalent wie der bürgerliche Geist insgesamt, der dem Individuum the pursuit of happiness garantieren und aus Arbeitsmoral verbieten möchte." GS 6, 253–54. English in original.

104. GS 6, 253.

105. "Das unterschiebt nicht nur die formale Logik der reinen Konsequenz als höchste moralische Instanz, sondern zugleich die Unterordnung jeglicher Regung unter die logische Einheit, ihren Primat über das Diffuse der Natur, ja über alle Vielfalt des Nichtidentischen." GS 6, 253.

106. "Alles Glück auf sinnliche Erfüllung abzielt und an ihr seine Objektivität gewinnt." GS 6, 202–3.

Chapter Three

1. Marx, "Economic and Philosophical Manuscripts of 1844," in MER, 66–125.

2. For an important discussion of Marx's materialism, see the study by Adorno's student, Alfred Schmidt, *Der Begriff der Natur in der Lehre von Marx* (Frankfurt am Main: Europäische Verlaganstalt, 1962).

3. MCP, English, 9. NGS, Abt. IV: Band 14: 21–22. Emphasis in original.

4. Martin Seel has raised a similar objection to Adorno's pretense of total negativism. He notes that Adorno also invokes "radically positive" experiences as the inspiration for his ethical commitments. "From his youth Adorno always insisted that, under present conditions, freedom and happiness, morality and justice, the individual and social good in general, could only be determined negatively. They could be recognized only in their inverted form. This is, however, a flagrant self-deception. For Adorno's ethics radically takes as its point of departure positive— and, moreover, radically positive—experiences. The Proustian and Benjaminian motifs of redeemed time are still at work here with great power." Martin Seel, *Adornos Philosophie der Kontemplation* (Frankfurt am Main: Suhrkamp, 2004).

5. On Horkheimer's assumption of the directorship and its change to a more expansive and interdisciplinary program of social philosophy, see Martin Jay, "Ungrounded: Horkheimer and the Founding of the Frankfurt School," in RFS, 137–51.

6. See the discussion of "mastery of nature," or *Naturbeherrschung*, in the eleventh "thesis" by Walter Benjamin, "Über den Begriff der Geschichte," *Gesammelte Schriften*, Band I, 2:691–706.

7. Adorno, *Philosophical Terminologie*, Band 2 (Frankfurt am Main: Suhrkamp, 1973), 253.

8. Quoted by Deborah Cook, *Adorno on Nature* (Slough: Acumen, 2011), 29.

9. This is a remark that Adorno made to Martin Jay, *The Dialectical Imagination: A History of the Frankfurt School and the Institute for Social Research, 1923-1950* (Boston: Little, Brown, 1973), 57.

10. Adorno, *Jargon der Eigentlichkeit*. GS 6, 435. On the paradoxical effort to apply quasi-sacred categories to secular life, see Gordon, *Adorno and Existence*, esp. 88–98.

11. Adorno, "Marx and the Basic Concepts of Sociological Theory (From a Seminar Transcript in the Summer Semester of 1962)," trans. Verena Erlenbusch-Anderson and Chris O'Kane, *Historical Materialism* (April 2018): 154–164; 164. My emphasis.

12. Adorno, "Marx and the Basic Concepts of Sociological Theory," 164.

13. For Adorno's reading of "the philosophies of bourgeois interiority," see Gordon, *Adorno and Existence.*

14. Adorno, "Résumé der Dissertation," in GS 1, 375–77; 376.

15. In his "Résumé der Dissertation," Adorno refers to the "schlechthingen Transcendenz der Dingwelt," in GS 1, 375–77; at 376.

16. Adorno, GS 1, 321. For a lucid exposition of the place of this study in Adorno's corpus and especially as an anticipation of his mature reflections on the dialectic between psyche and society, see Brandon Bloch, "The Origins of Adorno's Psycho-Social Dialectic: Psychoanalysis and Neo-Kantianism in the Young Adorno," *Modern Intellectual History* 16, no. 2 (2019): 501–29.

17. ND, "Vorrede," in GS 6, 10. My emphasis.

18. "Als dialektische muß Theorie—wie weithin die Marxische—*immanent* sein auch wenn sie schließlich die gesamte Sphäre negiert, in der sie sich bewegt." ND, GS 6, 197. My emphasis.

19. ND, GS 6, 197.

20. GS 6, 197.

21. "Materialismus ist nicht das Dogma, als das seine gewitzigten Gegner ihn verklagen, sondern Auflösung eines seinerseits als Dogmatisch Durchshauten; daher sein Recht in kritischer Philosophie." GS 6, 197.

22. GS 6, 184–87.

23. "die Wendung zum Subjekt . . . verschwindet nicht einfach mit ihrer Revision; diese erfolgt nicht zuletzt im subjektiven Interesse der Freiheit." SO, in CM, 245–58; quote from 249. GS 10.2, 746.

24. GS 10.2, 746. My emphasis.

25. SO, in CM, 249. GS 10.2, 746.

26. SO, in CM, 251.

27. GS, 10.2, 747. I follow Henry Pickford in this translation.

28. "Vermöge der Ungleichheit im Begriff der Vermittlung fällt das Subjekt ganz anders in Objekt als diese in jenes. Objekt kann nur durch Subjekt gedacht werden, erhält sich aber diesem gegenüber immer als Anders; Subjekt jedoch ist der eigenen Beschaffenheit nach vorweg auch Objekt. Vom Subjekt ist Objekt nicht einmal als Idee wegzudenken; aber vom Objekt Subjekt. Zum Sinn von Subjektivität rechnet es, auch Objekt zu sein; nicht ebenso zum Sinn von Objektivität, Subjekt zu sein." GS 6, 184.

29. GS 10.2, 747.

30. "immer auch *gebunden an das, was nicht selbst Denken ist.*" NPT, in CM, 127–34; quote from 129. GS 10.2, 601. My emphasis.

31. "Wo es wahrhaft produktiv ist, wo es erzeugt, dort ist es immer auch ein Reagieren. Passivität steckt im Kern des Aktiven. . . . Das ist sein Passivität. Seine Anstrengung fällt zusammen mit seiner Fähigkeit zu jener. Die Psychologie nennt sie Objektbeziehung oder Objektbesetzung. Sie reicht aber weit hinaus über die psychologische Seite des Denkvorgangs. Objektivität, die Wahrheit der Gedanken hängt an ihrer Relation zur Sache." NPT, in CM, 127–34; quote from 129. GS 10.2, 601.

32. GS 10.2, 601.

33. GS 10.2, 599–607; quote from 602. My emphasis.

34. The rather unusual suggestion that experience would mean "snuggling up to" the object is also found elsewhere in Adorno's work. In his introductory lectures on dialectics, for example, Adorno evokes the ideal of a "freedom which refrains from violently imposing aspects of our

own upon this reality, which opens itself up to this reality, which traces and responds to the object as it were [*dieser Realität sich zu überlassen und gewissermaßen den Objekt sich anzuschmiegen, dem Objekt zu folgen*]." He adds that "this kind of responsiveness [*Art der Schmiegsamkeit*], of productive passivity or spontaneous receptively [*der produktiven Passivität oder der spontanen Rezeptivität*]," is what the concept of experience consists in. Although Adorno ascribes this concept to Hegel, we can plausibly assume that Adorno too endorses this concept of experience. Quoted from ID, 81. ED, NGS Abt. IV, Band 2: 119.

35. SO, in CM, quote from 254. GS 10.2, 752.

36. GS 6, 186. My emphasis.

37. SO, in CM, quote from 254. GS 10.2, 752.

38. GS 6, 188.

39. For an exploration of this concept, see Martin Jay, *Songs of Experience: Modern European and American Variations on a Universal Theme* (Berkeley: University of California Press, 2005).

40. On the comparison to the Kantian schematism, see GS 3, 145–46. DE, English, 98.

41. MM (§19), 40. GS 4, 19. English following Jephcott's translation.

42. For a further discussion of "emphatic experience," see Lambert Zuidervaart, *Truth in Husserl, Heidegger, and the Frankfurt School: Critical Retrieval* (Cambridge, MA: MIT Press, 2017); and Bernstein, *Disenchantment and Ethics*, 420–29.

43. ED, 261. ID, 184. My emphasis.

44. "die Momente . . . wo die lebendige Erfahrung oder die lebendige Erkenntnis die Kruste der verdinglichten, und vorgegebenen konventionellen Anschauungen und Begriffe durchbricht." NGS, Abt. IV: Band 2: 144. ID, 98.

45. NGS, Abt. IV: Band 2: 145. ID, 98.

46. NGS, Abt. IV: Band 2: 144. ID, 98.

47. "das sich in uns vollzieht und lebendig vollzieht nur so und gerade in der Weise, wie wir nicht kontrolliert denken, wie wir noch etwas wie die Freiheit unseres Bewußtseins überhaupt uns bewahren, wie unser Denken nicht bereits zugerichtet ist von den Normen, denen es unterworfen werden soll." NGS, Abt. IV: Band 2: 144. ID, 98.

48. NGS, Abt. IV: Band 2: 145. ID, 98.

49. "Seiner Erkenntnis nähert sich der Akt, in dem das Subjekt den Schleier zerreißt, den es um das Objekt webt. Fähig dazu ist es nur wo es in angstloser Passivität der eigenen Erfahrung sich anvertraut. An den Stellen, wo die subjektive Vernunft subjektive Zufälligkeit wittert, schimmert der Vorrang des Objekts durch; das an diesem, was nicht subjektive Zutat ist." SO, in GS 10.2, 741–58; quote from 752. English in CM, 245–58, quote from 254. Translation modified; my emphasis on "experience."

50. Adorno elaborates on this same idea in many other places in his work. See, e.g., his comments on the true insight into the limitations of human freedom and subjectivity in cases of obsessional neurosis: "the ego that we regard as something substantial and given turns out not to have an existence of its own but to be highly precarious, and its vulnerability is deeply exposed by these neurotic experiences. On the other hand, however, the feeling is true because the ego knows that the *possibility* of its own existence is its true being and it is against this that the obsession offends. I could put it this way: the human subject knows that the inner causes underlying his impulses are not part of himself." Adorno concludes from this analysis that there is an antinomy in our concept of freedom: "we are simultaneously both free and unfree." HF, English, 218. NGS, Abt. IV, Band 13: 302.

51. MCP, 220; in English, 141. On the concept of "disappointment" in Adorno, see Max Pensky, "Critique and Disappointment: *Negative Dialectics* as Late Philosophy," in BC, 503–18.

52. Hartmut Rosa explores this theme in his sociological and phenomenological study of "uncontrollability." See, e.g., his remarks on the "world-relation of dynamic openness between subject and world [*einer Weltbeziehung welche von der dynamischen Offenheit im Verhältnis zwischen Welt und Subjekt*]" and our modern attempt "to eliminate the uncertainty associated with this openness [*einer Welthaltung, welche versucht, die damit verbundene Unsicherheit (die immer auch Risiken birgt) auszuschalten*]." Rosa urges us to accept this openness and what he calls "resonance [*Resonanz*]," even though "resonance implies vulnerability [*Resonanz impliziert Verletzbarkeit*]." Quotes from Rosa, *The Uncontrollability of the World* (Cambridge: Polity, 2020), 52–53. *Unverfügbarkeit* (Salzberg-Wien: Residenz Verlag, 2018), 60–62.

53. Britta Scholze writes that the self can only be characterized as happy "when it opens itself to objects in the broadest sense" and thereby overcomes the "ossification of the bourgeois subject." Quote from Scholze, "Adorno und das Glück," 457.

54. Habermas, ch. 5, "The Entwinement of Myth and Enlightenment," in PDM, 106.

55. "einen *positiven Begriff von ihr* [von der Aufklärung] vorbereiten, der sie aus ihrer Verstrickung in blinder Herrschaft lost." DE, Preface (1944), xviii. My emphasis. "Vorrede," in GS 3, 16.

56. DE, 31. GS 3, 57.

57. DE, English, 32. GS 3, 58. Translation modified, reading "Herrschaft" as "domination."

58. "Jeder Fortschritt der Zivilisation hat mit der Herrschaft auch jene Perspektive auf deren Beschwichtigung erneuert." DE, 32. GS 3, 57.

59. DE, 32. GS 3, 58.

60. DE, 32. GS 3, 58.

61. Adorno, "Progress," in CM, 145. My thanks to Iain Macdonald for alerting me to this passage.

62. This question has been the topic of an important study by Cook, *Adorno on Nature*, whose insights have immeasurably enriched my understanding of this theme.

63. "Die Aufhebung des Privateigentums ist daher die vollständige *Emanzipation* aller menschlichen Sinne und Eigenschaften; aber sie ist diese Emanzipation grade dadurch, daß diese Sinne und Eigenschaften *menschlich*, sowohl subjektiv als objektiv, geworden sind." Karl Marx, "Economic and Philosophic Manuscripts of 1844," in MER, 66–125; quoted from 87; emphasis in original. *Die Ökonomisch-philosophischen Manuskripte* (1844), 540.

64. Schmidt, *Der Begriff der Natur in der Lehre von Marx.*

65. See Agnes Heller, *The Theory of Need in Marx* (London: Verso, 2018).

66. GS 6, 243.

67. "Wer des Lotos Gewächs nun kostete, süßer als Honig, / Nicht an Verkündigung weiter gedachte der, noch an Zurückkunft; / Sondern sie trachteten dort in der Lotophagen Gesellschaft, / Lotos pflückend zu bleiben und abzusagen der Heimat." Homer's *Odyssey*, as quoted in GS, 3, 81.

68. DE, 48. GS 3, 81. My emphasis.

69. "Glück . . . enthält Wahrheit in sich." DE, 48. GS 3, 81. My emphasis.

70. MM (§37), 60–61. GS 4, 68.

71. MM (§37), 60–61. GS 4, 68.

72. Marcel Mauss, *Essai sur le Don: Forme et raison de l'échange dans les sociétés achaïques, L'Année Sociologique*, n.s., no. 1 (1924); republished the following year. In English as *The Gift: The Form and Reason for Exchange in Archaic Societies*, trans. W. D. Halls (New York: Norton, 1990).

73. Mauss, *The Gift*, 65.

74. "Wirkliches Schenken hatte sein Glück in der Imagination des Glücks des Beschenkten. Es heißt wählen, Zeit aufwenden, aus seinem Weg gehen, den anderen als Subjekt denken." MM (§21), 42. GS 4, 47.

75. MM (§21), 43; translation modified. GS 4, 47.

76. "[D]enn es gibt keinen heute, für den Phantasie nicht genau das finden könnte, was ihn durch und durch beglückt." MM (§21), 43. GS 4, 47.

77. MM (§21), 43. GS 4, 47.

78. MM (§21), 43. GS 4, 47.

79. MM (§21), 43. GS 4, 47.

80. Theodor Adorno and Max Horkheimer, *Toward a New Manifesto*, trans. Rodney Livingstone (London: Verso, 2019).

Chapter Four

1. See, e.g., Agnes Heller, *The Theory of Need in Marx* (London: Verso, 2018).

2. MCP, English, 116–17; translation modified. In German from NGS, 182–83.

3. Adorno, "Theses on Need," trans. Iain Macdonald and Martin Shuster, Adorno and Horkheimer, *Towards a New Manifesto*, 79–90; quote from 85 [hereafter cited as TN]. Original text: "Thesen über Bedürfnis" (1942), in GS 8, 392–96; quote from 394.

4. This is an insight that had already occurred to Adorno at the start of his career, namely, in his lecture on the idea of natural history where he argues that the very distinction between nature and history is not natural; it is historical. See Adorno, "Die Idee der Naturgeschichte," in GS 1, 345–65. On the concept of natural history, see Max Pensky, "Natural History: The Life and Afterlife of a Concept in Adorno," *Critical Horizons: A Journal of Philosophy and Social Theory* 5, no. 1 (2004): 227–58.

5. "*Wenn die Produktion unbedingt, schrankenlos sogleich auf die Befriedigung der Bedürfnisse, auch und gerade der vom Kapitalismus produzieren, umgestellt wird, werden sich eben damit die Bedürfnisse selbst entscheidend verändern.* Die Undurchdringlichkeit von echtem und falschem Bedürfnis gehört wesentlich zu der Klassenherrschaft. In ihr bilden die Reproduktion des Lebens und dessen Unterdrückung eine Einheit." TN, 85; GS 8, 392–96; 394. Emphasis in original.

6. TN, 87; GS 8, 395. Emphasis in original.

7. TN, 89; GS 8, 396.

8. HF, English, 213; my emphasis. NGS, Abt. IV: Band 13: 294.

9. HF, English, 213. NGS, Abt. IV: Band 13: 294.

10. Walter Benjamin, "On the Mimetic Faculty," in Walter Benjamin, *Selected Writings, Volume 2 (1927–1934)*, ed. Michael Jennings (Cambridge, MA: Harvard University Press, 1999), 720–22. "Über das mimetische Vermögen," in Walter Benjamin, *Gesammelte Schriften*, Band II, 1 (Frankfurt am Main: Suhrkamp, 1977), 210–13. For an account of the relationship between Benjamin and Adorno on mimesis, see Shierry Weber Nicholsen, "*Aesthetic Theory*'s Mimesis of Walter Benjamin," in *The Semblance of Subjectivity: Adorno's "Aesthetic Theory*," ed. Tom Huhn and Lambert Zuidervaart (Cambridge, MA: MIT Press, 1997), 55–92. For a general discussion of mimesis in Adorno, see Martin Jay, "Mimesis and Mimetology: Adorno and Lacoue-Labarthe," in Huhn and Zuidervaart, *The Semblance of Subjectivity*, 29–54.

11. See Adorno and Horkheimer, "So beschreiben Hubert und Mauß den Vorstellungsge-halt der 'Sympathie', der Mimesis: 'L'un est le tout, tout est dans l'un, la nature triomphe de la nature.'" H. Hubert and M. Mauß, *Théorie générale de la Magie, L'Année Sociologique* (1902–3): 100. As quoted in *Dialektik der Aufklärung*, GS 3, n. 20, following "Begriff der Aufklärung." DE 256. For an illuminating discussion of mimesis and its sources, see Anson Rabinbach, "The Cunning of Unreason: Mimesis and the Construction of Anti-Semitism in Horkheimer and Adorno's *Dialectic of Enlightenment*," in *In the Shadow of Catastrophe: German Intellec-tuals between Apocalypse and Enlightenment* (Berkeley: University of California Press, 1997), 166–98.

12. DE, English, 148. GS 3, 205.

13. On this theme, see Pierre-François Noppen, "The Anthropology in *Dialectic of Enlight-enment*," in BC, 207–20.

14. DE, English, 148. GS 3, 204.

15. DE, English, 148. GS 3, 204.

16. "Anstelle der leiblichen Angleichung an Natur tritt die 'Rekognition im Begriff.'" DE, English, 148. GS 3, 204.

17. GS 3, 206. DE, English, 149.

18. For an excellent discussion of this theme, see Fabian Freyenhagen, "Adorno and Hork-heimer on Anti-Semitism," in BC, 103–22.

19. DE, English, 152. GS 3, 209.

20. For a superb elucidation of the category of mimesis, see Owen Hulatt, "The Place of Mimesis in *Dialectic of Enlightenment*," in RFS, 351–64. I believe that Hulatt is mistaken to char-acterize mimesis as resulting in "only a hollow imitation of and 'merging' with the world around it." Adorno specifies that mimesis is *not* merging or fusion; rather, it is a relationship of similarity *across* difference. Also see Hulatt, "Reason, Mimesis, and Self-Preservation in Adorno," *Journal of the History of Philosophy* 54, no. 1 (2016): 135–52.

21. HF, English, 213. NGS, Abt. IV: Band 13: 294.

22. HF, English, 213. Emphasis in original. NGS, Abt. IV: Band 13: 294.

23. HF, English, 213. NGS, Abt. IV: Band 13: 295.

24. MM (§146), 227–28. GS 4, 259–61.

25. MM (§146), 228. GS 4, 260.

26. MM (§146), 228. GS 4, 260–61. My translation.

27. MM (§146), 228. GS 4, 261.

28. ND, English translation by Redmond. GS 6, 192.

29. For a further exposition of this concept, see Peter E. Gordon, "Adorno's Concept of Metaphysical Experience," in BC, 459–564.

30. NGS, Abt. IV: Band 16. *Vorlesung über Negative Dialektik.* See esp. lecture 8, "Begriff der geistigen Erfahrung," 114–28.

31. To be sure, this well-known stricture against metaphysical knowledge of world-transcendent entities (such as God or the immortal soul), however, does not prevent Kant from investigating the "metaphysical foundations" of natural science, "the metaphysics of morals," and so forth. But such inquiries do not yield genuine *knowledge* of objects that lie beyond the bounds of possible experience.

32. For another account of metaphysical experience, see J. M. Bernstein, "Why Rescue Sem-blance? Metaphysical Experience and the Possibility of Ethics," in Huhn and Zuidervaart, *The*

Semblance of Subjectivity, 177–212. Also see Gordon, "Adorno's Concept of Metaphysical Experience," in BC, 549–64.

33. GS 6, 366.

34. "Dem Kind ist selbstverständlich, daß, was es an seinem Lieblingsstädtchen entzückt, *nur dort, ganz allein und nirgends sonst* zu finden sei; es irrt, aber sein Irrtum stiftet das Modell der Erfahrung, eines Begriffs, welcher endlich der der Sache selbst wäre, nicht das Armselige von den Sachen Abgezogene." ND, trans. Redmond. GS 6, 366. My emphasis.

35. "it is only at a particular place that the experience of happiness can be had, of something that is not exchangeable, even if it later proves to be less than unique." See Adorno, "Amorbach," in GS 10.1, 302–9. Also see the remarkable passage from the concluding lecture of his 1965 course on metaphysics: "I myself have had a similar experience with such names. When one is on holiday as a child and reads or hears names such as Monbrunn, Reuenthal, Hambrunn, one has the feeling: 'if only one were there, at that place, that would be it.' This 'it'—what the 'it' is—is extraordinarily difficult to say; one will probably have to say, following Proust's tracks . . . that it is happiness [*daß es das Glück sei*]. When one later reaches such places, it is not there either, one does not find 'it.' Often they are just foolish villages. If there is a single stable door open in them and a smell of real live cow and dung and such things, to which this experience is no doubt attached, one must be very thankful today. . . . At such moments one has the curious feeling that something is receding. . . . I would say, therefore, that happiness—and there is an extremely deep constellation between metaphysical experience and happiness—is something within objects and, at the same time, remote from them." MCP, English 140. NGS, 218–19.

36. GS 6, 366.

37. GS 6, 366. My emphasis.

38. GS 6, 366.

39. GS 6, 366.

40. GS 6, 366.

41. "Was an Metaphysischen ohne Rekurs auf die Erfahrung des Subjekts, ohne sein unmittelbares Dabeisein verkündet wird, ist hilflos vor dem Begehren des autonomen Subjekts, nichts sich aufzwingen zu lassen, was nicht ihm selber einsichtig wäre." GS 6, 367. For the English I have followed Redmond's translation.

42. "Glück, das einzige an metaphysicher Erfahrung, was mehr ist denn ohnmächtiges Verlangen, gewährt das Innere der Gegenstände, als diesen zugleich Entrücktes." GS 6, 367. My emphasis and my translation.

43. For the alternative reading of "spiritual" experience, see Hent de Vries, "On the 'Spiritual' in Aesthetic Experience; or, The 'Nonfactual in Facticity,'" *New German Critique* 48, no. 2 (2021): 43–61.

44. On this point I agree with J. M. Bernstein's insightful remarks on "fugitive ethical events" and their embattled normative status. "Fugitive ethical events," he writes, "are Adorno's conception of the experience of normativity in late modernity: the domain of the normative, when fully, which is to say more than negatively, thought, is a domain of emphatic yet material experience; such experience is an experience of transcendence, and hence overlaps with what used to be thought under the title of metaphysics." Quoted from Bernstein, *Adorno: Ethics and Disenchantment*, 419.

45. "*die Metaphysik geschlüpft ist in das materielle Dasein.*" MCP (Vorlesung 15 [July 20, 1965]), English quoted from 116–17; translation modified. In NGS, Abt. IV: Band 14, 183.

46. See Rudolf Carnap, "Überwindung der Metaphysik durch logische Analyse der Sprache," *Erkenntnis* 2 (1931): 219–41. For a commentary, see Michael Friedman, *A Parting of the Ways:*

Carnap, Cassirer, and Heidegger (Chicago: Open Court, 2000). Also see Peter E. Gordon, *Continental Divide: Heidegger, Cassirer, Davos* (Cambridge, MA: Harvard University Press, 2010), 99, 327–28.

47. On the sublation [*Aufhebung*] of metaphysics in Adorno, see Theunissen, "Negativität bei Adorno," 59.

48. ND, English translation following Redmond. GS 6, 354.

49. GS 6, 354.

50. GS 6, 377–78.

51. GS 6, 400.

52. "Der Kant der Vernunftkritik hat in der Ideenlehre ausgesprochen, ohne Metaphysik sei Theorie nicht möglich. Daß sie aber möglich ist, impliziert jenes Recht zur Metaphysik, an dem der gleiche Kant festhielt, der sie, durch die Wirkung seines Werkes, zerschmetterte. Die Kantische Rettung der intelligiblen Sphäre ist nicht nur, wie alle wissen, protestantische Apologetik, sondern möchte auch in die Dialektik der Aufklärung dort eingreifen, wo sie in der Abschaffung von Vernunft selbst terminiert." ND, English translation following Redmond. GS 6, 377–78.

53. This was a charge that Heinrich Heine originally leveled against Kant: the resurrection of religion in the theory of postulates was seen as a concession to popular morality, since "old Lampe must have a God, otherwise the poor fellow can never be happy." Quoted from Heine, *On the History of Religion and Philosophy in Germany*, ed. Terry Pinkard (Cambridge: Cambridge University Press, 2007).

54. "Wieviel tiefer die Kantische Begierde des Rettens gründet denn einzig im frommen Wunsch, etwas von den traditionellen Ideen inmitten des Nominalismus und wider ihn in Händen zu halten, bezeugt die Konstruktion der Unsterblichkeit als eines Postulats der praktischen Vernunft. Es verurteilt die Unerträglichkeit des Bestehenden und bekräftigt den Geist der sie erkennt." ND, English following Redmond's translation. GS 6, 378.

55. ND, English following Redmond's translation. "Daß keine innerweltliche Besserung ausreiche, den Toten Gerechtigkeit widerfahren zu lassen; daß keine ans Unrecht des Todes rührte, bewegt die Kantische Vernunft dazu, gegen Vernunft zu hoffen. Das Geheimnis seiner Philosophie ist die Unausdenkbarkeit der Verzweiflung." GS 6, 378.

56. See, however, Adorno's conversation with Ernst Bloch. Adorno suggests that "without the notion of an unfettered life, freed from death, the idea of utopia, the idea of *the* utopia, cannot even be thought at all." There is certain contradiction in the idea of utopia, insofar as "it cannot be conceived at all without the elimination of death," but "where the threshold of death is not at the same time considered, there can actually be no utopia." Quoted from Adorno and Bloch, "Something's Missing," 10.

57. MCP, English, 116–117; translation modified. In German from NGS, 182–83.

58. MCP, English, 116–17; translation modified. In German from NGS, 182–83.

59. "Wenn ich Ihnen sage, daß eigentlich der Grund der Moral heute in[,] . . . in dem Körpergefühl, in der Identifikation mit dem unerträglichen Schmerz beruht, so zeige ich Ihnen damit etwas von einer anderen Seite her an, was ich Ihnen vorhin in einer viel abstrakteren Form anzudeuten versucht habe,—nämlich daß die Moral, das was man moralisch nennen kann, also *die Forderung nach dem richtigen Leben*, fortlebt in ungeschminkt materialistischen Motiven; daß gerade also das metaphysische Prinzip eines solchen '*Du sollst*'—und dies '*Du sollst*' ja ein metaphysisches, *ein über die bloße Faktizität hinausweisendes Prinzip*—, daß das selber seiner Rechtfertigung eigentlich finden kann nur noch in dem Rekurs auf die materielle

NOTES TO PAGES 141–146

Wirklichkeit, auf die leibhafte, physische Realität und nicht an seinem Gegenpol, als reiner Gedanke." MCP, English, 116–17; translation modified. In German from NGS, 182–83. My emphasis.

60. I owe this insight to Iain Macdonald (pers. comm.).

61. MM (Dedication), 15. Jephcott translates "richtiges Leben" as "the good life." GS 4, 13.

62. "Die kleinste Spur sinnlosen Leidens in der erfahrenen Welt *straft die gesamte Identitätsphilosophie Lügen.*" GS 6, 203. My emphasis.

63. GS 6, 203.

64. "Denn ist Objektivität, die auf dem Subjekt lastet." GS 6, 29.

65. "Bewußtsein könnte gar nicht über das Grau verzweifeln, hegte es nicht den Begriff von einer verschiedenen Farbe, deren versprengte Spur im negativen Ganzen nicht fehlt." GS 6, 370.

66. "Glück . . . ist wesentlich ein Resultat. Es entfaltet sich am aufgehobenen Leid." DE, GS 3, 81. The term "aufgehoben" (translated as "removed" in Jephcott's English edition from Stanford University Press) alerts us to what I have called the relation of dialectical entailment between suffering and happiness.

67. For a related argument, see the exceptionally thoughtful argument by Lambert Zuidervaart, "Metaphysics after Auschwitz: Suffering and Hope in Adorno's *Negative Dialectics,*" in *Adorno and the Need in Thinking,* ed. Donald Burke et al. (Toronto: University of Toronto Press, 2007), 133–62.

68. "Darum konvergiert das spezifisch Materialistische mit dem Kritischen, mit gesellschaft veränderder Praxis." GS 6, 203.

69. See, e.g., Axel Honneth, *The Struggle for Recognition: The Moral Grammar of Social Conflicts,* trans. Joel Anderson (Cambridge, MA: MIT Press, 1996); and Honneth, *Disrespect.*

70. "Das Bedürfnis, Leiden beredt werden zu lassen, ist Bedingung aller Wahrheit." GS 6, 29.

Chapter Five

1. Seyla Benhabib, *Critique, Norm, and Utopia: A Study of the Foundations of Critical Theory* (New York: Columbia University Press, 1987), 11. For a general discussion of this problem, see Robin Celikates, "Critical Theory and the Unfinished Project of Mediating Theory and Practice," in RFS, 206–20.

2. Walter Benjamin, "Left-Wing Melancholy," trans. Ben Brewster, in *Selected Writings,* ed. Michael W. Jennings (Cambridge, MA: Harvard University Press, 1996–2003), vol. 2 (1999), 423–27.

3. In his study of Adorno's practical philosophy Fabian Freyenhagen has relatively little to say about art, though he acknowledges that art "represents the real possibility that things could be different." See FF, 45 n. 54. But he nonetheless denies the central place of art as a source of normativity: "Adorno allows that art, theology, and metaphysics have a positive function to play. They remind and promise us that things could be different, that what we have now need not be all there could be. Yet, at the same time, it is an illusion to think that they, or the experiences involved in them bring us in touch with the good. It is not that we can actually transcend the totality of our current evil world in our experiences of engagement with art, theology, or metaphysics. Rather, their claim to transcendence enables us to see this totality for what it is: something which only *seems* to be unchangeable and without real alternative, but is, in fact, sustained by our action and both possible to and in need of change." FF, 227. Notice that Freyenhagen elevates the criterion of normativity in suggesting that art (along with theology and metaphysics), if they were to put us in touch with the good, would be required to "*actually transcend the totality of*

our current evil world" (my emphasis). Clearly Adorno imposes no such requirement. Even a partial glimpse of the good from *within* (and not transcendent to) our unfree social world would be sufficient for Adorno to qualify art as a specimen of normative truth.

4. Peter Hohendahl, "Autonomy of Art: Looking Back at Adorno's *Ästhetische Theorie*," *German Quarterly* 54, no. 2 (March 1981): 133–148; quote from 145.

5. Walter Benjamin and Theodor Adorno, *The Complete Correspondence, 1928–1940*, ed. Henri Lonitz, trans. Nicholas Walker (Cambridge, MA: Harvard University Press, 2001), 127–34; quote from 128. *Briefwechsel, 1928–1940*, ed. Henri Lonitz (Frankfurt am Main: Suhrkamp,1994), 168–77.

6. Benjamin and Adorno, *Briefwechsel*, 169. My emphasis.

7. Walter Benjamin and Gershom Scholem, *The Correspondence of Walter Benjamin and Gershom Scholem, 1932–1940*, ed. Gershom Scholem, trans. Gary Smith and Andre Lefevere (New York: Schocken Books, 1989), 84.

8. Benjamin, knowing that the habilitation would not be accepted, withdrew it from consideration. For details on this episode, see Howard Eiland and Michael Jennings, *Walter Benjamin: A Critical Life* (Cambridge, MA: Harvard University Press, 2016), 232.

9. For another excellent summary of this debate, see Michael Rosen, "Benjamin, Adorno, and the Decline of the Aura," in CC, 40–56.

10. AT, 29. GS 7, 50.

11. AT, 45. GS 7, 73.

12. "Nicht nur das Jetzt und Hier des Kunstwerks ist, nach Benjamins These, dessen Aura, sondern was immer daran über seine Gegebenheit hinausweist, sein Gehalt; *man kann nicht ihn abschaffen und die Kunst wollen*." AT, 45. GS 7, 73. My emphasis.

13. For a more detailed analysis, see Peter E. Gordon, "Social Suffering and the Autonomy of Art," *New German Critique* [Special issue on Adorno's *Aesthetic Theory*, guest editor Peter E. Gordon], no. 143 (August 2021): 125–46.

14. Karl Marx, "The Fetishism of the Commodity and its Secret," in *Capital*, vol. 1, trans. Ben Fowkes (London: Penguin Books, 1990), 163–77.

15. Theodor Adorno, "On the Fetish Character in Music and Regression in Listening," in *The Essential Frankfurt School Reader*, ed. Andrew Arato and Eike Gebhardt (London: Bloomsbury, 1978), 270–99, quote from 279; "Über den Fetischcharakter in der Musik und die Regression des Hörens," in GS 14, 14–50, quote from 25.

16. "Es ist *neimals* ein Dokument der Kultur, ohne *zugleich* ein solches der Barbarei zu sein." Walter Benjamin, "Über den Begriff der Geschichte," *Gesammelte Schriften*, Band I, 2, ed. Rolf Tiedemann and Hermann Schweppenhäuser (Frankfurt am Main: Suhrkamp, 1974), 691–704; quote from 696. My emphasis. The original English translation by Harry Zohn (misleadingly) substitutes "civilization" for "culture."

17. DE, 109. GS 3, 159.

18. DE, 127. GS 3, 180.

19. Quoted above; my emphasis on "crossed with."

20. For a helpful discussion, see Owen Hulatt, "Aesthetic Autonomy," in BC, 351–64.

21. GS 4, 260.

22. GS 4, 260.

23. Paraphrased from GS 7, 73.

24. For further thoughts on this theme, see Kathy J. Kiloh, "Adorno's Materialist Ethics of Love," in BC, 601–14.

25. GS 4, 260.

26. Immanuel Kant, *Critique of the Power of Judgment*, ed. Paul Guyer and Eric Matthews (Cambridge: Cambridge University Press, 2000).

27. DE, English, 128. GS 3, 181.

28. DE, English, 128. GS 3, 181.

29. AT, 317. GS 7, 469.

30. AT, 317. GS 7, 469.

31. AT, 317. GS 7, 470.

32. Paralipomena, AT 318; GS 7, 471. The text in question is Johan Huizinga, *Homo Ludens: A Study of the Play-Element of Culture* (London: Routledge and Kegan Paul, 1949); originally published in Dutch in 1938.

33. For a related argument, see Erica Weitzman, "No 'Fun': Aporias of Pleasure in Adorno's *Aesthetic Theory*," *German Quarterly* 81, no. 2 (Spring 2008): 185–202.

34. Paralipomena, AT 318. GS 7, 472. My emphasis.

35. See too the helpful comments in Fred Rush, "Adorno after Adorno," in *Art and Aesthetics after Adorno*, Townshend Center for the Humanities, no. 3 (Berkeley: University of California Press, 2010), 41–68, esp. the remark that "to be art is to be a necessary failure." Quote from 57.

36. "Der Begriff des Kunstwerks impliziert den des Gelingens. Mißlungene Kunstwerke sind keine." AT, 188. GS 7, 280.

37. "Das Bedürfnis, Leiden beredt werden zu lassen, ist Bedingung aller Wahrheit." GS 6, 29.

38. Marx, "Die entfremdete Arbeit," in *Ökonomisch-philosophische Manuskripte*. In English from Tucker, 76. It should be noted that Marx includes *aesthetic* labor in his capacious definition of human self-objectification. When the human subject creates the objective world he objectifies himself, and this is no less the case in artistic creation, in which "der Mensch formiert . . . auch nach den Gesetzen der Schönheit."

39. "Was aber wäre Kunst als Geschichtsschreibung, wenn sie das Gedächtnis des akkumulierten Leidens abschüttelte." AT, 261. GS 7, 387.

40. AT, 9. GS 7, 21.

41. AT, 141. GS 7, 213. My emphasis.

42. AT, 141. GS 7, 213.

43. "autonomer Gebilde *und* gesellschaftlicher Phänomene." AT, 248. GS 7, 368. My emphasis.

44. AT, 158. GS 7, 236.

45. "Sie ist für sich und ist es nicht, verfehlt ihre Autonomie ohne das ihr Heterogene." AT, 6; my translation. GS 7, 17.

46. AT, 236. GS 7, 350.

47. AT, 180. GS 7, 268.

48. "Insofern ist ihnen transzendent, kommt ihnen von außen zu, wodurch sie zu einem Immanenzzusammenhang überhaupt werden. Jene Katagorien werden aber dabei so weitgehend modifiziert, daß nur der Schatten von Bündigkeit übrig ist." AT, 180. GS 7, 268.

49. AT, 180. GS 7, 269.

50. AT, 180. GS 7, 269.

51. "Die ungelösten Antagonismen der Realität kehren wieder in den Kunstwerken als die immanenten Probleme ihre Form." AT, 6. GS 7, 16.

52. AT, 177. GS 7, 267. Translation modified.

53. AT, 190. GS 7, 283.

54. AT, 177. GS 7, 264.

55. AT, 177. GS 7, 264. I have reproduced this paragraph, with minor alterations, from my essay, "Social Suffering and the Autonomy of Art."

56. The literature on this controversy is vast. For a helpful survey of the relevant issues, see Richard Leppert, "Commentary," in Theodor W. Adorno, *Essays on Music* (Berkeley: University of California Press, 2002), 327–72. For the claim that Adorno should not have condemned all varieties of jazz as mere commodities, see Theodore A. Gracyk, "Adorno, Jazz, and the Aesthetics of Popular Music," *Musical Quarterly* 76, no. 4 (Winter 1992): 532–33. For a related commentary on Adorno's mistaken impression that jazz was widely popular, see Ulrich Schönherr, "Adorno and Jazz: Reflections on a Failed Encounter," *Telos* 87 (Spring 1991): 85–96. On Adorno's failure to comprehend improvisation, see Richard Quinn, "Playing with Adorno: Improvisation and the Jazz Ensemble," *Yearbook of Comparative and General Literature* 44 (1996): 57–67. Among the most recent and creative attempts to mobilize Adorno's insights is Fumi Okiji, *Jazz as Critique: Adorno and Black Expression Revisited* (Stanford, CA: Stanford University Press, 2018).

57. Adorno, "Perennial Fashion—Jazz," in PRSM, 123; GS 10.1, 125.

58. "Schon die Negro Spirituals, Vorformen des Blues, mögen als Sklavenmusik die Klage über die Unfreiheit mit deren unterwürfiger Bestätigung verbunden haben." Adorno, "Perennial Fashion—Jazz," in PRSM, 121; GS 10.1, 124.

59. "Das perennierende Leiden hat soviel Recht auf Ausdruck wie der Gemartete zu brüllen." ND, "After Auschwitz," in GS 6, 355.

60. CCS, 43. GS 10.1, 30.

61. But the suggestion that his opinions about jazz were a reflection of racism would need to be examined alongside critical remarks on racism elsewhere in his oeuvre, including what Richard Leppert calls the "bitterly ironic exchange" between Tom Sawyer and Huck Finn about the lynching of a black man in Adorno's never-completed libretto, *Der Schatz der Indianer Joe.* See Leppert, "Commentary," 60.

62. Adorno, "On Jazz"; quote from Leppert, "Commentary," 478.

63. MM (§153), 247. GS 4, 283.

64. AT, English, 3. GS 7, 13.

65. AT, 3. GS 7, 13. On the "withering of experience [*die verdorrte Erfahrung*]," see MM (§33), 55; GS 4, 61. For an important comment on this theme, see Martin Jay, "Is Experience Still in Crisis? Reflections on a Frankfurt School Lament," in CC, 129–47.

Chapter Six

1. AT, English 334; GS 7, 497.

2. AT, 334. GS 7, 497.

3. AT, 341. GS 7, 507.

4. AT, 341. GS 7, 507.

5. AT, 357. GS 7, 530. "Solange nicht in die Werke, nach dem Goetheschen Vergleich nach der Kappelle, eingetreten wird, bleibt die Rede von Objektivität in ästhetischen Dingen . . . bloße Behauptung."

6. MM (§128), 199. GS 4, 227.

7. As quoted in the afterword to Adorno, GS, 19, ed. Rolf Tiedemann and Klaus Schulz (Frankfurt am Main: Suhrkamp, 1984), 635. Emphasis in original.

8. Adorno, Letter to Thomas Mann (July 5, 1948), in *Correspondence, 1943–1955*, trans. Nicholas Walker (Cambridge: Polity, 2006), 24. My emphasis. In German as Adorno and Mann, *Briefwechsel, 1943–1955*, 33.

9. For a general discussion of Adorno's views on late style, see Peter E. Gordon, "The Artwork Beyond Itself: Adorno, Beethoven, and Late-Style," in *The Modernist Imagination: Essays in Intellectual History and Critical Theory in Honor of Martin Jay* (New York: Berghahn Books, 2008), 77–98.

10. We all owe an enormous debt to Adorno's student the recently deceased Rolf Tiedemann for assembling and editing Adorno's notes on Beethoven and making them available to readers in a legible form.

11. Scott Burnham, *Beethoven Hero* (Princeton, NJ: Princeton University Press, 1995).

12. Lewis Lockwood, *Beethoven: The Music and the Life* (New York: Norton, 2005), 149–50.

13. Adorno, BPM, "Towards a Theory of Beethoven," 13.

14. BPM, "Towards a Theory of Beethoven," 13. My emphasis.

15. BPM, "Towards a Theory of Beethoven," 13.

16. BPM, "Towards a Theory of Beethoven," 14. My emphasis.

17. BPM, "Towards a Theory of Beethoven," 14. My emphasis.

18. BPM, 152. In German as "Verfremdetes Hauptwerk," in *Moments musicaux*. GS 17, 159.

19. BPM, 152; German from "Spätstil Beethovens," in *Moments musicaux*. GS 17, 13–17; quote from 15.

20. "Late Style in Beethoven," in Leppert, *Essays on Music*, ed. Adorno, 566; German from "Spätstil Beethovens," GS 17, 13–17; quote from 15.

21. Adorno, MM (§153), 247; GS 4, 283.

22. "Man kann nicht mehr wie Beethoven komponieren, aber man muß so *denken* wie er komponierte." BPM, 160. NGS, Abt. 1, Band I: 321. Emphasis in original.

23. For a superb commentary, see Maynard Solomon, "The Ninth Symphony: A Search for Order," in *Beethoven Essays* (Cambridge, MA: Harvard University Press, 1990), 3–34.

24. See Solomon, "The Ninth Symphony," 18–19.

25. "die Möglichkeit der Wahrheit, welche im ästhetischen Bild verkörpert, wird ihm leibhaft." AT, 244–45; translation modified. GS 7, 363.

26. "Erschütterung, dem üblichen Erlebnisbegriff schroff entgegengesetzt, ist keine partikulare Befriedigung des Ichs, der Lust nicht ähnlich. Eher ist sie ein Memento des Liquidation des Ichs, das als erschüttertes der eigenen Beschränktheit und Endlichkeit innewird. Diese Erfahrung ist konträr zur Schwächung des Ichs, welche die Kulturindustrie betreibt. . . . Das Ich bedarf, damit es nur um ein Winziges über das Gefängnis hinausschaue, das es selbst ist, nicht der Zerstreuung, sondern der äußersten Anspannung; das bewahrt Erschütterung, übrigens ein unwillkürliches Verhalten, vor der Regression." AT, 245; GS 7, 364. For a further comment recommending Adorno's idea of concentration over distraction as the disposition best suited to aesthetic experience, see Hammer, *Adorno's Modernism*, 213.

27. AT, 245; GS 7, 364. "Memento der Liquidation des Ichs, das als erschüttertes der eigenen Beschränktheit und Endlichkeit innewird."

28. AT, 245; GS 7, 364.

29. For a related discussion, see Kathy Kiloh, "Towards an Ethical Politics: T. W. Adorno and Aesthetic Self-Relinquishment," *Philosophy and Social Criticism* 43, no. 6 (2017): 571–98.

30. Susan McClary, "Getting Down Off the Beanstalk: The Presence of a Woman's Voice in Janika Vandervelde's *Genesis II*," republished in *Feminine Endings: Music, Gender, and Sexuality* (Minneapolis: University of Minnesota Press,1991),112–31; quotes from 128.

31. The responses to McClary have ranged from the thoughtful and sympathetic to the dismissive and hostile. For an example of the former, see Robert Fink, "Beethoven Antihero: Sex, Violence, and the Aesthetics of Failure, or Listening to the Ninth Symphony as Postmodern Sublime," in *Beyond Structural Listening? Postmodern Modes of Hearing*, ed. Andrew Dell'Antonio (Berkeley: University of California Press, 2004), 109–53. For an example of the latter, see Pieter C. van den Toorn, "Politics, Feminism, and Contemporary Music Theory," *Journal of Musicology* 9, no. 3 (1991): 275–99. And see the nuanced intervention by Ruth Solie, "What Do Feminists Want? A Reply to Pieter van den Toorn," *Journal of Musicology* 9, no. 4 (1991): 399–410.

32. On the role of anthropomorphism in Adorno's interpretation of music, see Max Paddison, *Adorno's Aesthetics of Music* (Cambridge: Cambridge University Press, 1993). Although Paddison is partly correct, it is crucial to Adorno's interpretive method that ascribing agency or anthropomorphic characteristics to the music does not necessarily entail an identity between music and listener, and certainly not between the music and the composer.

33. BPM, 15.

34. As quoted by Joseph Kerman in *The Beethoven Quartets* (New York: Norton, 1966), 199.

35. As quoted by Joseph Kerman from a conversation between Stravinsky and Robert Craft, in Kerman, *The Beethoven Quartets*, 199.

36. Kerman, *The Beethoven Quartets*, 198.

37. Daniel K. L. Chua and Alexander Rehding, *Alien Listening: Voyager's Golden Record and Music from Earth* (Brooklyn, NY: Zone Books, 2021), 112.

38. BPM, "Appendix III," "Text 9: Beethoven's Late Style" (from impromptu radio talk, Norddeutscher Rundunk, 1966), in BPM, English edition, 193.

39. BPM, 192–93; my emphasis on "hope." On the status of hope it may be helpful to consider the contrast between Adorno and Ernst Bloch. Whereas Bloch believed that the concept of hope carries a religious imprint, Adorno abstained from acknowledging the legitimacy of explicitly religious concepts. If hope is given to us at all, he claims, it appears not in the immediacy of religious tradition, but only as refracted through material experience and in the secularized medium of art. In the sketches for his unfinished book on Beethoven, for example, Adorno offers an intriguing remark on the composer's Piano Sonata no. 26 in E♭ Major, whose name, "Les Adieux," derives from its musical "farewell" (*lebewohl*) to Beethoven's friend the archduke Rudolf, whose departure from Vienna is thematized in the sonata's three movements. The composer wished for his friend's swift return. Adorno writes of the sonata that "the clatter of horses' hooves moving away into the distance carries a greater degree of hope than the four Gospels." BPM, 174. For a related remark on the theme of hope and Beethoven's "Les Adieux," see AT, 358; GS 7, 531.

40. W. J. Verdenius, "A 'Hopeless' Line in Hesiod: *Works and Days* 96," *Mnemosyne*, 4th ser., 24, fasc. 3 (1971): 225–31.

41. For a superb discussion of the Cavatina, see Lewis Lockwood, "On the Cavatina of Beethoven's String Quartet in B-flat Major, Opus 130," ch. 10 in Lockwood, *Beethoven: Studies in the Creative Process* (Cambridge, MA: Harvard University Press, 1992; repr. 2014), 209–17.

42. BPM, 70–71.

43. See Adorno's analysis of the "shadow" as one of Beethoven's "most splendid formal means," in BPM, 70–71. For their assistance in deciphering Adorno's unusual analysis of the "shadow" effect in Beethoven's music, I am grateful to Alex Rehding and John Schott.

44. DE (English), 103; GS 3, 151.

45. For Adorno on Wagner, see Peter E. Gordon, "Wounded Modernism: Adorno on Wagner," *New German Critique* [Special Issue on Adorno and Music] 129, no. 3 (November 1916): 155–73.

46. AT 110; GS 7, 168.

47. AT, 110; GS 7, 168. For a different view, see James Gordon Finlayson's rejoinder to my claims regarding the transhistorical validity of late style, in Finlayson, "The Artwork and the *Promesse du Bonheur* in Adorno," *European Journal of Philosophy* 23, no. 3 (2012): 392–419; see n. 27.

48. MMP, 33; GS 13, 182.

49. "Frei wie nur einer, der selber von Kultur nicht ganz verschluckt ist, greift er auf muskalisch obdachlosen Zug nach dem zerbrochenen Glas auf der Landstraße und hält es gegen die Sonne, daß alle Farben darin sich brechen." MMP, 36; GS 13, 184.

50. MMP, 17; GS 13, 166.

51. MMP, 17; GS 13, 166.

52. MMP, 36; translation modified. GS 13, 184; my emphasis.

53. MMP, 37; GS 13, 186. Jephcott has included the German directions in the text; these are not printed in the original German version of Adorno's text.

54. MMP, 37; translation modified. GS 13, 186. My emphasis.

55. Alma Mahler, ed., *Gustav Mahler: Briefe, 1879–1911* (New York: Georg Olms Verlag, 1978), 198.

56. MMP, 9.

57. AT, 63; GS 7, 99. My translation. Hullot-Kentor uses the term "plenipotentiary," but in the German original Adorno writes: "Das Kunstwerk, durch und durch θέσει, ein Menschliches, vertritt, was φύσει, kein bloßes fürs Subjekt, was, kantisch gesprochen, Ding an sich wäre." Adorno's German verbal term "vertritt" may not warrant such an unusual English noun.

58. MMP, 8; GS 13, 157.

59. MMP, 9; GS 13, 157.

60. "Das Kunstwerk, gekettet an Kultur, möchte die Kette zerreißen, Barmherzigkeit üben am schäbigen Rest." MMP, 38; GS 13, 187.

61. "*verkörpern. . . . die Freiheit.*" MMP, 167. My emphasis.

62. GS 7, 309.

63. MMP, 51; GS 13, 200. My emphasis.

64. GS 6, 396. English following Redmond's translation.

65. "So hinfällig in ihm alle Spuren des Anderen sind; so sehr alles Glück durch seine Widerruflichkeit entstellt ist, das Seiende wird doch in den Brüchen, welche die Identität Lügen strafen, durchsetzt von den stets wieder gebrochenen Versprechungen jenes Anderen. Jegliches Glück ist Fragment des ganzen Glücks, das den Menschen sich versagt und das sie sich versagen." GS 6, 396. English following Redmond's translation. My emphasis.

66. MMP, 51; GS 13, 200.

67. See, e.g., Arnold Schoenberg, "Gustav Mahler (1912, 1948)," in Schoenberg, *Style and Idea: Selected Writings*, ed. Leonard Stein, trans. Leo Black (Berkeley: University of California Press, 1975), 449–72.

68. Schoenberg, "Gustav Mahler: In Memoriam (1912)," in Schoenberg, *Style and Idea*, 447–48.

69. For a helpful summary, see Sherry D. Lee, "Adorno and the Second Viennese School," in BC, 67–84.

70. It is well known that Schoenberg himself did not welcome such criticism, and he even confided in a letter to an acquaintance that notwithstanding his personal dislike for Stravinsky's music, he saw little legitimacy in Adorno's philosophical polemics. I will not dwell here on the debate as to whether Adorno's specific remarks on the contest between Schoenberg and

Stravinsky have any merit. Despite its professed admiration for Schoenberg's early work, the polemical character of Adorno's book did not appeal to the composer himself. Shortly after its publication, Schoenberg wrote to the critic Hans Stuckenschmidt to express his displeasure: "So modern music has a philosophy. It would been sufficient for it to have a philosopher. He attacks me quite vehemently in it. Another defector. . . . Disgusting the way he is treating Stravinsky. I am certainly no Stravinsky fan, though every now and then I do like some of his pieces—but you certainly don't have to write something like that." Quoted from Schoenberg, Letter to H. H. Stuckenschmidt (December 5, 1949); reprinted in *The Doctor Faustus Dossier: Arnold Schoenberg, Thomas Mann, and Their Contemporaries, 1930–1951,* ed. E. Randol Schoenberg (Berkeley: University of California Press, 2018), 192–93.

71. PNM, 88.

72. PNM, 89. For Adorno's views on Schoenberg, see, e.g., Robert Hullot-Kentor, "The Philosophy of Dissonance: Adorno and Schoenberg," in Huhn and Zuidervaart, *The Semblance of Subjectivity,* 309–19.

73. It could be fruitful, perhaps, to isolate a single composition from Schoenberg's early years such as *Verklärte Nacht* or the *Gurrelieder,* both of which Adorno singled out for special analysis in his 1955 Kranichstein lecture. See Adorno, "The Young Schoenberg," in Adorno, *The New Music: Kranichstein Lectures,* trans. Wieland Hoban, ed. Klaus Reichert and Michael Schwarz (Cambridge: Polity, 2021), 1–72.

74. Adorno, AE, *1958–59* (Polity), 6. NGS, Abt. IV, Band 3: 17.

75. KNM, 194. GS 16, 170–228; quote from 226.

76. KNM, 145–96; quote from 194–95. GS 16, 226.

77. Kant, *Critique of the Power of Judgment,* 144–45. As quoted by Adorno in "Kriterien," GS 16, 226.

78. Kant, *Critique of the Power of Judgment,* 145.

79. For Adorno's appeal to the category of the sublime, see, e.g., Wolfgang Welsch, "Adornos Ästhetik: Eine implizite Ästhetik des Erhabenen," in *Das Erhabene: Zwischen Grenzerfahrung und Größenwahn,* ed. Christine Priese (Berlin: Akademie Verlag, 1989), 185–216.

80. "Criteria," 194; GS 16, 227.

81. "Ohne die Illusion, es wäre durch dies Standhalten des Geistes ein Absolutes verbürgt." "Criteria," 195; GS 16, 227.

82. "Am Ende des bürgerlichen Zeitalters erinnert sich der Geist am vorweltliche Mimesis, die reflexhafte Nachahmung, die wie immer auch vergebliche Regung, aus der einmal entsprang, was anders ist als das Seiende: der Geist selber." Adorno, "Kriterien der neuen Musik," in GS 16, 227.

83. Not surprisingly, perhaps, Adorno's understanding of mimesis bears a certain debt to Benjamin's definition of mimesis and its survival in language as "non-sensuous resemblance." The mimetic moment in language, I would suggest, is that which permits language to gain a second-order critical stand toward the world without wholly breaking from the world.

84. "Am Ende des bürgerlichen Zeitalters erinnert sich der Geist an vorweltlichen Mimesis, die reflexhafte Nachahmung, die wie immer auch vergebliche Regung, aus der einmal entsprang, was anders ist als das Seiende: der Geist selber. Vor der Übermacht der Dingwelt versteckt er sich in dem rudimentärem Minimum, auf das zu regredieren die Dingwelt ihn nötigt. *Dies prekäre Glück indessen ist in der exponierten neuen Musik so gegenwärtig wie die Verzweiflung.*" KNM, 195; my emphasis. GS 16, 227; my emphasis.

85. "*Die vieltönigen Klänge tun nicht nur weh, sondern waren in ihrer schneidenden Gebrochenheit immer zugleich auch schön.*" KNM, 195, my translation. GS 16, 227; my emphasis.

86. KNM, 195; my translation. GS 16, 227.

87. KNM, 145–96; quote from 195. GS 16, 227.

88. "*daß er dieser Schönheit ohne Reservat sich überantwortet.*" KNM, 195; my translation. GS 16, 227. My emphasis.

89. "Trying to Understand *Endgame,*" in AR, 319–52; GS 11, 281–324.

90. "Kunstwerke sind keine göttlichen Manifestationen, sondern Menschenwerk und haben insofern allerdings ebenso ihre Grenze wie auch ihre Beziehung auf Menschliches." AE, *1958/59,* quote from 120. NGS, Abt. IV: Band 3: 192.

91. "Und wenn es gar keine Beziehung zum Glück in der Tat mehr in sich enthält, warum soll ich dann schließlich gehalten sein, mit den Kunstwerken mich abzugeben?" AE, from the English at 120; NGS, Abt. IV: Band 3: 192. My emphasis.

92. Baudelaire takes up Stendhal's phrase: "C'est pourquoi Stendhal, esprit impertinent, . . . s'est rapproché de la vérité plus que beaucoup d'autres, en disant que *le Beau n'est que la promesse du bonheur.*" See Baudelaire, "Le Peintre de la vie moderne," in *L'Art Romantique* (Paris: Calmann Lévy, 1885), 55. For the English version, see Baudelaire, "The Painter of Modern Life," in *Selected Writings on Art and Literature,* ed. and trans. P. E. Charvet (New York: Penguin, 1972), 390–435; quote from 393. For an excellent analysis of this phrase and its permutations in Stendhal and Baudelaire, see Finlayson, "The Artwork and the *Promesse du Bonheur* in Adorno."

93. "die promesse du bonheur, als welche man einmal Kunst definiert hat, ist nirgends mehr zu finden, als wo dem falschen Glück die Maske heruntergerissen wird." Quoted from "Fetisch-Charakter," in GS 14, see esp. the remark on "promesse du bonheur," at 19.

94. GS 7, 205; AT, 135–36. In the English translation, Hullot-Kentor introduces an intensifier into the claim that the promise is broken; he renders it, "Art is the *ever* broken promise of happiness" (my emphasis). This is not implausible, but it is an interpolation that does not appear in the German: "Aesthetic experience is that of some thing that spirit may find neither in the world nor in itself; it is possibility promised by its impossibility. Art is the ever broken promise of happiness" [*Die ästhetische Erfahrung ist die von etwas, was der Geist weder von der Welt noch von sich selbst schon hätte, Möglichkeit, verhießen von ihrer Unmöglichkeit. Kunst ist das Versprechen des Glücks, das gebrochen wird*]. GS 7, 205; AT, 135–36.

95. "Stendhals Diktum von der promesse du bonheur sagt, daß Kunst dem Dasein dankt, indem sie akzentuiert, was darin auf die Utopie vordeutet. Das aber wird stets weniger, das Dasein gleicht immer mehr bloß sich selber. Kunst kann darum immer weniger ihm gleichen. Weil alles Glück am Bestehenden und in ihm Ersatz und falsch ist, muß sie das Versprechen brechen, um ihm die Treue zu halten." Quoted from AT, 311 (parilipomena); GS 7, 461.

96. "Kunst ist Magie, befreit von der Lüge, Wahrheit zu sein." MM (§143), 222; GS 4, 254.

97. Finlayson, "The Artwork and the *Promesse du Bonheur* in Adorno."

98. I borrow the concept of "austere negativism" from Finlayson's essay, "The Artwork and the *Promesse du Bonheur* in Adorno."

99. AE, 140; NGS, Abt. IV: Band 3: 224.

100. AE, 140; NGS, Abt. IV: Band 3: 224. My emphasis.

101. AE, 142; NGS, Abt. IV: Band 3: 226.

102. AE, 142; NGS, Abt. IV: Band 3: 228.

103. "zugleich kritische und utopische Intention." AE, 170; NGS, 271. My emphasis.

104. "und daß es dort, wo es nicht mehr verletzt, sondern wo es ganz und gar in die geschlossene Oberfläche der Erfahrung sich einfügt, eigentlich aufgehört hat, überhaupt ein lebendiges Kunstwerk zu sein." AE, 170; NGS, Abt. IV: Band 3: 271. Translation modified.

105. AE, 214; NGS, Abt. IV: Band 3: 338. My emphasis.

106. "Und deshalb haftet an der Dissonanz nicht nur dieses Moment des Ausdrucks der Negativität, dieses Leidens, *sondern immer zugleich auch das Glück, der Natur ihre Stimme zu geben*, etwas nicht Erfaßtes zu finden, etwas in das Kunstwerk hereinzuziehen, was . . . noch nicht domeziert ist, sondern was gewissermaßen Neuschnee ist und was dadurch an das mahnt, was anders wäre als der immergleiche Betrieb der bürgerlichen Gesellschaft, in der wir alle Gefangene sind. . . . Das dissonierende Moment ist *Schmerz und Glück in eins*." AE, 39-40; NGS, Abt. IV: Band 3: 66-67. My emphasis.

107. AE, 204; NGS, 324-25; my emphasis.

108. AE, 204; NGS, 325.

109. AE, 95; NGS, 153.

110. AE, 95; NGS, 153. Translation modified.

111. "daß dieses Etablieren der ästhetischen Sphäre als einer jenseits des Begehrens über-haupt *stets prekär ist*." AE, 32; NGS, 55. My emphasis.

112. "Sie dürfen also auch etwa eine solche Bestimmung die die des Ausgegliedertseins des Ästhetischen aus der empirischen Realität nicht als ein Absolutum nehmen, sondern Sie müs-sen das selber auch nehmen als ein Moment, das in der geschichtlichen Dialektik steht und das prekär ist—ebenso prekär, wie ich Ihenen in einer der vorigen Studen gesagt habe, daß das sogenannte interesselose Wohlgefallen etwas Prekäres ist." AE, 50; NGS, 83.

113. See Rebecca Comay, "Adorno's Siren Song," *New German Critique*, no. 81 (Autumn 2000): 21-48.

114. "*Es liegt gewissermaßen in der Idee des Schönen selber . . . immer auch das Potential des Absturzes drin.*" AE, 95; NGS IV, Band 3: 153. My emphasis.

115. AT, Paralipomena, 269; GS 7, 400.

116. AE, 210; NGS IV, Band 3: 333.

117. AE, 124; NGS IV, Band 3: 198. My emphasis.

118. "Unter Durchbruch verstehe ich dabei, daß es dann Augenblicke gibt . . . in denen jenes Gefühl des Herausgehobenseins, jenes Gefühl, wenn Sie wollen, der Transzendenz gengenüber dem bloßen Dasein, sich intensiv zusammendrängt, sich aktualisiert, und in denen es uns so vorkommt, als ob das absolut Vermittelte, nämlich eben jene Idee des Befreitseins, doch ein Unmittelbares wäre, wo wir glauben, sie unmittelbar greifen zu können." AE, 122-23; NGS IV, Band 3: 196.

119. AE, 123; NGS IV, Band 3: 196.

120. AE, 123; NGS IV, Band 3: 197.

121. "Es ist dann so, wie wenn in diesen Augenblick—man könnte sie die Augenblicke des Weinens nennen—das Subjekt in sich erschüttert zusammenstürtzen würde. [Es sind] ei-gentlich Augenblicke, in denen das Subjekt sich selber auslöscht und sein Glück hat an dieser Auslöschung—und nicht etwa darin, daß ihm als einem Subjekt etwas zuteil werden." AE, 123; NGS IV, Band 3: 197.

122. AT, 269; GS 7, 401.

123. GS 7, 401; AT, 269. The full passage from *Aesthetic Theory* is worth quoting at length: "Although artworks offer themselves to observation, they at the same time disorient the observer who is held at the distance of a mere spectator; to him is revealed the truth of the work as if it must also be his own. The instant of this transition is art's highest. It rescues subjectivity, even subjective aesthetics, by the negation of subjectivity. The subject, convulsed by art, has real ex-periences; by the strength of insight into the artwork as artwork, these experiences are those in

which the subject's petrification in his own subjectivity dissolves and the narrowness of his self-positedness is revealed. *If in artworks the subject finds his true happiness in the moment of being convulsed, this is a happiness that is counterposed to the subject and thus its instrument is tears, which also express the grief over one's own mortality* [*Während die Kunstwerke der Betrachtung sich öffnen, beirren sie zugleich den Betrachter in seiner Distanz, der des bloßen Zuschauers; ihm geht die Wahrheit des Werkes auf als die, welche auch die Wahrheit seiner selbst sein sollte. Der Augenblick dieses Übergangs ist der oberste von Kunst. Er errettet Subjektivität, sogar subjektive Ästhetik durch ihre Negation hindurch. Das von Kunst erschütterte Subjekt macht reale Erfahrungen; nun jedoch, kraft der Einsicht ins Kunstwerk als Kunstwerk solche, in denen seine Verhärtung in der eigenen Subjektivität sich löst, seiner Selbstsetzung ihre Beschränktheit aufgeht.* Hat das Subjekt in der Erschütterung sein wahres Glück an den Kunstwerken, so ist es eines gegen das Subjekt; darum ihr Organ das Weinen, das auch die Trauer über die eigene Hinfälligkeit ausdrückt]." AT, 269; GS 7, 401. My emphasis.

124. AT, 105; GS 7, 161.

125. AT, 70–71.

126. "It would be more accurate to say that control over nature, along with the associated forms of domination in society, has actually increased the alienation of humans from one another and from nature, and that art, at every level, has the task of revoking this process." *Aesthetics, 1958/59,* quote from 147 (English).

127. In the 1958/59 lectures Adorno argues that art wishes "to give nature its due, albeit for now only a symbolic portion—namely the portion of memory, the memory of the suppressed, of that which becomes a victim, and also the memory of all those internal powers which are destroyed by the process of progressive human rationalization." AE, 47–48. My thanks to Jay Bernstein for alerting me to this passage. This thought anticipates Adorno's later claim in *Aesthetic Theory* that in art we come to experience "the primacy of the object." Although the artwork is culture and not nature, it is through the artwork that we are put into contact with the nature that subjective reason has dominated: "The primacy of the artwork is affirmed aesthetically only in the character of art as the unconscious writing of history, as anamnesis of the vanquished, of the repressed, and *perhaps of what is possible.* The primacy of the object, as the potential freedom from domination of what is, manifests itself in art as its freedom from objects." Thus the artwork is a "mediated plenipotentiary of immediacy." AT, 62; GS 7, 98.

128. AT, 258; GS 7, 383.

Conclusion

1. "heute . . . es gehört zur Moral, nicht bei sich selber zu Hause zu sein." MM (§18), 39; GS 4, 43.

2. MM (§21), 21; GS 4, 21.

3. RSGN, 293.

4. MM (§85), 131–32; GS 4, 149–50.

5. MM (§82), 126; GS 4, 144.

6. MM (§153), 247; GS 4, 283.

7. "Wir entwickeln der Welt aus den Prinzipien der Welt neue Prinzipien." MER, 14. Translation modified; my emphasis.

8. MM, 247, translation modified; GS 4, 283.

9. "Während er danach tastet, die eigene Existenz zum hinfälligen Bilde einer richtigen zu machen, sollte er dieser Hinfälligkeit eingedenk beliben und wissen, wie wenig das Bild *das richtige Leben* ersetzt." MM (§6), 26; GS 4, 27. My emphasis.

10. GS 10.2, 798.

11. "Philosophical aesthetics, the author states [by Ivo Frenzel in the *Encyclopedia of Philosophy*, ed. Fischer], lacks the secure foundation of other philosophical disciples. Now, I would argue that the secure foundation of the other philosophical disciplines is a somewhat precarious matter too." AE, English (Lecture 1), 1.

12. Adorno, "Marginalia to Theory and Practice," in CM (Pickford trans.); quote from 264. GS 10.2, 759–82; quote from 764.

13. MTP, in CM, Pickford trans.; quote from 264. GS 10.2, 759–82; quote from 765.

14. "Während Praxis verspricht, die Menschen aus ihrem Verschlossensein in such hinauszuführen, ist sie eh und je verschlossen; darum sind die Praktischen *unansprechbar*; die Objektbezogenheit von Praxis a priori unterhöhlt. Wohl ließe sich fragen ob nicht bis heute alle naturbeherrschende Praxis in ihrer Indifferenz gegens Objekt Scheinpraxis sei." MTP (Pickford trans.), 259; GS 10.2, 759–82; quote from 759. My emphasis on "unansprechbar."

15. Theodor W. Adorno et al., *The Authoritarian Personality* (New York: Harper & Brothers, 1950); hereafter cited as AP.

16. For comments on the implications of the study today, see Peter E. Gordon, "The Authoritarian Personality Revisited: Reading Adorno in the Age of Trump," in Wendy Brown, Peter E. Gordon, and Max Pensky, *Authoritarianism: Three Inquiries in Critical Theory* (Chicago: University of Chicago Press, 2018).

17. Max Horkheimer, AP, ix. It should be noted that Horkheimer places inverted commas around the term "anthropological," as if to signal that this is not meant to be taken literally.

18. AP, 973; my emphasis.

19. AP, 975.

20. AP, 975.

21. Adorno, "Remarks on *The Authoritarian Personality*," in AP (rev. ed. New York: Verso, 2019), xli–lxvi.

22. "Das gepriesene Hart-Sein, zu dem da erzogen werden soll, bedeutet Gleichgültigkeit gegen den Schmerz schlechthin." Quoted from "Erziehung nach Auschwitz," GS 10.2, 683.

"Being-hard [*Hart-Sein*], the vaunted quality education should inculcate, means absolute indifference toward pain as such." From Adorno, "Education after Auschwitz," in CM (Pickford trans.), 198; translation modified.

23. SO, in GS 10.2, 741–58; quote from 752. English in CM, 245–58; quote from 254.

24. "Ich betrachte das Nachleben des Nationalsozialismus in der Demokratie als potentiell bedrohlicher denn das Nachleben fascistischer Tendenzen *gegen* die Demokratie." Adorno, "The Meaning of Working through the Past" (1959), in CM, 89–103; quote from 90. Original emphasis. GS 10.2, 555–56. With this remark he remained more or less faithful to the spirit of Horkheimer's infamous dictum, that "whoever is not willing to talk about capitalism should also keep quiet about fascism." Max Horkheimer, "Die Juden und Europa," *Zeitschrift für Sozialforschung* (December 1939); reprinted in English as "The Jews and Europe" (1938), trans. Mark Ritter, in *Critical Theory and Society: A Reader*, ed. S. Bronner and D. Kellner (New York: Routledge, 1989).

25. Thus Adorno's striking remarks that in our moral deliberations "what is needed above all is that consciousness of our own *fallibility*." To this he adds, "If you to press me to follow the

example of the Ancients and make a list of the cardinal virtues, I would probably respond cryptically by saying that I could think of nothing except *modesty*." PMP, English, 169; NGS, 251. My emphasis on both words.

26. For further discussion of Adorno's interpretation of the Kantian postulates, see Bernstein, *Adorno: Ethics and Disenchantment*, 418.

27. "Hitler hat den Menschen im Stande ihrer Unfreiheit *einen neuen kategorischen Imperative* aufgezwungen: ihr Denken und Handeln so einzurichten, daß Auschwitz nicht sich wiederhole, nicht Ähnliches geschehe." GS 6, 358. My emphasis.

28. GS 6, 358.

29. Martin Heidegger, as quoted from the disputation at Davos. For a reconstruction and analysis of the disputation and a discussion of this specific remark, see Peter E. Gordon, *Rosenzweig and Heidegger: Between Judaism and German Philosophy*. (Berkeley: University of California Press, 2003), 287.

30. Martin Heidegger, *Anmerkungen I-V*, Gesamtausgabe, Band 97, ed. Peter Trawny, (Frankfurt am Main: Klostermann, 2015), 20. Also see Peter Trawny, *Heidegger and the Myth of a Jewish World Conspiracy*, trans. Andrew J. Mitchell (Chicago: University of Chicago Press, 2015). For an excellent commentary on Trawny's interpretation, see Taylor Carman, https://ndpr.nd.edu/reviews/heidegger-and-the-myth-of-a-jewish-world-conspiracy/#_ednref3. For a variety of critical essays, see Andrew Mitchell and Peter Trawny, eds., *Heidegger's Black Notebooks: Responses to Anti-Semitism* (New York: Columbia University Press, 2017); and Peter E. Gordon, "Heidegger in Black," *New York Review of Books* (October 9, 2014). For an attempt to summarize how Heidegger's philosophy might still be available for a critical appropriation, see "The Critical Appropriation of Heidegger's Philosophy: Five Motifs," ch. 4 in *After Heidegger*, New Heidegger Research, ed. Gregory Fried and Richard Polt (Lanham, MD: Rowman and Littlefield, 2017), 29–40.

31. On this topic, see the excellent summary by Lars Fischer, "The Frankfurt School and Fascism," in *The Sage Handbook of Frankfurt School Critical Theory*, ed. Beverly Best, Werner Bonefeld, and Chris O'Kane (London: Sage, 2018), 799–815. Fischer suggests that the early critical theorists did not wholly resolve their two countervailing interpretations; they saw fascism as "the extreme case of the administered world" but also as "the dysfunctional other of the administered world." Quote from 812.

32. MM, 46; GS 4, 51.

33. MM, 40; GS 4, 44.

34. "Daß der Faschismus nachlebt . . . rührt daher, daß die objektiven gesellschaftlichen Voraussetzungen fortbestehen, die den Faschismus zeitigen." Adorno, "The Meaning of Working through the Past" (Pickford trans.), 98; GS 10.2, 566.

35. For comparative treatments of Adorno and Foucault, see Cook, *Adorno, Foucault, and the Critique of the West*; and Allen, *The End of Progress*. For an excellent attempt to mediate between critical theory and genealogy, see Colin Koopman, *Genealogy as Critique: Foucault and the Problems of Modernity* (Bloomington: Indiana University Press, 2013). Also see Christoph Menke, "Genealogy and Critique: Two Forms of Ethical Questioning of Morality," in CC, 302–27. A superb collection of essays on Adorno and postmodernism is Max Pensky, ed., *The Actuality of Adorno: Critical Essays on Adorno and the Postmodern*, SUNY Series in Contemporary Continental Philosophy (Albany: SUNY Press, 1997).

36. "comme à la limite de la mer un visage de sable." Michel Foucault, *Les Mots et les choses: Une archéologie des sciences humaines* (Paris: Gallimard, 1966), 398.

37. For philosophical accounts of genealogy and its significance, see Raymond Geuss, "Nietzsche and Genealogy," in *Morality, Culture, and History: Essays on German Philosophy* (Cambridge: Cambridge University Press, 1999), 1–28; also see Richard Schacht, ed., *Genealogy, Morality, History: Essays on Nietzsche's Genealogy of Morals* (Berkeley: University of California Press, 1994); Wendy Brown, "Politics without Banisters: Genealogical Politics in Nietzsche and Foucault," in *Politics out of History* (Princeton, NJ: Princeton University Press, 2001), 91–120; Foucault, "Nietzsche, Genealogy, History," in *Language, Counter-Memory, Practice: Selected Essays and Interviews*, ed. D. F. Bouchard (Ithaca, NY: Cornell University Press, 1977), 139–64; and David Garland, "What Is a 'History of the Present'? On Foucault's Genealogies and their Critical Preconditions," *Punishment and Society* 16, no. 4 (2014): 365–84.

38. Michel Foucault, *Surveiller et punir: Naissance de la prison* (Paris: Gallimard, 1975).

39. Michel Foucault, *Histoire de la sexualité. 1. La volonté de savoir* (Paris: Gallimard, 1976). See especially the chapter, "Droit de mort et pouvoir sur la vie." For an analysis, see Alan Milchman and Alan Rosenberg, "Michel Foucault, Auschwitz and Modernity," *Philosophy and Social Criticism* 22, no. 1 (1996): 101–13.

40. Michel Foucault, *The Archaeology of Knowledge*, trans. A. M. Sheridan Smith (New York: Pantheon Books, 1972), 17.

41. For insightful comments on this problem, see David Owen, "Criticism and Captivity: On Genealogy and Critical Theory," *European Journal of Philosophy* 10, no. 2 (2002): 216–30. Owen argues that the general attitude of hostility among critical theorists toward Foucault's practice of genealogy is based on a misunderstanding, since Foucault does not mean to practice a species of ideology critique. Owen suggests that Foucault is better understood as providing us with insight into the "limitations of a picture" and that the work of historicizing genealogy is "to present rival pictures in order to see the limitations of one's own picture and the ways in which it inhibits self-government." While I am in agreement with this account of Foucault's project, the argument for "self-government" remains unclear and lacks normative motivation. For how are we to distinguish self-government from other modes of governmentality without drawing at least a minimal distinction between the subject and its social constitution? If Foucault rejects all normative language, he cannot explain why the mere fact that a picture is *limited* should count as criticism. Presumably Foucault believes that *all* pictures are limited. So he would still need to offer some account as to why we should prefer one picture over another.

42. It is of course one thing to say that human beings are *known* as x or y, but it is quite another thing to say that they simply *are* x or y. Ian Hacking has characterized this stronger language of ontology ("real," etc.) as "elevator" words, though it is doubtful that Foucault is philosophically committed to the stronger claim. See Hacking, *The Social Construction of What?* (Cambridge, MA: Harvard University Press, 1999), 21 ff.

43. GS 6, 10.

44. For a critique of Foucault's antirealist gestures, see Peter E. Gordon, "Agonies of the Real: Anti-Realism from Kuhn to Foucault," *Modern Intellectual History*, Special Issue on the 50th Anniversary of Kuhn's *Structure* (Guest Editor), 9, no. 1 (April 2012): 127–47. On the varieties of antirealism in Continental philosophy, see the scrupulous and exhaustive study by Lee Braver, *A Thing of This World: A History of Continental Anti-Realism* (Evanston, IL: Northwestern University Press, 2007).

45. It may be relevant to note that in 1983 Foucault confessed in an interview that he might have drawn instruction from critical theory. "If I had known about the Frankfurt School in time, I would have been saved a great deal of work. I would not have said a certain amount of nonsense and would not have taken so many false trails trying not to get lost, when the Frankfurt School had

already cleared the way." Michel Foucault, "Um welchen Preis sagt die Vernunft die Wahrheit? Ein Gespräch," *Spuren* 1 (1983): 24. As quoted in Rolf Wiggershaus, *The Frankfurt School: Its Histories, Theories, and Political Significance*, trans. Michael Robertson (Cambridge, MA: MIT Press, 1995), 4. This confession is interesting not least because it raises once again the question as to how the first-generation of critical theory should be understood: Did Foucault mean to imply that Adorno and his colleagues were allies in the project of a normatively indifferent genealogy that collapses the dialectical difference between subject and object? Or, on the contrary, did he mean that he might have avoided the "false trail" of a totalizing critique of reason that cannot explain the conditions of its own possibility in the society it describes? Because Foucault does not elaborate on the significance of this unrealized encounter, we can only speculate as to whether he would have seen in critical theory a mirror image for his own project or whether he would have recognized it as a salutary corrective. For important comments on the critical potential in Foucault's work, see, e.g., Koopman, *Genealogy as Critique*. Axel Honneth offers what I take to be a definitive summary: "Foucault's normative criteria remain on the whole so obscure and so overshadowed by epistemological perspectivism that the normative orientation of his critique of power can often only be deduced from his political-journalistic statements, and not from his theoretical writings." See Honneth, "Pathologies of the Social: The Past and Present of Social Philosophy," in *Disrespect*, 3–48; quote from 40.

46. Adorno, "Bürgerliche Oper," *Klangfiguren* (Darmstädter Gespräche, 1955; Suhrkamp, 1959). Reprinted in GS 16, 31. My emphasis. I hope it will be apparent to readers that the disagreement between Foucault and Adorno regarding the concept of the prison reflects a far more fundamental disagreement as to how philosophical critique is possible and what normative commitments it requires. In this book, I have tried to suggest that when we say that we can appeal to immanent sources of normativity we are not lapsing into a bad form of "utopianism," let alone what some critical theorists often disparage as "ideal theory." The question of how to think about imprisonment is a helpful paradigm for these broader philosophical questions. For a lucid discussion of these questions, see Tommie Shelby, The Idea of Prison Abolition (Princeton, NJ: Princeton University Press, 2022), esp. ch. 6, "Dreaming Big," 183–201.

47. Gordon, *Migrants in the Profane*.

48. Theunissen, "Negativität bei Adorno," 7.

49. GS 6, 353.

50. "säkularisiert Metaphysik in der säkularen Kategorie schechthin, der des Verfalls." GS 6, 353.

51. GS 6, 353.

52. "Kein Eingedenken an Transcendenz ist mehr möglich als kraft der Vergängnis; Ewigkeit erscheint nicht als solche sondern gebrochen durchs Vergänglichste hindurch." GS 6, 353; English translation by Dennis Redmond.

53. Adorno, "Theses upon Art and Religion Today" (originally in English, 1945), reprinted in *Notes to Literature: Volume Two*, trans. Shierry Weber Nicholsen (New York: Columbia University Press, 1992), 292–98; quotes from 297–98.

54. GS 6:396. English quotation from Redmond.

55. PMP, trans. Rodney Livingstone (Stanford), 175. PMP (Suhrkamp), 261.

56. Hent de Vries, *Minimal Theologies: Critiques of Secular Reason in Adorno and Lévinas* (Baltimore: Johns Hopkins University Press, 2005).

57. For an elaboration of this idea, see Gordon, *Migrants in the Profane*, 140.

58. "Gegenüber der Forderung, die damit an ihn ergeht, ist aber die Frage nach der Wirklichkeit oder Unwirklichkeit der Erlösung selber fast gleichgültig." MM, 247; GS 4, 283. I have slightly modified Jephcott's translation.

59. Gordon, *Migrants in the Profane*; also see Jürgen Habermas, *Auch eine Geschichte der Philosophie. Band II: Vernünftige Freiheit: Spuren des Diskurses über Glaben und Wissen* (Frankfurt am Main: Suhrkamp, 2019), 806–7.

60. ND, GS 6, 400.

61. W. Benjamin, "Über den Begriff der Geschichte," in *Gesammelte Schriften*, Band I, 2 (Frankfurt am Main: Suhrkamp, 1974), 691–704; quote from 693.

62. The categories of conventional religion have also lost their self-evidence: "even the existence of a saint is today precarious [*aber die Existenz eines Heiligen ist heute auch prekär*]." PMP, 168; NGS, 250.

63. "etwas von der Friedlichkeit, dem Mangel an Angst und Bedrohung, wie man es sich in einem chiliastischen Reich vorstellt." KC, in NaS, Abt. V, Band 1: *Vorträge (1949–1968)*, 156–76.

64. "Ein solcher emphatischer Begriff von Denken allerdings ist nicht gedeckt, weder von bestehenden Verhältnissen noch von zu erreichenden Zwecken, noch von irgendwelchen Battalionen." Quoted from "Resignation," GS 10.2, 794–99; quote from 798.

65. Adorno's reliance on phenomenological description is confirmed by Jürgen Habermas, who writes that "the sober moral theory confined to explaining the moral point of view needs to be supplemented by an appealing moral *phenomenology*. For an eye-opening phenomenology . . . the literary skills and sensibilities of great philosophical writers, such as Nietzsche or Adorno or Levinas, are more suitable than the analytical abilities of conventional philosophers." Jürgen Habermas, ch. 3, "Discourse Ethics," in *Philosophical Introductions: Five Approaches to Communicative Reason*, trans. Ciaran Cronin (Cambridge: Polity, 2018), 111. See also the perceptive remarks on "showing" rather than "saying," in James Gordon Finlayson, "Adorno on the Ethical and the Ineffable," *European Journal of Philosophy* 10, no. 1 (2002): 1–25, esp. 16.

66. In his own theoretical arguments for the role of justification in critical theory, Rainer Forst suggests that even Adorno recognizes the importance of the norm of justice. In the introduction to this book, I quoted Adorno's skeptical remarks from the 1963 lectures, *Problems of Moral Philosophy*: "We may not know what the absolute good is or the absolute norm, we may not even know what man is or the human or humanity—but what the inhuman is we know very well indeed." Forst wisely refuses to accept this skeptical claim at face value: "But here again the idea of justice, of a higher, better, and yet 'humane' form of justice, what Adorno calls 'social freedom' [. . .], remains the guiding concern. Thus we see as well that the criticism of the inhumane aspect of justice is primarily a criticism of a lack of justice *in the name of justice*." Quoted from Forst, ch. 7, "The Injustice of Justice: Normative Dialectics According to Ibsen, Cavell, and Adorno," in *Justification and Critique: Toward a Critical Theory of Politics*, trans. Ciaran Cronin (Cambridge: Polity, 2014), 162; my emphasis. When Adorno develops a critique of our normative failure, this critique presupposes some normative standard that has been violated.

67. RSGN, 293; GS 10.2, 798.

68. "so etwas wie ein richtiges Leben nicht denkbar ist, wenn man nicht zugleich auch an dem Gewissen und an der Verantwortung festhält. Man ist also an diesem Punkt selber wirklich und in allem Ernst in einer antinomischen Situation. *Man muß an den Normativen, an der Selbstkritik, an der Frage nach dem Richtigen oder Falschen und gleichzeitig an der Kritik der Fehlbarkeit der Instanz festhalten, die eine solche Art der Selbstkritik sich zutraut.*" PMP, English, 169; in NGS, Abt. IV: Band 10: 250. My emphasis.

69. RSGN, 289–93; quote from 293. GS 10.2, 794–99; quote from 799.

Index

abstract expressionism, 144. *See also* art; modernism, in art
"Actuality of Philosophy, The" (Adorno), 18
Adorno, Theodor Wiesengrund: on aesthetics, xx, 144–91; and critical theory, 22, 25, 34, 39, 43; on democratic pedagogy, 24–29, 235n90; and exaggeration, 27–30, 237n114; and Gnosticism, 38, 77, 215, 239n146, 252n4; on happiness, 3, 40, 69–105, 113, 250n79; and immanent critique, 25–27, 41–68; on materialism, 105–26, 155; on metaphysics, 127–43; on morality, 127–43, 155, 245n3; on music, 41–45, 145, 159, 265n32; on nature, 105–26; as a negativist, xvii–xviii, 1–7, 12–16, 23–27, 63, 77, 85, 90, 159–60, 235n90; and normativity, xix, 15, 37–38, 43, 258n44; philosophical legacy of, xiii–2; on reason, 9–11; as a skeptic, 17–20, 25, 40; and social theory, 19, 35, 41, 57, 108, 174, 192–216, 239n146; on suffering, 13–14, 17; and utopianism, 242n47, 259n56
Adorno's Practical Philosophy (Freyenhagen), 15
aesthetics, xix–xx, 35–36, 71, 82, 144–91. *See also* art; beauty; sublime, the
Aesthetic Theory (Adorno), 35, 82, 144–62, 167, 173–75, 184, 188–90, 248n41
À la recherche du temps perdu (Proust), 210
Allen, Amy, 83
animals, 153, 175–77
anticipation, 56–57
anti-foundationalism, 195–96, 202
anti-humanism, 205–9
Aristotelian, and neo-Aristotelian, 16–17, 23, 69
Aristotle, 69, 230n12
art: autonomous, 150–51, 155–61, 182–83, 186–88, 191; commodified, 150–51, 159–61, 186; form of, 156–58; and happiness, 162, 184–90; and heteronomy, 156–58; and suffering, 160–62; and

truth, 160–62, 167. *See also* abstract expressionism; aesthetics; modernism, in art; pop art
"Art and Religion Today" (Adorno), 210
aura, 146–49, 152, 261n9, 261n12. *See also* art: autonomous
Auschwitz, 17, 138, 180, 200–205; and new categorical imperative, 16–17
authoritarianism, 198–200. *See also* fascism
Authoritarian Personality, The (Adorno), 198–99

beauty, 187–91. *See also* aesthetics; *promesse du bonheur*; sublime, the
Becker, Hellmut, 23
Beckett, Samuel, 38–39, 154, 183
Beethoven, Ludwig van, xiv, 41–45, 88, 137, 164–75, 177; Cavatina from String Quartet no. 13 (Op. 130), 170–71, 175–77; "The Creatures of Prometheus" (Op. 43), 165; *Fidelio*, 41–45, 137, 169, 208; Symphony no. 9 in D Minor (Op. 125), 167–70
"Beethoven's Late-Style" (Adorno), 166
Benhabib, Seyla, 26
Benjamin, Walter, 107, 130, 142, 145–51, 161, 237n116, 267n83
Berg, Alban, xiv, 164, 178–79, 182, 187
Berkeley, Bishop, 208
Bernstein, J. M., 15, 107, 235n85; fugitive ethical events, 258n44
bio-politics, 207. *See also* Foucault, Michel
Bloch, Ernst, 259n56, 265n39
bourgeoisie, the, 21, 33–34, 41–43, 126, 146, 161, 166, 195, 204–5
"Bourgeois Opera" (Adorno), 41–42
Brave New World (Huxley), 19, 29
Brecht, Bertolt, 160
Brink, Bert van den, 28